JOACHIM DU BELLAY

The Regrets

with

The Antiquities of Rome,
Three Latin Elegies,
and
The Defense and Enrichment of
the French Language

JOACHIM DU BELLAY

The Regrets

with

The Antiquities of Rome,
Three Latin Elegies,
and
The Defense and Enrichment of the French Language

EDITED AND TRANSLATED BY
RICHARD HELGERSON

A Bilingual Edition

PENN

University of Pennsylvania Press
Philadelphia

Copyright © 2006 University of Pennsylvania Press
All rights reserved

10 9 8 7 6 5 4 3 2 1

Published by
University of Pennsylvania Press
Philadelphia, Pennsylvania 19104-4122

Library of Congress Cataloging-in-Publication Data

Du Bellay, Joachim, ca. 1522–1560.
[Regrets. English & French]
The regrets ; with, The antiquities of Rome, Three Latin Elegies and The defense and enrichment of the French language / Joachim du Bellay ; edited and translated Richard Helgerson. —A bilingual ed.
p. cm.
Includes bibliographical references and index.
ISBN-13: 978-0-8122-3941-6 (alk. paper)
ISBN-10: 0-8122-3941-5
1. Du Bellay, Joachim, ca. 1522–1560—Translations into English. I. Helgerson, Richard. II. Title.
PQ1668.R4 E5 2006
841.3 22
2006041848

For Max and Penelope,
future readers of du Bellay

Contents

Preface

One evening at dinner, a few months before I finished this translation, a friend asked a question that caught me off guard. What, he wanted to know, had most "amazed" me about du Bellay. Not knowing what to say, I mumbled something and nudged the conversation off in another direction. But the question stuck with me. There is much in du Bellay to be wondered at, as readers who spend time with this book will soon discover. His poems can be moving, funny, inspiring, thought-provoking, and troubling. They put us in touch with a world that is at once distant and familiar, and they speak with a rare intimacy and power. But, as I discovered after mulling over that unexpected question, what most amazes me about du Bellay is how quickly his poetic career passed and how enduring its effect has been.

In March 1549, the then unknown, twenty-six-year-old Joachim du Bellay published a manifesto calling for a radically new French poetry, his *Deffence et Illustration de la Langue Françoyse*, the book whose title I have translated as *The Defense and Enrichment of the French Language*. Just over a decade later, on the first of January 1560, du Bellay died. In those few years, he published an extraordinary amount of poetry, and together with such friends as Pierre de Ronsard, Jean Antoine de Baïf, Pontus de Tyard, Étienne Jodelle, Rémi Belleau, and Jacques Peletier du Mans—the group that famously named itself the Pléiade—he accomplished the transformation of French poetry he had called for, though he did it in ways the young author of the *Defense* could hardly have envisioned. Driven by needs that were both personal and more broadly communal and inspired by examples from ancient Greece and Rome as well as from modern Italy, du Bellay set forth a program whose tenets he both observed and violated in a decade of rapid, voluminous, and wonderfully unpredictable literary production. There have been other moments like this in literary history. Such rapid change has, in fact, become a hallmark of modernity. But few of those moments can match du Bellay's marvelous decade either for the sheer daring of the undertaking or for the lasting appeal of the work it produced.

Living with this work for the last several years has given me a privileged access to the energy and excitement of that intense moment. The aim of this volume is to make that experience more generally available to English-speaking readers, readers whose French may need a little assistance. The works I have chosen are those that many generations have found the most engaging and most memorable: the two, very different sonnet sequences that du Bellay wrote during the four years he spent in Rome as secretary to his distinguished kinsman, Cardinal Jean du Bellay, and that he published in 1558 shortly after his return to France. Those two sonnet sequences are *Les Regrets* (*The Regrets*) and *Les Antiquitez de Rome* (*The Antiquities of Rome*). To these I have added three Latin elegies that du Bellay also wrote during his stay in Rome and that have a particularly close relation to the sonnets of the *Regrets* and the *Antiquities*, his "Romae descriptio" (Description of Rome), "Ad P. Ronsardum" (To P. de Ronsard), and "Patriae desiderium" (Longing for His Fatherland). And in order to place all these poems, both French and Latin, in relation to du Bellay's revolutionary literary project and to make available one of the most influential manifestos of European literary history, I have also included the *Defense* itself.

As befits du Bellay's position as one of the great poets of the French Renaissance and one of the founders of modern French poetry, there are many excellent French editions of the *Regrets*, the *Antiquities*, and the *Defense*, and there is a fine edition of his Latin poems with a facing French translation. But there is no other modern English prose translation of any of these works. For all their very real interest, the translations that do exist—C. H. Sisson's and David R. Slavitt's recent verse renditions of the first 130 sonnets of the *Regrets*, Edmund Spenser's Elizabethan versions of the *Antiquities*, and Gladys M. Turquet's mock-Elizabethan *Defense* from the 1930s—are either very free or very far removed from modern English or (in the case of Spenser's) both. None can reliably guide a twenty-first-century reader through du Bellay's text. On the assumption that these works deserve and will richly reward a wider English-speaking readership than the existing translations allow, such reliable guidance is what this edition seeks to provide.

As du Bellay himself was keenly aware, even translation of the sort I attempt, literal prose translation that has no pretension of rivaling the original with a text of comparable poetic value, has difficulties to overcome. Du Bellay's historical, mythological, and contemporary references need elucidation; his echoes of ancient and modern works that he assumed would be well-known to his first readers need identification; and his sometimes contorted Latinate syntax needs frequent unscrambling. Some of these things can be done only in notes. Others affect the text itself and must be accomplished with sensitivity to the often intentional remoteness and rhetorical patterning of du Bellay's diction and syntax. Part of du Bellay's undertaking was to alienate French from vulgar usage, to remake French by making

it more like the poetic languages of Greece, Rome, and Renaissance Italy—in effect, to make French new by making it foreign. In respecting that purpose, the translator must resist the temptation of excessive familiarity. And in the case of the *Regrets*, excessive familiarity is a very real temptation, one to which recent verse translators have eagerly succumbed. Many of these poems are familiar in the quite obvious sense that they were written—or, at least, present themselves as having been written—as personal letters to close friends and colleagues of du Bellay's own age, and many others are comically satirical. What it takes to render them accurately is a language that can shift rapidly from intimacy to formality, from pathos to ridicule, from colloquial familiarity to artful elevation and that can sometimes combine all these qualities in a single brief poem.

And even when all possible stylistic accommodation has been made, there remain many words and expressions that have no adequate counterpart in modern English. The most obvious of these is the second of the paired words to which the title of du Bellay's *Defense* has given lasting currency in French, *illustration.* Breaking up the now hallowed couple, *défense et illustration,* and giving the Englished *defense* a new partner, as I have done, seems almost a desecration, particularly since both words have close English look-alikes. Why not just yield to tradition and call the book *The Defense and Illustration of the French Language*? Because, unfortunately, in neither French nor English does *illustration* now mean what du Bellay meant by it. And, even worse, what it does now mean runs directly counter to his original meaning. To defend and illustrate the French language would now mean to defend it and give examples of its greatness. But that is not at all what du Bellay does. Nor could he, for in his view French was not yet great and had little of value to show. He defends the potential greatness of French, not anything the language had actually accomplished. By *illustration* what du Bellay meant was "rendering illustrious" or "giving luster to," meanings the word no longer has. My *enrichment* can only accomplish half the task, and even at that substitutes a metaphor of wealth (a metaphor du Bellay himself sometimes uses) for one of luminosity. But no alternative I can find seems any better. And there are many other occasions in the course of these works where present-day English words will not do what du Bellay's sixteenth-century French words were doing. When in the *Defense* du Bellay echoes the proverbial Italian charge that translators are traitors, he must have had examples of this sort in mind. But in translating works as far removed in time, in place, and in language as his now are, some measure of treachery, however scrupulously we try to avoid it, is inevitable.

The best antidote I know to the treason of translation is having the original text on the facing page. This edition does just that not only for du Bellay's French and Latin poems but also for his prose treatise. These French and Latin texts are closely based on the first printed edition of each of the works. For the *Defense* this means the edition published in 1549 by Arnoul

l'Angelier, and for the *Regrets*, the *Antiquities*, and the Latin elegies, the editions published in 1558 by Féderic Morel. With the exceptions mentioned below, I have retained not only the language of these first editions but also their spelling and punctuation. I have done this not because they faithfully reproduce the spelling and punctuation of du Bellay's manuscripts—they almost certainly don't—but because they come far closer to his practice than a fully modernized edition could possibly do and because they better represent the sound and sometimes even the meaning of the words he used. The original punctuation in the French poems, which is often more rhetorical than logical—intended, that is, to guide readers in voicing du Bellay's verse rather than in perceiving its syntactic structures—is of particular value, but the spelling, with all its obvious inconsistencies, also provides a useful reminder of the unsettled state of the French language at the time he was writing. Language was itself a central issue not only in the *Defense* but in all du Bellay's work. Modernizing even its so-called "accidental" features thus hides from view a telling aspect of the very object he was addressing.

I have, however, felt it necessary to make a few small changes, none of which alter the substantive meaning of the original texts. I have brought the use of *u*, *v*, *i*, and *j* in du Bellay's French and *u* and *v* in his Latin in line with current practice; I have added cedillas to soft *c*'s in the *Defense* (the *Regrets* and *Antiquities* already have them); I have added accents in both the poems and the prose to make clear the difference between *ou* and *où*, *des* and *dès*, and *la* and *là* and in a few other places where the sense would be obscure without them; I have separated with a space or an apostrophe a few words sixteenth-century practice ran together; I have expanded abbreviations in both the French and Latin; I have reduced the distracting profusion of capital letters in the *Defense*, making it more nearly resemble the poems; in the poems themselves, I keep the capital letters from the Morel edition, though I use them more sparingly in the translations, and have added them following a full stop within a line of verse; with the *Defense*, where the original punctuation has no poetic value and is considerably more confusing and mechanical than with the poems, I have freely repunctuated; with the Latin I have adopted the alterations in punctuation and the very few other emendations introduced by Geneviève Demerson in her still-definitive edition; and I have followed all editors since Morel in numbering the sonnets in du Bellay's two sequences. To make the structure of du Bellay's poems and prose more apparent and to make it easier for readers to move back and forth from the French to the English, I have also made some changes in formatting, printing the sonnets of the *Regrets* and the *Antiquities* in the usual modern French manner with quatrains and tercets each set off as a separate stanza and introducing paragraph breaks within the chapters of the *Defense* and in the English translations of the three Latin elegies. With the help of these changes, with some practice,

and with the support of an English translation just across the way, readers who have even a smattering of French or Latin should be able to enjoy du Bellay's work very much as he wrote it, despite the initial unfamiliarity of the sixteenth-century spelling and, for the French poems, the sixteenth-century punctuation. Indeed, those now archaic features can, at the cost of a little additional effort, heighten that pleasure by marking the reader's entry into an intriguingly distant yet still accessible world.

In at least one significant regard, this edition follows its copy texts more closely than does any other modern edition. Not only do the spelling and punctuation of the *Regrets* and the *Antiquities* here correspond to those of the original Morel printings, but so does the page layout. In the case of the *Antiquities,* the reason for this is obvious and at least one modern edition, that of Daniel Aris and Françoise Joukovsky, has respected it. In the *Antiquities,* du Bellay alternates between sonnets in lines of ten syllables and sonnets in lines of the twelve-syllable alexandrine that he and Ronsard made the standard meter for French verse, and he arranges the poems so that a decasyllabic sonnet is in the top half of each page and one in alexandrines is in the bottom half, a pattern he reverses just once to mark the end of the *Antiquities* proper—that is, the part of the sequence that precedes the final fifteen apocalyptic sonnets of the *Songe,* or *Dream.* But if the reasons are less obvious, the significance of the original page layout is, if anything, still greater for the *Regrets.* Again and again a new departure in the sequence will begin with a sonnet placed in the upper left-hand position of the four poems that can be seen at any opening, and, similarly, sections frequently close with a sonnet placed in the lower right-hand position. And still more commonly the two poems on the same page or the four poems on facing pages will speak to one another in ways that make the page and the opening units of poetic meaning that are difficult to retrieve when they are broken up, as they are in every modern French edition. Given the constraints of a bilingual edition, I cannot put four French sonnets on facing pages, but I do maintain the individual page couplings for both the *Regrets* and the *Antiquities* and I print du Bellay's left-hand, verso pages and his right-hand, recto ones as they appear in the Morel editions. Thus readers encountering a poem in French at the top of a verso page should have a sense, however slight in most instances, of a possible new beginning, while in encountering one at the bottom of a recto page they should sense the possibility of an ending. And if readers wish to see all four facing poems together, as those poems would have been seen in the Morel editions, they can simply lift up the intervening leaf of English translations and look to either side of it.

For reasons I have already mentioned and for others I have not yet had occasion to specify, du Bellay's work requires annotation. I have, however, tried to keep this necessary clutter as light and unobtrusive as possible. Rather than dot even the English text with superscript numbers, I have sig-

naled notes with a catchword or phrase and placed them under each sonnet translation or, in the case of the few longer poems and the prose treatise, at the bottom of the relevant page. These notes have several tasks. They identify contemporary people, places, and events, explain unfamiliar classical allusions, point out sources, cross-reference passages from the Latin and French, and, in a few instances, attempt to compensate for unavoidable inadequacies in the translation. As a supplement to the notes, the name index allows readers to recover explanatory notes as well as to trace patterns of reference, allusion, and address. Though ultimately all the notes point back to it, the French text itself has been kept as free of direct annotation as it was in the original editions.

In the character and presentation of its notes and even more in its style of translation, this book has drawn continual inspiration from Robert Durling's now classic edition and translation of *Petrarch's Lyric Poems.* As a sonneteer, as a literary reformer, as a Renaissance humanist, as a fiercely engaged partisan and critic of Rome, and as a passionately desiring subject, du Bellay is very much the successor of Petrarch. If this volume can make du Bellay accessible to English-speaking readers in the way Durling has done for Petrarch, it will have done its work. I am also obliged to the many du Bellay critics whose works are listed in the bibliography and especially to du Bellay's twentieth- and twenty-first-century editors: Henri Chamard, S. de Sacy, Daniel Aris and Françoise Joukovsky, and J. Joliffe and M. A. Screech for the *Regrets* and the *Antiquities*; Chamard again, Jean-Charles Monferran, and Francis Goyet and Olivier Millet for the *Defense*; and Geneviève Demerson for the Latin elegies. My notes often borrow from theirs, and my translations would have been far less accurate without the help of their glosses and glossaries. And for pointing out the significance of du Bellay's page layout, I am grateful to George Hugo Tucker's books on the *Antiquities* and the *Regrets.*

Though unable adequately to repay them, I must also acknowledge a number of more personal debts. Edwin Duval read the first draft of my translations of the *Regrets* and the *Antiquities* and saved me from innumerable errors and infelicities. There is hardly a poem in those two collections whose English rendering has not benefited from his expert eye and unfailing ear. Elizabeth MacArthur gave my translations of all the French poems a careful second reading and served as the first reader for my translation of the *Defense.* Always clearheaded, always concerned for strict fidelity to du Bellay's text, she, too, deserves credit as a virtual co-translator of the works in this volume. Additional valuable suggestions for both the poems and the prose treatise came from Anne Lake Prescott, the leading student of literary relations between sixteenth-century France and England. Margaret Ferguson generously commented on my version of the *Defense*, a work to whose understanding her published scholarship has contributed so much. Michael O'Connell, who has been a vigilant reader of every book I have

written, once again came to the rescue with a careful review of my Latin translations, which were also given a very helpful reading by Sara Lindheim, who has written brilliantly of the very Roman poets du Bellay most closely followed. And both Michael O'Connell and Apostolos Athanassakis checked my Greek transcriptions, transliterations, and translation. Thanks are also due to Cassandre Gniady for saving me a great deal of typing by scanning the first copy text of du Bellay's French and Latin originals; to Robert Hamm for some timely research assistance; to Patricia Fumerton for insisting on the need for a name index; to Jessica Murphy for help with the indexing; to Noreen O'Connor-Abel for help managing a difficult text; to the staffs of the Musée Joachim du Bellay in Liré and the Bibliothèque Municipale in Lyon for their hospitality and help; to the Albert and Elaine Borchard Foundation for fellowship support and a beautiful place to work; to my editor, Jerome Singerman, for his interest and encouragement; and especially to my wife, Marie-Christine Helgerson, who patiently listened to my first halting attempts to translate du Bellay and who convinced me that this recreation might be a book.

And a final debt, the deepest of all, is to Joachim du Bellay himself. The delight and the fascination of his poems are what kept me going. The other recent English translators of the *Regrets*, C. H. Sisson and David Slavitt, have both emerged from the experience convinced that du Bellay—who constantly deferred to his friend Ronsard, who recognized and celebrated Ronsard's superior success, who saw in Ronsard the realization of the ideal he had imagined in the *Defense*—is in fact, as Sisson puts it, "a greater poet than Ronsard." Not having spent as long with Ronsard as I have with du Bellay, I can make no such magisterial pronouncement on their respective merits. But it does seem to me that du Bellay's work is marked by an intensity of desire, a distinguishing and passionate focus, an almost obsessive dedication that his more fluent friend and rival cannot match. In this, though Ronsard wrote far more love poetry, du Bellay, especially the du Bellay of the *Regrets* and the *Antiquities*, more nearly deserves the title of the French Petrarch. Certainly, in the time I have spent with it, du Bellay's work has come to seem steadily more compelling, more rewarding, more revealing with regard not only to du Bellay himself and his own immediate world but also to the self-consciously new poetry of sixteenth-century Europe generally and to movements for artistic change whenever and wherever they have occurred. In concert with his friends and fellow poets, du Bellay undertook a great project of literary renovation, a project closely dependent on the social, economic, technological, political, religious, and cultural changes of his time, and as a self-declared exile in Rome he lived that project more fully than did any but a very few of his contemporaries. To share that experience through his poems and prose treatise is a privilege I hope this edition will make possible for many who might hesitate to make the adventure on their own.

Introduction

A word du Bellay uses just a few times provides a key to understanding the ambition and accomplishment of all the works included in this volume. That word is *monarchie.* It occurs first in *The Defense and Enrichment of the French Language,* where he looks forward to the time "when," as he puts it, "this noble and powerful kingdom will in its turn seize the reins of *monarchie.*" And it appears again in *The Antiquities of Rome,* in a dedicatory sonnet to Henry II, where he wishes the king "the good fortune to rebuild in France" a greatness like that Rome once enjoyed. "Perhaps then," he continues, "your great majesty, recalling my verses, would say that they have been a blessed omen of your *monarchie.*" In both, he clearly means, as he does in his few other uses of the term, something quite different from what the French now mean by *monarchie,* what in English we mean by *monarchy.* France already had that. No, what he has in mind more nearly resembles Rome's "universal dominion," the phrase I use in both passages to translate *monarchie.* What du Bellay imagines is a rebirth of the Roman Empire with France as the new Rome. It is this thought that allows him in another of his poems to address Henry as a "Roman monarch" and to say that "the whole world"—*tout l'univers*—will be under Henry's powerful hand. And it is this thought that prompts, shapes, and enables much of what he wrote. For if France is to be the new Rome, the old Rome will need the kind of attention his poems and prose treatise give it and France itself will need a language and literature comparable to Rome's, the very language and literature he sets out to supply.

Du Bellay was not alone in this undertaking. His friend Pierre de Ronsard and the other members of the Pléiade shared his vision and his ambition. And similar projects, suggested by old ideas of the westward movement of empire and learning, modeled on the ancient Roman appropriation of Greek literature and culture, inspired more particularly by Petrarch's obsessive devotion to Rome and the undeniable appeal of his vernacular poetry, and given new immediacy by the rapid consolidation of the great monarchic states of western Europe, were either already under way or were soon to get under way in many parts of Europe, most notably in Italy, Spain, Portugal, and England. In 1492, just a month after Ferdinand and Isabella had completed the centuries-long reconquest of the Iberian Peninsula with the capture of Granada, the Spanish humanist An-

tonio de Nebrija introduced his *Castilian Grammar,* the first grammar of any European vernacular, with the resounding claim that "language has always been the companion of empire." And it was not long before poets like Juan Boscán and Garcilaso de la Vega were responding to Nebrija's call by remaking Spanish verse in open imitation of Petrarch and the Romans, as Pietro Bembo and his followers had already begun doing in Italy and as Luís de Camões would do in Portugal and Edmund Spenser and Sir Philip Sidney in England. The notion that universal empire might be restored in their time and place, that one or another of their hitherto uncultivated vernaculars might be called on to play a world-historical role like that of Latin, had, we may suppose, a more-or-less-realistic hope of accomplishment depending on the particular circumstances of each of these countries. But in each, thoughts of empire went hand in hand with plans for radical literary reform. However likely or unlikely their chances may have appeared, imperial yearnings prompted and justified their projects and shaped the form and content of much of the poetry they actually wrote.

But even in this broadly shared and intensely pursued undertaking, du Bellay stands apart. No other sixteenth-century European poet wrote as much about Rome, ancient or modern, as he did. No other wrote as passionate or as fully articulated a manifesto for the new imperial poetry as his *Defense.* No other, between Petrarch and Shakespeare, wrote as moving or as brilliantly innovative a sonnet sequence—the favorite form of the new poets—as his *Regrets,* and none at all wrote a sequence as directly concerned with the predicament of the modern poet. Nor did any other meditate as intensely on the fate of ancient Rome as he did in his *Antiquities* or foresee Rome's ultimate ruin with the apocalyptic fervor of the *Dream or Vision* he appended to that sequence. And were this not enough, du Bellay has a still further distinction, for no other sixteenth-century poet engaged as fully as he did in his Latin elegies with the interrelated prospects of empire and poetry in ancient Rome's own language. Whether as polemicist or as poet, whether regarding the distant past or the present and much-desired future, whether in French or in Latin, du Bellay took the common concerns of his time to an unequaled level of emotional complexity and literary expression. More than that of any of his contemporaries, his work gives voice to the aspirations and concerns that so fatefully brought the new poetry of sixteenth-century Europe into existence, endowing the various nations of Europe with their first distinctly modern, vernacular literatures.

Who then was Joachim du Bellay, and what form did he give the works that accomplished so much, the works by which he is now most remembered?

A Life in Letters

A few weeks before his death on the first of January 1560, du Bellay wrote a Latin elegy—his longest Latin poem—to his friend Jean Morel d'Embrun.

The immediate circumstance prompting the poem seems to have been a crisis in du Bellay's relations with his kinsman and longtime employer Cardinal Jean du Bellay. But he seizes the moment to offer a more general assessment of his life and present situation. About his work as a poet, he expresses considerable satisfaction. He has, he says, acquired glory and renown. His name is on the lips of the learned. Both the people and the court read him, and he takes pleasure in recalling that he was known and admired by King Henry II, who had died a few months earlier, as he is still by the late king's sister Margaret and all those who love Apollo and the muses. "For these reasons," he continues, "it seems to me that I am a king, that I have a place at the table of the gods, and that already in my lifetime I enjoy the future that awaits me." But for all this well-merited self-congratulation, he cannot refrain from thinking of another life that he might have had, that for a moment he seems even to suppose might still be within reach. What would that other life be? A life more like that of Cardinal du Bellay and the cardinal's late brother Guillaume, who in the reign of Francis I was a leading diplomat and governor of Piedmont—a life, that is, of eminent and richly rewarded service to the state.

Born in 1522 on his parents' estate in the Angevin village of Liré overlooking the western end of the Loire valley, du Bellay was always keenly aware of the noble accomplishments of his renowned elder kinsmen, Jean, Guillaume, and their brothers, the soldier Martin and the bishop René, as well as of his more distant ancestors, who had distinguished themselves in the fifteenth-century wars with the English. But from an early age, he was no less aware of the debilities and deprivations that prevented his following their illustrious example. He was a sickly child and suffered for much of his life from illnesses that in early manhood left him bedridden for two years and that resulted in intermittent deafness and persistent weakness. Nor was poor health his only complaint. By the time he was ten both his parents had died, and he was left in the care of his wastrel elder brother René, who, as du Bellay charged on more than one occasion, sorely neglected his education. And when in 1551 René himself died, du Bellay was made the guardian of his orphaned eleven-year-old nephew Claude, whose tangled and time-consuming property interests he was obliged to defend. No wonder then that du Bellay dreamed of empire and Rome. Such dreams and the poetry that expressed them helped fill the gap between his lofty aspirations and the often discouraging reality of his everyday life.

But all was not discouragement and deprivation. Sometime around 1546, perhaps with the idea of preparing himself for a diplomatic career, du Bellay went to Poitiers to study law at the university. Scholars differ over how much law he actually learned, but no one doubts that the time he spent in Poitiers gave shape to his poetic inclinations, for it was there that he met the humanist Marc Antoine Muret, the neo-Latin poet Salmon Macrin, and his future colleague in the remaking of French poetry Jacques

Peletier du Mans, who, as du Bellay later reported, first urged him to try the sonnet and the ode. But easily the most important encounter du Bellay had during his time in Poitiers was not with Muret, Macrin, or even Peletier but rather with Pierre de Ronsard, the man with whose name his would forever be linked. Tradition has it that the meeting took place by accident at a country inn outside the city. Wherever it took place, its effect was immediate and far reaching.

Within the year—1547—du Bellay left Poitiers and joined Ronsard in Paris at the College of Coqueret, whose new master, Jean Dorat, had been the tutor of Ronsard and of the youthful Jean-Antoine de Baïf, another of the students at Coqueret and another future French poet. And within that same year—the year of the death of Francis I and the succession of Henry II—Peletier, who had also come to Paris, brought out his *Poetic Works* (*Oeuvres Poétiques*) with an ode by Ronsard and an epigram by du Bellay, the first appearance of either in print. Clearly, the movement that would burst into prominence two years later with the publication of du Bellay's *Defense and Enrichment of the French Language* and of his and Ronsard's first collections of verse had already begun. Peletier himself anticipates its program. In a piece entitled "To a Poet Who Wrote Only in Latin," Peletier declares, "I write in my mother tongue and strive to improve it with the aim of rendering it eternal, as the ancients did with theirs." Having recently translated Horace's *Art of Poetry*, Peletier knew precisely what the ancients had done with their language, and the question he goes on to ask is one to which du Bellay and Ronsard would soon be ready to respond: "Why do we not do as they did, to become immortal like them?"

In the intervening two years, that extraordinary ambition gained substance and clarity under the direction of Jean Dorat and in the company of Peletier, who left Paris a year later, and of Baïf at the College of Coqueret and of two students from the neighboring College of Boucourt, Étienne Jodelle and Rémi Belleau. Together these young men militantly dubbed themselves the Brigade, before adopting a few years later the more transcendentally stellified title under which posterity has remembered them, the Pléiade. And together they studied the ancients and modern Italians and began writing the French verse that would, they hoped, make them and their native language immortal. At Coqueret in particular, Dorat led du Bellay, Ronsard, and Baïf through an intense study of the Greek language and of Greek literature, thus providing them with models they might otherwise not have encountered and sharpening their sense of Latin poetry's dependence on Greek. This last lesson had an especially marked effect on du Bellay, whose devotion to poetic renovation through imitation was greatly strengthened by his detailed knowledge of what the ancient Romans had done to make their own language new.

But the actual appearance of du Bellay's *Defense* in the spring of 1549 seems to have been less a matter of careful study reaching its natural culmi-

nation than of fear of having been unexpectedly preempted. Though du Bellay's hastily written and no less hastily published manifesto nowhere mentions Thomas Sébillet, it would appear to have been the publication of Sébillet's *Art of French Poetry* (*Art Poëtique François*) in 1548 that spurred du Bellay into action. The problem with Sébillet's book was not so much that it proposed an art of French poetry that in many ways anticipated what du Bellay, Ronsard, and their friends were contemplating, though that was bad enough, but rather that it claimed that such a poetry had already arrived. According to Sébillet, Clément Marot and his followers, the so-called "Marotiques," had given France the refined poetic art it needed. But if that were so, what place would there be for du Bellay and Coqueret's Brigade? I will discuss du Bellay's response to this challenge in greater detail in a later section. Here it is enough to recall his repeated insistence in the *Defense* that French poetry could not achieve greatness by imitating, as Sébillet suggested, any previous writing in French, including that of Marot. Such a course would lead only to continued mediocrity. Marot was too common and low, too ignorant of the classics, too artless, to merit imitation. And the other best-known French poets, Antoine Héroët, Mellin de Saint-Gelais, and Maurice Scève, were, though for other reasons, no better. Only imitation of the Greeks, Romans, and modern Italians would do, and such imitation had yet to be attempted.

This belligerently offensive declaration was bound to provoke controversy. And since the *Defense* was published simultaneously with du Bellay's first collection of poems—a small volume containing a sonnet sequence, *The Olive* (*L'Olive*), an antidote to love, *The Anti-Erotic* (*L'Antérotique*), and a book of odes, *The Lyric Verses* (*Les Vers lyriques*)—it too was drawn into the tussle, as was Ronsard's first book of poems, his *Odes*, which appeared early in 1550 with a preface advertising its author's close association with du Bellay ("whose judgment, similar study, long acquaintance, and ardent desire to awaken French poetry, prior to us weak and languishing . . . , has made us nearly identical in spirit, invention, and work") and his full agreement with du Bellay's disdain for the imitation of any existing poetry in French ("for the imitation of our [French poets] is so odious to me . . . that for that reason I have distanced myself from them . . . wishing to have nothing in common with so monstrous an error"). Now, neither du Bellay nor Ronsard maintained their hostility to all previous French poetry with perfect consistency. Even in the preface to his *Odes*, Ronsard makes a passing exception of Marot, Héroët, Scève, and Saint-Gelais, and du Bellay at various times would publish admiring poems about all four. Indeed, his *Lyric Verses* ends with an epitaph on Marot, and he would soon acknowledge Saint-Gelais's precedence in writing French sonnets. But the provocation offered by his *Defense* was nevertheless unmistakable, and the reaction was swift. Even before Ronsard came on the scene, Sébillet published a response mocking du Bellay's pretension and charging, accurately, that many of his

so-called novelties were "translated word for word from others." The mockery was then amplified to book length by Barthélemy Aneau, a schoolmaster from Lyon, whose *Quintil Horatian*—Quintilius was the frank and clear-sighted critic lauded by Horace and recalled in du Bellay's *Defense*—goes through the *Defense* chapter by chapter and through du Bellay's verse poem by poem making fun of whatever lent itself to ridicule. Nor did the mockery stop there. It was repeated in print by Guillaume des Autels and at court by Saint-Gelais, who was particularly annoyed by Ronsard.

Though these critics found much in the program and the poems of du Bellay and Ronsard to oppose, what most bothered them was the break these self-proclaimed "new" poets wanted to make with the French literary past—that and the claim that the only models worth following were foreign, whether Greek or Roman or modern Italian. Such views moved Aneau to call du Bellay's "defense and illustration" an "offense and denigration" and to charge du Bellay with rendering French poetry foreign to itself. He was not far wrong. At stake in the radical departure proposed by du Bellay and Ronsard was nothing less than the identity of France and of French letters. Guided by Dorat, Peletier, and their own ambition, du Bellay and Ronsard had gone into what might be thought of as internal exile. As Ronsard put it, "Seeing nothing in our French poets deserving imitation, I went to see foreigners." And having once taken this irreversible step, he and du Bellay were intent on bringing the rest of their countrymen, beginning with the intellectual and political elite, with them. In danger of being left behind, Sébillet, Aneau, and others who were committed to the literary identity France already had could hardly do other than object. Responding to du Bellay's repeated use of the Latinizing neologism *patrie*, Aneau thus proclaimed, "Qui ha *pays* n'ha que faire de *patrie*," which might be paraphrased, "Those, like us, who have a good French *country* don't need your pretentious, imported, Roman-style *fatherland*." But if France and French poetry were to be remade in the image of their imperial desire, that is exactly what du Bellay and Ronsard did need.

For du Bellay, the experience of something like exile had begun long before with ill health, the loss of his parents, and his brother's neglect, and it was soon to take a more literal form in his voyage to Rome. But before the opportunity to live in the capital of the ancient empire presented itself, du Bellay further immersed himself in Greek and Latin literature and continued to produce an extraordinary amount of poetry. In the four years between the simultaneous publication of the *Defense* and the *Olive* volume in March 1549 and his departure for Rome in April 1553, he brought out another five books of verse: in 1549 a *Collection of Poetry* (*Recueil de Poesie*); in 1550 a much augmented *Olive* with an important new preface and a *Battle Between the Muses and Ignorance* (*La Musagnoeomachie*); in 1551 a long poem mourning the death of Margaret of Valois (*Le Tombeau de Marguerite de Valois*); in 1552 a translation of the fourth book of the *Aeneid* with another im-

portant preface and other poetic works; and finally in 1553 a revised and augmented *Collection of Poetry*. For all its real interest, none of this work would have sufficed to keep du Bellay's memory alive. That would be the accomplishment of his Roman poems, poems whose striking vigor and originality these early collections only begin to suggest. But taken together this large body of verse does nevertheless provide a fascinating glimpse of du Bellay's struggle to turn high ambition into poetic reality. The sonnet and ode, the two forms recommended years earlier by Peletier, dominate these collections, which are also marked by repeated deference to the superior accomplishment of Ronsard, by disdain for the vulgar multitude, and by attempts to curry the favor of the great. And it is here in two long poems addressed to King Henry II that du Bellay most clearly defines both his expectations regarding France's imperial destiny and the role that as poet he hopes to play in "this new age, the mirror image of antiquity." With his military triumphs, Henry's crescent will fill, du Bellay says, until it stands for the whole world, and du Bellay himself will erect a poetic temple in the same emblematic form, a "work made of such strong material that it will outlast the ravages of time."

The real-life side of the imperial ambition so fantastically evoked in du Bellay's poems to the king was tied up in the Valois monarchy's military and diplomatic conflicts with England and, even more acutely, with the far-flung realms of the emperor Charles V. With his appointment as secretary and household intendant to Cardinal Jean du Bellay and his departure in the cardinal's service for Rome, du Bellay moved to one of the principal sites of those conflicts. In the nearly sixty years since the French first invaded Italy, the Italian peninsula had been the main testing ground for the rival pretensions of the Valois and the Habsburgs, and the papal court in Rome was where much of the most crucial diplomatic maneuvering went on. Tending to French interests in Rome was the cardinal's job, and, as his chief aide, du Bellay would, he might easily have supposed, be inevitably involved. But if he imagined, as he seems to have done, that his service in Rome would engage him in the great affairs of state and put him on the way to a career comparable to that of Jean or Guillaume, he was soon stripped of those illusions. Not that great affairs weren't afoot. They were. In the four years du Bellay spent in Rome, the papacy changed hands twice, from the Habsburg-leaning Julius III to the austere and virtuously reforming Marcellus II, whose pontificate lasted only twenty-one days, and then to the aggressively anti-Spanish Paul IV, who schemed with Henry II and the Guise faction in France to drive the Spanish and imperial forces from Italy. These years also included Charles V's illness and retirement and the unexpected Truce of Vaucelles between France and Spain, which radically undermined the militant Franco-papal alliance. But despite his high place as dean of the College of Cardinals, not even Cardinal du Bellay had much part in the most important of these negotiations, which were carried

out behind his back by Pope Paul's nephew, the notorious Cardinal Caraffa. And, as for du Bellay himself, he could do little more than watch from the sidelines and lament the folly of his misplaced hopes and ambitions.

But conditions that shut doors in one direction opened them in another. Though Rome disappointed du Bellay's political ambitions, it excited his literary imagination and prompted what is easily the finest poetry he was ever to write, his *Regrets*, his *Antiquities of Rome*, his *Various Rustic Pastimes* (*Divers Jeux rustiques*), and his Latin *Poemata* (*Poems*), all four of which were published in Paris in the early months of 1558, shortly after his return from Rome. Since childhood, du Bellay had dreamed of ancient Rome. And as his poetic and political ideas had matured, Rome had become an ever more compelling object of desire. "O," he had written in an ode to Cardinal du Bellay, "the great fervor I had to quench my thirst in that stream"—the Tiber—"whose bank once saw the spoils of all the world." Now he was living in Rome, walking the streets the ancient Romans had walked, seeing buildings and statues they had seen, even hearing, in the humanist and ecclesiastic circles in which he moved, the sounds of their ancient tongue. The initial excitement of this encounter is nowhere better expressed than in his "Description of Rome," one of the eight elegies that would eventually be published in his *Poemata*, a poem that ends with an ardent wish "that I, Frenchman that I am, might make your fountains flow once again, while I enjoy the more bountiful Genius of this clime. . . . To my ambition, Latin Camenae, grant your indulgence, join with the Muses of my fatherland, and here may a second harvest of my talent spring forth." That he writes this poem in Latin is a first evidence of the effect Rome was having on him. But there are many others. Indeed, virtually all the poetry he wrote in those four years bears the marks of his residence in Rome. The calamitous fate of ancient and perhaps of modern Rome as well is the very subject of his *Antiquities*. His *Regrets* are filled with the traveler's nostalgia for home and the outsider's disdain for papal corruption and intrigue. And even the least Roman of his Roman poems, the *Rustic Pastimes*, are shaped by literary contacts he made while away from France.

This stimulating, disillusioning, and enormously fruitful sojourn came to an end in the last months of 1557 when du Bellay was sent back to Paris to oversee Cardinal du Bellay's many interests there. These affairs, which embroiled du Bellay in a conflict with the new bishop of Paris, his cousin Eustache, and the continuing struggle over the inheritance of his nephew Claude demanded much of his energy in the ensuing two years. And during these years, he was also afflicted with the return of illnesses, including the total loss of his hearing, that had largely spared him during his time in Rome. But despite all this, he continued to write. Many—perhaps all—of the final sixty-one sonnets of the *Regrets* were produced after his return to France, and he also produced a number of occasional poems and prose

works on such events as the Truce of Vaucelles, the marriage of his patroness Margaret of France, the death of Henry II, the coronation of Francis II, and the birth of the duke of Beaumont, as well as a discourse to the king on poetry and another on the four estates of the kingdom of France, a wryly satirical verse account of *The Courtier Poet* (*Le Poete courtisan*), and the long Latin elegy to Morel on his own unhappy affairs. Running through these works is a mixture of resignation, frustration, and continuing high ambition, both literary and political, that seems never to have left him. It is thus not surprising that when he died of a stroke on the night of January 1, 1560, he was at his desk working.

The Regrets

The shifting yet persistent mix of sometimes contradictory attitudes and ambitions that characterizes du Bellay's life also characterizes his greatest work, his *Regrets.* Describing the work—a sequence of 192 sonnets preceded by a Latin epigram and a 108-line dedicatory poem—would, for example, appear simple. I have, after all, just done it. But that appearance is deceptive. The book's title on the first edition, an edition whose printing du Bellay obviously oversaw with great care, is not *The Regrets* but rather *The Regrets and Other Poetic Works* (*Les Regrets et Autres Oeuvres Poetiques*). So where does the *Regrets* stop and the *Other Poetic Works* begin? A little over thirty years ago, in the introduction to his richly annotated edition, M. A. Screech had an answer. The break comes after sonnet 130, with du Bellay's return to France. This suggestion has proved sufficiently plausible to have convinced the two English-language translators of the *Regrets,* C. H. Sisson and David R. Slavitt, to stop with sonnet 130. But nothing in the sequence as it originally appeared tells us that sonnet 130 signals the passage from one work to another. Unlike what we find in *The Antiquities of Rome,* where the break between the *Antiquities* proper and the *Dream or Vision* is clearly indicated, there is no metrical marker, no new title, no abrupt change in poetic style. Sonnet 131 still talks about Rome, and sonnets 132–138 retell du Bellay's voyage home, now by land whereas in sonnets 128 and 129 it was by sea. Nor is sonnet 130 the only place where the *Regrets* might be thought to give way to something else. *Regrets* is du Bellay's translation of *Tristia,* the title Ovid gave one of the two collections of his poems of exile, poems du Bellay begins by translating in the opening seventy-two lines of his dedicatory poem and whose elegiac manner dominates the first suite of sonnets, before shifting to satire somewhere around sonnet 61 and then to eulogy with sonnet 155. So why don't we call sonnet 61 the beginning of the *Other Poetic Works?* For the obvious reason that the *Regrets* is always both one work and many, a single sequence, divided in narrative terms between Rome and France, in which du Bellay adopts a wide variety of generically distinct, though often overlapping, authorial poses.

In this regard, the Ovidian pose is not even the most obvious. Seeing the title and noticing that this is a sonnet sequence, the first readers of the *Regrets* would have thought of Petrarch and his host of sixteenth-century imitators, the du Bellay of *Olive* among them. Nor would they have been altogether disappointed. Du Bellay has dropped the Petrarchan mistress, but the suffering, the misplaced youth, the unrequited desire, the loss, the vain hopes, are all still there, now with a country, the idealized France of du Bellay's nostalgic imagination, in the place of the lady. Only after registering the partial deflection of these Petrarchan expectations would an early reader have noticed du Bellay playing Ovid. And here too the imitated pose comes with a significant substitution. For where Ovid in his Pontic exile had lamented his absence from Rome, du Bellay *in Rome* laments his absence from France. France is thus made the new seat of empire, the new "mother," as he audaciously puts it in sonnet 9, "of arts, of arms, and of laws." And were that early reader sufficiently alert, he would almost immediately have remarked still another pose. In the Latin epigram "To the Reader," du Bellay tells us that we should expect to find "the taste of gall and honey mixed with salt." Then in the dedicatory poem, he names the literary genre that "salt" was meant to evoke, satire, and in sonnet 2 he hints at the ancient satirist who provides his model, Horace, whose satiric mode he defines more fully and more openly in the transitional sonnet 62. Petrarchan sonneteer, Ovidian elegist, and Horatian satirist. In the *Regrets*, du Bellay is all three. And from sonnet 155 to the end of the sequence, he is also a eulogist of the great, a pose that from the beginning of his career he had associated with Pindar, Horace, Ronsard, and the ode.

What then are we to make of du Bellay's insistence, particularly in the programmatic sonnets that open the sequence, that he no longer aspires to poetic greatness, no longer cares for posterity, no longer feels the breath of divine inspiration, no longer wants "to turn the pages of Greek models," "retrace the beautiful lines of a Horace," or "imitate the grace of a Petrarch or the voice of a Ronsard"? This too is a pose, a pose so conspicuously adopted as to have led François Rigolot, one of the best modern readers of the *Regrets*, to talk of du Bellay's "poetics of refusal." Much of the energy of the *Regrets* comes from this refusal. After years of working to fulfill the program for literary and linguistic renewal that he had proposed in the *Defense* and that his friend Ronsard seemed to be so brilliantly accomplishing, du Bellay gives up and claims only to be writing for himself and a few friends. But this refusal paradoxically accomplishes his original purpose far more effectively than any of the more obviously ambitious poetry he had published before his departure for Rome. Not only does he in fact imitate Petrarch, Ovid, Horace, Pindar, and Ronsard while pretending not to. He imitates them in such a way as radically to remake them and the whole poetic tradition for which they stood. Out of the poetics of refusal he creates a poetics of the everyday, a poetics that is nevertheless charged with heroic po-

tential. Already his assumption of Petrarchan, Ovidian, Horatian, Pindaric, and Ronsardian poses in circumstances so far removed from those imagined by those great ancient and modern poets achieves something heroic. But he goes well beyond this. As he presents it, his voyage to Rome is a modern epic, and he is himself a latter-day Ulysses, Jason, Aeneas, Hercules, and Ruggiero. Like Joyce's Leopold Bloom, wandering the streets of early twentieth-century Dublin, du Bellay in sixteenth-century Rome is an epic hero—or, perhaps better, a mock-epic hero—for a world that still dreams, as du Bellay himself certainly does, of a glorious imperial restoration but that lives oppressed by everyday necessities that are anything but glorious.

Everydayness is central to the extraordinary appeal of the *Regrets*. At the end of sonnet 1, a sonnet that rings with refusal, du Bellay asks that his verses be given no "more gallant names than those of daily jottings or chronicles." Daily jottings and chronicles are in fact what we find, particularly in the first 130 sonnets, those devoted to his stay in Rome. He several times recounts the pastimes of an ordinary day: the household cares, the nagging worries, the importunity of creditors, the tedious business of diplomatic service, the gossip, the comradeship, and the debauchery. He reports on what he sees at the papal court, on the exchange, in the streets, tells how Rome has changed in the years he has been there, and describes everything from a conclave to a carnival to an exorcism to a bullbaiting to the eating habits of Pope Julius III and the wanton behavior of Roman whores. He even includes a sonnet on a conversation with his barber and another on the laziness of his roommate. And he lets us experience the great offstage events—movements toward war, papal deaths and elections, diplomatic scheming, the retirement of Charles V, the Truce of Vaucelles—as they were felt in the antechambers and reception halls he frequented. The result is an immediacy, a sense of reality, that is rare in the poetry of the sixteenth century and that could hardly have been predicted from the literary program du Bellay and his friends set forth.

The immediacy of the *Regrets* comes at least in part from the prevalence of still another genre, the epistle. As well as being a Petrarchan sonnet sequence with strong elegiac, satiric, panegyric, and even heroic leanings, the *Regrets* is a collection of letters. Du Bellay did not write his daily jottings and chronicles only for himself. Many were addressed to friends, colleagues, and patrons in France and in Rome. Like the everydayness of the *Regrets*, the collection's epistolary character may come as a surprise. In the *Defense*, where he lists ancient and modern poetic genres deserving imitation, du Bellay specifically advises *against* the epistle. "This," he says, "is not a kind of poem that can greatly enrich our vulgar tongue, since they are normally about familiar and domestic matters." But in this, as in so many other ways, the *Regrets* deliberately violates its author's recommendations. The familiar and the domestic are precisely the subjects of the *Regrets*, and

verse letters are just the kind of poem needed to treat them, whatever the consequences of that choice may be for the enrichment of the French language.

That du Bellay actually sent these letters is suggested by several surviving responses, particularly from Ronsard and from Olivier de Magny, a fellow poet and secretary to Jean de Saint-Marcel d'Avanson, the French ambassador in Rome and the dedicatee of the *Regrets.* Ideally, an edition of the *Regrets* would find a place for these other poems so that we could hear all sides of the ongoing conversation. But even without them, we should think of the *Regrets* as an open rather than a closed work, a work whose characteristic stances are assumed in response to a whole series of social, literary, and political exchanges. And though Ronsard and Magny hold a large place in these exchanges, du Bellay had many other correspondents, including most conspicuously Pierre Paschal, Jean Morel, Jean-Antoine de Baïf, Oudart d'Illiers (or "Dilliers," as du Bellay called him), Jerome della Rovere (du Bellay's "Vineus"), and a certain "Gordes," who is probably Jean-Antoine de Simiane. About some of the dozens of men du Bellay addresses, we know little more than what we can gather from the poems. Others are well known to literary scholars and historians. But well known or not, they together constitute the large and varied community that gives the *Regrets* the feeling of intimate and lived experience. And since the epistolary mode of the *Regrets* continues well beyond the specifically Roman sonnets to encompass the voyage home, the cynically disillusioned response to the French court, and even the final eulogistic poems, it provides the sequence one of its most powerful unifying elements. Poems of a self in search of itself and its place in the world, these are also poems of a dynamically evolving community. From the first, du Bellay's literary project was a group project, a project devised and pursued in company. In the *Regrets,* the joys, distresses, affections, animosities, comradeship, and rivalry that animated that company and the larger social world of which it was part are made known with unparalleled richness and complexity.

Daily jottings, chronicles, letters, and satires: the very commonplace lowness the du Bellay of the *Defense* worked so hard to avoid marks all these forms. Prosaic and apparently artless, they are the signs of du Bellay's poetics of refusal and of the everyday. But the seeming artlessness of the *Regrets* is itself an artful pretense that any alert reader will easily unmask. After all, when du Bellay in sonnet 2 says that he has given up on poetic aspiration, that he wants only that whatever he writes "should be prose in rhyme or rhyme in prose," he deliberately echoes Horace, one of the most self-consciously artful of all Roman poets, and he echoes Horace again just a few lines later when he teasingly suggests that would-be imitators will find his plain style harder to copy than they expect. Du Bellay's style would in fact prove hard to imitate, as Magny's attempts to do just that in *The Sighs* (*Les Soupirs*), which he wrote while he and du Bellay were both in Rome, clearly

show. In its combination of "rhyme" and "prose," artifice and artlessness, alienation and intimacy, imitation and authenticity, the heroic and the pedestrian, the extraordinary and the everyday, the *Regrets* stands alone. No where else did du Bellay achieve this remarkable balance. He does not even sustain it throughout the *Regrets*. By the time we get to the eulogistic poems, the balance has tipped decisively away from the everyday. But while it lasts, its delicate workings wonderfully accomplish the goal du Bellay had defined years earlier in the preface to the augmented edition of *Olive*: "to enrich our vulgar tongue with a new, or rather an ancient renewed poetry."

Consider, for example, what is probably the best known of all du Bellay's poems, sonnet 31 of the *Regrets*, a poem few French schoolchildren in the last century and a half have been able to avoid learning by heart.

Heureux qui, comme Ulysse, a fait un beau voyage,
Ou comme cestuy là qui conquit la toison,
Et puis est retourné, plein d'usage et raison,
Vivre entre ses parents le reste de son aage!

Quand revoiray-je, helas, de mon petit village
Fumer la cheminee, et en quelle saison,
Revoiray-je le clos de ma pauvre maison,
Qui m'est une province, et beaucoup d'avantage?

Plus me plaist le sejour qu'ont basty mes ayeux,
Que des palais Romains le front audacieux,
Plus que le marbre dur me plaist l'ardoise fine:

Plus mon Loyre Gaulois, que le Tybre Latin,
Plus mon petit Lyré, que le mont Palatin,
Et plus que l'air marin la doulceur Angevine.

Happy the man who, like Ulysses, has traveled well, or like that man who conquered the fleece, and has then returned, full of experience and wisdom, to live among his kinfolk the rest of his life!

When, alas, will I again see smoke rising from the chimney of my little village and in what season will I see the enclosed field of my poor house, which to me is a province and much more still?

The home my ancestors built pleases me more than the grandiose facades of Roman palaces, fine slate pleases me more than hard marble,

My Gallic Loire more than the Latin Tiber, my little Liré more than the Palatine hill, and more than sea air, the sweetness of Anjou.

This poem could easily be taken as a manifesto—albeit a metaphoric manifesto—for the poetics of refusal and the everyday. What du Bellay refuses is Rome and its grandeur. What he embraces or hopes to embrace is the humble sweetness of his native Anjou. It would be hard to imagine a more deliberate reversal of the values for which he had argued so vehemently in the *Defense.* Instead of wanting to remake France in the image of Rome, he wants only to return to the unreformed France his ancestors built. Now, it is true that before the sequence reaches its end, he will reverse this reversal. In sonnets 157 and 158, sonnets that introduce his panegyric poems, he proposes to construct for the muses a palace comparable to the classically remodeled Louvre, a magnificent palace whose four apartments would each have its own ancient style, one Doric, one Attic, one Ionian, and one Corinthian—a palace, in short, that would in no way resemble his Angevin home. But in sonnet 31 refusal and the everyday work with great power to convince us of their utter sincerity. That, after all, is why generations of French schoolchildren have been made to learn this poem. Having apparently abandoned all thought of transforming France into an imperial *patrie,* du Bellay longs rather for the contentment of a thoroughly homely *pays,* and he succeeds brilliantly in getting his readers to share that longing.

But when we look more closely at the poem that so touchingly expresses these feelings, we quickly discover a continuing and pervasive allegiance to the estranging, Roman values he seems to be renouncing. This is no rondel, ballad, virelay, or any of the other kinds of French poem du Bellay mocked in the *Defense.* It is a sonnet, an Italian form rarely attempted in French, never in a full sequence, before du Bellay came along. And not only is it a sonnet, but it is an extraordinarily artful example of the form, one that takes full advantage of the sonnet's internal division of octave and sestet, of quatrains and tercets, beautifully fitting a single exclamatory sentence into the first quatrain, a plaintive interrogative one into the second, and an extended, gracefully varied, anaphoric comparison (*Plus . . . , / Que . . . , / Plus que . . . : / Plus . . . que . . . , / Plus . . . que . . . , / Et plus que . . .*) into the two tercets. In the *Defense,* du Bellay had applauded the alternation of masculine and feminine rhymes in Marot's translation of the Psalms without insisting that such a demanding nicety be scrupulously observed. In sonnet 31, he does it himself, as he does in all but a very few of the sonnets in the *Regrets.* And he also follows the strong recommendation of the *Defense* in favor "of the figure antonomasia, which," he said there, "is as common in the ancient poets as it is little used—indeed, unknown—among the French." "That man who conquered the fleece"—*cestuy là qui conquit la toison*—in the sonnet's second line could easily serve as a textbook example of this ancient trope.

Still more innovative and no less artful is the metrical line du Bellay chose for this poem and all the others in the *Regrets,* the twelve-syllable alexandrine that in the mid-1550s he and Ronsard retrieved from long

neglect and made into what would remain the dominant long line of French poetry for the next three and a half centuries. When he wrote the *Defense,* du Bellay had yet to discover the alexandrine and so says nothing of it. But years later in his retrospective *Summary of the Art of French Poetry* (*Abbregé de l'Art Poetique François*), Ronsard defined this newly revived meter as the French equivalent of Greek and Latin heroic verse, the kind of verse that might be used in an epic poem, and he insisted that the lines must be made grave and elevated if they were not to sink into prose. In the *Regrets,* du Bellay brilliantly exploits both ends of this stylistic spectrum, making the alexandrine the perfect vehicle for the alienated but familiar heroic "rhyme in prose" these poems aim at. This is an extraordinary feat, one whose artfulness is only underlined by du Bellay's unobtrusive yet perfectly regular observance of the sixth-syllable caesura. No wonder later generations of French poets acted as though the alexandrine had always been theirs. Du Bellay's art—his and Ronsard's—had succeeded in making it so.

But not only in its formal features does sonnet 31 declare its estrangement from familiar ways of writing French verse and its allegiance to foreign models. The opening "Heureux qui" translates the "Beatus ille" of Horace's second epode, and the allusions that follow maintain that pattern of classical association by putting du Bellay in the company of Ulysses and Jason. They thus pursue the work, already begun by the Virgilian echoes of sonnet 17, of making his stay in Rome a modern-day epic. And for those prepared to notice the imitation, he would have remained in ancient company just when his nostalgic imagination might be supposed to have brought him nearest to home, when he yearns to see smoke rising from the chimney of his little village. More than fifteen hundred years earlier, much the same smoke had risen from the chimneys of Rome in Ovid's *Ex Ponto,* and even then it was not new, for Ovid himself recalls Ulysses' prayer to see the smoke of his Ithacan home, smoke du Bellay will in his turn remember in sonnet 130. But perhaps most telling of all, though it is not something one could guess from the poem itself, du Bellay seems first to have written this most French of all poems in Latin. Translated, lines 49 and 50 of his "Patriae desiderium"—"Longing for His Fatherland"—read, "When will I see the smoke rise from the chimney of my own country house and when will I see the few acres of my own estate?" Is the du Bellay of sonnet 31 longing for his native French *pays*? Or is he rather intent, as he was in the *Defense,* on devising a newly Romanized *patrie*? The poem may say the first, but all its canny art points toward the second.

Nor is the artfulness of the *Regrets* confined to individual poems. Though even the best readers can talk, as M. A. Screech does, of the "disorder" of the collection, of its apparently haphazard organization, that too is little more than a deceptive appearance, part of the aesthetic of daily jottings and chronicles. Not only does the collection as a whole have a broad overall structure, its division into elegiac, satiric, and panegyric, but nearly

every page and every opening—that is, every sequence of two facing pages—has its own artful structure. It may well be that du Bellay wrote these poems much as he seems to be doing, one by one with little attention to the whole they might eventually make. In that respect, the *Regrets* can really be read as his collected correspondence. But when in 1558, on his return to Paris, he gathered the poems and took them to his printer, he had something more orderly and artful in mind.

Here again sonnet 31 is instructive, now not as an isolated poem but rather as one of four poems, sonnets 31 through 34, a sixteenth-century reader would have encountered together on facing pages. As we would expect from poems taken from this part of the sequence, strong links in theme and attitude bind these sonnets to one another. All four lament du Bellay's absence from France, and all four worry about his return. But the verbal connections are still more striking. The opening phrases, to start with what is most obvious, create a powerful chiasmus stretching across the two-page opening, tying sonnet 31 ("Heureux qui, comme Ulysse") to sonnet 34 ("Comme le marinier") and sonnet 32 ("Je me feray") to sonnet 33 ("Que feray-je"), connections that are reinforced by the more elevated tone shared by sonnets 31 and 34 and the more colloquial tone of sonnets 32 and 33. And once we have noticed these diagonal links, we may also see how *Ulysse* in the opening line of sonnet 31 is replaced by *Dubellay* in the penultimate line of sonnet 34 and how both sonnets 32 and 33 end with comic, proverbial allusions, herring for gold in 32 and a wolf by the ears in 33. But the links are not only diagonal. They are vertical as well. In its final lines, sonnet 32 repeats and reverses the opening rhymes—*voyage* and *aage*—of sonnet 31, as Ulysses' "beau voyage" (fine voyage) turns into du Bellay's "malheureux voyage" (unhappy voyage), while sonnets 33 and 34 both address "mon cher Morel" (my dear Morel).

Are these patterns merely accidental? I don't think so. Meaningful groupings of this sort are too frequent not to be the result of some fairly careful planning. Take, for example, the sonnet that most richly echoes sonnet 31, the sonnet Screech thought closed the *Regrets* proper, sonnet 130. As one might expect of a punctuating poem, one that marks closure (however provisional that closure may be), sonnet 130 is found in the lower right-hand corner of its opening. And it shares that opening with sonnets 128 and 129, which report on du Bellay's heroic, Ulysses-like return home, and with sonnet 127, whose final tercet alludes to the very abuse du Bellay hopes to revenge in the last line of 130. While the "great lord" in 127 (in all likelihood, Anne de Montmorency, the lord high constable of France, who was depriving du Bellay's nephew Claude of his inheritance) arms himself with "force and oppression," du Bellay begs for the counter arm of Dorat's satiric bow, and *vangence* (revenge), the last word of 130, slyly shoots a verbal arrow back across the opening at *tyrannie* (oppression), the last word of 127. Not every opening can be as fiercely dy-

namic as this one, but a great many, far more than could have happened by chance, do make significant use of the four-poem collocation. Page back from 127–130 and we immediately find four facing poems, the only four in the sequence, on the Truce of Vaucelles. Page forward and we find the first of two openings devoted to the overland version of du Bellay's trip home. In sonnet 131, he refers back to Rome; in 132, he reaches Urbino; in 133, Venice; in 134, the Grisons, a canton of Switzerland; in 135 and 136, other parts of Switzerland, probably including Geneva; in 137, Lyon; and in 138, Paris, for a second return home, a return that is appropriately located, as was the first in sonnet 130, in the lower right-hand corner of an opening. So here, at a crucial turning point in the sequence, four successive openings each have an order that can only be deliberate.

The 192 sonnets of the *Regrets* occupy forty-nine openings: one for the sonnet addressed to "My Book," which has a page all to itself, and, on the facing page, for the next two sonnets of the sequence, the sonnets that are now numbered 1 and 2; one for a final poem addressed to the king, sonnet 191, a poem that gets a page to itself with nothing across from it; and forty-seven for the remaining 188 sonnets, all of them arranged in groups of four. It would be tempting to discuss every one of these openings. Though some are more miscellaneous than others, all of them invite active reading back and forth between the juxtaposed poems, and most are strikingly unified. Without belaboring what will be quickly clear to any reader who is motivated to test that claim, let me just list a few obvious examples: 11–14 all concern writing poetry in the face of adversity; 27–30 all concern travel; 43–46 all concern du Bellay's virtue and the little good it has brought him; 51–54 all concern accepting fortune and leading the good life; 87–90 all concern Circean enchantment; 103–106 all concern papal corruption; 139–142 all provide cynical advice on how to get along at court; 155–158 all concern graver poetry; 159–174 (four successive openings) all praise various distinguished figures at court; 175–190 (four more openings) all praise Margaret of France.

And if, as I say, such openings invite active reading, we have only to look at the copy of du Bellay's collected works now in the municipal library of Lyon, a copy once owned and heavily annotated by du Bellay's contemporary, the humanist Henri Étienne, to find the invitation being accepted. Étienne notes that *pedantesque* (pedantic) in sonnet 68 and *mastin* (mastiff) in 69 connect these poems to one another and to sonnets 65 and 66 in the previous opening. He draws a line from 84 through 85 and 86 on the facing page to mark du Bellay's repeated use of the infinitive. He draws another line between 97 and 98 in recognition of their common subject. He draws two heavy lines between 117 and 118 to signal their repetition of *vrayement* (truly), and with another line he marks the repetition of *appartement* (apartment) from 157 to 158. And over each of the two facing pages containing 139–142, he writes "on the court"—*sur la court.* Page layout seems clearly to have guided his reading.

So is the *Regrets* ordered or disordered? In this, as in so many other ways, it is both. Through the greater part of the sequence, two quite different notions of poetic value are simultaneously in play, on one side the seemingly intimate and spontaneous poetics of refusal and the everyday and on the other the ambitious, imitative poetics of high art and imperial translation. Rome is central to both. Ancient Rome provides the model of empire and art, a model embodied in such exemplary figures as Ovid, Horace, Virgil, and another exile whose triumphant exploits du Bellay, like Petrarch before him, much admired, Scipio Africanus. But modern Rome, particularly the Rome of the papacy, threatens France's universalist aspirations, furnishes du Bellay with the object of his most scathing satire, and serves as the site of his own exile, the place from which he nostalgically looks back on the France of his frustrated desire. Refusal and the everyday belong to modern Rome. To ancient Rome belong ambition and imitation. In the *Regrets*, modern Rome and the poetics it provokes give the poems their subject and determine their attitude. Modern Rome surrounds du Bellay, presses itself on his often unwilling attention, annoys, amuses, enchants, and outrages him. The apparent disorder of the *Regrets* is the disorder of modern Rome, the disorder of du Bellay's everyday life there. But the urge to order, the urge that made him arrange his poems in the artfully unobtrusive way he did when he took them to the printer's, the urge to give them an enduring monumental structure came from ancient Rome. This is not to say that he had any ancient model for his use of pages and openings. Given the very different technologies of textual reproduction, that would be highly unlikely. But the very ambition to impose form on his scattered correspondence grew from his encounter with ancient Rome and its literature, and the individual poems, even the most colloquial of them, are shot through with Roman poses and allusions. Finding a way between these two Romes is the great undertaking of the *Regrets*, an undertaking du Bellay accomplishes with extraordinary and utterly unpredictable success.

The Antiquities of Rome

Datable events and statements like the "three years and more" of sonnet 10 suggest that the *Regrets* belongs to the last two years of du Bellay's stay in Rome and the first months following his return to France. Nothing in the other great sonnet sequence he published early in 1558, his *Antiquities of Rome*, allows us to date the writing of these poems with similar confidence. That fact points to a first obvious difference between these two very different collections. The poems in the *Regrets* are topical. Those in the *Antiquities* are not. Rome may be the subject of both sequences, but the Rome of the *Antiquities* is not the sixteenth-century Rome of du Bellay's everyday experience. Here he writes instead of ancient Rome, whose greatness he describes and whose fall he laments. And from this difference others flow.

The common or middle style of the *Regrets*—its *sermo pedestris*—gives way to the high style of the *Antiquities.* Where in the *Regrets* du Bellay wrote familiar letters to friends, he now apostrophizes in the most lofty terms the "Divine Spirits" of ancient Rome, Rome's "sacred hills" and "holy ruins," the "cruel stars" and "inhuman gods." Other than King Henry II, whose "universal dominion" du Bellay foresees in his dedicatory sonnet, he neither addresses nor even mentions any contemporary. And far from being shaped by a poetics of refusal, the *Antiquities* openly seeks inspiration, proclaims the highest of ambitions, and, in the *Dream* sequence with which the volume ends, claims to have been granted an apocalyptic vision comparable to that of the New Testament's Saint John. Nor is the resulting artfulness in any way hidden. Where, for example, the apparent spontaneity of the *Regrets* masks the collection's cunningly suggestive page layout, the pages of the *Antiquities,* each with a sonnet in decasyllabic verse on the top and a sonnet in alexandrines on the bottom, call immediate attention to the architectonic design that has arranged them that way.

Yet for all their differences, both sequences draw on a common Petrarchan legacy. If in the *Regrets* France takes the place of Petrarch's Laura, that place in the *Antiquities* is assumed by Rome. But in the *Antiquities* the relation between the poet and the object of his desire is even more complexly informed by the legacy of Petrarch than was the case in the *Regrets.* Consider, for example, poems from the two sequences that each open with an echo of Petrarch, *Regrets* 25 and *Antiquities* 5. Du Bellay's curse in *Regrets* 25 on the moment when he left France to go to Rome ("Malheureux l'an, le mois, le jour, l'heure, et le poinct") reverses Petrarch's blessing in Rime sparse 61 on the moment when he first saw Laura ("Benedetto sia 'l giorno e 'l mese et l'anno / e la stagione e 'l tempo et l'ora e 'l punto"), while his invitation in Antiquities 5 to admire in Rome all that nature, art, and heaven can do ("Qui voudra voir tout ce qu'ont peu nature, / L'art, et le ciel") simply translates, with the addition of "art," Petrarch's invitation in Rime sparse 248 to see the same marvel in Laura ("Chi vuol veder quantunque po Natura / e 'l Ciel"). To anyone who knew Petrarch—and these were among his most frequently imitated poems—the allusions would have been unmistakable. But they do not work in the same way. Where the first has an almost parodic relation to its source and is wryly self-mocking throughout, the second replicates not only the epiphanic wonder of Petrarch's poem but also its pathos. As so often in the *Rime sparse,* the menace of time obsesses Petrarch. If we don't hurry to see Laura, we will, he tells us, be too late, for death takes the best first. In the *Antiquities,* this obsession is also du Bellay's. "Rome is no more," he insists, "and if her ruins still show us some shade of Rome, it is like a body raised by magical powers from its sepulchre at night." Nor do the similarities stop here. As Petrarch ends by alluding to his own "rhymes" and their imperfect representation of Laura's beauty, so too du Bellay ends with the focus on writing, though not

on his own writing but rather on that of Rome and her poets: "But her writings, which in spite of time wrest her fairest praise from the grave, keep her specter wandering throughout the world."

These recurring elements—the wondrous beauty and/or greatness of the beloved object, that object's inevitable subjection to death and decay, and poetry's role in conferring whatever immortality may be achieved in this world—firmly bind the *Rime sparse* and the *Antiquities* to one another. Poetry needs death to define its power to preserve an absent transcendence, its power to keep the specter of that transcendence wandering throughout the world. And for both Petrarch and du Bellay, poetry has a still greater ambition, not only to memorialize but also to restore, to make the dead live again. In the *Rime sparse* this greater ambition is little more than a hint, though it was central to Petrarch's humanist scholarship. But inasmuch as Laura is made to recall the Venus of Virgil's *Aeneid,* as she is, for example, in the famous "Erano i capei d'oro" (*Rime sparse* 90), she points Petrarch toward an Italian restoration of Rome just as Venus directed Aeneas to Rome's original founding, which was also the restoration of vanished Troy. In this sense, Petrarch's Laura is already a figure for Rome even before du Bellay renames her. But, unlike Petrarch, du Bellay announces his ambition of effecting an imperial restoration right from the start, in that dedicatory sonnet to Henry II, where he hopes that his verses will one day be seen as "a blessed omen" of the king's "universal dominion." And he frames the collection with two "boasts": the first in the dedicatory sonnet to have "pulled from the tomb the dusty remains of the ancient Romans" and the second in sonnet 32 to have "sung, first among the French, the ancient honor of the long-robed people," a phrase that would have recalled a well-known line from the *Aeneid,* where Jupiter proclaims that the *gens togata*—"the long-robed people"—will be "lords of the world."

Did du Bellay really expect France to enjoy a similar destiny? Despite a number of quite explicit statements to that effect scattered through his work, scholars disagree about how seriously they are to be taken. But whatever du Bellay may have expected, thoughts of universal dominion clearly preoccupied him throughout his career, never more so than in the *Antiquities.* It is sometimes claimed that this *First Book of the Antiquities of Rome,* as the 1558 title has it, was to have been followed by a second book devoted to the French rebirth of Rome, in much the way that Janus Vitalis's epigram "Roma prisca" (Ancient Rome), from which du Bellay took the wonderful sonnet 3 of the *Antiquities,* was followed by a "Roma instaurata" (Rome Restored), on the sixteenth-century rebuilding of Rome. We do not, however, need to go so far to see how concerns for imperial renewal might have led du Bellay to his passionate meditation on the greatness of ancient Rome and on Rome's astounding ruin. Already in the preface to his 1492 *Castilian Grammar,* Antonio de Nebrija had coupled his claim that "language has always been the companion of empire" with an account of the succession

of empires and languages, the fall of one making way for the rise of another. Similarly, in his *Defense,* du Bellay, talking of how with great labor French can one day be made to equal or even surpass Greek and Latin, reminds his readers that God "gave as an inviolable law to all created things that they cannot endure forever but must pass ceaselessly from one state to another, the end and corruption of one being the beginning and generation of another." Insisting, as he does throughout the *Antiquities,* on the utter and catastrophic ruin of Rome, he thus discovers an imperial space that has opened for France, but also warns, at least implicitly, that France's empire will be no more lasting than Rome's.

In the final fifteen sonnets of the collection, the sequence du Bellay calls *A Dream or Vision* on the book's title page and simply *Dream* in the body of the text itself, he presents the pattern of greatness suddenly reduced to ruin with particular starkness. Here, again, Petrarch provided a model. In *Rime sparse* 323, the Italian poet describes a series of six visions—a wild creature, a ship with ropes of silk and sails of gold, a young laurel tree, a clear fountain, a wondrous phoenix, and a beautiful lady—all overcome by death or destruction and all, we suppose, representing Laura, whose own death was announced many poems earlier. From this canzone, du Bellay takes the idea of a series of emblematic visions and borrows two specific images, the fountain and the ship. At one point, he even mentions "the sad Florentine." But he had other sources as well, including most obviously the Bible and ancient Roman iconography. What he did with this heterogeneous material was to create a powerfully relentless, though often enigmatic vision of imperial ruin that starts with ancient Rome but reaches out to encompass modern papal Rome and, indeed, all worldly things, not excepting his own poetry, whose hopes for immortality he had entertained and questioned in sonnet 32 of the *Antiquities,* directly across the page opening from the first two sonnets of the *Dream.* Yet however far-reaching the ruin he describes may ultimately be, Rome, ancient and modern, is clearly the chief target, and it may at least be supposed from the echo of Virgil with which the *Dream* begins—an echo that puts du Bellay in the position of Aeneas—that, before the created universe finally returns to chaos, the fall of Rome will lead to the founding of a new imperial power.

But if that is so, if du Bellay is, however obliquely, casting himself as a new Aeneas, the *Antiquities* as a whole puts almost as many barriers in the way of his longed-for *translatio* as it opens possibilities. Not that he does not do a thorough job of insisting on Rome's fall. He does. Indeed, he is so much more intent on the sheer fact of ruin than he is on consistent historical explanation that he piles up far more causes for Rome's demise than can possibly be made to cohere. Does the fault lie, as he learned from Lucan's *Pharsalia,* with the civil wars that pitted Julius Caesar against Pompey? Or does it belong rather to the Gothic invasions that came centuries later? Rather than deciding, du Bellay embraces both and then for good measure

adds pride, destiny, a primal curse, the ravages of time, the animosity of the stars, the gods, envious heaven, and stepmother nature, and even the laws of physics. Rome simply got too big and came crashing down. But none of these causes, whether alone or combined, can quite account for the utter devastation du Bellay reports. In the *Antiquities,* Rome is "reduced to nothing but a dusty plain," to "dusty ashes," to "dusty tombs," to "dust" itself—in sum, to a waste more like what Rome made of Carthage than what Rome and all her enemies combined made of Rome herself. Nor is the likeness to ruined Carthage without reason. As Rome's universalist ambitions required her rival's obliteration, so du Bellay's ambitions for France require the obliteration of Rome. The death of imperial Rome makes possible the birth of imperial France.

The problem is that Rome refuses to stay dead. Even in the *Dream,* where ruin is so abrupt and so final, three poems allow a return. In sonnet 5, the "scorned stump" of the Dodonian oak sprouts "twin trees"; in sonnet 7, the incinerated eagle is reborn, "like a worm from his ashes," as an owl; and in sonnet 13, the sunken boat reemerges, as it fails to do in du Bellay's Petrarchan source. How are we to understand these revivals? With nothing to prove the contrary, the recovered boat could be a much-desired French succession. But the other two are not so promising. The twin trees would seem to represent the papacy and the Holy Roman Empire, while the owl, like the crow in *Antiquities* 17, is almost surely that same Germanic empire. And even without an obviously hostile succession to block France's way, the sixteenth-century rebuilding of Rome that du Bellay observed at first hand suggests, as he says in *Antiquities* 27, that "the spirit of Rome still strives with a fated hand to resurrect these dusty ruins." Such intimations of continued vitality—or if not of literal vitality, then of overwhelming preeminence even in death—run through the sequence. Rome's writings keep, as we have seen, "her specter wandering throughout the world"; "the greatness of the nothing" that is now Rome "still amazes the world"; true to the omen discovered at her foundation, Rome remains the *caput mundi,* the head of the world; even in desolation, "among the cities which most flourish now, the ancient and dusty honor of this city is the most honored"; "Rome was the whole world, and the whole world is Rome"; "alive Rome was the ornament of the world, and dead she is the world's tomb." Given all this, it should be no surprise that in a sonnet shot through with Virgilian recollections, du Bellay feels compelled to deny the very hope on which his project of imperial rebirth was based. "Rome alone could resemble Rome," he says in *Antiquities* 6. "No greatness equal to her greatness, except her own, will ever be seen again." If this is so, what hope can there be for France?

At this distance, we may find it difficult to comprehend the intensity of desire and intimidation Rome could provoke in a humanistically educated and culturally ambitious sixteenth-century poet like du Bellay. After all, wasn't imperial Rome's collapse already a full millennium old? A passage

from Lorenzo Valla's *On the Elegances of the Latin Language*, a book that was known and admired throughout Europe, may help. Identifying himself with Rome, Valla insists that "subject peoples may have thrown off the yoke of Roman arms, but they remain under the yoke of the Latin language. . . . Italy, France, Spain, Germany . . . and many other countries are still ours. Wherever the language of Rome dominates, the Roman Empire lives on." That continued dominance and the struggle to overcome it underlies du Bellay's career from start to finish. But nowhere does he confront his Roman dilemma, a dilemma he shared with poets all over Europe, more directly than in the two sequences that make up the *Antiquities of Rome*: the *Antiquities* proper and the *Dream or Vision on the Same Subject*. Where the *Regrets* claims, however disingenuously, to have renounced ambition and to content itself with reporting on its author's daily life in present-day Rome, the *Antiquities* takes on the idea of ancient imperial Rome in all its tragic grandeur. Du Bellay's "antiquities" are not so much the physical remains of Rome—to these he pays surprisingly little attention—as they are Rome's towering cultural and political remains, and those exist more in his mind than in any external reality. As a result, the whole volume, and not only its final *Dream* sequence, has a powerful visionary quality, a vision in which the poet and his own vernacular culture are deeply implicated in the fate of the "pale spirits" he summons from their graves. On those spirits he depends for his inspiration. But he depends no less on their standing aside to make way for a successor empire and its poets. If in the *Antiquities* the inspiration is richly granted, the succession has yet to be won.

Three Latin Elegies

In the *Defense*, du Bellay identifies two main enemies of the French language. First are ignorant writers who use French. Second are learned ones who don't, who choose instead to write in Latin. Neither can be can be expected to enrich French in the ways du Bellay thinks necessary. The first debase the language, the second neglect it. And as for the notion that the French nation can be rendered illustrious by Frenchmen writing in Latin, that is no more than an idle fancy. We will never, du Bellay insists, be able to rival, much less surpass, the ancients in their own language, and continued dependence on that language will only prolong our cultural servitude.

Given these views and the vehemence with which he had expressed them, du Bellay had some explaining to do when he began writing in Latin himself, as he did almost as soon as he arrived in Rome. In response to chiding from Ronsard, he weakly pleads the necessity of his present situation. You have made French the equal of the ancient tongues, he says to his friend, but here no one understands it. And in a poem—a Latin poem—addressed to the readers of his *Poemata*, he more wittily confesses his transgression and explains that while French is his wife, Latin is his mistress, and

just now he finds the mistress more exciting. But whether he thought of writing in Latin as a hard necessity or a stimulating adventure, the ancient language of empire remained an integral, even central part of the extraordinarily productive poetic life he led during the four crucial years he spent in Rome. Indeed, from the very start, long before he went to Rome, his plan for remaking French had been based on a Latin model, and the great poets of Rome, especially Virgil, Horace, and Ovid, had been constantly in his mind as he worked. What the direct experience of Rome and the humanist circle he encountered there did was to add a new dimension to this sometimes anxious relation. That experience made him a Latin poet. And it was in that foreign guise that he first responded to Rome and first expressed the feelings of radical estrangement and loss that eventually reshaped his vernacular poetry. Through Latin, du Bellay became the French poet we now best remember, the poet of the *Regrets* and the *Antiquities of Rome.*

The three elegies included in this edition all come from the *Poemata,* the collection of Latin poetry du Bellay published in 1558 along with the *Regrets,* the *Antiquities,* and the *Various Rustic Pastimes.* Together with five other elegies and a pastoral eclogue, these three poems make up the first book of the *Poemata,* whose three other books are the *Epigrammata* (*Epigrams*), many of them sharing the topical and epistolary character of the *Regrets,* the *Amores* (*Loves*), most devoted to a tumultuous affair with a certain Faustina, and the *Tumuli* (*Tombs*), sometimes eulogistic, sometimes satiric funeral poems, beginning with an epitaph for ancient Rome. Though many of these poems, particularly the *Loves* of Faustina, venture into territory du Bellay reserved for Latin, many others appear to be Latin drafts for poems he later wrote in French. Thus the epitaph on ancient Rome in the *Tombs* got reworked as the fourth sonnet of the *Antiquities*; the account of his voyage to Rome in the first elegy supplied the account of his voyage home in sonnet 128 of the *Regrets*; and *Epigrams* 1, 50, and 61 to Henry II, Margaret of France, and Jean Dorat were transformed into *Regrets* 191, 174, and 130. But none of the Latin poems has a deeper or more complex relation to du Bellay's French poetry and to his whole poetic enterprise than do the three elegies I have reprinted and translated here. Not only do specific poems in the *Regrets* and *Antiquities* draw on them directly, but together they represent the three poles that most decisively oriented du Bellay's literary career: Rome, Ronsard, and France.

The "Description of Rome"—elegy 2, as these poems are now commonly numbered—was probably written shortly after du Bellay's arrival in Rome and is charged with an excitement that had largely turned to disillusionment by the time he wrote the *Regrets.* The poem begins and ends with stirring reaffirmations of poetic vocation, just the opposite of the poetics of refusal that was to mark the later sonnet sequence. And du Bellay makes clear that the renewed fervor of his ambition has been ignited by Rome it-

self, by what he calls "the more bountiful Genius of this clime." For him, that Genius is animated almost equally by ancient and by modern Rome—or, perhaps better, by the heady mixture of the two. Though he eventually moves to an *Antiquities*-like meditation on the ruin of Rome and the continuing power of ancient Roman poetry, the Rome he describes seems anything but dead. The galleries of the Vatican and Saint Peter's Cathedral with Michelangelo's great dome still under construction are evoked along side the Mausoleum of Hadrian, the Pantheon, and the Aqua Virgo. The arts of Athena, armed combat and horse races, endless political intrigue, the spectacle of Fortune's power, and, most of all, Venus and her amorous games are as much part of modern Rome as they ever were of the ancient city, and the statues of antiquity—the *Laocoön*, the *Apollo Belvedere*, the *Capitoline Wolf*, the *Spinario*, the *Dioscuri*, and many others—are still to be seen more than a millennium after their creation. "Here great Tully was accustomed to reign," but here too the vicar of Rome, "who holds the keys to highest Olympus," reigns still, "august in his miter." "Rome dead is now her own tomb," he says, but Rome alive breathes through every line of this elegy. Though expressed nowhere else with quite the exuberance of first contact that we find here, that paradox—Rome's continuing life in death—remains among the abiding concerns of du Bellay's poetry. Rome dead provides the opportunity he seizes, while Rome alive furnishes the inspiration to pursue it.

Not inspiration, but rather its loss is featured in the other two elegies I reproduce here, the one addressed to Ronsard (elegy 6) and the one—"Patriae desiderium"—on his longing for France (elegy 7). Written in the last year or two of his stay in Rome, these two poems contributed directly to at least nine sonnets in the *Regrets*—6, 7, 10, 19, 20, 24, 30, 31, and 40—and have close thematic connections to the whole opening section of that sequence. Here, as there, du Bellay is obsessed with the very different trajectories his career and Ronsard's have followed. And here, as there, absence from home puts him in the company of wandering Ulysses and banished Ovid. For him, Latin, the language of radical self-estrangement, seems to have served as the language of a surprisingly heroic self-discovery that could then be expressed still more poignantly, if no more affirmatively, in his vernacular sonnets.

In these elegies, he does not, however, point toward his sonnets or toward any of the other French poems he may by then have written during his stay in Rome as the fulfillment of the high ambitions he had laid out in the *Defense* and renewed in his "Description of Rome." Instead, he identifies Ronsard as the poet who is accomplishing the task they had together assumed. By merit, Ronsard holds "the highest place in the Aonian troop" and enjoys "the favor of people and kings alike." Already the victory is assuredly his. Already a sacred crown encircles his head. But in that very proclamation of Ronsard's enviable apotheosis, du Bellay defines his friend

and the expectations that surround him in such a way as to make a place for himself and his own newly emerging countercareer. Elegy 6 ends with du Bellay calling on Ronsard to "write, be bold, and let France boast at last of a work to which Greece gives way and Italy as well." That work was to be the *Franciade*, the uncompleted epic Ronsard was then writing. As du Bellay sets out the terms, Ronsard must move beyond the Pindaric odes and Petrarchan love poems that had so far dominated his verse and take on the part of the French Virgil, a part that, as he hints in sonnet 23 of the *Regrets*, Ronsard may not have been ready to play. And meanwhile, even as he renounces his own ambition and laments his loss of inspiration, du Bellay slyly crafts for himself a part that recalls not only Ulysses and Ovid but also Aeneas in the underworld on his way to the founding of Rome. Though du Bellay would never dare to say as much—he may not even have dared to think it—he in his Roman and Latin Hades may have been better positioned to reach their shared imperial goal than Ronsard in his courtly French Elysium. In forcing him to write in Latin, the Genius of Rome may have done du Bellay—and us—a greater favor than he could recognize or acknowledge.

The benefits of that favor are immediately apparent in the beautiful seventh elegy, his "Patriae desiderium" (Longing for His Fatherland), and in the cluster of French sonnets from the *Regrets* that draw on it. It is here, in this Latin elegy, that du Bellay first sounds the Ovidian note that will so hauntingly ring through the *Regrets*, here that he first imagines the smoke rising from the chimneys of his native village, first defines his stay in Rome as exile, first takes alienation as his great subject, first compares himself to wandering Ulysses, and first dresses "the banks of the Loire, the pastures, the leafy woods, the rich products of the Angevin soil" in the garb of nostalgia. But he does something else here as well, something that has no counterpart in his French poems. Like Saint Paul in the Acts of the Apostles, he claims Roman citizenship. "Rome," he says, "is the fatherland"—the *patria*—"of the world, and he who dwells within the walls of high Rome lives—he too—on his own soil." Writing in Latin, he assumes one of the prerogatives of that citizenship. And even when he translates, as he will soon do, bits of his Latin into French, he is a Roman citizen still, a Romanized Frenchman bent on transforming the language and literature of France in imitation of a Roman model. For du Bellay, bilingualism and its inner accompaniment, spiritual dual-citizenship, provide, to use one of his own favorite horticultural metaphors, the well-cultivated ground from which a new imperial culture and, with it, a new identity and new allegiance can grow.

The Defense and Enrichment of the French Language

Were the order of my introduction chronological, I would already have discussed du Bellay's *Defense*, for it was written and published well before the

Regrets, the *Antiquities*, or the Latin elegies. But I have instead followed the order of this edition, which gives priority to the poetry. Chronological inversion does, however, have an advantage. Coming to the *Defense* after reading the Roman poems, we are better able to measure the distance du Bellay traveled in the years that separate one from the other. Viewed from one perspective, that distance appears enormous. The *Regrets* would seem to renounce, at least for du Bellay himself, the high ambition defined by the *Defense*; the Latin poems specifically defy the call issued in the *Defense* to write in French; and even the *Antiquities* raises questions as to whether imitation of the sort proposed by the *Defense* can, in fact, be accomplished. But seen from another angle, there would seem to be no distance at all between the manifesto and the poems. The ambition proclaimed in the Latin "Description of Rome" is at one with what du Bellay says in the *Defense*, and the actual accomplishment of the French poems, the triumphant realization of a vernacular art of poetry based on and comparable to, yet independent from the poetic art of ancient Greece and Rome and of modern Italy, wonderfully fulfills that ambition.

So what does the *Defense* actually do? As its title suggests, it defends the French language—not its accomplishment, but rather its potential—and proposes a way of making French poetry illustrious. Each of these tasks is assigned its own book: a book for the defense and a book for the *illustration*—what I have translated as the "enrichment." This overall structure, as suggested by the division of each of the books into twelve chapters, has heroic overtones. Twelve is the number of books in the *Aeneid*; twice twelve, the number of books in the *Iliad* and the *Odyssey*. Following in the trace of the *Aeneid*, the *Defense*, in the words of a recent editor, Jean-Charles Monferran, "wishes to participate in the foundation of a second Rome of which it claims to be the origin." The book's militant tone clearly supports this heroic pretension. Framed by a commendatory poem by Jean Dorat that hails du Bellay's manifesto as comparable to his ancestors' feats on the battlefield and by an epilogue that calls on Frenchmen to "march courageously on that proud Roman city and from her captured spoils . . . adorn your temples and altars," the *Defense* assumes an aggressively offensive posture. Indeed, unlike Aeneas, who in Virgil's poem only reports the Greek destruction of Troy before going on to found Rome, du Bellay was seen by contemporary opponents like Barthélemy Aneau as having himself perpetrated the devastation he then proposes to remedy. "Who is accusing or who has accused the French language?" Aneau asks. "Certainly no one, at least not in writing." On this point, modern scholars have tended to side with Aneau. French literary culture in the 1540s, the culture Thomas Sébillet celebrated in his *Art of French Poetry*, was in far better shape than du Bellay allowed. Du Bellay's heroic militancy can thus easily appear, as it did to both Aneau and Sébillet, willfully misdirected. In declaring French poetry a wasteland, little better than a ruined Troy, du Bellay does not so much

describe reality as invent an occasion for himself and his friends to found a second Rome that in the view of people like Aneau and Sébillet did not need founding.

To understand du Bellay's militancy, it is useful to remember not only his personal sense of deprivation, the heroic legacy associated with his name, and the hothouse environment of the College of Coqueret, where his ambition and Ronsard's were nourished, but also the broader literary and linguistic setting of mid-sixteenth-century Europe, and particularly of France's great cultural model and rival, Italy. Nowhere is that setting more fully laid out than in the book du Bellay seized on in his need as he hastily composed his *Defense*, the book from which he lifted without acknowledgment some twenty-eight passages totaling about fifteen pages of text, Sperone Speroni's 1542 *Dialogo delle Lingue* (*Dialogue on Languages*). Pierre Villey's discovery of this wholesale borrowing early in the twentieth century—or rather *re*discovery, since some of du Bellay's contemporaries were clearly aware of it—led first to the shocked denial of du Bellay's originality. Since then, critics have pointed out how unlike Speroni's dialogue du Bellay's manifesto really is. Though the two books share many passages, some of them stretching over a page or more, they put the passages to very different uses. And Speroni scarcely hints at the theory of cultural imitation that is among du Bellay's most fundamental ideas. But here I am less interested in reasserting du Bellay's originality, which seems to me by now well enough established to stand on its own, than in examining the particular provocation Speroni's book afforded. Though it may be, as Aneau says, that no one in France was accusing French of deficiencies that required du Bellay's defense, the speakers of Speroni's *Dialogue* do casually assume the barbarity of the French, and they talk of their own linguistic situation in ways that could hardly have failed to stimulate du Bellay's thinking about France.

Speroni's *Dialogue* is divided into two parts. In the first, Lazaro Bonamico, who had recently been appointed to the chair of Greek and Latin in Padua, Pietro Bembo, the famous churchman, humanist, and poet, and an unnamed courtier discuss the respective merits of the languages that were then competing for literary favor: the classical languages of Greece and Rome, the Tuscan of Petrarch and Boccaccio, and the various vernacular dialects of contemporary Italy. In the second, a hitherto silent student, also unnamed, repeats a conversation that took place several years earlier between his master, the Aristotelian philosopher Pietro Pomponazzi, and the Hellenist Giovanni Lascari over the question of whether philosophy should only be studied in Greek or whether Latin and even vernacular translations would serve. From Pomponazzi's defense of the vernacular—any vernacular—as a potentially philosophical language, du Bellay made his largest borrowings, including a crucial passage in the first chapter of book 1 of the *Defense* on the inherent equality of languages, large parts of the long tenth

chapter of book 1 on the suitability of the vernacular for philosophy, and several important passages in the following chapter on the impossibility of equaling the ancients in their own languages. But he also drew freely on Bembo's interventions in the first half. From these he took passages scattered through book 1 of the *Defense* and the third chapter of book 2 on such topics as the contemporary burgeoning of vernacular literary study, the deliberate cultivation the Romans gave Latin, the inevitable mutation of all things, the advantages of belated growth, and the necessity of hard work for a poet who wishes to attain immortality.

Yet significant as these direct borrowings undoubtedly are, they are no more significant than the impact on du Bellay and the *Defense* of a number of passages he did *not* borrow. As Lazaro and Bembo define it, the great question at issue between them is what language can serve to attain everlasting literary fame. For Lazaro, the answer is simple. Only Greek and Latin have that potential. For Bembo, things are more complicated. In his view, another contender has proved its strength: the fourteenth-century Tuscan perfected by Petrarch and Boccaccio. But for both, the question of language is intimately linked to the ancient fall of the Roman Empire and the more recent invasions of Italy, especially by the French. Linguistic and literary superiority, whatever the language, provides the sole consolation for Italy's political and military ruin. We "live and talk with barbarians," says Bembo, "without becoming barbarian." Reading these words and many other allusions to the French as barbarians—indeed, as the most barbarous of the many barbarians who have ravaged Italy over the centuries—du Bellay would have had reason enough to think his nation and his language needed defending. The terms he chose were clearly fitted to Speroni's attack. "That the French Language should not be called barbarous" is, after all, the title of one of his first chapters. And throughout the *Defense,* he adopts the standards of judgment shared by Lazaro and Bembo. Like them, he takes immortal fame to be the goal. Like them, he associates literary fame with imperial prowess. And like them, he argues that only a language that has attained the artful cultivation of Greek and Latin can support such an ambition. He even accepts something of their belittling characterization of France and the French.

When du Bellay argues that the French language should not be called barbarous, he does not deny its woeful lack of cultivation. On the contrary, that very lack is his subject. Following Speroni's Pomponazzi, he claims only that French is not barbarous by nature. Against the Lazaros of the world, he denies that Greek and Latin are uniquely suited for literary expression. French, like any other language, can also attain such greatness if those who speak and write it will properly apply themselves to the task. It is here that du Bellay strikes out into territory for which Speroni provides only implicit guidance. Speroni's interlocutors are concerned with the choice of language. They say nothing of how to transform a barbarous

tongue into a cultivated one. But their repeated insistence on the accomplishment of Greek, Latin, and, for Bembo, fourteenth-century Tuscan points toward a possibility, one du Bellay eagerly embraces. If French can imitate the cultivation of those languages, it too may become as illustrious as they are. That it should in fact do so is suggested by the very political and military calamity Lazaro and Bembo lament. At present, as du Bellay puts it, "France, whether in peace or in war, is by far to be preferred over Italy, now the slave and mercenary of those she used to command." The literary superiority that provides Lazaro and Bembo their consolation for Italy's defeat is, in du Bellay's view, a mere vestige of a long-departed political superiority that shows no sign of returning. Now that the former slaves have become the masters, their language should also achieve mastery.

But that will not happen, du Bellay insists, if the French continue along the path of mediocrity in which they have been content to remain. Invading Italy, marching into Rome, and occupying various parts of the Italian peninsula, as the French had been doing since the 1490s, is one thing. Surpassing or even rivaling the cultural greatness of Italy, a greatness that descended from ancient Rome and that was vigorously renewed in the fourteenth, fifteenth, and early sixteenth centuries, is quite another. For that, France had first to acknowledge the radical deficiency of its own literary culture and then to begin anew by imitating the Greeks, Romans, and modern Italians. On both fronts, du Bellay moves with breathtaking conviction. With regard to the present state of French letters, he combines relentless, if often sly mockery with unqualified vituperation, vituperation he justifies as required by the magnitude of the ill. "That ulcer and rotten flesh of bad poetry is so ingrown that it can be removed only with a knife and cauterizing iron." As for the future, he presents a program aimed at supplying France with a wholly new poetry. Instead of "all those old French poetic forms, such as rondels, ballads, virelays, royal airs, songs, and other such spices," he recommends Greek, Latin, and Italian genres: epigrams, elegies, odes, sonnets, eclogues, comedies, tragedies, and especially the epic, to which he devotes an entire chapter. He also recommends the importation of new words, the recuperation of old ones, more scrupulous attention to rhyme and meter, and the adoption of Greek and Latin turns of phrase and ways of speaking, such things as infinitives for nouns, substantive adjectives, infinitives following verbs that usually don't take them, adjectives for adverbs, and elaborate periphrastic figures.

In all this, du Bellay's objective is plain: to remove French verse from its familiar patterns and make it more artful, make it more like the poetry of those languages that have already produced works deserving immortality. And just as Speroni's *Dialogue* provided the shock of alienation that forced du Bellay to see his own language as others bred in less barbarous climes might see it, so the ancient Roman experience and that of more recent Italians gives him a model to emulate. Among the moderns, he cites Pe-

trarch, Boccaccio, Bembo, Ariosto, Sannazaro, and Luigi Alamanni, and among the ancients, Virgil, Ovid, Horace, Cicero, Martial, Tibullus, and Propertius. But two books seem to have done most to shape his thinking, Horace's *Art of Poetry* and Cicero's *Orator*. From each he takes numerous specific bits, though not nearly so many as he does from Speroni and none of them so long. What he does take is a pervasive sense of how a language and its poetry can be made capable of the most artful expression. In Horace, he finds a great poet laying out the secrets of his art. And in Cicero, he finds a great orator—along with the poets, the other chief masters of eloquence—putting his more specific recommendations in the context of a large cultural transformation based on the Roman imitation of Greece. Francis Goyet, in the lengthy commentary that accompanies his recent edition of the *Defense*, identifies Cicero's *Orator* as a single most important "matrix text" underlying du Bellay's manifesto. He may well be right. Certainly, in the 215 tightly printed pages Goyet devotes to the topic, he uncovers a remarkably dense tissue of connections between the two works. But Horace counts too. In much the way that Petrarch, Ovid, Horace, Pindar, Homer, Virgil, Ariosto, and the book of Revelation inform the *Regrets* and the *Antiquities*, so Horace and Cicero inform the *Defense*. Thus, even in his manifesto, du Bellay not only preaches the doctrine of cultural imitation. He also practices it. As much as any of his later poetic works, the *Defense* is an exercise in imitation.

A newly refined French language and a new French poetry, both based on imitation: these are then the explicit objectives of du Bellay's *Defense*, objectives he repeats and elaborates again and again over the course of the book's twenty-four chapters. But, as scholars have often pointed out, he has other, less explicit objectives as well. Most obviously, he wants to promote himself, Ronsard, and their friends. Though the *Defense* nowhere mentions his own soon-to-be-published poetic work or Ronsard's, it has from the first been recognized by friends and enemies alike as a prolegomenon to that work, a book that calls attention to what he and Ronsard were doing, justifies and even exaggerates their departure from previous French poetry, and claims for this enterprise an importance that the poems—his *Olive* and Ronsard's *Odes*—could not easily have sustained on their own. But narrow self-promotion is not du Bellay's only aim. As his mocking dismissal of the Floral Games of Toulouse and the Confraternity of Rouen, both active centers of vernacular poetic production, suggests, he also favored the capital over the provinces. And as we may guess from the fun he has at the expense of the "venerable druids" of the faculties of theology, the unfit troops marshaled behind the standard of Marot, the blinkered Latinists who scorned the vernacular, and the indolent court rhymsters whose "fair and dainty works" are destined for instant oblivion, he was intent as well on advancing a new intellectual elite, an elite located close to the royal center of power, independent of traditional academic institutions, devoted at

once to humanist learning and to the national vernacular, and prepared as occasion should arise either to give undying luster to France with its verse or to assume the most burdensome and distinguished positions in the state. For an example of someone who had followed the second course, we need look no further than the manifesto's dedicatee, Cardinal Jean du Bellay. And for an example of the first, we have Joachim himself. Both are identified as possessing heroic, Herculean strength. Where in the dedication the cardinal is said to bear on his robust shoulders the weightiest affairs of state just as Hercules bore the heavens on his, so in the "Conclusion to the Whole Work" du Bellay's own project of remaking French is associated with the "Gallic Hercules, who drew the nations after him by their ears with a chain attached to his tongue." Literary eloquence here joins state service as the two sides of a single enterprise bent on making France in the sixteenth century what Rome was a millennium and a half earlier.

And if such an imperial restoration seems far more than any literary reform could possibly hope to accomplish, remember the values expressed in Speroni's *Dialogue*, values du Bellay would have found echoed in Horace, Cicero, and a whole host of more recent humanist writers, including his own teacher Jean Dorat. As Speroni's Lazaro puts it, Rome owed more to the eloquence of Cicero than to the victories of Caesar, more to Virgil than to Augustus. From this perspective, Joachim's literary undertaking has even greater importance for France than Jean's diplomatic activity, and the *Defense* is itself a work of enormous national and possibly even imperial significance.

"Bellay, First Garland of Free Poësie"

That significance was quickly acknowledged. Even before the publication of du Bellay's Roman works, Étienne de la Boétie was writing of how French poetry has been "reborn through our Ronsard, our Baïf, our Bellay. These poets," he continues, "are defending our language so well that I dare to believe that very soon neither the Greeks nor the Latins will in this respect have any advantage over us except possibly that of seniority." With the publication of the *Regrets* and the *Antiquities of Rome*, François Olivier, the chancellor of France, thought the much-desired superiority over the ancients might in fact have been achieved. "By an indescribable something"—*un je ne sais quoi*—"the author outdoes even the Greeks and Latins. Of those who write in the same vein, I know none that du Bellay does not surpass." And a few years later, Michel de Montaigne, in listing recent accomplishments of the French, said that, as to vernacular poetry, "I think they have raised it to the highest point it will ever attain, and in the areas in which Ronsard and du Bellay excel, I find them scarcely removed from ancient perfection." If *translatio imperii* was still a work in progress—and with the death of Henry II and the outbreak of the Wars of Religion that project

seemed to have been put on indefinite hold—its other side, *translatio studii*, had, thanks to the efforts of du Bellay and Ronsard, been accomplished.

Looked at from our more distant vantage point, du Bellay, still more than Ronsard, can be seen not so much as having revived antiquity in sixteenth-century France, though certainly that was his aim, as having given early expression to what we now recognize as some of the most characteristic elements of French national culture: its revolutionary, universalist, and strongly centralizing tendencies, the place it accords an intellectual elite, the value it invests in literary culture, and the affection it has for radical manifestos. How much du Bellay had to do with all this is impossible to say, but he clearly provided a model that has stuck in the French imagination. And in many of his poems, poems like *Regrets* 9 ("France, mother of arts, of arms, and of laws") or *Regrets* 31 ("Happy the man who, like Ulysses, has traveled well"), he sounded a note that has continued to echo down the centuries. Nor is he remembered only for his Roman-inspired nationalist strain. As suggested by this brief exchange from Agnès Varda's 2000 documentary *Les Glaneurs et la glaneuse* (The Gleaners and I), he also figures—and in this *Regrets* 9 and 31 play their part—as a poet of the French *terroir*, the French soil and countryside.

An elderly winegrower. Gleaning was very beautiful. "Like the gleaner who, walking step by step, gathers the remains of what falls behind the harvester." You recognize it?
Varda. Du Bellay?
The winegrower. Du Bellay. Yes, that's it. Du Bellay.
Varda. It's wonderful that you know it by heart.

The poem is *Antiquities* 30. Its subject, the fall of Rome. But what the winegrower's memory retrieves has nothing to do with Rome. Instead, it is a resonant image of ordinary rural life. A token of cultural solidarity—"You recognize it?" "Du Bellay?"—du Bellay evokes for the French both an undeniable aspiration to grandeur and an equally undeniable love of plain, everyday pursuits. No wonder he remains among their favorite poets. He is, after all, a poet who has given them and continues to give them much of themselves.

But here, in this edition intended for English-speaking readers, I want to end not with the French reception of du Bellay but with the English. For du Bellay had as large a role in shaping England's new Renaissance poetry as any continental poet of the sixteenth century. With one of the leaders of that movement, Sir Philip Sidney, the connection is only conjectural, though the anti-Petrarchan Petrarchism of Sidney's *Astrophil and Stella* can often sound very much like the du Bellay of the *Regrets* and Sidney's writing of a defense—his *Defence of Poesie*—to accompany his poetic works is sug-

gestively reminiscent of the relation between du Bellay's poems and his *Defense.* But with the other great founder of England's new poetry, Edmund Spenser, the connection is unquestionable. Spenser's first published work, a series of visionary poems for Jan van der Noot's *Theatre for Worldlings,* printed in 1569 when Spenser was still a schoolboy, includes eleven sonnets translated from the *Dream* section of du Bellay's *Antiquities of Rome.* More than twenty years later, Spenser went back to the *Dream* and retranslated these eleven sonnets, now in rhymed verse, and added the four he had not originally included. At the same time, he translated all thirty-two sonnets of the *Antiquities* itself. Both sequences were featured in the 1591 volume of Spenser's *Complaints,* the *Dream* as *The Visions of Bellay* and the *Antiquities* as the *Ruines of Rome: by Bellay.* And in 1579, midway between Spenser's schoolboy debut and his mature exercise in translation, he brought out his own self-presentational work, *The Shepheardes Calender,* with fanfare that recalls that of du Bellay's inaugural acts and with introduction and notes that repeatedly echo du Bellay's *Defense.* Clearly, Spenser's very sense of himself as a poet, his sense of what a poet should be and do, owed much to his ambitious French predecessor.

At the conclusion of the *Ruines of Rome,* Spenser adds a sonnet of his own composition in honor of the poet he has been translating.

> Bellay, first garland of free Poësie
> That France brought forth, though fruitfull of brave wits,
> Well worthie thou of immortalitie,
> That long hast traveld by thy learned writs,
> Olde Rome out of her ashes to revive,
> And give a second life to dead decayes:
> Needes must he all eternitie survive,
> That can to other give eternall dayes.
> Thy dayes therefore are endles, and thy prayse
> Excelling all, that ever went before;
> And after thee, gins Bartas hie to rayse
> His heavenly Muse, th'Almightie to adore.
> Live happie spirits, th'honour of your name,
> And fill the world with never dying fame.

Coming from as ardent a Protestant as Spenser, the turn in the last few lines toward the recent Huguenot poet Guillaume de Salluste du Bartas may suggest that du Bellay's Gallican opposition to papal hegemony contributed significantly to his appeal. But the word that to me seems most mysterious and most telling in this poem, the adjective *free* in line 1, has, I suspect, a still broader meaning. Freedom from domination by the bishop of Rome is certainly part of it. But so is freedom from ancient Rome's cul-

tural dominance, the freedom associated with the founding of a vernacular poetry equal or superior to that of antiquity.

Such freedom was a persistent preoccupation in sixteenth-century Europe. To get an idea of why that might have been so, we need only recall Lorenzo Valla's proud boast that as long as Latin remained the universal language of learning, the various countries of Europe would remain in thrall to Rome. For an Italian follower of Valla's like Speroni's Lazaro, viewing the linguistic situation of his native land after the French invasions and the imperial sack of Rome, this story had another side. If the continuing preeminence of Latin represented the continuing preeminence of Rome, the Italian vernacular stood for Italy's defeat. The product of what Lazaro calls "our calamity," corrupted by contact over many centuries with barbarians like the Franks and their French descendants, the Italian language is, he says, "nothing but a demonstrative sign of Italian slavery." But elsewhere in Europe the vernacular meant just the opposite. Spenser's teacher Richard Mulcaster, an active and enthusiastic reader of du Bellay, who may well have been responsible for encouraging his pupil's translations of the French poet, put it best. After reminding his readers that "the Roman authority first planted the Latin tongue among us here by force of their conquest," he asks with rebellious energy, "Is it not indeed a marvelous bondage to become servants to one tongue for learning sake . . . whereas we may have the very same treasure in our own tongue, . . . our own bearing the joyful title of liberty and freedom, the Latin tongue remembering us of our thralldom and bondage?" When Spenser hails du Bellay as the "first garland of *free* Poësie," he recognizes in him a champion of the cause Mulcaster promoted, the cause to which his own vernacular poetry remains devoted.

But what has such freedom to do with *monarchie,* the term that at the outset of this introduction I identified as offering a key to understanding du Bellay's work? Very little, one might suppose. But, in fact, they are intimately linked. Crudely put, freedom means dominating others while not being dominated oneself. In this sense, Rome stands for both. Empire—*monarchie,* as du Bellay used the word—is the very condition of freedom. Thus when in 1533 the England of Henry VIII declared its independence from the pope in Rome, Parliament proclaimed: "This realm of England is an empire, and so hath been accepted in the world." Now, with the Roman model in mind, many in England imagined, as did many in France and Spain, that full imperial sovereignty—full imperial freedom—would necessarily entail universal dominion of the sort Rome had once exercised. This is not what Parliament was saying, but one idea of empire—full sovereignty—easily called up the other—universal dominion. Du Bellay entertained both, and so on occasion did Spenser. But whether the aim was limited to national sovereignty or stretched all the way to world dominance, an illustrious language and a "free Poësie" were thought essential to its ac-

complishment. Giving France such a language and such a poetry is what Spenser thinks du Bellay has done and what he hopes he can do for England.

It is thus striking that what we may remember most about each is not untrammeled freedom but rather exile and alienation. Spenser in Ireland and du Bellay in Rome figure a modernity in which vernacular poetry is more often a vehicle for painful contradiction than for imperial triumph. "I love liberty," du Bellay says in *Regrets* 39, "and languish in servitude. I do not like the court and have to play the courtier. I dislike feigning and must wear a mask. I love straightforwardness and learn only malice." Though Spenser never draws in any direct way on the *Regrets* and may not even have known this part of du Bellay's work, the sentiments du Bellay expresses will be familiar to any reader of *The Shepheardes Calender, Colin Clouts Come Home Againe,* or even *The Faerie Queene.* Both poets of empire, Spenser and du Bellay are also both poets of imperial disillusionment. Exile and estrangement are not accidents that coincidentally link them to one another—and, for that matter, link both to such other founders of a new vernacular poetry as Garcilaso de la Vega, Luís de Camões, and even Petrarch himself. That all five of these poets—du Bellay, Spenser, Garcilaso, Camões, and Petrarch—were exiles in a more literal sense merely enforced and gave outward expression to an inner estrangement that was essential to the heroic labor they accomplished. To remake one's culture, as each of these poets did, one must first be removed from it. For du Bellay, as for the others, this is what it meant to be the "first garland of free Poësie."

Les Regrets
et
Autres Oeuvres Poetiques

The Regrets
and
Other Poetic Works

Ad Lectorem

Quem, Lector, tibi nunc damus libellum,
Hic fellísque simul, simúlque mellis,
Permixtúmque salis refert saporem.
Si gratum quid erit tuo palato,
Huc conviva veni: tibi hæc parata est
Cœna. Sin minus, hinc facesse, quæso:
Ad hanc te volui haud vocare cœnam.

To the Reader

This little book, Reader, that we give you now has at once the taste of gall and honey mixed with salt. If it pleases your palate, come as a guest. This feast has been prepared for you. If not, please go away. I did not mean to invite you to the feast.

To Monsieur d'Avanson

Councillor to the King in his Privy Council

If I no longer am favored by the Muse, and if my lines are found to be imperfect, the place, the time, the age at which I wrote them, and my troubles will serve as their excuse.

I was in Rome in the midst of war, already beyond my most active years, seeking some rest from my labors, not to acquire praise or favor.

So the man who on the plain herds cattle or toils on the ramparts rejoices and with an artless poem he has made relieves the burden of his labor.

Likewise he, who on the galley makes the sea around him foam, accords his sad songs to his rowing, so that his oar will seem lighter.

They say that Achilles, brooding on his anger, with pleasures of this sort used to converse with himself, easing the sad remembrance of his mistress with the humming of his lyre.

Monsieur d'Avanson: Jean de Saint-Marcel, lord of Avanson, named French ambassador to the Holy See in 1555

If I no longer am favored by the Muse: the first eighteen stanzas of this dedicatory poem closely echo the *Tristia* (4.1.1–44) of Ovid, with whose exile from Rome du Bellay identifies through much of the *Regrets*

of his mistress: Briseis, taken by Agamemnon

A Monsieur d'Avanson

Conseiller du Roy
en son Privé Conseil

Si je n'ay plus la faveur de la Muse,
Et si mes vers se trouvent imparfaits,
Le lieu, le temps, l'aage où je les ay faits,
Et mes ennuis leur serviront d'excuse.

J'estois à Rome au milieu de la guerre,
Sortant desja de l'aage plus dispos,
A mes travaulx cherchant quelque repos,
Non pour louange ou pour faveur acquerre.

Ainsi voit-on celuy qui sur la plaine
Picque le bœuf, ou travaille au rampart,
Se resjouir, et d'un vers fait sans art
S'esvertuer au travail de sa peine.

Celuy aussi qui dessus la galere
Fait escumer les flots à l'environ,
Ses tristes chants accorde à l'aviron,
Pour esprouver la rame plus legere.

On dit qu'Achille en remaschant son ire
De tels plaisirs souloit s'entretenir,
Pour addoulcir le triste souvenir
De sa maistresse, aux fredons de sa lyre.

Ainsi flattoit le regret de la sienne
Perdue helas pour la seconde fois,
Cil qui jadis aux rochers et aux bois
Faisoit ouir sa harpe Thracienne.

La Muse ainsi me fait sur ce rivage,
Où je languis banny de ma maison,
Passer l'ennuy de la triste saison,
Seule compagne à mon si long voyage.

La Muse seule au milieu des alarmes
Est asseuree, et ne pallist de peur,
La Muse seule au milieu du labeur
Flatte la peine, et desseiche les larmes.

D'elle je tiens le repos et la vie,
D'elle j'apprens à n'estre ambitieux,
D'elle je tiens les saincts presens des Dieux,
Et le mespris de fortune, et d'envie.

Aussi sçait-elle, aiant dès mon enfance
Tousjours guidé le cours de mon plaisir,
Que le devoir, non l'avare desir,
Si longuement me tient loing de la France.

Je voudrois bien (car pour suivre la Muse
J'ay sur mon doz chargé la pauvreté)
Ne m'estre au trac des neuf sœurs arresté,
Pour aller veoir la source de Meduse.

Mais que feray-je à fin d'eschapper d'elles?
Leur chant flatteur a trompé mes esprits,
Et les appaz aux quels elles m'ont pris,
D'un doulx lien ont englué mes ælles.

In the same way he who once made the rocks and woods listen to his Thracian harp relieved his sorrow for his mistress, lost, alas, for the second time.

So the Muse helps me endure the trouble of this sad time on this shore where I languish, banished from my home, my only companion on this long, long voyage.

The Muse alone in the midst of alarms is confident and does not go pale with fright; the Muse alone in the midst of labor eases pain and dries my tears.

From her I get rest and life; from her I learn not to be ambitious; from her I get the holy gifts of the gods and contempt for fortune and envy.

And she knows, having from my childhood always guided the course of my pleasure, that duty, not greedy desire, has for so long kept me far from France.

I wish—for in following the Muse I have assumed the burden of poverty—that I had not set myself in the path of the nine sisters to visit the Medusaean spring.

But what can I do to escape them? Their flattering song has misled my wit, and the charms with which they have captured me have limed my wings with a sweet bond.

---

he who once made the rocks and woods listen to his Thracian harp: Orpheus
for his mistress: Eurydice
the nine sisters: the Muses
the Medusaean spring: the Hippocrene

Not otherwise than with such a sweet force were the companions of Ulysses bound and, with no thought of their forgotten labors, loved the fruit that was their bait.

He who has foolishly tasted the bittersweet poison of the love-inducing drink knows his sickness and, forced to love it, seeks out the bond that keeps him enslaved.

Because of this, sweet poetry pleases me, as does the sweet dart by which I was wounded. From the cradle, the Muse left that thorn in my fancy.

I accept that people call the holy goddess the madness of our wits, but it is not without some benefit that such error so sweetly binds us.

She dazzles the eyes of thought so as sometimes to blind us to our unhappiness and with a sweet charm enchants away the grief with which our soul is afflicted night and day.

Thus, too, the wine-drugged priestess, who with her cries fills Ida, does not feel the blow of the wand that wounds her, nor do I feel the misery that oppresses me.

Someone will say: "Of what use are these complaints?" As each tree gives birth to its own kind of fruit, so the fruits of grief are unfeigned sighs and tears.

---

the wine-drugged priestess: the priestess of Dionysius

Of what use: from Andrea Navagero's Latin epigram "Ex Philemone," on which du Bellay also based *Regrets* 52

Non autrement que d'une doulce force
D'Ulysse estoient les compagnons liez,
Et sans penser aux travaulx oubliez
Aymoient le fruict qui leur servoit d'amorce.

Celuy qui a de l'amoureux breuvage
Gousté mal sain le poison doulx-amer,
Cognoit son mal, et contraint de l'aymer
Suit le lien qui le tient en servage.

Pour ce me plaist la doulce poësie,
Et le doulx traict par qui je fus blessé:
Dès le berceau la Muse m'a laissé
Cest aiguillon dedans la fantaisie.

Je suis content qu'on appelle folie
De noz esprits la saincte deité,
Mais ce n'est pas sans quelque utilité,
Que telle erreur si doulcement nous lie.

Elle esblouit les yeulx de la pensee
Pour quelque fois ne veoir nostre malheur,
Et d'un doulx charme enchante la douleur
Dont nuict et jour nostre ame est offensee.

Ainsi encor' la vineuse prestresse,
Qui de ses criz Ide va remplissant,
Ne sent le coup du thyrse la blessant,
Et je ne sents le malheur qui me presse.

Quelqu'un dira, de quoy servent ces plainctes?
Comme de l'arbre on voit naistre le fruict,
Ainsi les fruicts que la douleur produict,
Sont les souspirs et les larmes non feinctes.

De quelque mal un chacun se lamente,
Mais les moiens de plaindre sont divers:
J'ay, quant à moy, choisi celuy des vers
Pour desaigrir l'ennuy qui me tormente.

Et c'est pourquoy d'une doulce satyre
Entremeslant les espines aux fleurs,
Pour ne fascher le monde de mes pleurs,
J'appreste icy le plus souvent à rire.

Or si mes vers meritent qu'on les loüe,
Ou qu'on les blasme, à vous seul entre tous
Je m'en rapporte icy, car c'est à vous,
A vous Seigneur, à qui seul je les voüe:

Comme celuy qui avec la sagesse
Avez conjoint le droit et l'æquité,
Et qui portez de toute antiquité
Joint à vertu le tiltre de noblesse:

Ne desdaignant, comme estoit la coustume,
Le long habit, lequel vous honnorez,
Comme celuy qui sage n'ignorez
De combien sert le conseil et la plume.

Ce fut pourquoy ce sage et vaillant Prince,
Vous honnorant du nom d'Ambassadeur,
Sur vostre doz deschargea sa grandeur,
Pour la porter en estrange province:

Recompensant d'un estat honnorable
Vostre service, et tesmoignant assez
Par le loyer de voz travaulx passez
Combien luy est tel service aggreable.

Everyone complains of some suffering, but the ways of lamenting are many. As for me, I have chosen verse to take the bitterness from the trouble that torments me.

And that is why, mixing thorns among the flowers in a sweet satire so as not to annoy the world with my weeping, I aim here most often at laughter.

Now whether my verses deserve praise or blame, to you alone among all I here defer, for it is to you, to you alone, my Lord, that I dedicate them,

To you who have wisely joined law and equity and who have worn from time immemorial, together with virtue, the title of nobility,

Not disdaining, as was once the custom, the long robe which you honor, as one who wisely knows what counsel and the pen can do.

That was why that wise and valiant prince, honoring you with the name of ambassador, charged you with his greatness for you to carry into a foreign land,

Rewarding your service with an honorable position and amply testifying by this payment for your former labors how much he values such service.

---

the long robe: the mark of civil, as opposed to military, office

that wise and valiant prince: Henry II (1519–1559; king of France, 1547–1559)

Let my book be no less welcome to you than with an open heart I here offer it to you. I then will little fear from evil tongues and will be sure to live forever.

Qu'autant vous soit aggreable mon livre
Que de bon cueur je le vous offre icy:
Du mesdisant j'auray peu de soucy,
Et seray seur à tout jamais de vivre.

A son livre

Mon livre (et je ne suis sur ton aise envieux)
Tu t'en iras sans moy voir la court de mon Prince.
He chetif que je suis, combien en gré je prinsse,
Qu'un heur pareil au tien fust permis à mes yeulx!

Là si quelqu'un vers toy se monstre gracieux,
Souhaitte luy qu'il vive heureux en sa province:
Mais si quelque malin obliquement te pince,
Souhaitte luy tes pleurs, et mon mal ennuieux.

Souhaitte luy encor' qu'il face un long voyage,
Et bien qu'il ait de veüe elongné son mesnage,
Que son cueur, où qu'il voise, y soit tousjours present:

Souhaitte qu'il vieillisse en longue servitude,
Qu'il n'esprouve à la fin que toute ingratitude,
Et qu'on mange son bien pendant qu'il est absent.

To his book

My book (and I do not begrudge your good fortune), you will go without me to see my prince's court. Ah, miserable as I am, how thankful I would be were such happiness as yours granted to my eyes.

There, if someone treats you graciously, wish him a happy life in his own country. But if some malicious person underhandedly attacks you, wish on him your tears and my heavy suffering.

Wish as well that he take a long journey and that, though his home be far from view, his heart, wherever he goes, be always there.

Wish that he grow old in prolonged service, that in the end he experience only ingratitude, and that his estate be devoured while he is away.

My book: echoes the opening lines of Ovid's *Tristia*

1

I do not want to pry into nature's bosom. I do not want to seek out the spirit of the universe. I do not want to sound the hidden depths nor draw the beautiful architecture of heaven.

I do not paint my works with such rich colors and do not seek such high subjects for my verse. But attending only to what happens here, whether good or bad, I write at random.

I complain to my verses if I have some sorrow. I laugh with them. I tell them my secret, as the most trustworthy confidants of my heart.

Nor do I want to comb and curl them much or to mask them under more gallant names than those of daily jottings or chronicles.

I do not want: du Bellay distinguishes himself from his friend Ronsard, who addresses these lofty topics in his *Hymnes* (1555)

2

Someone more learned than I, Paschal, will go dream with the Ascrean poet on the double-domed mount and, to be renowned among men, will dive naked into the Hippocrene.

As for me, I do not want to rack my brain to stretch out a line or file down my wit to polish a rhyme, or pound on the table or gnaw at my nails.

What I want, Paschal, is that whatever I write should be prose in rhyme or rhyme in prose, and for that I do not aspire to a laurel crown—

And perhaps that someone who thinks himself particularly clever and judges the style of my verse unusually easy will work in vain trying to imitate me.

Paschal: Pierre Paschal (1522–1565), royal historiographer to Henry II and friend of Ronsard and du Bellay

the Ascrean poet: Hesiod

the double-domed mount: Parnassus

the Hippocrene: "the Fountain of the Horse," sacred to the Muses, on Mount Helicon

What I want: the final six lines echo Horace, *Satires* 1.4.38–41 and *Epistles* 2.3.240

1

Je ne veulx point fouiller au sein de la nature,
Je ne veulx point chercher l'esprit de l'univers,
Je ne veulx point sonder les abysmes couvers,
Ny desseigner du ciel la belle architecture.

Je ne peins mes tableaux de si riche peinture,
Et si haults arguments ne recherche à mes vers:
Mais suivant de ce lieu les accidents divers,
Soit de bien, soit de mal, j'escris à l'adventure.

Je me plains à mes vers, si j'ay quelque regret,
Je me ris avec eulx, je leur dy mon secret,
Comme estans de mon cœur les plus seurs secretaires.

Aussi ne veulx-je tant les pigner et friser,
Et de plus braves noms ne les veulx desguiser,
Que de papiers journaulx, ou bien de commentaires.

2

Un plus sçavant que moy (Paschal) ira songer
Aveques l'Ascrean dessus la double cyme:
Et pour estre de ceulx dont on fait plus d'estime,
Dedans l'onde au cheval tout nud s'ira plonger.

Quant à moy, je ne veulx pour un vers allonger,
M'accoursir le cerveau: ny pour polir ma ryme,
Me consumer l'esprit d'une songneuse lime,
Frapper dessus ma table, ou mes ongles ronger.

Aussi veulx-je (Paschal) que ce que je compose
Soit une prose en ryme, ou une ryme en prose,
Et ne veulx pour cela le laurier meriter.

Et peult estre que tel se pense bien habile,
Qui trouvant de mes vers la ryme si facile,
En vain travaillera, me voulant imiter.

3

N'estant, comme je suis, encor' exercité
Par tant et tant de maulx au jeu de la Fortune,
Je suivois d'Apollon la trace non commune,
D'une saincte fureur sainctement agité.

Ores ne sentant plus ceste divinité,
Mais picqué du soucy qui fascheux m'importune,
Une adresse j'ay pris beaucoup plus opportune
A qui se sent forcé de la necessité.

Et c'est pourquoy (Seigneur) ayant perdu la trace
Que suit vostre Ronsard par les champs de la Grace,
Je m'adresse où je voy le chemin plus battu:

Ne me bastant le cœur, la force, ny l'haleine
De suivre, comme luy, par sueur et par peine
Ce penible sentier qui meine à la vertu.

4

Je ne veulx fueilleter les exemplaires Grecs,
Je ne veulx retracer les beaux traicts d'un Horace,
Et moins veulx-je imiter d'un Petrarque la grace,
Ou la voix d'un Ronsard, pour chanter mes regrets.

Ceulx qui sont de Phœbus vrais poëtes sacrez,
Animeront leurs vers d'une plus grand' audace:
Moy, qui suis agité d'une fureur plus basse,
Je n'entre si avant en si profonds secretz.

Je me contenteray de simplement escrire
Ce que la passion seulement me fait dire,
Sans rechercher ailleurs plus graves arguments.

Aussi n'ay-je entrepris d'imiter en ce livre
Ceulx qui par leurs escripts se vantent de revivre,
Et se tirer tous vifz dehors des monuments.

3

Not yet worn down, as I am now, by so many losses in the game of Fortune, I used to follow the little-traveled track of Apollo, sacredly moved by a sacred fury.

But now that I no longer feel that divinity, but am spurred by the gnawing care that torments me, I have chosen a path far better suited to one who is driven by necessity.

And that, my lord, is why, having lost the track your Ronsard follows through the fields of the Grace, I turn to a path that I see is more beaten:

For neither my heart, nor my strength, nor my breath suffices to follow, as he does, in sweat and in pain, that arduous trail that leads to virtue.

---

sacred fury: the divine frenzy or inspiration sought by Renaissance poets

my lord: has been variously identified as Charles de Guise, cardinal of Lorraine; Jean, lord of Avanson; and Odet de Coligny, cardinal of Châtillon

Ronsard: Pierre de Ronsard (1524–1585), poet, leader of the Pléiade, and close friend of du Bellay

the fields of the Grace: from the opening lines of Ronsard's "Ode à Michel de l'Hopital," where the term is associated with Pindar and Pindaric poetry

4

I do not want to turn the pages of Greek models; I do not want to retrace the beautiful lines of a Horace; and still less do I want to imitate the grace of a Petrarch or the voice of a Ronsard to sing my regrets.

Those who are true poets sacred to Apollo will quicken their verses with greater audacity. I, who am moved by a less elevated frenzy, do not delve so far into such deep secrets.

I will content myself with simply writing what passion alone makes me say, without seeking graver subjects elsewhere.

For I have not undertaken in this book to imitate those who boast that by their writings they will live again and raise themselves alive from their tombs.

I do not want: du Bellay here rejects the very advice he gives (in imitation of Horace's *Ars poetica*) in *Defense* 2.4

5

Those who are in love will sing their loves. Those who love honor will sing of glory. Those who are near the king will publicize his victory. Those who are courtiers will boast of their favors.

Those who love the arts will speak of learning. Those who are virtuous will make themselves known for it. Those who love wine will talk of drinking. Those who have leisure will write tales.

Those who speak ill of others will take pleasure in slander. Those who are less irksome will tell jokes for a laugh. Those who are more valiant will boast of their valor.

Those who are overly pleased with themselves will sing their own praises. Those who wish to flatter will make an angel of a devil. I, who am unhappy, will complain of my unhappiness.

6

Alas, where now is that contempt for Fortune? Where is that heart victorious over all adversity, that noble desire for immortality, and that noble flame so rarely found in the vile masses?

Where are those sweet pleasures that in the radiant night the Muses gave me, when in freedom on the green carpet of a secluded shore, I led them in dance by the light of the moon?

Now Fortune rules me; and my heart, once proud to be master of itself, is the slave of the thousand pains and regrets that torment me.

I no longer care for posterity; nor have I any longer that divine frenzy; and the Muses, like strangers, flee from me.

Alas, where now: compare du Bellay's Latin elegies, "Ad P. Ronsardum," lines 37–38, and "Patriae desiderium," 55–60

5

Ceulx qui sont amoureux, leurs amours chanteront,
Ceulx qui ayment l'honneur, chanteront de la gloire,
Ceulx qui sont pres du Roy, publiront sa victoire,
Ceulx qui sont courtisans, leurs faveurs vanteront:

Ceulx qui ayment les arts, les sciences diront,
Ceulx qui sont vertueux, pour tels se feront croire,
Ceulx qui ayment le vin, deviseront de boire,
Ceulx qui sont de loisir, de fables escriront:

Ceulx qui sont mesdisans, se plairont à mesdire,
Ceulx qui sont moins fascheux, diront des mots pour rire,
Ceulx qui sont plus vaillans, vanteront leur valeur:

Ceulx qui se plaisent trop, chanteront leur louange,
Ceulx qui veulent flater, feront d'un diable un ange:
Moy, qui suis malheureux, je plaindray mon malheur.

6

Las, où est maintenant ce mespris de Fortune?
Où est ce cœur vainqueur de toute adversité,
Cest honneste desir de l'immortalité,
Et ceste honneste flamme au peuple non commune?

Où sont ces doulx plaisirs, qu'au soir sous la nuict brune
Les Muses me donnoient, alors qu'en liberté
Dessus le verd tapy d'un rivage escarté
Je les menois danser aux rayons de la Lune?

Maintenant la Fortune est maistresse de moy,
Et mon cœur qui souloit estre maistre de soy,
Est serf de mille maulx et regrets qui m'ennuyent.

De la posterité je n'ay plus de soucy,
Ceste divine ardeur, je ne l'ay plus aussi,
Et les Muses de moy, comme estranges, s'enfuyent.

7

Ce pendant que la court mes ouvrages lisoit,
Et que la sœur du Roy, l'unique Marguerite,
Me faisant plus d'honneur que n'estoit mon merite,
De son bel œil divin mes vers favorisoit, 4

Une fureur d'esprit au ciel me conduisoit
D'une ælle qui la mort et les siecles evite,
Et le docte troppeau qui sur Parnasse habite,
De son feu plus divin mon ardeur attisoit. 8

Ores je suis muet, comme on voit la Prophete
Ne sentant plus le Dieu, qui la tenoit sugette,
Perdre soudainement la fureur et la voix. 11

Et qui ne prend plaisir qu'un Prince luy commande?
L'honneur nourrit les arts, et la Muse demande
Le theatre du peuple, et la faveur des Roys. 14

8

Ne t'esbahis Ronsard, la moitié de mon ame,
Si de ton Dubellay France ne lit plus rien,
Et si aveques l'air du ciel Italien
Il n'a humé l'ardeur qui l'Italie enflamme. 4

Le sainct rayon qui part des beaux yeux de ta dame,
Et la saincte faveur de ton Prince et du mien,
Cela (Ronsard) cela, cela merite bien
De t'eschauffer le cœur d'une si vive flamme. 8

Mais moy, qui suis absent des raiz de mon Soleil,
Comment puis-je sentir eschauffement pareil
A celuy qui est pres de sa flamme divine? 11

Les costaux soleillez de pampre sont couvers,
Mais des Hyperborez les eternelz hyvers
Ne portent que le froid, la neige, et la bruine. 14

7

As long as the court read my works and the king's sister, the incomparable Margaret, honoring me beyond my deserts, favored my verses with her beautiful eye divine,

A frenzy of the mind carried me to heaven on a wing that escapes death and time, and the learned troop that lives on Parnassus ignited my fervor with its most holy fire.

Now I am mute, like the prophetess who, no longer feeling the god who subjected her, suddenly loses her inspiration and her voice.

And who does not take pleasure in a prince's command? Honor nurtures the arts, and the Muse requires a popular audience and the favor of kings.

As long as the court: compare "Patriae desiderium," lines 61–68

the incomparable Margaret: Margaret of France (1523–1574), daughter of Francis I and sister of Henry II

the learned troop: the Muses

the prophetess: the Sibyl

the Muse requires: compare "Patriae desiderium," 77

8

Do not wonder, Ronsard, you who are half my soul, if France no longer reads anything from your du Bellay and if with the air of the Italian sky he has not breathed in the ardor that inflames Italy.

The sacred rays that shine from the beautiful eyes of your lady, and the sacred favor of your prince and mine, that, Ronsard, that, that has the power to warm your heart with such a lively flame.

But I, who am absent from the rays of my sun, how can I feel warmth like one who is near his divine flame?

Sunny hills are covered with vines, but endless Hyperborean winters bring only cold, snow, and mist.

9

France, mother of arts, of arms, and of laws, you long nourished me with the milk of your breast. Now, like a lamb that calls for its nurse, I fill the caves and woods with the sound of your name.

If you once acknowledged me as your child, why do you not answer me now, O cruel one? France, France, answer my sad complaint. But no one, save Echo, answers my voice.

Among cruel wolves, I wander on the plain. I feel the coming of winter, whose cold breath makes my skin bristle with a trembling fright.

Alas, your other lambs do not lack pasture. They do not fear the wolf, the wind, or the cold. Yet I am not the worst of the flock.

France, mother of arts: du Bellay here applies to France praise normally reserved for Italy

10

It is not the Tuscan river with its proud banks, it is not the Roman air or the Palatine hill, that now, my Ronsard, makes me speak Latin, changing my native language for a foreign tongue.

It is the misery of seeing myself three years and more, like a Prometheus, nailed to the Aventine, where a wretched hope and my cruel fate, not the yoke of love, hold me in servitude.

And yet, Ronsard, and yet, if on a foreign shore Ovid dared to trade his language for a barbarian tongue so as to be understood, who can blame me

For a more fortunate trade? No one, since French, though you have made it the equal of Greek and Latin, cannot be understood on this Roman shore.

It is not: du Bellay responds to a sonnet by Ronsard (*Amours* 2.5) where Ronsard talks of du Bellay's writing in Latin

the Tuscan river: the Tiber, which descends from the Tuscan land of Etruria

the Palatine hill . . . the Aventine: two of the Seven Hills of Rome

Ovid: compare "Patriae desiderium," lines 73–76

9

France mere des arts, des armes, et des loix,
Tu m'as nourry long temps du laict de ta mamelle:
Ores, comme un aigneau qui sa nourrice appelle,
Je remplis de ton nom les antres et les bois.

Si tu m'as pour enfant advoué quelquefois,
Que ne me respons-tu maintenant, ô cruelle?
France, France respons à ma triste querelle:
Mais nul, sinon Echo, ne respond à ma voix.

Entre les loups cruels j'erre parmy la plaine,
Je sens venir l'hyver, de qui la froide haleine
D'une tremblante horreur fait herisser ma peau.

Las, tes autres aigneaux n'ont faute de pasture,
Ils ne craignent le loup, le vent, ny la froidure:
Si ne suis-je pourtant le pire du troppeau.

10

Ce n'est le fleuve Thusque au superbe rivage,
Ce n'est l'air des Latins ny le mont Palatin,
Qui ores (mon Ronsard) me fait parler Latin,
Changeant à l'estranger mon naturel langage:

C'est l'ennuy de me voir trois ans et d'avantage,
Ainsi qu'un Promethé, cloué sur l'Aventin,
Où l'espoir miserable et mon cruel destin,
Non le joug amoureux, me detient en servage.

Et quoy (Ronsard) et quoy, si au bord estranger
Ovide osa sa langue en barbare changer
Afin d'estre entendu, qui me pourra reprendre

D'un change plus heureux? Nul, puis que le François,
Quoy qu'au Grec et Romain egalé tu te sois,
Au rivage Latin ne se peult faire entendre.

11

Bien qu'aux arts d'Apollon le vulgaire n'aspire,
Bien que de tels thresors l'avarice n'ait soing,
Bien que de tels harnois le soldat n'ait besoing,
Bien que l'ambition tels honneurs ne desire:

Bien que ce soit aux grands un argument de rire,
Bien que les plus rusez s'en tiennent le plus loing,
Et bien que Dubellay soit suffisant tesmoing,
Combien est peu prisé le mestier de la lyre:

Bien qu'un art sans profit ne plaise au courtisan,
Bien qu'on ne paye en vers l'œuvre d'un artisan,
Bien que la Muse soit de pauvreté suivie,

Si ne veulx-je pourtant delaisser de chanter,
Puis que le seul chant peult mes ennuys enchanter,
Et qu'aux Muses je doy bien six ans de ma vie.

12

Veu le soing mesnager, dont travaillé je suis,
Veu l'importun soucy, qui sans fin me tormente,
Et veu tant de regrets, desquels je me lamente,
Tu t'esbahis souvent comment chanter je puis.

Je ne chante (Magny) je pleure mes ennuys:
Ou, pour le dire mieulx, en pleurant je les chante,
Si bien qu'en les chantant, souvent je les enchante:
Voila pourquoy (Magny) je chante jours et nuicts.

Ainsi chante l'ouvrier en faisant son ouvrage,
Ainsi le laboureur faisant son labourage,
Ainsi le pelerin regrettant sa maison,

Ainsi l'advanturier en songeant à sa dame,
Ainsi le marinier en tirant à la rame,
Ainsi le prisonnier maudissant sa prison.

11

Though the vile masses do not aspire to the arts of Apollo, though greed does not care for such treasures, though the soldier does not need such armor, though ambition does not desire such honors,

Though to the great a subject of laughter, though the most cunning stay furthest away, and though du Bellay is witness enough to how little valued is the craft of the lyre,

Though an art without profit cannot please a courtier, though you cannot pay with a poem for the work of a craftsman, though the Muse is followed by poverty,

Nevertheless I do not wish to abandon singing, for song alone can charm away my troubles, and to the Muses I owe a good six years of my life.

---

the craft of the lyre: poetry

song alone can charm: here and in the following poem, du Bellay plays on *chanter* (to sing) and *enchanter* (to charm) in a way that English does not allow

12

Given the household cares with which I am oppressed, given the nagging worry that endlessly torments me, and given the many regrets of which I complain, you often wonder how I can sing.

I do not sing, Magny, I cry my troubles. Or, to put it better, I sing them crying, so that in singing them, I often charm them away. That is why, Magny, I sing night and day.

So sings the worker while doing his work; so the plowman plowing the field; so the pilgrim longing for home;

So the soldier of fortune dreaming of his lady; so the seaman pulling the oar; so the prisoner cursing his prison.

Magny: Olivier de Magny (1529–1561), poet and secretary to d'Avanson

13

Now I forgive the sweet frenzy that made me waste the best years of my life without any other profit from my thankless work than the vain pastime of such a prolonged error.

Now I forgive that pleasant toil, because it alone numbs the care that affronts me and because it alone in the midst of the storm, as it has done before, keeps me from trembling with fear.

If poetry has been the abuse of my youth, poetry will also be the support of my old age. If it was my folly, it will be my reason.

If it was my wound, it will be my Achilles. If it was my poison, it will be the useful scorpion, the only cure for my ill.

---

my thankless work: work (*ouvrage*) in the sense of a literary work

such a prolonged error: echoes Petrarch's sense of his love for Laura and the poetry it produced as a "lungo error" (*Rime sparse* 224)

my Achilles: the spear of Achilles whose rust could alone cure the wounds it gave

the useful scorpion: the scorpion was thought to provide the only antidote for its own bite

14

If the importunity of a creditor annoys me, poetry relieves the vexation of the annoying creditor. And if I am annoyed by an annoying servant, poring over poetry, Boucher, I suddenly free myself from annoyance.

If someone unleashes his anger on me, into poems I vomit the poison in my heart. And if my feeble wit is worn out with work, poetry brings me refreshed back to my task.

Poetry drives lazy idleness from me. Poetry makes me love sweet liberty. Poetry sings for me what I dare not say.

So if I reap such diverse benefits from it, how can you ask, Boucher, of what use is poetry, and what good I get from the poems I write?

Boucher: Étienne Boucher, churchman and secretary to the French ambassador in Rome

13

Maintenant je pardonne à la doulce fureur,
Qui m'a fait consumer le meilleur de mon aage,
Sans tirer autre fruict de mon ingrat ouvrage,
Que le vain passetemps d'une si longue erreur. 4

Maintenant je pardonne à ce plaisant labeur,
Puis que seul il endort le soucy qui m'oultrage,
Et puis que seul il fait qu'au milieu de l'orage
Ainsi qu'auparavant je ne tremble de peur. 8

Si les vers ont esté l'abus de ma jeunesse,
Les vers seront aussi l'appuy de ma vieillesse,
S'ils furent ma folie, ils seront ma raison, 11

S'ils furent ma blesseure, ils seront mon Achille,
S'ils furent mon venim, le scorpion utile,
Qui sera de mon mal la seule guerison. 14

14

Si l'importunité d'un crediteur me fasche,
Les vers m'ostent l'ennuy du fascheux crediteur:
Et si je suis fasché d'un fascheux serviteur,
Dessus les vers (Boucher) soudain je me défasche. 4

Si quelqu'un dessus moy sa cholere délasche,
Sur les vers je vomis le venim de mon cœur:
Et si mon foible esprit est recreu du labeur,
Les vers font que plus frais je retourne à ma tasche. 8

Les vers chassent de moy la molle oisiveté,
Les vers me font aymer la doulce liberté,
Les vers chantent pour moy ce que dire je n'ose. 11

Si donq j'en recueillis tant de profits divers,
Demandes-tu (Boucher) dequoy servent les vers,
Et quel bien je reçoy de ceulx que je compose? 14

15

Panjas, veuls-tu sçavoir quels sont mes passetemps?
Je songe au lendemain, j'ay soing de la despense
Qui se fait chacun jour, et si fault que je pense
A rendre sans argent cent crediteurs contents:

Je vays, je viens, je cours, je ne perds point le temps,
Je courtise un banquier, je prens argent d'avance,
Quand j'ay despesché l'un, un autre recommence,
Et ne fais pas le quart de ce que je pretends.

Qui me presente un compte, une lettre, un memoire,
Qui me dit que demain est jour de consistoire,
Qui me rompt le cerveau de cent propos divers:

Qui se plainct, qui se deult, qui murmure, qui crie,
Aveques tout cela, dy (Panjas) je te prie,
Ne t'esbahis-tu point comment je fais des vers?

16

Cependant que Magny suit son grand Avanson,
Panjas son Cardinal, et moy le mien encore,
Et que l'espoir flateur, qui noz beaux ans devore,
Appaste noz desirs d'un friand hamesson,

Tu courtises les Roys, et d'un plus heureux son
Chantant l'heur de Henry, qui son siecle decore,
Tu t'honores toymesme, et celuy qui honore
L'honneur que tu luy fais par ta docte chanson.

Las, et nous ce pendant nous consumons nostre aage
Sur le bord incogneu d'un estrange rivage,
Où le malheur nous fait ces tristes vers chanter:

Comme on voit quelquefois, quand la mort les appelle,
Arrengez flanc à flanc parmy l'herbe nouvelle,
Bien loing sur un estang trois cygnes lamenter.

15

Panjas, do you want to know how I spend my time? I plan ahead. I worry about each day's expenses, and whether with no money I need to find a way to appease a hundred creditors.

I come. I go. I run. I waste no time. I pay court to a banker. I borrow money in advance. When I have taken care of one of them, another starts up. And I do not pay out a quarter of what I seem to.

One gives me a bill, a letter, an invoice. One tells me the consistory meets tomorrow. One makes my head ache with a hundred stray remarks.

One complains. One mourns. One grumbles. One shouts. With all that, please tell me, Panjas, are you not amazed how I write any poems?

Panjas: Jean de Pardeillan, lord of Panjas, poet and secretary to the cardinal of Armagnac in Rome

consistory: the council of the pope and cardinals

16

While Magny follows his great Avanson, Panjas his cardinal, and I mine, too, and while flattering hope that devours our best years tempts our desires with its baited hook,

You pay court to kings, and with a happier note, singing the good fortune of Henry, the ornament of his age, you bring honor to yourself and to him who honors the honor that you do him with your learned song.

Alas! and we all the while waste the prime of our life on the unknown bank of a foreign shore, where misery makes us sing these sad songs,

As, when death calls them, set side by side in the new grass, far off on a pond, three swans are sometimes seen to lament.

---

mine: Cardinal Jean du Bellay

You: Ronsard

17

After wandering for so long on the shore where so many miserable courtiers lament, you have reached the bank toward which everyone strives, fleeing the painful bondage of poverty.

We, meanwhile, standing along that shore, reach out our hands in vain toward the deaf boatman, who chases us off, for, to win his favor, we haven't an obol to pay our passage.

And so you enjoy blessed rest, and, like those learned lovers in the underworld, you lose yourself deep in a wood with your lady.

You drink long forgetfulness of your past labors, without thinking anymore of those you have left behind crying in the port or straining at the oar.

---

the bank toward which everyone strives: these and other images in this poem recall Aeneas's descent into the underworld in book 6 of Virgil's *Aeneid*

you: Ronsard

the deaf boatman: Charon

an obol: in du Bellay's *quatrin* there may be a pun on the Latin *quadrans* (obol, a small coin) and the French *quatrain* (as in English, a four-line poem or stanza)

18

If you do not know, Morel, what I am doing here, I am not making love nor doing any other such work. I pay court to my master, and do still more, being in charge of his house.

"My God," you will say, "what miracle is this, to see du Bellay busy with housework and writing poems in another language! Wolves and lambs get along just as well."

Here is how things stand, Morel. Sweet poetry accompanies me everywhere, so that no other fancy can distract me from such pleasant labor.

But you will answer, "If you are wise, put an aging horse out to pasture while there is still time, for fear he will get worse and become broken-winded."

Morel: Jean Morel d'Embrun (1511–1581), noted humanist and steward to Henry II

put an aging horse: from Horace's *Epistles* 1.1.8–9

17

Apres avoir long temps erré sur le rivage,
Où lon voit lamenter tant de chetifs de court,
Tu as attaint le bord, où tout le monde court,
Fuyant de pauvreté le penible servage.

Nous autres ce pendant le long de ceste plage
En vain tendons les mains vers le Nautonnier sourd,
Qui nous chasse bien loing: car, pour le faire court,
Nous n'avons un quatrin pour payer le naulage.

Ainsi donc tu jouis du repos bienheureux,
Et comme font là bas ces doctes amoureux,
Bien avant dans un bois te perds avec ta dame:

Tu bois le long oubly de tes travaux passez,
Sans plus penser en ceulx que tu as delaissez,
Criant dessus le port, ou tirant à la rame.

18

Si tu ne sçais (Morel) ce que je fais icy,
Je ne fais pas l'amour, ny autre tel ouvrage:
Je courtise mon maistre, et si fais d'avantage,
Ayant de sa maison le principal soucy.

Mon Dieu (ce diras tu) quel miracle est-ce cy,
Que de veoir Dubellay se mesler du mesnage,
Et composer des vers en un autre langage!
Les loups, et les aigneaux s'accordent tout ainsi.

Voila que c'est (Morel) la doulce poësie
M'accompagne par tout, sans qu'autre fantaisie
En si plaisant labeur me puisse rendre oisif.

Mais tu me respondras: donne, si tu es sage,
De bonne heure congé au cheval qui est d'aage,
De peur qu'il ne s'empire, et devienne poussif.

19

Ce pendant que tu dis ta Cassandre divine,
Les louanges du Roy, et l'heritier d'Hector,
Et ce Montmorancy, nostre François Nestor,
Et que de sa faveur Henry t'estime digne:

Je me pourmene seul sur la rive Latine,
La France regretant, et regretant encor
Mes antiques amis, mon plus riche tresor,
Et le plaisant sejour de ma terre Angevine.

Je regrete les bois, et les champs blondissans,
Les vignes, les jardins, et les prez verdissans,
Que mon fleuve traverse: icy pour recompense

Ne voiant que l'orgueil de ces monceaux pierreux,
Où me tient attaché d'un espoir malheureux,
Ce que possede moins celuy qui plus y pense.

20

Heureux, de qui la mort de sa gloire est suivie,
Et plus heureux celuy, dont l'immortalité
Ne prend commencement de la posterité,
Mais devant que la mort ait son ame ravie.

Tu jouis (mon Ronsard) mesmes durant ta vie,
De l'immortel honneur que tu as merité:
Et devant que mourir (rare felicité)
Ton heureuse vertu triomphe de l'envie.

Courage donc (Ronsard) la victoire est à toy,
Puis que de ton costé est la faveur du Roy:
Ja du laurier vainqueur tes temples se couronnent,

Et ja la tourbe espesse à l'entour de ton flanc
Resemble ces esprits, qui là bas environnent
Le grand prestre de Thrace au long sourpely blanc.

19

While you sing your divine Cassandre, the praises of the king and Hector's heir, and Montmorency, our French Nestor, and while Henry judges you worthy of his favor,

I wander alone on the Latin shore, longing for France, and longing, too, for my old friends, my richest treasure, and for my pleasant Angevin home.

I miss the woods and the ripening fields, the vines, the gardens, and the meadows turning green through which my river runs: here, instead of all that,

Seeing only the pride of these piles of stone, where I am held by a vain hope for that which he least attains who desires it most.

---

you: Ronsard
Cassandre: the subject of Ronsard's *Amours de Cassandre*
Hector's heir: Francus, the hero of Ronsard's epic poem, the *Franciade*
Montmorency: Anne de Montmorency (1493–1567), the constable of France
Nestor: king of Pylos, noted at Troy for his age and wise counsel
my river: the Loire
piles of stone: Roman ruins

20

Happy the man whose death is followed by glory, and happier still he whose immortality begins not with posterity but before death has snatched away his soul.

You, my Ronsard, enjoy even during your lifetime the undying honor you have deserved, and before death—rare felicity!—your fortunate virtue triumphs over envy.

Then take heart, Ronsard. Victory is yours, for the king's favor is on your side. Already triumphant laurel crowns your head.

And already the throng that crowds around you resembles those spirits who in the underworld surround the high priest of Thrace in his long white robe.

Happy the man: compare du Bellay's Latin elegy "Ad P. Ronsardum," lines 13–22
the high priest of Thrace: Orpheus

21

Count, you who never took any account of greatness, your du Bellay is no more. There is only a stump that lies with bended back over a stream and shows no more life than a sprig of greenness.

Though I sometimes write, I write without passion. I simply write down everything that touches my heart, whether good or bad, just as it comes into my head, in a style as slow as my coldness of heart is slow.

You, meanwhile, painters of nature, whose art is not confined to a portrait, imitate the most beautiful works of the ancients.

As for me, I do not aspire to such high praise, and next to your paintings my portraits are no more than a Janet next to a Michelangelo.

Count: Nicolas Denisot, who, in an anagram of his name, called himself "Conte d'Alsinois," poet, painter, and schoolmate of du Bellay

Janet: François Clouet (1515–1572), called "Janet," portrait painter in the court of Henry II

22

Now, more than ever, I am glad that I love the Muse, whether I write in French or in the Roman tongue, since the judgment of a prince so full of humanity grants such great favor to letters.

Thus the sacred craft at which your spirit plays will no longer be a vain exercise, and the long-delayed labor your hand promises us will, for Francus, no longer have any excuse.

In the meantime, my Ronsard, to beguile my troubles, and not to enrich myself, I will imitate, if I can, the humblest songs of your weary Muse.

For not everyone has deserved, as you have, that the largess of a king gild his bow or decorate his lyre with an abbot's crook.

---

for Francus: for the as yet undelivered Francus, the hero of Ronsard's unfinished *Franciade.*

gild his bow: reward him for his song

decorate his lyre with an abbot's crook: Ronsard sought, less successfully than du Bellay seems to have thought, the benefice of an abbey for his *Franciade*

21

Conte, qui ne fis onc compte de la grandeur,
Ton Dubellay n'est plus. Ce n'est plus qu'une souche
Qui dessus un ruisseau d'un doz courbé se couche,
Et n'a plus rien de vif, qu'un petit de verdeur.

Si j'escry quelquefois, je n'escry point d'ardeur,
J'escry naïvement tout ce qu'au cœur me touche,
Soit de bien, soit de mal, comme il vient à la bouche,
En un stile aussi lent, que lente est ma froideur.

Vous autres ce pendant peintres de la nature,
Dont l'art n'est pas enclos dans une protraiture,
Contrefaites des vieux les ouvrages plus beaux.

Quant à moy je n'aspire à si haulte louange,
Et ne sont mes protraits aupres de voz tableaux,
Non plus qu'est un Janet aupres d'un Michelange.

22

Ores, plus que jamais, me plaist d'aymer la Muse,
Soit qu'en François j'escrive, ou langage Romain,
Puis que le jugement d'un Prince tant humain,
De si grande faveur envers les lettres use.

Donq le sacré mestier où ton esprit s'amuse,
Ne sera desormais un exercice vain,
Et le tardif labeur que nous promets ta main,
Desormais pour Francus n'aura plus nulle excuse.

Ce pendant (mon Ronsard) pour tromper mes ennuys,
Et non pour m'enrichir, je suivray, si je puis,
Les plus humbles chansons de ta Muse lassee.

Aussi chacun n'a pas merité que d'un Roy
La liberalité luy face, comme à toy,
Ou son archet doré, ou sa lyre crossee.

23

Ne lira-lon jamais, que ce Dieu rigoureux?
Jamais ne lira-lon que ceste Idaliene?
Ne voira-lon jamais Mars sans la Cypriene?
Jamais ne voira-lon, que Ronsard amoureux?

Retistra-lon tousjours, d'un tour laborieux
Ceste toile, argument d'une si longue peine?
Revoira-lon tousjours Oreste sur la scene,
Sera tousjours Roland par amour furieux?

Ton Francus, ce pendant a beau haulser les voiles,
Dresser le gouvernail, espier les estoiles,
Pour aller où il deust estre ancré desormais:

Il a le vent à gré, il est en equippage,
Il est encor pourtant sur le Troien rivage,
Aussi croy-je (Ronsard) qu'il n'en partit jamais.

24

Qu'heureux tu es (Baif) heureux et plus qu'heureux,
De ne suivre abusé ceste aveugle Deesse,
Qui d'un tour inconstant et nous haulse et nous baisse,
Mais cest aveugle enfant qui nous fait amoureux!

Tu n'esprouves (Baif) d'un maistre rigoureux,
Le severe sourcy: mais la doulce rudesse
D'une belle, courtoise, et gentile maistresse,
Qui fait languir ton cœur doulcement langoureux.

Moy chetif ce pendant loing des yeux de mon Prince,
Je vieillis malheureux en estrange province,
Fuyant la pauvreté: mais las ne fuyant pas

Les regrets, les ennuys, le travail, et la peine,
Le tardif repentir d'une esperance vaine,
Et l'importun souci, qui me suit pas à pas.

23

Will we never read anything but that cruel god? Never read anything but the Idalian? Will we never see Mars without the Cyprian? Never see Ronsard except in love?

Will that same cloth, the subject of such prolonged suffering, always be rewoven in the same laborious way? Will we always see Orestes on stage? Will Orlando always be driven out of his wits by love?

Meanwhile your Francus hoists his sails in vain, sets the rudder, checks the stars to go where he should have been at anchor long ago.

The wind is favorable, his crew is ready, and yet he is still on the Trojan shore. I believe, Ronsard, that he never left it.

---

that cruel god: Cupid

the Idalian: Venus

the Cyprian: Venus

that same cloth: the shroud woven and unwoven by Penelope in Homer's *Odyssey*

Orestes: the son of Agamemnon, often represented on stage as mad for love

Orlando: the love-crazed hero of Ariosto's *Orlando furioso*

he never left it: may allude either to the slow progress Ronsard was making on his *Franciade* or to the mythical character of the poem's protagonist, Francus, who "never left" the Trojan shore because he never existed

24

How lucky you are, Baïf, lucky, and more than lucky, not to be among the deceived followers of that blind goddess, who with her fickle wheel raises us up and drops us down, but rather of that blind child who makes us fall in love!

You do not suffer, Baïf, the severe frown of a stern master, but the sweet harshness of a beautiful, courteous, and gentle mistress, who makes your sweetly languishing heart pine.

Meanwhile miserable I, far from the eyes of my prince, am growing old, unhappy, in a foreign land, fleeing poverty, but not, alas, fleeing

The longings, the troubles, the torment, and the suffering, the belated repentance for a vain hope, and the nagging care that pursues me step by step.

Baïf: Jean-Antoine de Baïf (1532–1589), poet, classmate, and fellow member of the Pléiade with du Bellay and Ronsard

that blind goddess: Fortune

that blind child: Cupid

Meanwhile miserable I: compare "Ad P. Ronsardum," lines 33–36

25

Cursed be the year, the month, the day, the hour, and the instant, and cursed be the flattering hope, when to come here I left France, France and my Anjou, for which longing torments me.

Truly I was not led by a bird of good fortune, and my heart gave me plenty of warning that the heavens were charged with bad influence and that Mars was then housed with Saturn.

A hundred times good advice tried to draw me back, but fate always pulled me the other way, and had desire not blinded my reason,

Was it not enough to cancel my trip when—sinister omen!—I injured my foot on the doorstep as I was leaving the house?

Cursed be the year: alludes with ironic humor to the opening lines of Petrarch's *Rime sparse* 61, where Petrarch blesses "the day and the month and the year and the season and the time and the hour and the instant" when he first saw Laura

26

If someone preparing to take a long journey must believe one who has already traveled and who, after being long beaten by the waves, has pulled himself wet and dripping from the wreck,

You will believe me, Ronsard, though you are wiser and (I believe) a little bit older, because I have sailed this sea before you and because my ship already has the shore in sight.

Thus I warn you that this Roman sea, full of dangerous reefs and shoals, hides a thousand perils, and that here very often,

Misled by the enticing song of the Sicilian monsters, trying to avoid Charybdis, you will fall onto Scylla, unless you know how to sail in all weathers.

---

a little bit older: Ronsard seems, in fact, to have been two years younger than du Bellay

the Sicilian monsters: the Sirens, who, like Charybdis and Scylla, menaced Homer's Odysseus

25

Malheureux l'an, le mois, le jour, l'heure, et le poinct,
Et malheureuse soit la flateuse esperance,
Quand pour venir icy j'abandonnay la France:
La France, et mon Anjou dont le desir me poingt.

Vrayment d'un bon oiseau guidé je ne fus point,
Et mon cœur me donnoit assez signifiance
Que le ciel estoit plein de mauvaise influence,
Et que Mars estoit lors à Saturne conjoint.

Cent fois le bon advis lors m'en voulut distraire,
Mais tousjours le destin me tiroit au contraire:
Et si mon desir n'eust aveuglé ma raison,

N'estoit ce pas assez pour rompre mon voyage,
Quand sur le sueil de l'huis, d'un sinistre presage,
Je me blessay le pied sortant de ma maison?

26

Si celuy qui s'appreste à faire un long voyage,
Doit croire cestuy là qui a ja voyagé,
Et qui des flots marins longuement oultragé,
Tout moite et degoutant s'est sauvé du naufrage,

Tu me croiras (Ronsard) bien que tu sois plus sage,
Et quelque peu encor (ce croy-je) plus aagé,
Puis que j'ay devant toy en ceste mer nagé,
Et que desja ma nef descouvre le rivage.

Donques je t'advertis, que ceste mer Romaine,
De dangereux escueils et de bancs toute pleine,
Cache mille perils, et qu'icy bien souvent

Trompé du chant pippeur des monstres de Sicile
Pour Carybde eviter tu tomberas en Scylle,
Si tu ne sçais nager d'une voile à tout vent.

27

Ce n'est l'ambition, ny le soing d'acquerir,
Qui m'a fait delaisser ma rive paternelle,
Pour voir ces monts couvers d'une neige eternelle,
Et par mille dangers ma fortune querir. 4

Le vray honneur qui n'est coustumier de perir,
Et la vraye vertu qui seule est immortelle,
Ont comblé mes desirs d'une abondance telle,
Qu'un plus grand bien aux dieux je ne veulx requerir. 8

L'honneste servitude, où mon devoir me lie,
M'a fait passer les monts de France en Italie,
Et demourer trois ans sur ce bord estranger, 11

Où je vy languissant. Ce seul devoir encore
Me peult faire changer France à l'Inde et au More,
Et le ciel à l'enfer me peult faire changer. 14

28

Quand je te dis adieu, pour m'en venir icy,
Tu me dis (mon Lahaye) il m'en souvient encore,
Souvienne toy Bellay de ce que tu es ore,
Et comme tu t'en vas retourne t'en ainsi. 4

Et tel comme je vins, je m'en retourne aussi:
Hors mis un repentir qui le cœur me devore,
Qui me ride le front, qui mon chef decolore,
Et qui me fait plus bas enfoncer le sourcy. 8

Ce triste repentir qui me ronge, et me lime,
Ne vient (car j'en suis net) pour sentir quelque crime,
Mais pour m'estre trois ans à ce bord arresté: 11

Et pour m'estre abusé d'une ingrate esperance,
Qui pour venir icy trouver la pauvreté,
M'a fait (sot que je suis) abandonner la France. 14

27

Neither ambition nor greed made me leave my paternal shore to see those peaks covered with everlasting snow and to seek my fortune in the midst of a thousand dangers.

True honor, which rarely dies, and true virtue, which alone is immortal, have satisfied my desires with such abundance that I do not wish to beg the gods for any greater good.

The honorable service to which duty binds me made me cross the mountains from France to Italy and abide three years on this foreign shore

Where languishing I live. This duty alone could even make me exchange France for India or Africa and make me exchange heaven for hell.

---

those peaks: the Alps

three years: places the composition of this sonnet in 1556

28

When I bid you farewell to come here, you said to me, my La Haye, I remember it still, "Remember, Bellay, what you are now, and as you leave, return the same."

And, as I left, I return the same, save for a regret that devours my heart, that wrinkles my brow, that whitens my hair, and that deepens my frown.

This sad regret, that gnaws at me and wears me down, does not come from the sense of any crime (for of that I am free), but rather from having stayed three years on this shore,

And from having deceived myself with a thankless hope that made me (fool that I am) leave France to come here and find poverty.

La Haye: Robert de La Haye, counselor to the Parlement of Paris and admirer of du Bellay and Ronsard

29

I hate worse than death a young stay-at-home, who, except on holidays, never goes out and, fearing daylight more than a wild beast, makes himself a prisoner in his own house.

But I cannot love an old traveler, who runs here and there and never stops, but, on the contrary, less light on his feet than light in his head, never stays in one place any longer than a messenger.

The one, without tormenting himself, remains in safety. The other, who never rests until he dies, passes through a thousand dangerous places night and day.

The one happily spends his life rich and foolish. The other, more needy than a poor beggar, acquires in traveling unhappy knowledge.

30

Whoever, my Bailleul, remains for long under an unknown sky, and whoever can bear to go from port to port in search of his fortune and live as a stranger in another land,

Who can consign to forgetfulness the love of his family, the love of his mistress, and the love that nature inspires in us for the place where we were nurtured, and always travel with no thought of a return,

He is the son of a stone or of a cruel bear and worthy to have suckled at the breast of an inhuman tigress; yet do we not see

That wild animals return to their lairs and that those that live domesticated among us are always pricked by a sweet longing for home?

Whoever: compare du Bellay's Latin elegy "Patriae desiderium," lines 1–10 and 47–48

Bailleul: Louis Bailleul, friend of du Bellay in Rome

29

Je hay plus que la mort un jeune casanier,
Qui ne sort jamais hors, sinon au jour de feste,
Et craignant plus le jour qu'une sauvage beste,
Se fait en sa maison luy mesmes prisonnier.

Mais je ne puis aymer un vieillard voyager,
Qui court deça dela, et jamais ne s'arreste,
Ains des pieds moins leger, que leger de la teste
Ne sejourne jamais non plus qu'un messager.

L'un sans se travailler en seureté demeure,
L'autre qui n'a repos jusques à tant qu'il meure,
Traverse nuict et jour mille lieux dangereux.

L'un passe riche et sot heureusement sa vie,
L'autre plus souffreteux qu'un pauvre qui mendie,
S'acquiert en voyageant un sçavoir malheureux.

30

Quiconques (mon Bailleul) fait longuement sejour,
Soubs un ciel incogneu, et quiconques endure
D'aller de port en port cherchant son adventure,
Et peult vivre estranger dessoubs un autre jour:

Qui peult mettre en oubly de ses parents l'amour,
L'amour de sa maistresse, et l'amour que nature
Nous fait porter au lieu de nostre nourriture,
Et voyage tousjours sans penser au retour:

Il est fils d'un rocher, ou d'une ourse cruelle,
Et digne qui jadis ait succé la mamelle
D'une tygre inhumaine. Encor ne voit-on point

Que les fierts animaux en leurs forts ne retournent,
Et ceulx qui parmy nous domestiques sejournent,
Tousjours de la maison le doulx desir les poingt.

31

Heureux qui, comme Ulysse, a fait un beau voyage,
Ou comme cestuy là qui conquit la toison,
Et puis est retourné, plein d'usage et raison,
Vivre entre ses parents le reste de son aage!

Quand revoiray-je, helas, de mon petit village
Fumer la cheminee, et en quelle saison,
Revoiray-je le clos de ma pauvre maison,
Qui m'est une province, et beaucoup d'avantage?

Plus me plaist le sejour qu'ont basty mes ayeux,
Que des palais Romains le front audacieux,
Plus que le marbre dur me plaist l'ardoise fine:

Plus mon Loyre Gaulois, que le Tybre Latin,
Plus mon petit Lyré, que le mont Palatin,
Et plus que l'air marin la doulceur Angevine.

32

Je me feray sçavant en la philosophie,
En la mathematique, et medicine aussi,
Je me feray legiste, et d'un plus hault souci
Apprendray les secrets de la theologie:

Du lut et du pinceau j'ebateray ma vie,
De l'escrime et du bal. Je discourois ainsi,
Et me vantois en moy d'apprendre tout cecy,
Quand je changeay la France au sejour d'Italie.

O beaux discours humains! je suis venu si loing,
Pour m'enrichir d'ennuy, de vieillesse, et de soing,
Et perdre en voyageant le meilleur de mon aage.

Ainsi le marinier souvent pour tout tresor
Rapporte des harencs en lieu de lingots d'or,
Aiant fait, comme moy, un malheureux voyage.

31

Happy the man who, like Ulysses, has traveled well, or like that man who conquered the fleece, and has then returned, full of experience and wisdom, to live among his kinfolk the rest of his life!

When, alas, will I again see smoke rising from the chimney of my little village and in what season will I see the enclosed field of my poor house, which to me is a province and much more still?

The home my ancestors built pleases me more than the grandiose facades of Roman palaces, fine slate pleases me more than hard marble,

My Gallic Loire more than the Latin Tiber, my little Liré more than the Palatine hill, and more than sea air, the sweetness of Anjou.

Happy the man: compare "Patriae desiderium," lines 45–56
that man who conquered the fleece: Jason and the Golden Fleece
smoke rising: echoes Ovid's *Ex Ponto* 1.3.33–34

32

"I will become learned in philosophy, in mathematics, and medicine, too. I will become a jurist, and with a still higher ambition, I will learn the secrets of theology.

"I will brighten my life with the lute and the paintbrush, with fencing and dancing." Such were my thoughts, boasting to myself that I would learn all this, when I left France for a stay in Italy.

O fine reasonings of men! I came all this way to enrich myself with trouble, age, and care and to waste in travel the best years of my life.

Thus the seaman often brings back, as his only treasure, a load of herring instead of bars of gold, having made, like me, an unlucky trip.

---

an unlucky trip: du Bellay's *aage / voyage* echoes and reverses the first rhymes of the preceding sonnet

33

What shall I do, Morel? Tell me, if you know. Shall I stretch out my stay here still further? Or shall I go see the fields of France once again, when the snows have melted in the springtime sun?

If I stay here, alas, I waste my time feeding in vain on a long-protracted hope. And if I choose to seek my fortune elsewhere, I cheat my labor of the wages I expect.

But must I live thus on a vain hope? But must I lose thus a good three years of my toil? I will not budge then. No, no, I will leave.

Still, I will stay, if that is what you advise. Alas, my dear Morel, tell me what I should do, for I have, as they say, the wolf by the ears.

---

the wolf by the ears: a Latin proverb from Erasmus's *Adagia* 1.5.25

34

As the sailor, whom the cruel storm has long tossed on the high seas, having finally, by dint of rowing, secured his vessel from the danger of shipwreck,

Sees from the port, no longer fearing the rage of the waves or the winds, the foaming water and someone else far off in danger of going down, vainly reaching his hands out toward the shore,

So, my dear Morel, having reached the port, you look out to sea and view in safety its waves twisted in a thousand swirls.

You see it often mounting to the sky and see your du Bellay, at the mercy of the wind, seated at the tiller in a ship full of holes.

33

Que feray-je, Morel? Dy moy, si tu l'entends,
Feray-je encor icy plus longue demeurance,
Ou si j'iray reveoir les campaignes de France,
Quand les neiges fondront au soleil du printemps? 4

Si je demeure icy, helas je perds mon temps
A me repaistre en vain d'une longue esperance,
Et si je veulx ailleurs fonder mon asseurance,
Je fraude mon labeur du loyer que j'attens. 8

Mais fault-il vivre ainsi d'une esperance vaine?
Mais fault-il perdre ainsi bien trois ans de ma peine?
Je ne bougeray donc. Non, non, je m'en iray. 11

Je demourray pourtant, si tu le me conseilles.
Helas (mon cher Morel) dy moy que je feray,
Car je tiens, comme on dit, le loup par les oreilles. 14

34

Comme le marinier que le cruel orage
A long temps agité dessus la haulte mer,
Aiant finablement à force de ramer
Garanty son vaisseau du danger du naufrage, 4

Regarde sur le port sans plus craindre la rage
Des vagues ny des vents, les ondes escumer:
Et quelqu'autre bien loing au danger d'abysmer
En vain tendre les mains vers le front du rivage: 8

Ainsi (mon cher Morel) sur le port arresté
Tu regardes la mer, et vois en seureté
De mille tourbillons son onde renversee: 11

Tu la vois jusqu'au ciel s'eslever bien souvent,
Et vois ton Dubellay à la mercy du vent
Assis au gouvernail dans une nef percee. 14

35

La nef qui longuement a voyagé (Dillier)
Dedans le seing du port à la fin on la serre,
Et le bœuf, qui long temps a renversé la terre,
Le bouvier à la fin luy oste le collier:

Le vieil cheval se voit à la fin deslier,
Pour ne perdre l'haleine, ou quelque honte acquerre,
Et pour se reposer du travail de la guerre,
Se retire à la fin le vieillard chevalier:

Mais moy, qui jusqu'icy n'ay prouvé que la peine,
La peine et le malheur d'une esperance vaine,
La douleur, le souci, les regrets, les ennuis,

Je vieillis peu à peu sur l'onde Ausonienne,
Et si n'espere point, quelque bien qui m'advienne,
De sortir jamais hors des travaux où je suis.

36

Depuis que j'ay laissé mon naturel sejour,
Pour venir où le Tybre aux flots tortuz ondoye,
Le ciel a veu trois fois par son oblique voye
Recommencer son cours la grand' lampe du jour.

Mais j'ay si grand desir de me voir de retour,
Que ces trois ans me sont plus qu'un siege de Troye,
Tant me tarde (Morel) que Paris je revoye,
Et tant le ciel pour moy fait lentement son tour:

Il fait son tour si lent, et me semble si morne,
Si morne, et si pesant que le froid Capricorne
Ne m'accoursit les jours, ny le Cancre les nuicts.

Voila (mon cher Morel) combien le temps me dure
Loing de France et de toy, et comment la nature
Fait toute chose longue aveques mes ennuis.

35

The ship that has long sailed, Dilliers, is finally gathered to the bosom of the port. And from the ox that has long furrowed the field, the plowman finally takes the yoke.

The old horse is finally set free to prevent its being broken-winded or otherwise shamed. And to rest from the labor of war, the old knight finally retires.

But I, who until now have known only suffering, suffering and the misery of a vain hope, pain, care, regrets, troubles,

I grow old little by little on the Ausonian shore and have no hope, whatever good may come my way, that I will ever escape these travails.

The ship: images taken from Propertius 2.25.3–9

Dilliers: Oudart d'Illiers, gentleman ordinary of the king and friend of du Bellay and Magny

Ausonian shore: Italy

36

Since I left my native home to come where the twisting Tiber flows, the heavens have thrice seen the great lamp of day begin its course along its oblique path.

But I have such a great desire to return home that these three years have seemed longer to me than a siege of Troy, so impatient am I, Morel, to see Paris again, and so slowly for me the heavens make their round.

They make their round so slowly and seem to me so dreary, so dreary and so leaden, that for me cold Capricorn does not shorten the days, nor Cancer the nights.

That, my dear Morel, is how time hangs on me far from France and from you, and how nature stretches out everything with my troubles.

Since I left: from Ovid's *Tristia* 5.10.1–10

its course along its oblique path: the sun's annual progress through the zodiac

Capricorn and Cancer: the signs of the winter and summer solstices

37

There was a time when I had only to live unto myself, without wanting to be more than that which I am, and when I had to be happy with the little I have and live content with my pen and book.

But it did not please the gods to permit me to follow my youthful liberty nor to allow me since then to live as free from toil and trouble as I was free and exempt from ambition.

It did not please them that in old age I would know the joy of living at home, of living with my own family without fear or envy.

It did please them, alas, that on this foreign shore I would see my liberty transformed into a prison and the flower of my years turned into the winter of my life.

38

O happy the man who can spend his life with people like himself, and who, without feigning, without fear, without envy, and without ambition, reigns peacefully in his own poor household!

The miserable trouble of acquiring more does not tyrannize over his free inclinations, and his greatest desire, a desire without passion, reaches no further than his own inheritance.

He does not trouble himself with the business of others. His chief hope depends only on himself. He is his own court, his king, his benefactor, and his master.

He does not devour his wealth in a foreign country. He does not put his life in danger for others. And he would not want to be richer than he is.

37

C'estoit ores c'estoit qu'à moy je devois vivre,
Sans vouloir estre plus, que cela que je suis,
Et qu'heureux je devois de ce peu que je puis,
Vivre content du bien de la plume, et du livre.

Mais il n'a pleu aux Dieux me permettre de suivre
Ma jeune liberté, ny faire que depuis
Je vesquisse aussi franc de travaux et d'ennuis,
Comme d'ambition j'estois franc et delivre.

Il ne leur a pas pleu qu'en ma vieille saison
Je sceusse quel bien c'est de vivre en sa maison,
De vivre entre les siens sans crainte et sans envie:

Il leur a pleu (helas) qu'à ce bord estranger
Je veisse ma franchise en prison se changer,
Et la fleur de mes ans en l'hyver de ma vie.

38

O qu'heureux est celuy qui peult passer son aage
Entre pareils à soy! et qui sans fiction,
Sans crainte, sans envie, et sans ambition
Regne paisiblement en son pauvre mesnage.

Le miserable soing d'acquerir d'avantage
Ne tyrannise point sa libre affection,
Et son plus grand desir, desir sans passion,
Ne s'estend plus avant que son propre heritage.

Il ne s'empesche point des affaires d'autruy,
Son principal espoir ne depend que de luy,
Il est sa court, son roy, sa faveur, et son maistre.

Il ne mange son bien en païs estranger,
Il ne met pour autruy sa personne en danger,
Et plus riche qu'il est ne voudroit jamais estre.

39

J'ayme la liberté, et languis en service,
Je n'ayme point la court, et me fault courtiser,
Je n'ayme la feintise, et me fault deguiser,
J'ayme simplicité, et n'apprens que malice: 4

Je n'adore les biens, et sers à l'avarice,
Je n'ayme les honneurs, et me les fault priser,
Je veulx garder ma foy, et me la fault briser,
Je cherche la vertu, et ne trouve que vice: 8

Je cherche le repos, et trouver ne le puis,
J'embrasse le plaisir, et n'esprouve qu'ennuis,
Je n'ayme à discourir, en raison je me fonde: 11

J'ay le corps maladif, et me fault voyager,
Je suis né pour la Muse, on me fait mesnager,
Ne suis-je pas (Morel) le plus chetif du monde? 14

40

Un peu de mer tenoit le grand Dulichien,
D'Ithaque separé, l'Apennin porte-nue,
Et les monts de Savoye à la teste chenue
Me tiennent loing de France au bord Ausonien: 4

Fertile est mon sejour, sterile estoit le sien,
Je ne suis des plus fins, sa finesse est cogneue,
Les siens gardans son bien attendoient sa venue,
Mais nul en m'attendant ne me garde le mien: 8

Pallas sa guide estoit, je vays à l'aventure,
Il fut dur au travail, moy tendre de nature,
A la fin il ancra sa navire à son port, 11

Je ne suis asseuré de retourner en France,
Il feit de ses haineux une belle vengeance,
Pour me venger des miens je ne suis assez fort. 14

39

I love liberty and languish in servitude. I do not like the court and have to play the courtier. I dislike feigning and must wear a mask. I love straightforwardness and learn only malice.

I do not worship worldly goods and serve greed. I do not love honors and must prize them. I want to keep my word and must break it. I seek virtue and find only vice.

I seek rest and cannot find it. I embrace pleasure and experience only pain. I do not like arguing and must justify everything I say.

I have a sickly body and must travel. I was born for the Muse and am forced to run a household. Am I not, Morel, the most pitiful man in the world?

40

A bit of sea stood between the great Dulichian and Ithaca; the cloud-capped Apennines and the hoary-headed peaks of Savoy keep me far from France on the Ausonian shore.

My home is fertile; his was barren. I am not very clever; his cleverness is famous. His people, watching over his estate, awaited his coming; but no one, waiting for me, watches over mine.

Pallas was his guide; I go haphazardly. He was hardened to his task; I am tender by nature. In the end he anchored his ship in his home port;

I am not assured of my return to France. He achieved a great revenge over his enemies; I am not strong enough to avenge myself on mine.

A bit of sea: inspired by Ovid's *Tristia* 1.5.57–84, but compare also du Bellay's Latin elegy "Patriae desiderium," lines 41–44

the great Dulichian: Ulysses

41

Not satisfied with my woes, and wanting me to become hateful to myself, Fortune took the friend I loved most and without whom I had no desire to live.

Thus everlasting night has snatched away your brightness, and I have not followed you into those dim regions—you, who loved me more than your life and your eyes; you, whom I loved more than my eyes and my life.

Alas, dear companion, why can I not be the brother of Pollux, you that of Castor, since our friendship was more than fraternal?

Receive then these tears as proof of my faithfulness and these verses, which, unless I deceive myself, will make the memory of such a rare friendship eternal.

---

the friend: this friend has not been securely identified

Pollux and Castor: brothers who loved one another so deeply that Jupiter allowed them to share the immortality that belonged by right only to Pollux

42

It is now, my Vineus, my dear Vineus, it is now that of all the pitiful, I am the most pitiful, and that what I was I can no longer be, having wasted my time and with it my youth.

Poverty follows me. Care devours me. Sad are my days, and still sadder the nights. O how burdened am I with regrets and troubles! Would to God I were a Pasquino or Marforio;

I would not feel the misery that pierces me. My pen would be free, and I would not fear that someone greater than I would turn his anger against me.

You can be sure, Vineus, that he alone is king on whom not even kings can impose their law and who can write what he likes about anyone.

Vineus: Jerome della Rovere, lord of Vineus (Vinovo), a prelate and ambassador in Rome

Pasquino or Marforio: statues in Rome on which satiric verses were often pinned

41

N'estant de mes ennuis la fortune assouvie,
Afin que je devinsse à moymesme odieux,
M'osta de mes amis celuy que j'aymois mieux,
Et sans qui je n'avois de vivre nulle envie. 4

Donc l'eternelle nuict a ta clarté ravie,
Et je ne t'ay suivy parmy ces obscurs lieux?
Toy qui m'as plus aymé que ta vie et tes yeux,
Toy, que j'ay plus aymé que mes yeux et ma vie. 8

Helas, cher compaignon, que ne puis-je estre encor
Le frere de Pollux, toy celuy de Castor,
Puis que nostre amitié fut plus que fraternelle? 11

Reçoy donques ces pleurs, pour gage de ma foy,
Et ces vers qui rendront, si je ne me deçoy,
De si rare amitié la memoire eternelle. 14

42

C'est ores, mon Vineus, mon cher Vineus, c'est ore
Que de tous les chetifs le plus chetif je suis,
Et que ce que j'estois plus estre je ne puis,
Aiant perdu mon temps, et ma jeunesse encore. 4

La pauvreté me suit, le souci me devore,
Tristes me sont les jours, et plus tristes les nuicts,
O que je suis comblé de regrets, et d'ennuis!
Pleust à Dieu que je fusse un Pasquin ou Marphore. 8

Je n'aurois sentiment du malheur qui me poingt,
Ma plume seroit libre, et si ne craindrois point
Qu'un plus grand contre moy peust exercer son ire. 11

Asseure toy Vineus, que celuy seul est Roy,
A qui mesmes les Roys ne peuvent donner loy,
Et qui peult d'un chacun à son plaisir escrire. 14

43

Je ne commis jamais fraude, ne malefice,
Je ne doutay jamais des poincts de nostre foy,
Je n'ay point violé l'ordonnance du Roy,
Et n'ay point esprouvé la rigueur de justice: 4

J'ay fait à mon seigneur fidelement service,
Je fais pour mes amis ce que je puis et doy,
Et croy que jusqu'icy nul ne se pleint de moy,
Que vers luy j'aye fait quelque mauvais office. 8

Voila ce que je suis. Et toutefois, Vineus,
Comme un qui est aux Dieux et aux hommes haineux,
Le malheur me poursuit, et tousjours m'importune: 11

Mais j'ay ce beau confort en mon adversité,
C'est qu'on dit que je n'ay ce malheur merité,
Et que digne je suis de meilleure fortune. 14

44

Si pour avoir passé sans crime sa jeunesse,
Si pour n'avoir d'usure enrichi sa maison,
Si pour n'avoir commis homicide ou traïson,
Si pour n'avoir usé de mauvaise finesse, 4

Si pour n'avoir jamais violé sa promesse,
On se doit resjouir en l'arriere saison,
Je dois à l'advenir, si j'ay quelque raison,
D'un grand contentement consoler ma vieillesse. 8

Je me console donc en mon adversité,
Ne requerant aux Dieux plus grand' felicité,
Que de pouvoir durer en ceste patience. 11

O Dieux, si vous avez quelque souci de nous,
Ottroyez moy ce don, que j'espere de vous,
Et pour vostre pitié, et pour mon innocence. 14

43

I have never committed fraud or sorcery. I have never doubted the articles of our faith. I have not violated the king's edicts and have never felt the law's rigor.

I have served my lord faithfully. I do for my friends what I can and should, and believe that up to now no one has complained that I have done him wrong.

That is what I am. And yet, Vineus, misery pursues me and continually harasses me like one who is hated by gods and men.

But I have this good consolation in my adversity: that people say I have not deserved this misery and am worthy of better fortune.

44

If for having spent his youth without crime, if for having not increased his fortune by usury, if for having not committed murder or treason, if for having not used any subterfuge,

If for having never broken his word one should rejoice in later days, I should in the future, if I am at all right, solace my old age with great happiness.

I thus console myself in my adversity, not asking greater felicity of the gods than to be able to persist in this state of patience.

O Gods, if you have any care for us, grant me this gift I ask of you, moved by your pity and my innocence.

45

O stepmother nature (and a cruel stepmother you are for not bringing me into the world wiser or more fortunate), why did you not make me my own master, free to do as I wish and be my own man?

I see two paths, the bad and the good. I know that virtue calls me toward the right-hand side, and yet I am obliged to turn toward the left, to follow a false hope that has made me all its own.

And what has it profited me? O handsome reward! I have ruined myself with vain expense and have acquired nothing but sorrow and trouble.

A stranger gathers in the fruit of my service. I wear down my body in unworthy business and bear on my forehead another's shame.

I see two paths: recalls the myth of Hercules at the crossroads

46

If by hard work and sweat and by loyalty, by humble service and long patience, expending body and goods, wit and conscience, and utterly neglecting one's own interests,

If by never wheedling for a benefice or other compensation, one should get rich, I will (as I think) have some reward in the end, for I have deserved it.

But if one must get ahead by theft, by lying, by flattery, by cheating one's master, and by often doing worse than all that,

I know that I am sowing on a barren shore, that I am trying to sift water, and that I am beating the wind, and that I am, Vineus, a useless servant.

45

O marastre nature (et marastre es-tu bien,
De ne m'avoir plus sage ou plus heureux fait naistre)
Pourquoy ne m'as tu fait de moymesme le maistre,
Pour suivre ma raison, et vivre du tout mien? 4

Je voy les deux chemins, et de mal, et de bien:
Je sçay que la vertu m'appelle à la main dextre,
Et toutefois il fault que je tourne à senestre,
Pour suivre un traistre espoir, qui m'a fait du tout sien. 8

Et quel profit en ay-je? ô belle recompense!
Je me suis consumé d'une vaine despence,
Et n'ay fait autre acquest que de mal et d'ennuy, 11

L'estranger recueillist le fruict de mon service,
Je travaille mon corps d'un indigne exercice,
Et porte sur mon front la vergongne d'autruy. 14

46

Si par peine, et sueur, et par fidelité,
Par humble servitude, et longue patience,
Employer corps, et biens, esprit, et conscience,
Et du tout mespriser sa propre utilité, 4

Si pour n'avoir jamais par importunité
Demandé benefice, ou autre recompense,
On se doit enrichir, j'auray (comme je pense)
Quelque bien à la fin, car je l'ay merité. 8

Mais si par larrecin advancé l'on doit estre,
Par mentir, par flater, par abuser son maistre,
Et pis que tout cela faire encor' bien souvent: 11

Je cognois que je seme au rivage infertile,
Que je veux cribler l'eau, et que je bas le vent,
Et que je suis (Vineus) serviteur inutile. 14

47

Si onques de pitié ton ame fut atteinte,
Voiant indignement ton amy tormenté,
Et si onques tes yeux ont experimenté
Les poignans esguillons d'une douleur non feinte, 4

Voy la mienne en ces vers sans artifice peinte,
Comme sans artifice est ma simplicité:
Et si pour moy tu n'es à pleurer incité,
Ne te ry pour le moins des souspirs de ma pleinte. 8

Ainsi (mon cher Vineus) jamais ne puisse-tu
Esprouver les regrets qu'esprouve une vertu,
Qui se void defrauder du loyer de sa peine: 11

Ainsi l'œil de ton Roy favorable te soit,
Et ce qui des plus fins l'esperance deçoit,
N'abuse ta bonté d'une promesse vaine. 14

48

O combien est heureux, qui n'est contreint de feindre
Ce que la verité le contreint de penser,
Et à qui le respect d'un qu'on n'ose offenser,
Ne peult la liberté de sa plume contreindre! 4

Las pourquoy de ce nœu sens-je la mienne estreindre,
Quand mes justes regrets je cuide commencer?
Et pourquoy ne se peult mon ame dispenser
De ne sentir son mal, ou de s'en pouvoir pleindre? 8

On me donne la genne, et si n'ose crier,
On me voit tormenter, et si n'ose prier
Qu'on ait pitié de moy. Ô peine trop sugette! 11

Il n'est feu si ardent, qu'un feu qui est enclos,
Il n'est si facheux mal, qu'un mal qui tient à l'os,
Et n'est si grand' douleur, qu'une douleur muette. 14

47

If ever your soul was touched by pity, seeing your friend undeservedly tormented, and if ever your eyes have felt the sharp prick of an unfeigned sorrow,

See mine painted without artifice in these verses, since my sincerity is without artifice, and if you are not moved to weep for me, at least do not laugh at the sighs of my lament.

Thus, my dear Vineus, may you never feel the regrets felt by a virtue that sees itself robbed of the reward for its trouble.

Thus may the eye of your king look on you with favor and may your goodness not be taken in by a vain promise, which deceives the hope of even the sharpest.

48

O how happy the man who is not forced to dissemble what truth forces him to think and whose pen cannot be coerced by deference to one he dares not offend!

Alas, why do I feel mine tied by this knot when I wish to write my just regrets? And why can my soul not refrain either from feeling its pain or from complaining of it?

I am put to torture, yet I dare not cry out. I am seen in torment, yet I dare not beg for pity. O too servile suffering!

There is no fiercer fire than a fire contained. There is no more vexing pain than a pain deep in the bone, and no greater suffering than suffering in silence.

49

If after forty years of faithful service that he whom I serve has performed in various places, employing freely all the greatest and best he has in affairs of highest responsibility,

The invidious malice of a hateful stranger directs its odious force against him and, with respect for neither men nor gods, sets ignorance and vice against virtue,

Should I be distraught, I who am less than nothing, if, because of someone who is perhaps jealous of what I have, I do not receive the timely favor I crave?

I therefore comfort myself, and in such a sea, observing my dear lord in danger of going down, I am pleased to risk the same fortune.

---

he whom I serve: Cardinal Jean du Bellay
a hateful stranger: Cardinal Carlo Caraffa, nephew of Pope Paul IV

50

Let us leave, Dilliers, let us leave. Let us give way to envy, and henceforth flee civic strife, since we see that the most craven and vile are prized and the best side is the least followed.

Let us go where virtue and destiny invite us, even if we have to see Scythia or the source of the Nile, and let us rather give ourselves over to everlasting exile than stain with a single spot the honor of our life.

Up then, and before the cruel conqueror makes a show of us for the mocking crowd, let us banish virtue in voluntary exile.

And yet, do you not know that the banished Roman, though he was expelled by his own inhuman people, was nevertheless adored by barbarian pirates?

Scythia or the source of the Nile: for the Romans, whom du Bellay echoes, the ends of the world
the banished Roman: Scipio Africanus

49

Si apres quarante ans de fidele service,
Que celuy que je sers a fait en divers lieux,
Emploiant, liberal, tout son plus et son mieux
Aux affaires qui sont de plus digne exercice, 4

D'un hayneux estranger l'envieuse malice
Exerce contre luy son courage odieux,
Et sans avoir souci des hommes ny des dieux,
Oppose à la vertu l'ignorance et le vice, 8

Me doy-je tormenter, moy qui suis moins que rien,
Si par quelqu'un (peult estre) envieux de mon bien
Je ne treuve à mon gré la faveur opportune? 11

Je me console donc, et en pareille mer,
Voiant mon cher Seigneur au danger d'abysmer,
Il me plaist de courir une mesme fortune. 14

50

Sortons (Dilliers) sortons, faisons place à l'envie,
Et fuions desormais ce tumulte civil,
Puis qu'on y voit priser le plus lasche et plus vil,
Et la meilleure part estre la moins suivie. 4

Allons où la vertu, et le sort nous convie,
Deussions nous voir le Scythe, ou la source du Nil,
Et nous donnons plus-tost un eternel exil,
Que tacher d'un seul poinct l'honneur de nostre vie. 8

Sus donques, et devant que le cruel vainqueur
De nous face une fable au vulgaire moqueur,
Banissons la vertu d'un exil volontaire. 11

Et quoy? ne sçais-tu pas que le bany Romain
Bien qu'il fust dechassé de son peuple inhumain,
Fut pourtant adoré du barbare coursaire? 14

51

Mauny, prenons en gré la mauvaise fortune,
Puis que nul ne se peult de la bonne asseurer,
Et que de la mauvaise on peult bien esperer,
Estant son naturel, de n'estre jamais une.

Le sage nocher craint la faveur de Neptune,
Sachant que le beau temps long temps ne peult durer:
Et ne vault il pas mieulx quelque orage endurer,
Que d'avoir tousjours peur de la mer importune?

Par la bonne fortune on se trouve abusé,
Par la fortune adverse on devient plus rusé:
L'une esteint la vertu, l'autre la fait paroistre:

L'une trompe noz yeux d'un visage menteur,
L'autre nous fait l'amy cognoistre du flateur,
Et si nous fait encor' à nous mesmes cognoistre.

52

Si les larmes servoient de remede au malheur,
Et le pleurer pouvoit la tristesse arrester,
On devroit (Seigneur mien) les larmes acheter,
Et ne se trouveroit rien si cher que le pleur.

Mais les pleurs en effect sont de nulle valeur,
Car soit qu'on ne se veuille en pleurant tormenter,
Ou soit que nuict et jour on veuille lamenter,
On ne peult divertir le cours de la douleur.

Le cœur fait au cerveau ceste humeur exhaler,
Et le cerveau la fait par les yeux devaller,
Mais le mal par les yeux ne s'allambique pas.

Dequoy donques nous sert ce fascheux larmoyer?
De jetter, comme on dit l'huile sur le foyer,
Et perdre sans profit le repoz et repas.

51

Mauny, let us accept bad fortune willingly, since no one can be certain of good, and since with the bad one can always hope, its nature being never to stay the same.

The wise sailor fears the favor of Neptune, knowing that good weather cannot last for long. And is it not better to endure an occasional storm than to be always afraid of the importunate sea?

By good fortune we are deceived. By adverse fortune we are made more wily. One extinguishes virtue. The other reveals it.

One tricks our eyes with a lying face. The other teaches us to know a friend from a flatterer and also teaches us to know ourselves.

Mauny: probably Matthieu de Mauny, clerk in the household of Cardinal du Bellay

52

If tears were a remedy for unhappiness, and crying could stop sorrow, we would, my lord, have to buy tears, and nothing would be as expensive as a good cry.

But, in fact, crying has no value, for whether you do not want to torment yourself by crying or you want to cry night and day, you cannot alter the course of suffering.

The heart makes the brain give vent to this humor, and the brain makes it pour down from the eyes, but the pain is not distilled away through the eyes.

Of what use then is this tedious weeping? To throw, as they say, oil on the fire and to lose, without profit, rest and repast.

If tears were a remedy: based on Andrea Navagero's Latin epigram "Ex Philemone"

To throw, as they say, oil on the fire: from Erasmus's *Adagia* 1.2.9

53

Let us live, Gordes, let us live, let us live, and let us not, for the opinion of a few old men, abandon our good cheer. Let us live, since life is so brief and so dear and since even kings have only a limited claim on it.

Day fades out at evening and in the morning brightens again, and the seasons always follow their usual course. But when man has lost that sweet light, death makes him sleep an everlasting night.

Shall we then imitate the life of a beast? No, but always lifting our heads toward heaven, we shall sometimes taste the sweetness of pleasure.

He is truly mad who, trading the certainty of a present good for a doubtful hope, wishes always to deny his own desire.

Let us live: from Catullus's "Vivamus, mea Lesbia, atque amemus" (*Carmina* 5)

Gordes: Jean-Antoine de Simiane (1525–1562), lord of Cabanes and of Gordes, or his elder brother Bertrand-Rambaud de Simiane (1513–1578), baron of Caseneuve and of Gordes

54

Maraud, you who are a marauder in name only, he who calls you wise speaks the truth. But your countenance gives the lie to him who says that care to avoid poverty gnaws at your mind.

He is truly rich and lives happily who, distancing himself from either extreme, places a limit on his desires. For true wealth is contentment.

Then up, my dear Maraud, while our master, whom nature brought into the world for the public good, torments his mind with the business of others.

Lead the way to the vineyard to prepare the salad. Who knows who will be dead or sick tomorrow? He alone lives who lives today.

Maraud: Charles Maraud or Marault, member of the household of Cardinal du Bellay

53

Vivons (Gordes) vivons, vivons, et pour le bruit
Des vieillards ne laissons à faire bonne chere:
Vivons, puis que la vie est si courte et si chere,
Et que mesmes les Roys n'en ont que l'usufruit. 4

Le jour s'esteint au soir, et au matin reluit,
Et les saisons refont leur course coustumiere:
Mais quand l'homme a perdu ceste doulce lumiere,
La mort luy fait dormir une eternelle nuict. 8

Donq imiterons-nous le vivre d'une beste?
Non, mais devers le ciel levans tousjours la teste,
Gousterons quelque fois la doulceur du plaisir. 11

Celuy vrayement est fol, qui changeant l'asseurance
Du bien qui est present en douteuse esperance,
Veult tousjours contredire à son propre desir. 14

54

Maraud, qui n'es maraud que de nom seulement,
Qui dit que tu es sage, il dit la verité:
Mais qui dit que le soing d'eviter pauvreté
Te ronge le cerveau, ta face le desment. 4

Celuy vrayement est riche et vit heureusement,
Qui s'esloignant de l'une et l'autre extremité,
Prescrit à ses desirs un terme limité:
Car la vraye richesse est le contentement. 8

Sus donc (mon cher Maraud) pendant que nostre maistre,
Que pour le bien publiq la nature a fait naistre,
Se tormente l'esprit des affaires d'autruy, 11

Va devant à la vigne apprester la salade:
Que sçait-on qui demain sera mort, ou malade?
Celuy vit seulement, lequel vit aujourdhuy. 14

55

Montigné (car tu es aux procez usité)
Si quelqu'un de ces Dieux, qui ont plus de puissance,
Nous promit de tous biens paisible jouissance,
Nous obligeant par Styx toute sa deité, 4

Il s'est mal envers nous de promesse acquitté,
Et devant Juppiter en devons faire instance:
Mais si lon ne peult faire aux Parques resistance,
Qui jugent par arrest de la fatalité, 8

Nous n'en appellerons, attendu que ne sommes
Plus privilegiez, que sont les autres hommes
Condemnez, comme nous, en pareille action: 11

Mais si l'ennuy vouloit sur nostre fantaisie,
Par vertu du malheur faire quelque saisie,
Nous nous opposerions à l'execution. 14

56

Baif, qui, comme moy, prouves l'adversité,
Il n'est pas tousjours bon de combatre l'orage,
Il fault caler la voile, et de peur du naufrage,
Ceder à la fureur de Neptune irrité. 4

Mais il ne fault aussi par crainte et vilité
S'abandonner en proye: il fault prendre courage,
Il fault feindre souvent l'espoir par le visage,
Et fault faire vertu de la necessité. 8

Donques sans nous ronger le cœur d'un trop grand soing,
Mais de nostre vertu nous aidant au besoing,
Combatons le malheur. Quant à moy, je proteste 11

Que je veulx desormais Fortune despiter,
Et que s'elle entreprend le me faire quitter,
Je le tiendray (Baif) et fust-ce de ma reste. 14

55

Montigné (for you are accustomed to legal proceedings), if one of those gods who has greatest power promised us the peaceful enjoyment of all the world's goods, swearing by Styx to place his deity in our service,

He has badly fulfilled the promise he made us, and we should bring suit for it before Jupiter. But if one cannot resist the Fates, who judge by implacable decree,

We will not lodge an appeal, since we have no greater privilege than other men condemned, as we are, in a similar case.

But if anxiety, by force of misery, tried to seize our imagination, we would resist the execution of that seizure.

Montigné: has not been identified

56

Baïf, you who suffer adversity, as I do, it is not always good to fight the storm. One must strike the sail and, for fear of shipwreck, give way to the fury of angry Neptune.

But, still, one must not abandon oneself to destruction out of fear and cowardice. One must take courage. One must often put on a feigned air of hopefulness and make virtue of necessity.

Thus, without consuming our hearts with excessive care, but arming ourselves with virtue as needed, let us fight misery. As for me, I pledge

That from now on I intend to spite Fortune and if she tries to make me give it up, I will persist, Baïf, whatever the cost.

57

While you pursue the hare on the plain, the wild boar through the woods, and the kite in the sky, and while watching the falcon or sparrow hawk fly, you exercise your body with pleasant labor,

We unlucky ones follow the Roman court, where we no longer hear talk, as in your time, of laughter, games, dancing, and balls but of blood, fire, and inhuman war.

Now the only pleasure of your Gordes and me is to long for you and talk of you and to read some author or write a few verses.

Aside from that, my Dagaut, we experience here only trouble, only torment, only longing and care, and nothing, except le Breton, can make us laugh.

Dagaut: has not been identified
le Breton: Nicolas le Breton, secretary to Cardinal du Bellay

58

Le Breton is learned and can write very well in French and Italian, in Greek and Latin. In his speech he is amusing and very humane. He is good company and keeps us laughing.

He has good judgment and can easily tell white from black. He is a good writer, and can compose and write out a letter as well as one could imagine.

But he is indolent and so fears his profession that he would rather, I think, fast for a whole month than work for only a quarter of an hour.

In short, he is so lazy that, to describe him well, during the four months he has lodged in my room, his very shadow makes me act lazy.

57

Ce pendant que tu suis le lievre par la plaine,
Le sanglier par les bois, et le milan par l'aer,
Et que voiant le sacre, ou l'espervier voler,
Tu t'exerces le corps d'une plaisante peine, 4

Nous autres malheureux suivons la court Romaine,
Où, comme de ton temps, nous n'oyons plus parler
De rire, de saulter, de danser, et baller,
Mais de sang, et de feu, et de guerre inhumaine. 8

Pendant, tout le plaisir de ton Gorde, et de moy,
C'est de te regreter, et de parler de toy,
De lire quelque autheur, ou quelque vers escrire. 11

Au reste (mon Dagaut) nous n'esprouvons icy,
Que peine, que travail, que regret, et soucy,
Et rien, que le Breton, ne nous peult faire rire. 14

58

Le Breton est sçavant, et sçait fort bien escrire
En François, et Thuscan, en Grec, et en Romain,
Il est en son parler plaisant et fort humain,
Il est bon compaignon, et dit le mot pour rire: 4

Il a bon jugement, et sçait fort bien eslire
Le blanc d'avec le noir: il est bon escrivain,
Et pour bien compasser une lettre à la main,
Il y est excellent autant qu'on sçauroit dire: 8

Mais il est paresseux, et craint tant son mestier,
Que s'il devoit jeusner, ce croy-je, un mois entier,
Il ne travailleroit seulement un quart d'heure. 11

Bref il est si poltron, pour bien le deviser,
Que depuis quatre mois, qu'en ma chambre il demeure,
Son umbre seulement me fait poltronniser. 14

59

Tu ne me vois jamais (Pierre) que tu ne die
Que j'estudie trop, que je face l'amour,
Et que d'avoir tousjours ces livres à l'entour,
Rend les yeux esblouïs, et la teste eslourdie.

Mais tu ne l'entends pas: car ceste maladie
Ne me vient du trop lire, ou du trop long sejour,
Ains de voir le bureau, qui se tient chacun jour:
C'est, Pierre mon amy, le livre où j'estudie.

Ne m'en parle donc plus, autant que tu as cher
De me donner plaisir, et de ne me fascher:
Mais bien en ce pendant que d'une main habile

Tu me laves la barbe, et me tonds les cheveulx,
Pour me desennuyer, conte moy, si tu veulx,
Des nouvelles du Pape, et du bruit de la ville.

60

Seigneur, ne pensez pas d'ouir chanter icy
Les louanges du Roy, ny la gloire de Guyse,
Ny celle que se sont les Chastillons acquise,
Ny ce Temple sacré au grand Montmorancy.

N'y pensez voir encor' le severe sourcy
De madame Sagesse, ou la brave entreprise,
Qui au Ciel, aux Demons, aux Estoilles s'est prise,
La Fortune, la Mort, et la Justice aussi,

De l'Or encore moins, de luy je ne suis digne:
Mais bien d'un petit Chat j'ay fait un petit hymne,
Lequel je vous envoye: autre present je n'ay.

Prenez le donc (Seigneur) et m'excusez de grace,
Si pour le bal ayant la musique trop basse,
Je sonne un passepied, ou quelque branle gay.

59

You never see me, Pierre, without saying that I study too much, that I should make love, and that always having these books around makes for bleary eyes and a heavy head.

But you do not understand. For that illness comes not from too much reading or from sitting still too long, but from seeing to the office that is open for business every day. That, Pierre my friend, is the book I study.

Then say no more about it, if you wish to give me pleasure and not to annoy me. But while with a skillful hand

You wash my beard and cut my hair, to cheer me up, tell me, if you like, news of the pope and gossip of the town.

Pierre: du Bellay's barber in Rome

60

My lord, do not expect to hear the praises of the king sung here, nor the glory of Guise, nor that which the Châtillons have acquired, nor that temple consecrated to great Montmorency,

And do not expect to see here the austere brow of Lady Wisdom, or a bold expedition to heaven, to the daemons, to the stars, nor fortune, death, and justice either,

Still less of gold, of which I am unworthy. But I have written instead a little hymn about a little cat which I am sending you. I have no other gift.

Take it then, my Lord, and please excuse me if, with music too low for a ball, I play a jig or some gay country dance.

Guise: Charles de Guise, cardinal of Lorraine, and/or François de Guise, duke of Lorraine

Châtillons: Odet de Coligny (1517–1571), cardinal of Châtillon, and his family

daemons, stars, fortune, death, justice, and gold: subjects of Ronsard's *Hymnes*

a little hymn about a little cat: du Bellay's "Épitaphe d'un chat" in his *Divers Jeux rustiques* (1558)

61

"Close to the heart means close to the purse." That is what you will hear from some frank and bold borrower, who, freely spending other people's money, is himself rushing to the poorhouse.

But consider this: that no spring is so plentiful that it cannot be exhausted, nor is any creditor so rich that he cannot in the end be turned into a borrower, when dealing with people who have no means.

Gordes, if you want to live happily as a Roman, be generous with your favor, but be careful not to be too openhanded with everyone who comes along.

By the first, you can win over even an enemy. By the second, you can often lose a good friend, and when you lose money too, it is a double loss.

62

That wily Calabrian jokes at his friend's every vice, whatever it may be, without sparing anyone, and, making even those he pricks laugh, sports with the heart of him who invites him in.

So if some subtle reader notices that in my poems I bite while laughing, let no one call me a false friend to those I needle. For whoever judges me thus is badly mistaken.

Satire, Dilliers, is a public display where, as in a mirror, the wise man sees all that in him is ugly or beautiful.

Let no one read me then, or else let him who reads me not be annoyed if he sees something of himself comically portrayed in this painting.

That wily Calabrian: Horace, who is described in these terms by Persius, *Satires* 1.116–118

61

Qui est amy du cœur est amy de la bourse,
Ce dira quelque honneste et hardy demandeur,
Qui de l'argent d'autruy liberal despendeur
Luymesme à l'hospital s'en va toute la course.

Mais songe là dessus, qu'il n'est si vive source,
Qu'on ne puisse espuiser, ny si riche presteur,
Qui ne puisse à la fin devenir emprunteur,
Ayant affaire à gens qui n'ont point de resource.

Gordes, si tu veuls vivre heureusement Romain,
Sois large de faveur, mais garde que ta main
Ne soit à tous venans trop largement ouverte.

Par l'un on peult gaigner mesmes son ennemy,
Par l'autre bien souvent on perd un bon amy,
Et quand on perd l'argent, c'est une double perte.

62

Ce ruzé Calabrois tout vice, quel qu'il soit,
Chatouille à son amy, sans espargner personne,
Et faisant rire ceulx, que mesme il espoinçonne,
Se jouë autour du cœur de cil qui le reçoit.

Si donc quelque subtil en mes vers apperçoit
Que je morde en riant, pourtant nul ne me donne
Le nom de feint amy vers ceulx que j'aiguillonne,
Car qui m'estime tel, lourdement se deçoit.

La Satyre (Dilliers) est un publiq exemple,
Où, comme en un miroir, l'homme sage contemple
Tout ce qui est en luy ou de laid, ou de beau.

Nul ne me lise donc, ou qui me vouldra lire,
Ne se fasche s'il voit par maniere de rire,
Quelque chose du sien protrait en ce tableau.

63

Quel est celuy qui veult faire croire de soy
Qu'il est fidele amy? mais quand le temps se change,
Du costé des plus forts soudainement se range,
Et du costé de ceulx qui ont le mieux dequoy.

Quel est celuy qui dit qu'il gouverne le Roy?
J'entends quand il se voit en un païs estrange,
Et bien loing de la court: quel homme est-ce, Lestrange?
Lestrange, entre nous deux je te pry dy le moy.

Dy moy, quel est celuy qui si bien se deguise,
Qu'il semble homme de guerre entre les gens d'eglise,
Et entre gens de guerre aux prestres est pareil?

Je ne sçay pas son nom: mais quiconqu'il puisse estre,
Il n'est fidele amy, ny mignon de son maistre,
Ny vaillant chevalier, ny homme de conseil.

64

Nature est aux bastards volontiers favorable,
Et souvent les bastards sont les plus genereux,
Pour estre au jeu d'amour l'homme plus vigoreux,
D'autant que le plaisir luy est plus aggreable.

Le donteur de Meduse, Hercule l'indontable,
Le vainqueur Indien, et les Jumeaux heureux,
Et tous ces Dieux bastards jadis si valeureux
Ce probleme (Bizet) font plus que veritable.

Et combien voyons nous aujourdhuy de bastards,
Soit en l'art d'Apollon, soit en celuy de Mars
Exceller ceux qui sont de race legitime?

Bref tousjours ces bastards sont de gentil esprit:
Mais ce bastard (Bizet) que lon nous a descrit,
Est cause, que je fais des autres moins d'estime.

63

What is the man who wants to be thought a faithful friend, but who, when times change, suddenly goes over to the side of those who are stronger, and the side of those who have the greatest means?

What is the man who says he rules the king—I mean when he finds himself in a foreign country and far from court? What man is this, Lestrange? Lestrange, just between us, please tell me.

Tell me what is the man who disguises himself so well that he seems like a soldier among churchmen and among soldiers passes for a priest?

I do not know what to call him, but whatever he may be, he is neither a true friend, nor the favorite of his master, nor a valiant knight, nor a trustworthy counselor.

Lestrange: Charles de Lestrange (d. 1565), minor poet and representative of Cardinal de Guise

64

Nature gladly favors bastards, and often bastards are the most noble, for in illicit love-play a man has greater vigor, seeing that pleasure is more pleasurable then.

The conqueror of Medusa, the unconquerable Hercules, the Indian vanquisher, and the fortunate twins, and all those bastard gods who were once so valiant make this paradox, Bizet, more than credible.

And how many bastards do we see today, whether in the art of Apollo or that of Mars, surpass those of legitimate birth?

In short, these bastards still have a noble mind. But that bastard, Bizet, who was described to us, makes me think less of the others.

The conqueror of Medusa: Perseus
the Indian vanquisher: Bacchus
the fortunate twins: Castor and Pollux
Bizet: probably Odoard Bizé, secretary of François de Guise
the art of Apollo or that of Mars: poetry or war
that bastard: has not been identified

65

You do not fear the fury of my inspired pen, thinking that I have nothing to say against you except what your rage vomited up against me, gnashing, like a mastiff, your envenomed teeth.

You think that I know you only by reputation and that when I have said that you are utterly faithless, that you are a cheat, that you are a traitor to the king, I will have spent all my ammunition against you.

You think I have nothing I can use to avenge myself, except that you were made only to eat and drink. But I do have something still more biting.

And what would that be? The love of Orpheus? And that you have never known what it is to believe in God? No. What vice is it then? It is, in a word, that you are a pedant.

You: sometimes identified as the humanist Louis le Roy, though this identification has been contested

The love of Orpheus: pederasty

a pedant: in this poem and in *Regrets* 66 and 68 du Bellay's *pedante* plays on our modern English sense of *pedant* and the now archaic sense that was then still current of a pedant as a schoolmaster

66

Do not be at all surprised that he scorns everyone, that he disdains one and all, that he esteems only himself, that he wants to criticize the works of everyone else, and, like an Aristarchus, approves only his own.

Paschal, he is a pedant, and though he disguise himself, he will always be a pedant. A pedant and a king—do you not think that they have something in common and that one resembles the other?

The subjects of a pedant are his pupils; his classes, his states; his prefects, officers; his school, Paschal, is like his province.

And that is why long ago the Syracusan, having lost the name of Sicilian king, wanted to be a pedant, since he could not be a prince.

Aristarchus: du Bellay's mention of this ancient Greek critic may suggest that his target in this and the poems that surround it is Barthélemy Aneau, principal of the Collège de la Trinité in Lyon, who in his attack on du Bellay's *Defense,* his *Quintil Horatian* (1550), identified himself with Aristarchus

and a king: if Louis le Roy is the target of this poem, "a king" (*un roi*) would be a pun on his name

the Syracusan: Dionysius the Younger

65

Tu ne crains la fureur de ma plume animee,
Pensant que je n'ay rien à dire contre toy,
Sinon ce que ta rage a vomy contre moy,
Grinssant comme un mastin la dent envenimee.

Tu crois que je n'en sçay que par la renommee,
Et que quand j'auray dict que tu n'as point de foy,
Que tu es affronteur, que tu es traistre au Roy,
Que j'auray contre toy ma force consommee.

Tu penses que je n'ay rien dequoy me vanger,
Sinon que tu n'es fait que pour boire et manger:
Mais j'ay bien quelque chose encore plus mordante,

Et quoy? l'amour d'Orphee? et que tu ne sceus oncq
Que c'est de croire en Dieu? Non. Quel vice est-ce doncq?
C'est, pour le faire court, que tu es un pedante.

66

Ne t'esmerveille point que chacun il mesprise,
Qu'il dedaigne un chacun, qu'il n'estime que soy,
Qu'aux ouvrages d'autruy il veuille donner loy,
Et comme un Aristarq' luymesme s'auctorise.

Paschal, c'est un pedant': et quoy qu'il se desguise,
Sera tousjours pedant'. Un pedant' et un roy
Ne te semblent-ilz pas avoir je ne sçay quoy
De semblable, et que l'un à l'autre symbolise?

Les subjects du pedant' ce sont ses escoliers,
Ses classes ses estatz, ses regents officiers,
Son college (Paschal) est comme sa province.

Et c'est pourquoy jadis le Syracusien
Aiant perdu le nom de roy Sicilien,
Voulut estre pedant', ne pouvant estre prince.

67

Magny, je ne puis voir un prodigue d'honneur
Qui trouve tout bien fait, qui de tout s'esmerveille,
Qui mes faultes approuve, et me flatte l'oreille
Comme si j'estois prince, ou quelque grand seigneur. 4

Mais je me fasche aussi d'un fascheux repreneur,
Qui du bon et mauvais fait censure pareille,
Qui se list voluntiers, et semble qu'il sommeille
En lisant les chansons de quelque autre sonneur. 8

Cestui-là me deçoit d'une faulse louange,
Et gardant qu'aux bons vers les mauvais je ne change,
Fait qu'en me plaisant trop à chacun je desplais: 11

Cestui-cy me degouste, et ne pouvant rien faire
Qui luy plaise, il me fait egalement desplaire
Tout ce qu'il fait luymesme, et tout ce que je fais. 14

68

Je hay du Florentin l'usuriere avarice,
Je hay du fol Sienois le sens mal arresté,
Je hay du Genevois la rare verité,
Et du Venetien la trop caute malice: 4

Je hay le Ferrarois pour je ne sçay quel vice,
Je hay tous les Lombards pour l'infidelité,
Le fier Napolitain pour sa grand' vanité,
Et le poltron Romain pour son peu d'exercice: 8

Je hay l'Anglois mutin, et le brave Escossois,
Le traistre Bourguignon, et l'indiscret François,
Le superbe Espaignol, et l'yvrongne Thudesque: 11

Bref, je hay quelque vice en chaque nation,
Je hay moymesme encor' mon imperfection,
Mais je hay par sur tout un sçavoir pedantesque. 14

67

Magny, I cannot stand a spendthrift of praise, who thinks everything is well done, who is amazed at everything, who applauds my faults and fills my ear with flattery, as though I were a prince or some great lord.

But I am also annoyed by an annoying faultfinder, who criticizes the good and the bad alike, who gladly reads his own stuff and looks as though he is falling asleep when he reads the songs of any other rhymester.

The first misleads me with a false accolade, and by keeping me from changing bad verses into good ones, makes me so pleasing to myself that I displease everyone else.

The second leaves me discouraged, and since I am unable to do anything that pleases him, he makes me equally displeased with everything he does himself and with everything I do.

68

I hate the Florentine's usurious greed. I hate the crazy Sienese's lack of judgment. I hate the Genovese's rare truthfulness, and the Venetian's excessively sly malice.

I hate the Ferraran for I know not what vice. I hate all Lombards for disloyalty, the proud Neapolitan for his great vanity, and the lazy Roman for working so little.

I hate the unruly Englishman and the blustering Scot, the treacherous Burgundian and the gossipy Frenchman, the haughty Spaniard and the drunken German.

In short, I hate some vice in every nation. I even hate myself for my imperfection. But above all, I hate pedantic learning.

69

Why do you snarl at me, you starving old mastiff, as though du Bellay could not defend himself? Why do you wrong me, when I have done you no wrong, except sometimes to have thought too highly of you?

Who set you, you jealous dog, so much against me—against me, while I am away? Do you think that my vengeance cannot easily shoot an arrow more envenomed with rage than yours from here as far as France?

I spare your name, so as not to dirty my book with a name unworthy to live by my verses. You will not, you wretch, get that much favor from me.

But if your rage persists any longer, I will send you from here a whip, a Megaera, a serpent, a rope to avenge myself on you.

Why do you snarl: inspired by Horace's *Epode* 6

Megaera: one of the three Furies or Eumenides

70

Had Pirithous not gone down to hell, Theseus's friendship would be buried, and Nisus would not have ennobled his by his death had he not seen Euryalus lying on the field.

Pylades' name would not be known without the rage of Orestes, and Pythias's loyalty would not have been brought to light in so many writings had Damon not taken his place.

And I would not have known how mutable yours is had Fortune not turned against me. So what can I do to avenge myself on you?

The ill I wish you is that one day, in similar circumstances, but in a more generous manner, I can make you recognize your fault and acknowledge my faithfulness.

Had Pirithous: imitates Ovid's *Tristia* 1.5.19–24

Pirithous and Theseus, Nisus and Euryalus, Pylades and Orestes, and Pythias and Damon: ancient exemplars of heroically loyal friendship

69

Pourquoy me gronde-tu, vieux mastin affamé,
Comme si Dubellay n'avoit point de defense?
Pourquoy m'offense-tu, qui ne t'ay fait offense,
Sinon de t'avoir trop quelquefois estimé?

Qui t'ha, chien envieux, sur moy tant animé,
Sur moy, qui suis absent? croy-tu que ma vangeance
Ne puisse bien d'icy darder jusques en France
Un traict, plus que le tien, de rage envenimé?

Je pardonne à ton nom, pour ne souiller mon livre
D'un nom, qui par mes vers n'a merité de vivre:
Tu n'auras, malheureux, tant de faveur de moy:

Mais si plus longuement ta fureur persevere,
Je t'envoiray d'icy un foet, une Megere
Un serpent, un cordeau, pour me vanger de toy.

70

Si Pirithois ne fust aux enfers descendu,
L'amitié de Thesé' seroit ensevelie,
Et Nise par sa mort n'eust la sienne ennoblie,
S'il n'eust veu sur le champ Eurial' estendu:

De Pylade le nom ne seroit entendu
Sans la fureur d'Oreste, et la foy de Pythie
Ne fust par tant d'escripts en lumiere sortie,
Si Damon ne se fust en sa place rendu:

Et je n'eusse esprouvé la tienne si muable,
Si Fortune vers moy n'eust esté variable.
Que puis-je faire donc, pour me vanger de toy?

Le mal que je te veulx, c'est qu'un jour je te puisse
Faire en pareil endroit, mais par meilleure office,
Recognoistre ta faulte, et voir quelle est ma foy.

71

Ce Brave qui se croit, pour un jacque de maille
Estre un second Roland, ce dissimulateur,
Qui superbe aux amis, aux ennemis flateur,
Contrefait l'habile homme, et ne dit rien qui vaille,

Belleau, ne le croy pas: et quoy qu'il se travaille
De se feindre hardy d'un visage menteur,
N'ajouste point de foy à son parler vanteur,
Car oncq homme vaillant je n'ay veu de sa taille.

Il ne parle jamais que des faveurs qu'il a,
Il desdaigne son maistre, et courtise ceulx la
Qui ne font cas de luy: il brusle d'avarice,

Il fait du bon Chrestien, et n'a ny foy ny loy:
Il fait de l'amoureux, mais c'est, comme je croy,
Pour couvrir le soupçon de quelque plus grand vice.

72

Encores que lon eust heureusement compris
Et la doctrine Grecque, et la Romaine ensemble,
Si est-ce (Gohory) qu'icy, comme il me semble,
On peult apprendre encor', tant soit-on bien appris.

Non pour trouver icy de plus doctes escripts
Que ceulx que le François songneusement assemble,
Mais pour l'air plus subtil qui doucement nous amble
Ce qui est plus terrestre, et lourd en noz esprits.

Je ne sçay quel Demon de sa flamme divine
Le moins parfait de nous purge, esprouve, et affine,
Lime le jugement, et le rend plus subtil.

Mais qui trop y demeure, il envoye en fumee
De l'esprit trop purgé la force consumee,
Et pour l'esmoudre trop, luy fait perdre le fil.

71

This brave fellow, who, for a coat of mail, thinks he is another Roland, this faker, who, arrogant with his friends and flattering with his enemies, plays the clever man but says nothing of any worth,

Belleau, do not believe him, and however he strains with assumed airs to pass himself off as bold, give no credit to his boasting speech, for I have never seen a valiant man of his build.

He never speaks but of the favors he has won. He scorns his master and makes up to those who care nothing for him. He burns with greed.

He pretends to be a good Christian and has neither faith nor law. He pretends to be a lover, but it is, I think, to cover the trace of some greater vice.

Roland: given his frequent allusions to the *Orlando furioso,* it is likely that du Bellay's *Roland* refers to Ariosto's Orlando rather than to the hero of the *Chanson de Roland*

Belleau: Rémi Belleau (1528–1577), poet and member with du Bellay and Ronsard of the Pléiade

72

Even if one has happily understood the teachings of both the Greeks and the Romans, it seems to me, Gohory, that here one can learn more, however well-schooled one may be.

Not because there are more learned writings here than have been carefully assembled in France, but because the subtler air gradually steals away what is most earthy and heavy in our minds.

I do not know what daemon with his divine flame purges what is least perfect in us, tempers and refines, polishes our judgment and makes it more subtle,

But he sends up in smoke the exhausted strength of the overly purified mind of whoever stays here too long, and from having sharpened it too much, makes it lose its edge.

Gohory: Jacques Gohory, poet, translator, and friend of du Bellay and Magny

what daemon: the *genius loci* of Rome

73

Gordes, I am horrified by a vicious old man, who imitates the blind appetite of youth, and, already cooled by years, forces himself to live fastidiously in idle repose.

But I fear nothing more than an ambitious young man, who plays the hermit to get ahead and, veiling his faithlessness with a hypocrite's mask, broods a malicious heart under a fine appearance.

There is nothing, as the popular proverb has it, as dirty as an old billy goat or as quick to do evil as a young wolf. And, to put it better,

When I consider the nature of each of them, one, like a filthy pig, offends my eyes, while I am on guard against the other, as with a sly fox.

74

You say that du Bellay is getting above himself and that he no longer cares for his friends. But I am not a lord, prince, marquis, or count and have not changed my rank or status.

Up to now I have not known what ambition is and do not blush for shame because I am not one of the great. And my place in the world does not fall or rise, for I am subject only to my own disposition.

I do not know how to converse with a master, how to act like a courtier, and still less how to live among the great, as they live today.

I am polite to everyone and annoy no one. If someone gives me a greeting, I give him four in return. If someone pays no attention to me, I pay no attention to him.

73

Gordes, j'ay en horreur un vieillard vicieux,
Qui l'aveugle appetit de la jeunesse imite,
Et ja froid par les ans de soymesme s'incite
A vivre delicat en repoz ocieux.

Mais je ne crains rien tant qu'un jeune ambicieux,
Qui pour se faire grand contrefait de l'hermite,
Et voilant sa traïson d'un masque d'hypocrite,
Couve soubs beau semblant un cœur malicieux.

Il n'est rien (ce dit-on en proverbe vulgaire)
Si sale qu'un vieux bouq, ne si prompt à mal faire
Comme est un jeune loup: et pour le dire mieux,

Quand bien au naturel de tous deux je regarde,
Comme un fangeux pourceau l'un desplaist à mes yeux,
Comme d'un fin renard de l'autre je me garde.

74

Tu dis que Dubellay tient reputation,
Et que de ses amis il ne tient plus de compte:
Si ne suis-je Seigneur, Prince, Marquis, ou Conte,
Et n'ay changé d'estat ny de condition.

Jusqu'icy je ne sçay que c'est d'ambition,
Et pour ne me voir grand ne rougis point de honte,
Aussi ma qualité ne baisse ny ne monte,
Car je ne suis subject qu'à ma complexion.

Je ne sçay comme il fault entretenir son maistre,
Comme il fault courtiser, et moins quel il fault estre
Pour vivre entre les grands, comme on vid aujourdhuy.

J'honnore tout le monde, et ne fasche personne,
Qui me donne un salut, quatre je luy en donne,
Qui ne fait cas de moy je ne fais cas de luy.

75

Gordes, que Dubellay ayme plus que ses yeux,
Voy comme la nature, ainsi que du visage,
Nous a fait differents de meurs et de courage,
Et ce qui plaist à l'un, à l'autre est odieux.

Tu dis: je ne puis voir un sot audacieux,
Qui un moindre que luy brave à son avantage,
Qui s'escoute parler, qui farde son langage,
Et fait croire de luy, qu'il est mignon des Dieux.

Je suis tout au contraire, et ma raison est telle:
Celuy, dont la doulceur courtoisement m'appelle,
Me fait oultre mon gré courtisan devenir:

Mais de tel entretien le brave me dispense,
Car n'estant obligé vers luy de recompense,
Je le laisse tout seul luymesme entretenir.

76

Cent fois plus qu'à louer on se plaist à mesdire:
Pource qu'en mesdisant on dit la verité,
Et louant, la faveur, ou bien l'auctorité
Contre ce qu'on en croit fait bien souvent escrire.

Qu'il soit vray, prins-tu onq tel plaisir d'ouir lire
Les louanges d'un prince, ou de quelque cité,
Qu'ouir un Marc Antoine à mordre exercité
Dire cent mille mots qui font mourir de rire?

S'il est donques permis, sans offense d'aucun,
Des meurs de nostre temps deviser en commun,
Quiconques me lira, m'estime fol, ou sage:

Mais je croy qu'aujourdhuy tel pour sage est tenu,
Qui ne seroit rien moins que pour tel recogneu,
Qui luy auroit osté le masque du visage.

75

Gordes, you whom du Bellay loves more than his own eyes, see how nature has made us different in manners and taste, as in appearance, and that what one likes the other hates.

You say, "I cannot stand an impudent fool who defies his inferior to make himself look good, who speaks just to hear himself, who dolls up his language, and pretends he is the darling of the gods."

I am just the opposite, and here is my reason: he whose sweet manner courteously calls out to me makes me more of a courtier than I want to be.

But the impudent fellow frees me from any such obligation, for owing him no reply, I leave him all alone to talk to himself.

76

It is a hundred times more enjoyable to speak ill than to praise, for in speaking ill we speak the truth, while in praising, favor or power often makes us write the opposite of what we believe.

As proof, have you ever enjoyed hearing someone read the praises of a prince or of some city as much as hearing a Marc Antony, who has lots of practice at biting, come out with a hundred thousand sallies that make you die with laughter?

So if we are allowed, without offending anyone, to talk together of the manners of our time, let whoever reads me judge me foolish or wise,

But I think that today some are thought to be wise who would be recognized as anything but by him who had stripped the mask from his face.

---

a Marc Antony: an Italian street satirist

77

I do not reveal here the sacred mysteries of the holy priests of Rome. I do not want to write anything that a blushing virgin would be ashamed to read. I want to touch lightly on less hidden vices.

But you will say that I misname these *Regrets*, seeing that most often I write in a comic vein. But I say that the sea does not always roar out its anger and that Apollo does not always shoot his arrows at the Greeks.

So if you encounter some laughter here, do not label as false complaints the poems I sigh out on the Ausonian shore.

My complaint, Dilliers, is true. If I laugh, it is as one laughs in company. For I laugh, as they say, with a Sardonic laugh.

I do not reveal: the first of a suite of sonnets satirizing papal Rome from du Bellay's Gallican perspective

Apollo does not always shoot: from Horace, *Odes* 2.10.19–20

78

I will not tell you about Bologna and Venice, about Padua and Ferrara, or about Milan either, about Naples, about Florence and which are the best for war or trade.

I will tell you about the Holy See, which makes idleness its richest treasure and which, under the pride of the triple crown of gold, breeds ambition, hate, and dissimulation.

I will tell you that here happiness and misery, vice, virtue, pleasure, pain, honorable learning and ignorance abound.

In short, I will say that here, as in that primal chaos, are to be found, Peletier, confusedly gathered all that one sees of good and bad in this world.

---

triple crown: the three-tiered crown worn by the pope

Peletier: Jacques Peletier du Mans (1517–1582), poet, translator of Horace, and friend of du Bellay and Ronsard

77

Je ne descouvre icy les mysteres sacrez
Des saincts prestres Romains, je ne veulx rien escrire
Que la vierge honteuse ait vergongne de lire,
Je veulx toucher sans plus aux vices moins secretz.

Mais tu diras que mal je nomme ces regretz,
Veu que le plus souvent j'use de mots pour rire,
Et je dy que la mer ne bruit tousjours son ire,
Et que tousjours Phœbus ne sagette les Grecz.

Si tu rencontre donc icy quelque risee,
Ne baptise pourtant de plainte desguisee
Les vers que je souspire au bord Ausonien.

La plainte que je fais (Dilliers) est veritable:
Si je ry, c'est ainsi qu'on se rid à la table,
Car je ry, comme on dit, d'un riz Sardonien.

78

Je ne te conteray de Boulongne, et Venise,
De Padoue, et Ferrare, et de Milan encor',
De Naples, de Florence, et lesquelles sont or'
Meilleures pour la guerre, ou pour la marchandise:

Je te raconteray du siege de l'eglise,
Qui fait d'oysiveté son plus riche tresor,
Et qui dessous l'orgueil de trois couronnes d'or
Couve l'ambition, la haine, et la feintise:

Je te diray qu'icy le bon heur, et malheur,
Le vice, la vertu, le plaisir, la douleur,
La science honorable, et l'ignorance abonde.

Bref je diray qu'icy, comme en ce vieil Caos,
Se trouve (Peletier) confusément enclos
Tout ce qu'on void de bien, et de mal en ce monde.

79

Je n'escris point d'amour, n'estant point amoureux,
Je n'escris de beauté, n'aiant belle maistresse,
Je n'escris de douceur, n'esprouvant que rudesse,
Je n'escris de plaisir, me trouvant douloureux:

Je n'escris de bon heur, me trouvant malheureux,
Je n'escris de faveur, ne voyant ma Princesse,
Je n'escris de tresors, n'aiant point de richesse,
Je n'escris de santé, me sentant langoureux:

Je n'escris de la court, estant loing de mon Prince,
Je n'escris de la France, en estrange province,
Je n'escris de l'honneur, n'en voiant point icy:

Je n'escris d'amitié, ne trouvant que feintise,
Je n'escris de vertu, n'en trouvant point aussi,
Je n'escris de sçavoir, entre les gens d'eglise.

80

Si je monte au Palais, je n'y trouve qu'orgueil,
Que vice desguisé, qu'une cerimonie,
Qu'un bruit de tabourins, qu'une estrange armonie,
Et de rouges habits un superbe appareil:

Si je descens en banque, un amas et recueil
De nouvelles je treuve, une usure infinie,
De riches Florentins une troppe banie,
Et de pauvres Sienois un lamentable dueil:

Si je vais plus avant, quelque part où j'arrive,
Je treuve de Venus la grand' bande lascive
Dressant de tous costez mil appas amoureux:

Si je passe plus oultre, et de la Rome neufve
Entre en la vieille Rome, adonques je ne treuve
Que de vieux monuments un grand monceau pierreux.

79

I do not write of love, not being a lover. I do not write of beauty, not having a beautiful mistress. I do not write of sweetness, knowing only harshness. I do not write of pleasure, finding myself in pain.

I do not write of happiness, finding myself miserable. I do not write of favor, not seeing my princess. I do not write of treasures, having no wealth at all. I do not write of health, feeling myself languishing.

I do not write of the court, being far from my prince. I do not write of France in a foreign land. I do not write of honor, seeing none of it here.

I do not write of friendship, finding only hypocrisy. I do not write of virtue, finding none of that either. I do not write of learning among men of the church.

---

my princess: Margaret of France
my prince: King Henry II

80

If I go up to the palace, I find nothing there but pride, but dissimulated vice, but pomp, but a noise of drums, but a strange harmony, and a vainglorious show of scarlet apparel.

If I go down to the exchange, I find a huge gathering of news, endless usury, a banished troop of rich Florentines, a sad cortege of poor Sienese.

If I go further, wherever I arrive, I find Venus's great lascivious gang, displaying on every side a thousand amorous charms.

If I go further still and from the new Rome enter the old Rome, then I find only a great stony heap of old monuments.

---

the palace: the Vatican
Venus's great lascivious gang: prostitutes

81

It is fun to see, Paschal, a crowded conclave, and one room just like the one next to it, serving as antechamber, hall, and kitchen, in a little nook ten feet square.

It is fun to see the palace walled up, and the godly troop scheming inside, one moved by ambition, another by likely appearance, and out of spite for one, another adored.

It is fun to see outside all the town in arms, shouting "The pope is made," giving out false alarms, sacking a palace. But more than all that,

It is fun to see who boasts of one, who another, who bets on this one, who bets on that, and for less than an ecu ten cardinals for sale.

---

a crowded conclave: du Bellay was in Rome for two conclaves, the first at the death of Pope Julius III for the election of Marcellus II (April 1555), the second at the death of Marcellus for the election of Paul IV (May 1555)

crowded: du Bellay's *serré* could also mean *locked*

the godly troop: the College of Cardinals

sacking a palace: it was common to sack the Roman palace of the cardinal elected as pope

82

Do you want to know, Duthier, what sort of place Rome is? Rome is a public scaffold for all the world, a stage, a theater, where nothing is lacking that men can do.

Here we see the game of Fortune and how her hand keeps us turning, now down, now up. Here everyone shows himself and cannot, however cunning he may be, prevent the populace from calling him what he is.

Here rumor spreads quickly, whether false or true. Here courtiers make love and pay court. Here ambition and trickery abound.

Here freedom makes the lowborn man bold. Here idleness makes the good man vicious. Here the base porter holds forth on worldly affairs.

Duthier: Jean du Thier, counselor to the king, secretary of state, and patron of poets, including du Bellay's friend Magny

the game of Fortune: an allusion to Fortune's wheel

81

Il fait bon voir (Paschal) un conclave serré,
Et l'une chambre à l'autre egalement voisine
D'antichambre servir, de salle, et de cuisine,
En un petit recoing de dix pieds en carré: 4

Il fait bon voir autour le palais emmuré,
Et briguer là dedans ceste troppe divine,
L'un par ambition, l'autre par bonne mine,
Et par despit de l'un, estre l'autre adoré: 8

Il fait bon voir dehors toute la ville en armes,
Crier le Pape est fait, donner de faulx alarmes,
Saccager un palais: mais plus que tout cela 11

Fait bon voir, qui de l'un, qui de l'autre se vante,
Qui met pour cestui-cy, qui met pour cestui-là,
Et pour moins d'un escu dix Cardinaux en vente. 14

82

Veuls-tu sçavoir (Duthier) quelle chose c'est Rome?
Rome est de tout le monde un publique eschafault,
Une scene, un theatre, auquel rien ne default
De ce qui peult tomber es actions de l'homme. 4

Icy se void le jeu de la Fortune, et comme
Sa main nous fait tourner ores bas, ores haut:
Icy chacun se monstre, et ne peult, tant soit caut,
Faire que tel qu'il est, le peuple ne le nomme. 8

Icy du faulx et vray la messagere court,
Icy les courtisans font l'amour et la court,
Icy l'ambition, et la finesse abonde: 11

Icy la liberté fait l'humble audacieux,
Icy l'oysiveté rend le bon vicieux,
Icy le vil faquin discourt des faicts du monde. 14

83

Ne pense (Robertet) que ceste Rome cy
Soit ceste Rome là, qui te souloit tant plaire,
On n'y fait plus credit, comme lon souloit faire,
On n'y fait plus l'amour, comme on souloit aussi. 4

La paix, et le bon temps ne regnent plus icy,
La musique et le bal sont contraints de s'y taire,
L'air y est corrompu, Mars y est ordinaire,
Ordinaire la faim, la peine, et le soucy. 8

L'artisan desbauché y ferme sa boutique,
L'ocieux advocat y laisse sa pratique,
Et le pauvre marchand y porte le bissac: 11

On ne voit que soldartz, et morrions en teste,
On n'oit que tabourins, et semblable tempeste,
Et Rome tous les jours n'attend qu'un autre sac. 14

84

Nous ne faisons la court aux filles de Memoire,
Comme vous qui vivez libres de passion:
Si vous ne sçavez donc nostre occupation,
Ces dix vers ensuivans vous la feront notoire: 4

Suivre son Cardinal au Pape, au consistoire,
En capelle, en visite, en congregation,
Et pour l'honneur d'un prince, ou d'une nation,
De quelque ambassadeur accompagner la gloire: 8

Estre en son rang de garde aupres de son seigneur,
Et faire aux survenans l'accoustumé honneur,
Parler du bruit qui court, faire de l'habile homme: 11

Se pourmener en housse, aller voir d'huis en huis
La Marthe, ou la Victoire, et s'engager aux Juifz:
Voila, mes compagnons, les passetemps de Rome. 14

83

Do not think, Robertet, that this Rome is the Rome you used to like so much. They no longer extend credit here, as they used to do. They no longer make love here, as they used to do.

Peace and happy times no longer reign here. Music and balls here are forced to fall silent. The air here is corrupted. Mars is common here. Common are hunger, suffering, and care.

The unemployed artisan here closes his shop. The idle lawyer here abandons his practice. And the poor merchant here goes around with an alms bag.

We see only soldiers and helmets on heads. We hear only drums and similar tempests. And every day Rome awaits only another sack.

Robertet: Florimond Robertet, baron of Alluye

another sack: alluding to the notorious imperial sack of Rome in 1527 and the fear in 1556 and 1557 of another attack

84

We do not court the daughters of Memory, as do you who live free from turmoil. So if you do not know what keeps us busy, the next ten lines will make it plain to you.

Following one's cardinal to the pope, to the consistory, in the chapel, on visits, in the congregation, and, for the honor of a prince or a nation, waiting on the pomp of some ambassador,

Taking one's place in the service of one's lord and paying the usual respects to those who appear, talking of the gossip that goes around, pretending to be in the know,

Riding with a stately saddlecloth, passing from door to door to visit Martha or Victoria, and running up a debt with the Jews. These, my friends, are the pastimes of Rome.

---

the daughters of Memory: the Muses

the consistory: a gathering of cardinals presided over by the pope

the congregation: a gathering of prelates for some specific purpose

Martha or Victoria: prostitutes

85

To flatter a creditor to gain some more time; to court a banker; to seem a hopeful prospect; not to speak as freely as in France; to reflect for a quarter of an hour before answering a word;

Not to ruin your health with too much drinking and eating; not to spend wildly without a good reason; not to tell anyone who comes along whatever you think; and to manage a stranger without saying much;

To know dispositions; to know who is asking; and, the more freedom you have, to be all the more wary not to be caught out;

To get along with everyone; to take everyone's measure: that, my dear Morel (I blush with shame to admit it), is all the good I have learned in three years in Rome.

86

To walk with a solemn step and a solemn brow and to greet everyone with a solemn smile; to weigh every word; to answer with a nod and a *Messer non* or else a *Messer si*;

To slip in here and there a little *È cosi*, and with a *son Servitor* to pass for polite; to hold forth, as though you had had your part in the victory, on Florence and on Naples as well;

To treat everyone like a lord with a kiss on the hand; and, imitating the manner of a Roman courtier, to hide your poverty under a fine appearance.

These are the greatest virtues of this court, from which—often badly mounted, in bad health, and badly dressed—beardless and moneyless, one returns to France.

Messer non/Messer si: no, sir/yes, sir
È cosi: so it is
son Servitor: your servant
beardless: a sign of venereal disease

85

Flatter un crediteur, pour son terme alonger,
Courtiser un banquier, donner bonne esperance,
Ne suivre en son parler la liberté de France,
Et pour respondre un mot, un quart d'heure y songer:

Ne gaster sa santé par trop boire et manger,
Ne faire sans propos une folle despence,
Ne dire à tous venans tout cela que lon pense,
Et d'un maigre discours gouverner l'estranger:

Cognoistre les humeurs, cognoistre qui demande,
Et d'autant que lon a la liberté plus grande,
D'autant plus se garder que lon ne soit repris:

Vivre aveques chacun, de chacun faire compte:
Voila, mon cher Morel (dont je rougis de honte)
Tout le bien qu'en trois ans à Rome j'ay appris.

86

Marcher d'un grave pas, et d'un grave sourci,
Et d'un grave soubriz à chacun faire feste,
Balancer tous ses mots, respondre de la teste,
Avec un Messer non, ou bien un Messer si:

Entremesler souvent un petit, Et cosi,
Et d'un son Servitor' contrefaire l'honneste,
Et comme si lon eust sa part en la conqueste,
Discourir sur Florence, et sur Naples aussi:

Seigneuriser chacun d'un baisement de main,
Et suivant la façon du courtisan Romain,
Cacher sa pauvreté d'une brave apparence:

Voila de ceste court la plus grande vertu,
Dont souvent mal monté, mal sain, et mal vestu,
Sans barbe et sans argent on s'en retourne en France.

87

D'où vient cela (Mauny) que tant plus on s'efforce
D'eschapper hors d'icy, plus le Demon du lieu
(Et que seroit-ce donq si ce n'est quelque Dieu?)
Nous y tient attachez par une doulce force?

Seroit-ce point d'amour ceste allechante amorse,
Ou quelque autre venim, dont apres avoir beu
Nous sentons noz esprits nous laisser peu à peu,
Comme un corps qui se perd sous une neuve escorse?

J'ay voulu mille fois de ce lieu m'estranger,
Mais je sens mes cheveux en fueilles se changer,
Mes bras en longs rameaux, et mes piedz en racine.

Bref, je ne suis plus rien qu'un vieil tronc animé,
Qui se pleint de se voir à ce bord transformé,
Comme le Myrte Anglois au rivage d'Alcine.

88

Qui choisira pour moy la racine d'Ulysse?
Et qui me gardera de tomber au danger
Qu'une Circe en pourceau ne me puisse changer,
Pour estre à tout jamais fait esclave du vice?

Qui m'estreindra le doy de l'anneau de Melisse,
Pour me desenchanter comme un autre Roger?
Et quel Mercure encor' me fera desloger,
Pour ne perdre mon temps en l'amoureux service?

Qui me fera passer sans escouter la voix
Et la feinte douceur des monstres d'Achelois?
Qui chassera de moy ces Harpyes friandes?

Qui volera pour moy encor' un coup aux cieux,
Pour rapporter mon sens, et me rendre mes yeux?
Et qui fera qu'en paix je mange mes viandes?

87

How does it happen, Mauny, that the more one tries to get away from here, the more the daemon of the place (and what then could it be, if it is not some god?) keeps us bound with a sweet enchantment?

Would that alluring bait be of love or some other venom that after having drunk, we feel our wits slip away from us little by little, like a body that disappears under a new bark?

I have wanted to escape from this place a thousand times, but I feel my hair changing into leaves, my arms into long branches, and my feet into roots.

In short, I am no longer anything but an old, animated tree trunk, who laments to see himself transformed on this shore, like the English myrtle on Alcina's bank.

---

the English myrtle: Astolfo, who was transformed into a myrtle by the enchantress Alcina in Ariosto's *Orlando furioso,* 6.23ff.

88

Who will find me Ulysses' root? And who will keep me from succumbing to the danger that a Circe will transform me into a swine, to be forever made a slave to vice?

Who will put Melissa's ring on my finger to disenchant me, like another Ruggiero? And what Mercury will make me, too, steal away so as not to waste my time in amorous service?

Who will help me pass by without listening to the voice and feigned sweetness of the monsters of Achelous? Who will drive from me these rapacious Harpies?

Who will once more fly to the heavens for me to bring back my reason and restore my sight? And who will make it possible for me to eat my meals in peace?

Ulysses' root: moly, given Ulysses by Mercury to ward off Circe's enchantments in book 10 of Homer's *Odyssey*

Melissa's ring: the ring that breaks the spell under which the Circean Alcina holds Ruggiero in Ariosto's *Orlando furioso,* 7.68

will make me, too, steal away: like Aeneas warned by Mercury to leave Dido in Virgil's *Aeneid* 4.219ff.

the monsters of Achelous: the Sirens, who tempt Odysseus (Ulysses) in book 12 of the *Odyssey*

fly to the heavens: echoes *Orlando furioso,* 34.1, which follows Astolfo's flight to the moon to retrieve Orlando's lost wits

89

Gordes, I seem to have awoken, like someone who, terrified by a horrible dream, wakes with a start and lies on his bed amazed that he has slept so long.

Ruggiero was, I think, similarly amazed, and I think that shame eats at me the same way it did at him, when he discovered the deceit of the magical disguise that had blinded him.

And like him, I too want to change my behavior and live from now on in the bosom of Logistilla, who is the common support of languishing hearts.

Up then, Gordes. Get up. Hoist the sail. Seize the oar. Let us flee. Let us get to sea. I see the beautiful lady who with a happy sign calls us to her port.

---

the magical disguise: the disguise of the enchantress Alcina in Ariosto's *Orlando furioso,* 7.69–74

Logistilla: the figure of reason and truth opposed to the witch Alcina in *Orlando furioso,* 10.45ff.

the beautiful lady: Logistilla

90

Do not think, Bouju, that the Roman nymphs, by hiding their treachery under a modest familiarity, nor by masking their complexion with a false beauty, make me forget our Angevin nymphs.

The sweetness of the Angevin women, their heavenly speech, their apparel which is free from all lewdness, their grace, their youth, and their simplicity take away my appetite, Bouju, for these old Alcinas.

Whoever sees them from the outside can see nothing more beautiful. But the inside resembles the inside of a tomb, or whatever fouler thing we might think of.

O what greed! O what indigence! O what a horror to see their impurity! To see them is truly the salvation of a young man.

Bouju: Jacques Bouju, poet from du Bellay's native Anjou

Alcinas: enchantresses, like the enchantress in Ariosto's *Orlando furioso,* here representing Roman courtesans bearing the threat of venereal disease

89

Gordes, il m'est advis que je suis esveillé,
Comme un qui tout esmeu d'un effroyable songe
Se resveille en sursault, et par le lict s'alonge,
S'esmerveillant d'avoir si long temps sommeillé.

Roger devint ainsi (ce croy-je) esmerveillé:
Et croy que tout ainsi la vergongne me ronge,
Comme luy, quand il eut descouvert la mensonge
Du fard magicien qui l'avoit aveuglé.

Et comme luy aussi je veulx changer de stile,
Pour vivre desormais au sein de Logistile,
Qui des cœurs langoureux est le commun support.

Sus donc (Gordes) sus donc, à la voile, à la rame,
Fuions, gaignons le hault, je voy la belle Dame
Qui d'un heureux signal nous appelle à son port.

90

Ne pense pas (Bouju) que les Nymphes Latines
Pour couvrir leur traison d'une humble privauté,
Ny pour masquer leur teint d'une faulse beauté,
Me facent oublier noz Nymphes Angevines.

L'Angevine douceur, les paroles divines,
L'habit qui ne tient rien de l'impudicité,
La grace, la jeunesse, et la simplicité
Me desgoustent (Bouju) de ces vieilles Alcines.

Qui les voit par dehors, ne peult rien voir plus beau,
Mais le dedans resemble au dedans d'un tombeau,
Et si rien entre nous moins honneste se nomme.

O quelle gourmandise! ô quelle pauvreté!
O quelle horreur de voir leur immundicité!
C'est vrayment de les voir le salut d'un jeune homme.

91

O beaux cheveux d'argent mignonnement retors!
O front crespe, et serein! et vous face doree!
O beaux yeux de crystal! ô grand' bouche honoree,
Qui d'un large reply retrousses tes deux bordz!

O belles dentz d'ebene! ô precieux tresors,
Qui faites d'un seul riz toute ame enamouree!
O gorge damasquine en cent pliz figuree!
Et vous beaux grands tetins, dignes d'un si beau corps!

O beaux ongles dorez! ô main courte, et grassette!
O cuisse delicatte! et vous gembe grossette,
Et ce que je ne puis honnestement nommer!

O beau corps transparent! ô beaux membres de glace!
O divines beautez! pardonnez moy de grace,
Si pour estre mortel, je ne vous ose aymer.

92

En mille crespillons les cheveux se frizer,
Se pincer les sourcilz, et d'une odeur choisie
Parfumer hault et bas sa charnure moisie,
Et de blanc et vermeil sa face desguiser:

Aller de nuict en masque, en masque deviser,
Se feindre à tous propos estre d'amour saisie,
Siffler toute la nuict par une jalousie,
Et par martel de l'un, l'autre favoriser:

Baller, chanter, sonner, folastrer dans la couche,
Avoir le plus souvent deux langues en la bouche,
Des courtisannes sont les ordinaires jeux.

Mais quel besoing est-il que je te les enseigne?
Si tu les veuls sçavoir (Gordes) et si tu veuls
En sçavoir plus encor', demande à la Chassaigne.

91

O beautiful silver hair prettily curled! O forehead wrinkled and serene! And you, golden face! O beautiful crystal eyes! O honorable large mouth that twists up with a big crease on each side!

O beautiful ebony teeth! O precious treasures that with a single smile can make any soul fall in love! O damasked throat crossed with a hundred folds! And you, beautiful big breasts, worthy of such a beautiful body!

O beautiful golden nails! O hand short and plump! O delicate thigh! And you thick leg, and that which I cannot decorously name!

O beautiful lucent body! O beautiful limbs of ice! O divine beauties! Forgive me, please, if, as a mortal, I dare not love you.

O beautiful silver hair: from an Italian burlesque sonnet by Francesco Berni

92

Curling her hair in a thousand ringlets, plucking her eyebrows, and with a special scent perfuming her moldy flesh from top to toe, and with white and red disguising her face,

Going out masked at night, chatting in a mask, always pretending to be possessed by love, whistling all night through a lattice screen, and out of jealousy for one, favoring another,

Dancing, singing, strumming, frolicking in bed, having most often two tongues in her mouth, these are the ordinary games of courtesans.

But what need is there for me to teach them to you? If you want to know them, Gordes, and if you want to know still more on the subject, ask Chassaigne.

Chassaigne: a Roman courtesan

93

Sweet mother of love, wanton Cyprian, you who make all powers submit to your power and who, from the banks of the Xanthus to this foreign shore, guided with your son your Dardanian people,

If I return to France, O Idalian mother, as I arrived here, without succumbing to the danger of seeing my old skin changed into another skin and my French beard into an Italian beard,

I swear here and now to hang on your altar not the lily, nor the flower of the immortal Amaranth, nor that flower dyed with your blood,

But rather the fairest fleece from my chin, proud to have done more than Jason did when he carried away the prize of the Golden Fleece.

Sweet mother of love: Venus, who is also the "wanton Cyprian" and the "Idalian mother"
from the banks of the Xanthus to this foreign shore: from Troy to Latium
your son: Aeneas
your Dardanian people: the Trojans
another skin/an Italian beard: symptoms of venereal disease
that flower dyed with your blood: the rose

94

Happy the man who can long go to war without death, without a wound, or without a long stay in prison! Happy the man who lives long far from his home without depleting his wealth or selling his land!

Happy the man who can win some favor at court without fearing envy or treachery! Happy the man who without danger of poison can long enjoy a scarlet cap or the keys of Saint Peter!

Happy the man who without peril can frequent the sea! Happy the man who without going to trial can haunt the palace! Happy the man who without suffering can live out his allotted years!

Happy the man who can keep his treasure without care, his wife without suspicion, and happier still the man who without losing his hair can live three years in Rome!

---

a scarlet cap: of a cardinal
the keys of Saint Peter: the sign of the pope
losing his hair: a symptom of venereal disease

93

Doulce mere d'amour, gaillarde Cyprienne,
Qui fais sous ton pouvoir tout pouvoir se ranger,
Et qui des bordz de Xanthe, à ce bord estranger
Guidas avec ton filz ta gent Dardanienne,

Si je retourne en France, ô mere Idalienne!
Comme je vins icy, sans tomber au danger
De voir ma vieille peau en autre peau changer,
Et ma barbe Françoise en barbe Italienne,

Dès icy je fais veu d'apprendre à ton autel
Non le liz, ou la fleur d'Amarante immortel,
Non ceste fleur encor' de ton sang coloree:

Mais bien de mon menton la plus blonde toison,
Me vantant d'avoir fait plus que ne feit Jason
Emportant le butin de la toison doree.

94

Heureux celuy qui peult long temps suivre la guerre
Sans mort, ou sans blesseure, ou sans longue prison!
Heureux qui longuement vit hors de sa maison
Sans despendre son bien, ou sans vendre sa terre!

Heureux qui peult en court quelque faveur acquerre
Sans crainte de l'envie, ou de quelque traison!
Heureux qui peult long temps sans danger de poison
Jouir d'un chapeau rouge, ou des clefz de sainct Pierre!

Heureux qui sans peril peult la mer frequenter!
Heureux qui sans procez le palais peult hanter!
Heureux qui peult sans mal vivre l'aage d'un homme!

Heureux qui sans soucy peult garder son tresor!
Sa femme sans souspçon, et plus heureux encor'
Qui a peu sans peler vivre trois ans à Rome!

95

Maudict soit mille fois le Borgne de Libye,
Qui le cœur des rochers perçant de part en part
Des Alpes renversa le naturel rampart,
Pour ouvrir le chemin de France en Italie.

Mars n'eust empoisonné d'une eternelle envie
Le cœur de l'Espaignol, et du François soldart,
Et tant de gens de bien ne seroient en hasart
De venir perdre icy et l'honneur et la vie.

Le François corrompu par le vice estranger
Sa langue et son habit n'eust appris à changer,
Il n'eust changé ses mœurs en une autre nature.

Il n'eust point esprouvé le mal qui fait peler,
Il n'eust fait de son nom la verole appeler,
Et n'eust fait si souvent d'un bufle sa monture.

96

O Deesse, qui peuls aux Princes egaler
Un pauvre mendiant, qui n'a que la parole,
Et qui peuls d'un grand roy faire un maistre d'escole,
S'il te plaist de son lieu le faire devaller:

Je ne te prie pas de me faire enroller
Au rang de ces messieurs que la faveur accolle,
Que lon parle de moy, et que mon renom vole
De l'aile dont tu fais ces grands Princes voler:

Je ne demande pas mille et mille autres choses,
Qui dessous ton pouvoir sont largement encloses,
Aussi je n'eu jamais de tant de biens soucy.

Je demande sans plus que le mien on ne mange,
Et que j'aye bien tost une lettre de change,
Pour n'aller sur le bufle au departir d'icy.

95

Cursed a thousand times over be the one-eyed Libyan, who, cutting through the heart of the mountains from one end to the other, broke down the natural rampart of the Alps, to open the road from France to Italy.

Mars would not have poisoned with incessant desire the heart of the Spanish and French soldier, and so many honest people would not have risked coming here to lose both honor and life.

The Frenchman, corrupted by foreign vice, would not have learned to alter his language and his dress. He would not have exchanged his customs for a second nature.

He would not have known the disease that makes your hair fall out. He would not have given his name to the pox, and would not so often have ridden an ox.

---

the one-eyed Libyan: Hannibal
the illness that makes your hair fall out: venereal disease
the pox: known as "the French illness"
ridden an ox: riding an ox seems to have been a punishment for unpaid debts

96

O Goddess, who can raise a poor beggar who has nothing but words to the level of a prince and who can make a schoolmaster of a great king if you feel like toppling him from his place,

I do not pray that you inscribe me in the register of those gentlemen whom favor embraces, so that people will speak of me and so that my fame will fly on the wing on which you make those great princes fly.

I do not ask for thousands and thousands of other things that are easily within your power, for I have never craved such an abundance of goods.

I ask only that what is mine not be devoured and that I soon get a bill of exchange, so that when I leave here I will not have to ride an ox.

Goddess: Fortune
a schoolmaster of a great king: an allusion to Dionysius the Younger of Syracuse

97

Doulcin, when I sometimes see those poor girls who are possessed by the devil, or seem to be, convulse their bodies and heads in a terrifying way and act as they say the ancient Sibyls did,

When I see the strongest become enfeebled, vainly trying to exercise their mad power, and when I see even those confounded who in your art are thought to be most able,

When I hear them dreadfully screaming, and when I see the whites of their rolling eyes, my hair stands on end and I no longer know what to say.

But when I see a monk with his Latin feeling them up and down, belly and breast, that fear passes and I am forced to laugh.

Doulcin: Rémy Doulcin, priest and medical doctor

those poor girls: may refer to an episode of mass possession at the Roman hospital for orphaned girls (the "convent" of *Regrets* 98) in 1554

in your art: medicine

98

How does it happen that we so often see in Rome these madwomen, and most of them not old, Ronsard, but the age of young maidens, and always in a single convent?

Who speaks through their voices? What demon keeps them from answering those they do not know? And how does it happen that suddenly they no longer seem that way when they have put out a candle with their breath?

How does it happen that holy places increase such frenzies? How does it happen that so many spirits torment just one girl? And that when some leave her, the rest do not?

Please tell me, Ronsard, you who know their nature, are those who thus torment these poor creatures the highest spirits, the middle ones, or the lowest?

---

you who know their nature: alludes to Ronsard's hymn "Les Daimons"

97

Doulcin, quand quelquefois je voy ces pauvres filles,
Qui ont le diable au corps, ou le semblent avoir,
D'une horrible façon corps et teste mouvoir,
Et faire ce qu'on dit de ces vieilles Sibylles:

Quand je voy les plus forts se retrouver debiles,
Voulant forcer en vain leur forcené pouvoir:
Et quand mesme j'y voy perdre tout leur sçavoir
Ceulx qui sont en vostre art tenuz des plus habiles:

Quand effroyablement escrier je les oy,
Et quand le blanc des yeux renverser je leur voy,
Tout le poil me herisse, et ne sçay plus que dire.

Mais quand je voy un moine avec son Latin
Leur taster hault et bas le ventre et le tetin,
Ceste frayeur se passe, et suis contraint de rire.

98

D'où vient que nous voyons à Rome si souvent
Ces garses forcener, et la pluspart d'icelles
N'estre vieilles (Ronsard) mais d'aage de pucelles,
Et se trouver tousjours en un mesme convent?

Qui parle par leur voix? quel Demon leur defend
De respondre à ceulx-là qui ne sont cogneuz d'elles?
Et d'où vient que soudain on ne les voit plus telles
Ayant une chandelle esteinte de leur vent?

D'où vient que les saincts lieux telles fureurs augmentent?
D'où vient que tant d'espritz une seule tormentent?
Et que sortans les uns, le reste ne sort pas?

Dy je te pry (Ronsard) toy qui sçais leurs natures,
Ceulx qui faschent ainsi ces pauvres creatures,
Sont-ilz des plus haultains, des moiens, ou plus bas?

99

Quand je vays par la rue, où tant de peuple abonde,
De prestres, de prelatz, et de moines aussi,
De banquiers, d'artisans, et n'y voiant, ainsi
Qu'on voit dedans Paris, la femme vagabonde: 4

Pyrrhe, apres le degast de l'universelle onde,
Ses pierres (di-je alors) ne sema point icy:
Et semble proprement, à voir ce peuple cy,
Que Dieu n'y ait formé que la moitié du monde. 8

Car la dame Romaine en gravité marchant',
Comme la conseilliere, ou femme du marchand
Ne s'y pourmene point, et n'y voit on que celles, 11

Qui se sont de la court l'honneste nom donné:
Dont je crains quelquefois qu'en France retourné,
Autant que j'en voiray ne me resemblent telles. 14

100

Ursin, quand j'oy nommer de ces vieux noms Romains,
De ces beaux noms cogneus de l'Inde jusqu'au More,
Non les grands seulement, mais les moindres encore,
Voire ceulx-là qui ont les ampoulles aux mains: 4

Il me fasche d'ouir appeler ces villains
De ces noms tant fameux, que tout le monde honnore:
Et sans le nom Chrestien, le seul nom que j'adore,
Voudrois que de telz noms on appellast noz Saincts. 8

Le mien sur tous me fasche, et me fasche un Guillaume,
Et mil autres sotz noms communs en ce royaume,
Voiant tant de faquins indignement jouir 11

De ces beaux noms de Rome, et de ceulx de la Grece,
Mais par sur tout (Ursin) il me fasche d'ouir
Nommer une Thaïs du nom d'une Lucrece. 14

99

When I pass through the street where there are so many people—priests, prelates, and monks too, bankers, artisans—and do not see there, as one would in Paris, any women walking about,

I then say that Pyrrha, after the destruction of the universal flood, did not sow any of her stones here, and it certainly seems, to judge from this crowd, that God fashioned only half of humankind.

For the dignified Roman lady, like the lawyer's wife or the merchant's wife, does not walk around here at all, and we see only those

Who have given themselves the honorable name of the court, for which I sometimes fear that, once back in France, all the women I see will seem to me of their sort.

Pyrrha: after the flood that destroyed all humankind but them, Deucalion scattered stones to regenerate men and his wife, Pyrrha, scattered stones to regenerate women

only those: courtesans

100

Ursin, when I hear not only the great but the lowest as well, even those who have calluses on their hands, named with those ancient Roman names, with those fine names known from India to North Africa,

It annoys me to hear those peasants called by famous names that everyone honors, and, except for the name "Christian," the only name I worship, I would want our saints to be called by such names.

Mine especially annoys me, and a William annoys me, and a thousand other foolish names that are common in this kingdom, seeing so many scoundrels unworthily enjoy

Those fine names from Rome and from Greece. But above all, Ursin, it annoys me to hear a Thaïs called by the name of Lucretia.

Ursin: probably Charles Juvenal des Ursins, chaplain in the household of Cardinal du Bellay

this kingdom: France

a Thaïs: a courtesan

Lucretia: the heroic model of ancient Roman chastity, here a possible allusion to the notorious Lucretia Borgia

101

What shall we say, Mellin, of this Roman court, where we see everyone following a different path, and the lowest reaching the highest honors, by vice, by virtue, by work, or without effort?

One goes to useless expense to get ahead. Another by this means sees himself become great. One promotes himself by severity. Another wins hearts with his humane sweetness.

One gets ahead by not pushing himself forward. Another by pushing himself forward gets left behind. And what harms one benefits another.

Some say that learning is the road to honor. Some say that ignorance attracts good fortune. Which of the two, Mellin, is truer?

Mellin: Mellin de Saint-Gelais (1487–1558), poet, mocked by du Bellay in *Defense* 2.2

102

"You cannot make a statue of Mercury from just any kind of wood," says the old proverb. But we see here a pope made of any wood and cardinals too, and assume in three days a completely different appearance.

Princes and kings are great by nature, so they are not as worried about their greatness as are these new gods, who have only a frown to make us revere their greatness, which does not last long.

Paschal, I have seen a man who lately drew all Rome behind him whenever he went out, with three lackeys making his way down the street,

And bearing in his wake his long Roman pride, a man whose father has callused hands and, with a prod in his fist, bends over the plow.

101

Que dirons nous (Melin) de ceste court Romaine,
Où nous voions chacun divers chemins tenir,
Et aux plus haults honneurs les moindres parvenir,
Par vice, par vertu, par travail, et sans peine?

L'un fait pour s'avancer une despence vaine,
L'autre par ce moyen se voit grand devenir,
L'un par severité se sçait entretenir,
L'autre gaigne les cœurs par sa doulceur humaine:

L'un pour ne s'avancer se voit estre avancé,
L'autre pour s'avancer se voit desavancé,
Et ce qui nuit à l'un, à l'autre est profitable:

Qui dit que le sçavoir est le chemin d'honneur,
Qui dit que l'ignorance attire le bon heur,
Lequel des deux (Melin) est le plus veritable?

102

On ne fait de tout bois l'image de Mercure,
Dit le proverbe vieil: mais nous voions icy
De tout bois faire Pape, et Cardinaulx aussi,
Et vestir en trois jours tout une autre figure.

Les princes, et les rois, viennent grands de nature,
Aussi de leurs grandeurs n'ont-ilz tant de souci,
Comme ces Dieux nouveaux, qui n'ont que le sourci,
Pour faire reverer leur grandeur, qui peu dure.

Paschal, j'ay veu celuy qui n'agueres trainoit
Toute Rome apres luy, quand il se pourmenoit,
Aveques trois valletz cheminer par la rue:

Et trainer apres luy un long orgueil Romain
Celuy, de qui le pere a l'ampoulle en la main,
Et l'aiguillon au poing se courbe à la charrue.

103

Si la perte des tiens, si les pleurs de ta mere,
Et si de tes parents les regrets quelquefois,
Combien, cruel Amour, que sans amour tu sois,
T'ont fait sentir le dueil de leur compleinte amere:

C'est or' qu'il fault monstrer ton flambeau sans lumiere,
C'est or' qu'il fault porter sans flesches ton carquois,
C'est or' qu'il fault briser ton petit arc Turquois,
Renouvelant le dueil de ta perte premiere.

Car ce n'est pas icy qu'il te fault regretter
Le pere au bel Ascaigne: il te fault lamenter
Le bel Ascaigne mesme, Ascaigne, ô quel dommage!

Ascaigne que Caraffe aymoit plus que ses yeux,
Ascaigne qui passoit en beaulté de visage
Le beau Couppier Troyen, qui verse à boire aux Dieux.

104

Si fruicts, raisins, et bledz, et autres telles choses
Ont leur tronc, et leur sep, et leur semence aussi,
Et s'on voit au retour du printemps addoulci
Naistre de toutes partz violettes, et roses:

Ny fruicts, raisins, ny bledz, ny fleurettes descloses
Sortiront (Viateur) du corps qui gist icy:
Aulx, oignons, et porreaux, et ce qui fleure ainsi,
Auront icy dessous leurs semences encloses.

Toy donc, qui de l'encens et du basme n'as point,
Si du grand Jules tiers quelque regret te poingt,
Parfume son tombeau de telle odeur choisie:

Puis que son corps, qui fut jadis egal aux Dieux,
Se souloit paistre icy de telz metz precieux,
Comme au ciel Jupiter se paist de l'ambrosie.

103

If the loss of those close to you, if your mother's tears, and if the sorrows of your kinfolk have sometimes made you feel the mourning of their bitter lamentation, however lacking in love you are, cruel Love,

Now is the time to show your torch unlit, now is the time to bear your quiver without arrows, now is the time to break your little Turkish bow, renewing the mourning of your first loss,

For it is not here that you must mourn the father of beautiful Ascanius. You must now bewail beautiful Ascanius himself, Ascanius, O what a loss!

Ascanius, whom Caraffa loved more than his own eyes. Ascanius, the beauty of whose face surpassed the beautiful Trojan cupbearer who poured drinks for the gods.

---

your mother's tears: the tears of Venus
cruel Love: Cupid
your first loss: the death of Cupid's half brother Aeneas
Ascanius: both the son of Aeneas and the boy lover of Cardinal Caraffa
the beautiful Trojan cupbearer: Ganymede, the boy lover of Jove

104

If fruits, grapes, and wheat, and other such things have their trunks and their vine-stocks and their seeds, and if we see at the sweet return of spring violets and roses bursting forth on every side,

Neither fruits, grapes, nor wheat, nor blooming little flowers will spring, Passerby, from the body that lies here. Garlic, onions, and leeks, and whatever smells like them, will germinate here below.

You therefore, who have no incense or balm, if you are pierced by some sorrow for the great Julius the Third, perfume his tomb with odors of that sort,

Since his body, which was once equal to the gods, used to feed here on such precious dishes, as Jupiter in heaven feeds on ambrosia.

Julius the Third: pope (1550–1555), had a well-known taste for onions and garlic

105

To see an honest courtier the king's favorite, to see a poor younger son wearing the chain of the order, a low fellow rise to a position of state, this is not, Morel, the sort of thing that deserves a celebration.

But to see a footman, a child, a beast, a braggart, a skulker become cardinal, and a Ganymede wear scarlet on his head for taking good care of a monkey,

To see him who is called by the name of Saint Peter high on a ladder with a rope around his neck, put there by the hands of a Spanish soldier,

To see a scoundrel in three days climb to the level of princes and then to see him fall from there in three days, these miracles, Morel, happen only in Rome.

To see an honest courtier: because of the daring of their satire, this and the following seven sonnets were not included in most early copies of the *Regrets*

the order: the Order of Saint Michael

a Ganymede: a boy lover, here Cardinal del Monte, a young favorite of Julius III, who took care of the pope's monkey

him who is called by the name of Saint Peter: an incident in the life of Julius III before he became pope, when he served as a hostage in the place of Pope Clement VII

a scoundrel: has not been identified

106

Who will deny, Gillebert, if he does not want to set himself against common opinion, that the see of Peter, which can rightly be called an earthly paradise, has, as does heaven, its great Jupiter?

The Greeks made one live on Olympus, from where he often loosens his thunderbolts on us. The other releases his thunder from the Vatican, when some king has stirred his resentment.

They boast of the heavenly Jupiter's Ganymede. The Tuscan Jupiter has more than fifty of them. One gets drunk on Nectar; the other on good wine.

Both claim the eagle for their escutcheon. But one hates tyrants; the other favors them. In this, the mortal is not like the god.

Who will deny: satirically comparing the pope to Jupiter, as du Bellay does here, would have smacked of dangerously Protestant or at least Gallican ideas

Gillebert: Pierre Gillebert, minor poet and counselor to the Parlement of Grenoble

The other releases his thunder: Julius III threatened to excommunicate King Henry II

the other favors them: alludes to Julius III's alliance with Emperor Charles V

105

De voir mignon du Roy un courtisan honneste,
Voir un pauvre cadet l'ordre au col soustenir,
Un petit compagnon aux estatz parvenir,
Ce n'est chose (Morel) digne d'en faire feste.

Mais voir un estaffier, un enfant, une beste,
Un forfant, un poltron Cardinal devenir,
Et pour avoir bien sçeu un singe entretenir
Un Ganymede avoir le rouge sur la teste:

S'estre veu par les mains d'un soldat Espagnol
Bien hault sur une eschelle avoir la corde au col
Celuy, que par le nom de Sainct-Pere lon nomme:

Un belistre en trois jours aux princes s'égaller,
Et puis le voir de là en trois jours devaller:
Ces miracles (Morel) ne se font point qu'à Rome.

106

Qui niera (Gillebert) s'il ne veult resister
Au jugement commun, que le siege de Pierre
Qu'on peult dire à bon droit un Paradis en terre,
Aussi bien que le ciel, n'ait son grand Juppiter?

Les Grecz nous ont fait l'un sur Olympe habiter,
Dont souvent dessus nous ses fouldres il desserre:
L'autre du Vatican délasche son tonnerre,
Quand quelque Roy l'a fait contre luy despiter.

Du Juppiter celeste un Ganymede on vante,
Le Thusque Juppiter en a plus de cinquante:
L'un de Nectar s'enyvre, et l'autre de bon vin.

De l'aigle l'un et l'autre a la defense prise,
Mais l'un hait les tyrans, l'autre les favorise:
Le mortel en cecy n'est semblable au divin.

107

Où que je tourne l'œil, soit vers le Capitole,
Vers les baings d'Antonin, ou Diocletien,
Et si quelqu'œuvre encor dure plus ancien,
De la porte sainct Pol jusques à Ponte-mole:

Je deteste apart-moy ce vieil Faucheur, qui vole,
Et le Ciel, qui ce tout a reduit en un rien:
Puis songeant que chacun peult repeter le sien,
Je me blasme, et cognois que ma complainte est fole.

Aussi seroit celuy par trop audacieux,
Qui vouldroit accuser ou le Temps ou les Cieux,
Pour voir une medaille, ou columne brisee.

Et qui sçait si les Cieulx referont point leur tour,
Puis que tant de Seigneurs nous voyons chacun jour
Bastir sur la Rotonde, et sur le Collisee?

108

Je fuz jadis Hercule, or Pasquin je me nomme,
Pasquin fable du peuple, et qui fais toutefois
Le mesme office encor que j'ay fait autrefois,
Veu qu'ores par mes vers tant de monstres j'assomme.

Aussi mon vray mestier c'est de n'espargner homme,
Mais les vices chanter d'une publique voix:
Et si ne puis encor, quelque fort que je sois,
Surmonter la fureur de cet Hydre de Rome.

J'ay porté sur mon col le grand Palais des Dieux,
Pour soulager Atlas, qui sous le faiz des cieux
Courboit las et recreu sa grande eschine large.

Ores au lieu du ciel, je porte sur mon doz
Un gros moyne Espagnol, qui me froisse les oz,
Et me poise trop plus que ma premiere charge.

107

Wherever I turn my eye, whether toward the Capitol, toward the baths of Antoninus or Diocletian, or toward any still older monument that yet survives from the gate of Saint Paul to the Milvian bridge,

I inwardly curse that old reaper, who flies, and heaven, which has reduced this all to nothing. Then recalling that everyone has a right to claim his due, I repent and recognize that my complaint is foolish.

And indeed anyone who would accuse Time or the heavens every time he sees a broken medallion or column would be far too presumptuous.

And who knows if the heavens will not renew their course, since we see so many lords every day building on the Rotunda and the Coliseum.

---

that old reaper, who flies: Time, with a possible pun on du Bellay's *qui vole,* which can also mean "who robs"

the Rotunda: the Pantheon

108

I used to be Hercules, but now I call myself Pasquino—Pasquino, the people's laughingstock—though I still perform the same labor I did before, in that now with my verses I beat to death so many monsters.

My true calling is thus to spare no one, but to sing out vices with a public voice. And yet, however strong I may be, I can still not overcome the rage of that Hydra of Rome.

I bore on my shoulders the great palace of the gods to ease Atlas, whose broad, strong back, tired and worn out, bent under the weight of the heavens.

Now, instead of the heavens, I bear on my back a fat Spanish monk, who bruises my bones and weighs much more than my original load.

---

now I call myself Pasquino: Pasquino, the Roman statue on which satirical verses were hung, was thought to have been originally a statue of Hercules

that Hydra of Rome: the papal court

the great palace of the gods: the heavens

a fat Spanish monk: possibly Cardinal Alvarez of Toledo, president of the Holy Inquisition

109

Like one who would clean out a dirty sewer, often choked by the terrible stench, remains buried in the deep filth, unless he arms his nose to ward off the smell,

So the good Marcellus, having pulled out the stopper to drain away the thick slime of accumulated vices with which his predecessor had for the previous six years poisoned the world,

The poor fellow, overcome by such an odor, fell dead in the midst of the work he had undertaken, without having cleared away even half that filth.

But whoever brings that task to completion will be able to boast that he has done much more than the man who purged the Augean stables.

---

the good Marcellus: Pope Marcellus II (April-May 1555)
his predecessor: Pope Julius III (1550–1555)
the man who purged the Augean stables: Hercules

110

When my Caracciolo releases from their prison Mars, winds, and winter, a blazing fury, an imperious tempest, a quaking horror scorches, overturns, and contracts souls, waves, humors.

But when it pleases him to shut up war, storms, and cold, a loving ardor, a long calm, a mild warmth burns, quiets, and melts hearts, waves, and the earth.

Thus in one moment he sets peace against Mars, fair weather against storm, spring against winter, by comparing Paul the Fourth with Julius the Third.

And, truly, never were two ages more unlike, nor can the verso better reveal the recto than by putting Julius the Third back-to-back with Paul the Fourth.

Caracciolo: Antoine Caracciolo (1515–1570), bishop of Troyes, wrote a poem comparing Pope Julius III and Pope Paul IV, which du Bellay also evokes in a Latin epigram (*Poemata* 2.33)

Mars, winds, and winter: the first of eight coordinated triplets that run through the first eight lines of this sonnet are in what the French call *vers rapportés*

109

Comme un, qui veult curer quelque Cloaque immunde,
S'il n'a le nez armé d'une contresenteur,
Estouffé bien souvent de la grand' puanteur
Demeure ensevely dans l'ordure profonde:

Ainsi le bon Marcel ayant levé la bonde,
Pour laisser escouler la fangeuse espesseur
Des vices entassez, dont son predecesseur
Avoit six ans devant empoisonné le monde:

Se trouvant le pauvret de telle odeur surpris,
Tomba mort au milieu de son œuvre entrepris,
N'ayant pas à demy ceste ordure purgee.

Mais quiconques rendra tel ouvrage parfait,
Se pourra bien vanter d'avoir beaucoup plus fait,
Que celuy qui purgea les estables d'Augee.

110

Quand mon Caraciol de leur prison desserre
Mars, les ventz, et l'hyver: une ardente fureur,
Une fiere tempeste, une tremblante horreur
Ames, ondes, humeurs, ard, renverse, et reserre.

Quand il luy plait aussi de renfermer la guerre,
Et l'orage, et le froid: une amoureuse ardeur,
Une longue bonasse, une doulce tiedeur
Brusle, appaise, et resoult les cœurs, l'onde, et la terre.

Ainsi la paix à Mars il oppose en un temps,
Le beautemps à l'orage, à l'hyver le printemps,
Comparant Paule quart, avec Jules troisieme.

Aussi ne furent onq' deux siecles plus divers,
Et ne se peult mieulx voir l'endroit par le revers,
Que mettant Jules tiers avec Paule quatrieme.

111

Je n'ay jamais pensé que ceste voulte ronde
Couvrist rien de constant: mais je veulx desormais,
Je veulx (mon cher Morel) croire plus que jamais,
Que dessous ce grand Tout rien ferme ne se fonde.

Puis que celuy qui fut de la terre et de l'onde
Le tonnerre et l'effroy, las de porter le faiz
Veult d'un cloistre borner la grandeur de ses faicts,
Et pour servir à Dieu abandonner le monde.

Mais quoy? que dirons-nous de cet autre vieillard,
Lequel ayant passé son aage plus gaillard
Au service de Dieu, ores Cesar imite?

Je ne sçay qui des deux est le moins abusé:
Mais je pense (Morel) qu'il est fort mal aisé,
Que l'un soit bon guerrier, ny l'autre bon hermite.

112

Quand je voy ces Seigneurs, qui l'espee et la lance
Ont laissé pour vestir ce sainct orgueil Romain,
Et ceulx-là, qui ont pris le baston en la main,
Sans avoir jamais fait preuve de leur vaillance:

Quand je les vois (Ursin) si chiches d'audience,
Que souvent par quatre huiz on la mendie en vain:
Et quand je voy l'orgueil d'un Camerier hautain,
Lequel feroit à Job perdre la patience:

Il me souvient alors de ces lieux enchantez,
Qui sont en Amadis, et Palmerin chantez,
Desquelz l'entree estoit si cherement vendue.

Puis je dis: ô combien le Palais que je voy
Me semble different du Palais de mon Roy,
Où lon ne trouve point de chambre deffendue!

111

I never thought this round vault covered anything stable. But I am determined from now on, my dear Morel, I am determined to believe more than ever that beneath the great All nothing lasting can exist,

Since he who was the thunder and terror of earth and sea, tired of bearing the burden, wants to confine the greatness of his deeds in a cloister and abandon the world to serve God.

But then what shall we say of that other old man who, having spent the most vigorous years of his life in the service of God, now imitates Caesar?

I do not know which of the two is less deluded. But I think, Morel, that it is highly unlikely that the one will be a good soldier or the other a good hermit.

---

this round vault: of the heavens

he who was the thunder and terror of earth and sea: Emperor Charles V, who gave up his offices and retired to a monastery in 1557

that other old man: Pope Paul IV, who was known as a warrior pope

112

When I see those lords who have abandoned sword and lance to assume the holy pride of Rome and those who have taken in hand the staff of command without having ever given proof of their valor,

When I see them, Ursin, so sparing of their presence that often in vain you beg an audience with them at four different doors, and when I see the arrogance of a haughty chamberlain who would make Job lose his patience,

I then remember those enchanted places that are sung in *Amadis* and *Palmerin*, to which entrance was sold so dearly.

Then I say, "O how different is the palace I see from the palace of my king, where there is no forbidden room!"

Amadis and *Palmerin*: popular chivalric romances

my king: Henry II

113

To have seen a triple mountain collapse, a deer appear and suddenly disappear, and over the tomb of a Roman emperor an old carafe raised as an ensign.

To see nothing but soldiers come and go on campaign, lords imprisoned for an uncertain crime, exiles return, and the Neapolitan lord it over the pride of Spain,

Many new lords, of whom the most prominent are the closest relatives of his holiness, and many cardinals, whose names we hardly know,

Many fine horses, and many high collars, and many favorites, who were only lackeys. That, my dear Dagaut, is the news from Rome.

To have seen: alludes to the events of 1555 when two popes died in quick succession

a triple mountain: Pope Julius III, whose family name was del Monte (mountain)

a deer: Pope Marcellus II, whose family name was Cervini (deer)

the tomb of a Roman emperor: Castello San Angelo, the tomb of the Emperor Hadrian

an old carafe: Pope Paul IV, whose family name was Caraffa (carafe)

the Neapolitan: Pope Paul IV, who detested the Spanish

114

O three and four times unhappy the land whose prince sees only through the eyes of others, hears only through those who answer for him, more blind, deaf, and mute than a stone!

Such are those, my lord, who are today shut up idle in their room, as if in a box, to make them last longer and to keep them from feeling the misery that their poor people feel, overwhelmed by war.

They play like children with trumpets and cannons, fifes, drums, ensigns, banners, and seeing their land besieged by enemies.

Such was he who, from the top of a tower, watching flames lick all around, to amuse himself sang the burning of Troy.

O three and four times unhappy: echoes and reverses Virgil's *Aeneid* 1.94

he who . . . sang the burning of Troy: Nero

113

Avoir veu devaller une triple Montagne,
Apparoir une Biche, et disparoir soudain,
Et dessus le tombeau d'un Empereur Romain
Une vieille Caraffe eslever pour enseigne:

Ne voir qu'entrer soldardz, et sortir en campagne,
Emprisonner seigneurs pour un crime incertain,
Retourner forussiz, et le Napolitain
Commander en son rang à l'orgueil de l'Espagne:

Force nouveaux seigneurs, dont les plus apparents
Sont de sa Saincteté les plus proches parents,
Et force Cardinaulx, qu'à grand'peine lon nomme:

Force braves chevaulx, et force haults colletz,
Et force favoriz, qui n'estoient que valletz,
Voila (mon cher Dagaut) des nouvelles de Rome.

114

O trois et quatre fois malheureuse la terre,
Dont le prince ne voit que par les yeux d'autruy,
N'entend que par ceulx-là, qui respondent pour luy,
Aveugle, sourd, et mut, plus que n'est une pierre!

Telz sont ceulx-là (Seigneur) qu'aujourd'huy lon reserre
Oisifz dedans leur chambre, ainsi qu'en un estuy,
Pour durer plus long temps, et ne sentir l'ennuy,
Que sent leur pauvre peuple accablé de la guerre.

Ilz se paissent enfans de trompes et canons,
De fifres, de tabours, d'enseignes, gomphanons,
Et de voir leur province aux ennemis en proye.

Tel estoit cestui-là, qui du hault d'une tour,
Regardant undoyer la flamme tout autour,
Pour se donner plaisir chantoit le feu de Troye.

115

O que tu es heureux, si tu cognois ton heur,
D'estre eschappé des mains de ceste gent cruelle,
Qui soubz un faulx semblant d'amitié mutuelle
Nous desrobbe le bien, et la vie, et l'honneur! 4

Où tu es (mon Dagaud) la secrette ranqueur,
Le soing qui comme un' hydre en nous se renouvelle,
L'avarice, l'envie, et la haine immortelle
Du chetif courtisan n'empoisonnent le cœur. 8

La molle oisiveté n'y engendre le vice,
Le serviteur n'y perd son temps et son service,
Et n'y mesdit on point de cil qui est absent: 11

La justice y a lieu, la foy n'en est banie,
Là ne sçait-on que c'est de prendre à compagnie,
A change, à cense, à stoc, et à trente pour cent. 14

116

Fuions (Dilliers) fuions ceste cruelle terre,
Fuions ce bord avare, et ce peuple inhumain,
Que des Dieux irritez la vangeresse main
Ne nous accable encor' soubs un mesme tonnerre. 4

Mars est desenchainé, le temple de la guerre
Est ouvert à ce coup, le grand prestre Romain
Veult fouldroier là bas l'heretique Germain,
Et l'Espagnol marran, ennemis de sainct Pierre. 8

On ne voit que soldartz, enseignes, gonphanons,
On n'oit que tabourins, trompettes, et canons,
On ne voit que chevaux courans parmy la plaine: 11

On n'oit plus raisonner que de sang, et de feu,
Maintenant on voira, si jamais on l'a veu,
Comment se sauvera la nacelle Romaine. 14

115

O how happy you are, if you know your happiness, to have escaped from the hands of that cruel race that, under the false appearance of mutual friendship, strips away our goods, and our life, and our honor!

Where you are, my Dagaut, hidden rancor, care that like a Hydra is constantly reborn in us, avarice, jealousy, and the undying hate of a worthless courtier does not poison your heart.

There slack idleness does not engender vice. The servant does not there waste his time and his service. And there people do not speak ill of whoever is absent.

Justice has a place there. Faith is not banished. There no one knows what it means to borrow with interest, with a bill of exchange, against land, against stock, and at thirty percent.

O how happy you are: echoes Virgil's *Georgics* 2.458
that cruel race: the Romans, especially Roman churchmen
Where you are: in France

116

Let us flee, Dilliers, let us flee this cruel land. Let us flee this miserly shore and this inhuman people, so that the avenging hand of the angry gods does not again destroy us all with the same thunderbolt.

Mars has been unchained. The temple of war has now been opened. The great Roman priest wants to strike down the German heretic and the Spanish converso, enemies of Saint Peter.

We see only soldiers, ensigns, banners. We hear only drums, trumpets, and cannons. We see only horses running in the plain.

We hear only talk of blood and fire. Now, if ever, we shall see whether the Roman skiff can be saved.

---

the great Roman priest: Pope Paul IV
the German heretic: German Protestants
the Spanish converso: Paul IV accused Spaniards of being converted Jews and Moors
the Roman skiff: the ship of state addressed by Horace in *Odes* 1.14

117

He was truly both wise and well taught who, knowing that the divine seeds of fire are the first source of living things, said that our minds are made of fire.

The body is the brand lit with that heat, which, as its matter is more refined, makes a brighter flame and makes the mind more worthy to show what it contains.

This celestial fire, humble in its birth, rises little by little to the level of its essential being, until it has attained the height of its greatness.

Then it abates and, its strength exhausted, reduced to ashes through lack of fuel, suddenly feels its languishing ardor fail.

He was truly both wise and well taught: Heraclitus

118

When I see those lords, whose authority, each according to his rank, now commands here, marching proudly side by side, I seem to see so many gods.

But seeing them go pale when his holiness spits in a basin and with a frightened look surreptitiously check whether there is any blood, then with a little smile pretend to be reassured,

O how miserable, I say then, is the greatness I see compared to the greatness of a king! Unhappy the man who buys such honor so dearly.

Truly a death-dealing blade and a rock, too, hang over the heads of these lords, since all their happiness depends on an old thread.

---

his holiness: probably Julius III, who in 1555 died of a catarrh

an old thread: the thread of the aged pope's life with an allusion to both the sword of Damocles and the rock hanging over the heads of the condemned in Virgil's underworld (*Aeneid* 6.602–603)

117

Celuy vrayement estoit et sage et bien appris,
Qui cognoissant du feu la semence divine
Estre des Animans la premiere origine,
De substance de feu dit estre noz espritz.

Le corps est le tison de ceste ardeur espris,
Lequel, d'autant qu'il est de matiere plus fine,
Fait un feu plus luisant, et rend l'esprit plus digne
De monstrer ce qui est en soymesme compris.

Ce feu donques celeste, humble de sa naissance
S'esleve peu à peu au lieu de son essence,
Tant qu'il soit parvenu au poinct de sa grandeur:

Adonc' il diminue, et sa force lassee
Par faulte d'aliment en cendres abbaissee
Sent faillir tout à coup sa languissante ardeur.

118

Quand je voy ces Messieurs, desquelz l'auctorité
Se voit ores icy commander en son rang,
D'un front audacieux cheminer flanc à flanc,
Il me semble de voir quelque divinité.

Mais les voiant pallir lors que sa Saincteté
Crache dans un bassin, et d'un visage blanc
Cautement espier s'il y a point de sang,
Puis d'un petit soubriz feindre une seureté:

O combien (di-je alors) la grandeur que je voy,
Est miserable au pris de la grandeur d'un Roy!
Malheureux qui si cher achete tel honneur.

Vrayement le fer meurtrier, et le rocher aussi
Pendent bien sur le chef de ces Seigneurs icy,
Puis que d'un vieil filet depend tout leur bonheur.

119

Brusquet à son retour vous racontera (Sire)
De ces rouges prelatz la pompeuse apparence,
Leurs mules, leurs habitz, leur longue reverence,
Qui se peult beaucoup mieulx representer que dire.

Il vous racontera, s'il les sçait bien descrire,
Les mœurs de ceste court, et quelle difference
Se voit de ces grandeurs à la grandeur de France,
Et mille autres bons poincts, qui sont dignes de rire.

Il vous peindra la forme, et l'habit du sainct Pere,
Qui, comme Jupiter, tout le monde tempere
Aveques un clin d'œil: sa faconde et sa grace,

L'honnesteté des siens, leur grandeur et largesse,
Les presentz qu'on luy feit, et de quelle caresse
Tout ce que se dit vostre à Rome lon embrasse.

120

Voicy le Carneval, menons chacun la sienne,
Allons baller en masque, allons nous pourmener,
Allons voir Marc Antoine, ou Zany bouffonner,
Avec son Magnifique à la Venitienne:

Voyons courir le pal à la mode ancienne,
Et voyons par le nez le sot buffle mener,
Voyons le fier taureau d'armes environner,
Et voyons au combat l'adresse Italienne:

Voyons d'œufz parfumez un orage gresler,
Et la fusee ardent' siffler menu par l'aer.
Sus donc depeschons nous, voicy la pardonnance:

Il nous fauldra demain visiter les saincts lieux,
Là nous ferons l'amour, mais ce sera des yeux,
Car passer plus avant c'est contre l'ordonnance.

119

At his return, Brusquet will tell Your Majesty about the pompous show of these scarlet prelates, their slippers, their costumes, and their elaborate bows, which can be much better shown than told.

He will tell you, if he can describe them well, about the manners of this court and what a difference there is between these grandeurs and the grandeur of France, and a thousand other good things that are worth a laugh.

He will paint for you the appearance and dress of the Holy Father, who, like Jupiter, keeps everyone in control with a wink, his copious eloquence and his grace,

The honesty of his family, their greatness and generosity, the gifts that were given him, and with what attentive care all that claims allegiance to you is embraced in Rome.

Brusquet: the king's jester, who was in Rome with the cardinal of Lorraine in 1557

120

It's carnival! Let's each take a girl. Let's go to a masked ball. Let's stroll around. Let's go see a Marc Antony or Zany play the buffoon with his Magnifico in the Venetian manner.

Let's watch a traditional race for the *palio,* and let's watch a foolish ox led by the nose. Let's watch a proud bull encircled with arms, and let's watch the Italian skill at fencing.

Let's watch a hailstorm of scented eggs and a flaming rocket whistle sharply through the air. Up then! Let's hurry. Here is our pardon.

Tomorrow we will have to visit holy sites. There we will make love, but only with our eyes, for to go further is against the decree.

Marc Antony . . . Zany . . . Magnifico: figures from Italian street comedy
the *palio*: a decorated cloth that was the traditional prize in a race
Tomorrow: Ash Wednesday, the day after Mardi Gras
the decree: Paul IV had issued a decree forbidding lewd behavior

121

Being bored all day by a tedious bullbaiting, seeing a brave bull surrounded by a large ring of spectators, astonished to see so many men on every side, and fifty pikemen standing up to his courage,

Seeing him charge with his head down, flee and return with a still bolder attack, then seeing him caught at last by some maneuver, run through with a thousand thrusts, filling the square with blood,

Seeing them run with torches, but without bumping into each other, give three sword blows, display their arms, and all around the camp a wall of Teutons,

Seeing them go through a big preparation, make everyone wait a long time, then finally present a poor show: there you have all the fun of Roman festivals.

122

While in the courthouse you talk of trials, of lawyers, procurators, presidents, councillors, statutes, judgments, of new court officers, of corrupt judges, and such surprises,

We talk here of towns taken, of banking news, of new dispatches, of new cardinals, of mules, of footmen, of copes, of surplices, of ceremonial staffs and valises.

And now, Sébillet, as I write this to you, we talk of bulls and of oxen too, of masks, of banquets, and of such expenses.

Tomorrow we will talk of visiting shrines, of *motu proprio,* of reformations, of decrees, of pastoral letters, of papal bulls and dispensations.

---

in the courthouse: the Palais de Justice in Paris

mules: figured in the solemn processions of cardinals, but du Bellay's *mules* could also mean the slippers worn by high churchmen

valises: ornamented velvet sacks in which cardinals' vestments were kept and which were carried by their servants in processions

Sébillet: Thomas Sébillet (1512–1589), lawyer and author of *Art Poetique françois* (1548), which had a large part in prompting du Bellay's *Defense*

motu proprio: a papal edict decided on by the pope personally

121

Se fascher tout le jour d'une fascheuse chasse,
Voir un brave taureau se faire un large tour
Estonné de se voir tant d'hommes alentour,
Et cinquante picquiers affronter son audace: 4

Le voir en s'elançant venir la teste basse,
Fuïr et retourner d'un plus brave retour,
Puis le voir à la fin pris en quelque destour
Percé de mille coups ensenglanter la place: 8

Voir courir aux flambeaux, mais sans se rencontrer,
Donner trois coups d'espee, en armes se monstrer,
Et tout autour du camp un rampart de Thudesques: 11

Dresser un grand apprest, faire attendre long temps,
Puis donner à la fin un maigre passetemps:
Voila tout le plaisir des festes Romanesques. 14

122

Ce pendant qu'au Palais de procez tu devises,
D'advocats, procureurs, presidents, conseillers,
D'ordonnances, d'arrestz, de nouveaux officiers,
De juges corrompuz, et de telles surprises: 4

Nous devisons icy de quelques villes prises,
De nouvelles de banque, et de nouveaux courriers,
De nouveaux Cardinaulx, de mules, d'estaffiers,
De chappes, de rochetz, de masses, et valises: 8

Et ores (Sibilet) que je t'escry ceci,
Nous parlons de taureaux, et de buffles aussi,
De masques, de banquetz, et de telles despences: 11

Demain nous parlerons d'aller aux stations,
De motu-proprio, de reformations,
D'ordonnances, de briefz, de bulles, et dispenses. 14

123

Nous ne sommes faschez que la trefve se face:
Car bien que nous soyons de la France bien loing,
Si est chacun de nous à soymesme tesmoing,
Combien la France doit de la guerre estre lasse.

Mais nous sommes faschez que l'Espagnole audace,
Qui plus que le François de repoz a besoing,
Se vante avoir la guerre et la paix en son poing,
Et que de respirer nous luy donnons espace.

Il nous fasche d'ouir noz pauvres alliez
Se plaindre à tous propoz qu'on les ait oubliez,
Et qu'on donne au privé l'utilité commune:

Mais ce qui plus nous fasche est que les estrangers
Disent plus que jamais que nous sommes legers,
Et que nous ne sçavons cognoistre la Fortune.

124

Le Roy (disent icy ces baniz de Florence)
Du sceptre d'Italie est frustré desormais,
Et son heureuse main cet heur n'aura jamais
De reprendre aux cheveulx la fortune de France.

Le Pape mal content n'aura plus de fiance
En tous ces beaux desseings trop legerement faictz,
Et l'exemple Sienois rendra par ceste paix
Suspecte aux estrangers la Françoise alliance.

L'Empereur affoibly ses forces reprendra,
L'Empire hereditaire à ce coup il rendra,
Et paisible à ce coup il rendra l'Angleterre.

Voila que disent ceulx, qui discourent du Roy:
Que leur respondrons-nous? Vineus, mande le moy,
Toy, qui sçais discourir et de paix et de guerre.

123

We are not annoyed that the truce has been concluded. For though we are far from France, yet each one of us bears witness to himself how weary France must be of war.

But we are annoyed that audacious Spain, which needs respite more than the French, boasts of having war and peace in hand, and that we are giving her a chance to catch her breath.

It annoys us to hear our poor allies complain at every opportunity that we have forgotten them and that the general good is being sacrificed for private interest.

But what annoys us most is that foreigners say more than ever that we are frivolous and that we do not know Fortune when we see her.

---

the truce: the Truce of Vaucelles, concluded in 1556 between King Henry II of France and Emperor Charles V

our poor allies: Paul IV and Cardinal Caraffa, who favored a more bellicose policy

124

The king, say the Florentine exiles here, will from now on be denied the Italian scepter, and his lucky hand will never have the good luck to seize back by the forelock the fortune of France.

The angry pope will no longer trust all those fine plans too lightly proposed, and the example of Siena will, as a result of this peace, make foreigners mistrust a French alliance.

The weakened emperor will regain his strength. He will now make the empire hereditary. And he will now pacify England.

That is what they say who talk of the king. What shall we answer? Tell me, Vineus, you who know how to speak of both peace and war.

The king: Henry II, who dreamed of conquering the kingdom of Naples, then held by the Spanish

the angry pope: Paul IV

the example of Siena: the Truce of Vaucelles was understood to have violated the French alliance with Siena

125

In the dark womb, where was once enclosed all that has since filled the great void—air, earth, fire, and the liquid element—and all that Atlas bears on his back,

The seeds of the Universe were still confusedly mixed, the hot with the dry, the cold with the wet, and the harmony, which has since bridled them, had not yet opened the door of Chaos,

For war had jammed the lock, and the key was so rusted with age, that this great body struggled in vain to get out,

Without the truce, my lord, the harbinger of peace, which found the secret, and with an agile hand let out peace along with love.

In the dark womb: draws on both the opening of Ovid's *Metamorphoses* and Virgil's *Aeneid* 6.724ff.

126

Welcome to you, O blessed truce! Truce that a Christian cannot praise too much, for you alone have the power to charm away the painful memory of our former sufferings.

You are set to last five years—and may envy choke with rage!—for if indulgent heaven allows you to give birth to what we expect of you, you will be able to boast of having made a peace that will not be so brief.

But if this common respite gives the favorite greater opportunity from now on to accuse the innocent so as to snatch away his land,

If the fruit of this peace, so much desired by the people, belongs only to the greedy lawyer, then go in peace, truce, and let war return.

---

the favorite: possibly Anne de Montmorency, the constable of France, who was involved in a legal maneuver to seize the land of du Bellay's nephew and ward

125

Dedans le ventre obscur, où jadis fut encloz
Tout cela qui depuis a remply ce grand vide,
L'air, la terre, et le feu, et l'element liquide,
Et tout cela qu'Atlas soustient dessus son doz,

Les semences du Tout estoient encor' en gros,
Le chault avec le sec, le froid avec l'humide,
Et l'accord, qui depuis leur imposa la bride,
N'avoit encor' ouvert la porte du Caos:

Car la guerre en avoit la serrure brouillee,
Et la clef en estoit par l'aage si rouillee,
Qu'en vain, pour en sortir, combatoit ce grand corps.

Sans la trefve (Seigneur) de la paix messagere,
Qui trouva le secret, et d'une main legere
La paix avec l'amour en fit sortir dehors.

126

Tu sois la bien venue, ô bienheureuse trefve!
Trefve, que le Chrestien ne peult assez chanter,
Puis que seule tu as la vertu d'enchanter
De noz travaulx passez la souvenance greve.

Tu dois durer cinq ans: et que l'envie en creve,
Car si le ciel bening te permet enfanter
Ce qu'on attend de toy, tu te pourras vanter
D'avoir fait une paix, qui ne sera si breve.

Mais si le favory en ce commun repoz
Doit avoir desormais le temps plus à propoz
D'accuser l'innocent, pour luy ravir sa terre:

Si le fruict de la paix du peuple tant requis
A l'avare advocat est seulement acquis,
Trefve, va t'en en paix, et retourne la guerre.

127

Icy de mille fards la traison se desguise,
Icy mille forfaitz pullulent à foison,
Icy ne se punit l'homicide ou poison,
Et la richesse icy par usure est acquise:

Icy les grands maisons viennent de bastardise,
Icy ne se croid rien sans humaine raison,
Icy la volupté est toujours de saison,
Et d'autant plus y plaist, que moins elle est permise.

Pense le demourant. Si est-ce toutefois
Qu'on garde encor' icy quelque forme de loix,
Et n'en est point du tout la justice bannie:

Icy le grand seigneur n'achete l'action,
Et pour priver autruy de sa possession
N'arme son mauvais droit de force et tyrannie.

128

Ce n'est pas de mon gré (Carle) que ma navire
Erre en la mer Tyrrhene: un vent impetueux
La chasse maulgré moy par ces flots tortueux,
Ne voiant plus le pol, qui sa faveur t'inspire.

Je ne voy que rochers, et si rien se peult dire
Pire que des rochers le hurt audacieux:
Et le phare jadis favorable à mes yeux
De mon cours egaré sa lanterne retire.

Mais si je puis un jour me sauver des dangers
Que je fuy vagabond par ces flots estrangers,
Et voir de l'Ocean les campagnes humides,

J'arresteray ma nef au rivage Gaulois,
Consacrant ma despouille au Neptune François,
A Glauque, à Melicerte, et aux sœurs Nereïdes.

127

Here treason disguises itself with a thousand masks. Here a thousand crimes multiply in abundance. Here they do not punish homicide or poison. And riches are here acquired by usury.

Here great houses descend from bastardy. Here they believe nothing without human reason. Here sensual pleasure is always in fashion, and the less it is permitted, the more desirable it is.

You can imagine the rest. Yet they do still retain some form of law, and justice is not entirely banished.

Here the great lord does not buy a judgment, and to deprive another of his property does not arm his weak claim with force and oppression.

Here: in Rome

the great lord: as in *Regrets* 126, a possible allusion to Anne de Montmorency

128

It is not by my choice, Carle, that my ship wanders in the Tyrrhenian Sea. A violent wind drives it against my will through these tortuous waves, no longer seeing the pole that inspires you with its favor.

I see only rocks and whatever can be called worse than the terrible crashing of rocks. And the lighthouse that once showed me its favor withdraws its beam from my errant course.

But if I can one day save myself from the dangers I flee wandering in these foreign seas and can find the liquid fields of the Ocean,

I will anchor my boat on the Gallic shore, dedicating my remains to the French Neptune, to Glaucus, to Melicertes, and to the Nereides sisters.

It is not: this and the following two sonnets imagine a Ulysses-like return to France by sea rather than the less heroic land itinerary du Bellay actually followed and that he describes in *Regrets* 132–138

Carle: Lancelot de Carle (1500–1568), bishop of Riez, whose support of Ronsard is evoked in du Bellay's Latin elegy "Ad P. Ronsardum," lines 7–10

the Ocean: the Atlantic

Glaucus: a sea god, like Neptune, Melicertes, and the Nereides

129

I see, Dilliers, I see the tempest subside. I see old Proteus shut up his flock. I see green Triton sporting on the sea. And I see the twinned stars flaming over my head.

Already a wind favorable to my return is beginning to blow. Already I begin rowing toward the mouth of the harbor. And I already see so many friends that I cannot name them, stretching their arms toward me, rejoicing on the shore.

I see my great Ronsard. I recognize him from here. I see my dear Morel and my Dorat too. I see my de La Haye and also my Paschal.

And a little farther off I see (if I am not mistaken) my divine Mauléon, whom, without having seen, I worship for his grace, his learning, and his virtue.

I see: modeled on Ariosto's *Orlando furioso,* 46.1–19

the twinned stars: the Gemini

Dorat: Jean Dorat (1508–1588), humanist and teacher of du Bellay, Ronsard, and Baïf at the College Coqueret in Paris

Mauléon: Michel-Pierre de Mauléon, counselor to the Parlement of Paris and friend of Paschal and Ronsard

130

And I too thought what Ulysses thought: that there was nothing sweeter than for a man one day to see again smoke rising from his chimney and after a long absence to find himself once more in the bosom of the land that nursed him.

I rejoiced to have escaped from vice, from the Circes of Italy, from the Sirens of love and to have brought back to France on my return the honor one acquires from faithful service.

Alas, but after the weariness of such a long time away, I find in my house a thousand biting cares that gnaw at my heart without hope of relief.

So adieu, Dorat, I am a Roman still, unless you lend me here the bow the nine sisters put into your hand so I can take my revenge.

And I too thought: based on a Latin epigram du Bellay wrote to Dorat (*Poemata* 2.61)

the bow the nine sisters put into your hand: alluding at once to Dorat's gift for satiric poetry and to Odysseus's triumph over the suitors on his return to Ithaca

129

Je voy (Dilliers) je voy serener la tempeste,
Je voy le vieil Proté son troppeau renfermer,
Je voy le verd Triton s'egaier sur la mer,
Et voy l'Astre jumeau flamboier sur ma teste.

Ja le vent favorable à mon retour s'appreste,
Ja vers le front du port je commence à ramer,
Et voy ja tant d'amis, que ne les puis nommer,
Tendant les bras vers moy, sur le bord faire feste.

Je voy mon grand Ronsard, je le cognois d'ici,
Je voy mon cher Morel, et mon Dorat aussi,
Je voy mon Delahaie, et mon Paschal encore:

Et voy un peu plus loing (si je ne suis deceu)
Mon divin Mauleon, duquel, sans l'avoir veu,
La grace, le sçavoir et l'a vertu j'adore.

130

Et je pensois aussi ce que pensoit Ulysse,
Qu'il n'estoit rien plus doulx que voir encor' un jour
Fumer sa cheminee, et apres long sejour
Se retrouver au sein de sa terre nourrice.

Je me resjouissois d'estre eschappé au vice,
Aux Circes d'Italie, aux Sirenes d'amour,
Et d'avoir rapporté en France à mon retour
L'honneur que lon s'acquiert d'un fidele service.

Las mais apres l'ennuy de si longue saison,
Mille souciz mordants je trouve en ma maison,
Qui me rongent le cœur sans espoir d'allegence.

Adieu donques (Dorat) je suis encor' Romain,
Si l'arc que les neuf Sœurs te misrent en la main
Tu ne me preste icy, pour faire ma vangence.

131

Morel, dont le sçavoir sur tout autre je prise,
Si quelqu'un de ceulx là, que le Prince Lorrain
Guida dernierement au rivage Romain,
Soit en bien, soit en mal, de Rome te devise: 4

Dy, qu'il ne sçait que c'est du siege de l'eglise,
N'y aiant esprouvé que la guerre, et la faim,
Que Rome n'est plus Rome, et que celuy en vain
Presume d'en juger, qui bien ne l'a comprise. 8

Celuy qui par la ruë a veu publiquement
La courtisanne en coche, ou qui pompeusement
L'a peu voir à cheval en accoustrement d'homme 11

Superbe se monstrer: celuy qui de plein jour
Aux Cardinaulx en cappe a veu faire l'amour,
C'est celuy seul (Morel) qui peult juger de Rome. 14

132

Vineus, je ne viz onc si plaisante province,
Hostes si gracieux, ny peuple si humain,
Que ton petit Urbin, digne que soubs sa main
Le tienne un si gentil et si vertueux Prince. 4

Quant à l'estat du Pape, il fallut que j'apprinse
A prendre en patience et la soif et la faim:
C'est pitié, comme là le peuple est inhumain,
Comme tout y est cher, et comme lon y pinse. 8

Mais tout cela n'est rien au pris du Ferrarois,
Car je ne vouldrois pas pour le bien de deux roys
Passer encor' un coup par si penible enfer. 11

Bref je ne sçay (Vineus) qu'en conclure à la fin,
Fors, qu'en comparaison de ton petit Urbin,
Le peuple de Ferrare est un peuple de fer. 14

131

Morel, you whose learning I prize above all else, if one of those men the prince of Lorraine recently led to the Roman shore speaks to you of Rome, whether favorably or unfavorably,

Say that he does not know what the seat of the church is, having only known war and hunger there, that Rome is no longer Rome, and that he presumes in vain to judge it who has not understood it well.

He who in the streets has seen a courtesan in a coach, or who has seen her magnificently on horseback dressed like a man

Proudly showing herself, he who has seen her in full daylight making love to cloaked cardinals, it is he alone, Morel, who can judge Rome.

---

the prince of Lorraine: the duke of Guise, who led an expedition to Naples in 1557

132

Vineus, I have never seen such a pleasant country, such gracious hosts, nor such humane people as in your little Urbino, which deserves to be governed by such a noble and virtuous prince.

As for the papal state, I had to learn to bear patiently both thirst and hunger. It is a pity how the people there are inhumane, how everything there is expensive, and how they steal there.

But all that is nothing compared to Ferrara, for I would not want to travel through such a cruel hell again for the wealth of two kings.

In short, Vineus, I do not know what to conclude in the end other than that in comparison to your little Urbino, the people of Ferrara are a people of iron.

Vineus, I have never seen: the first of seven sonnets tracing du Bellay's overland return to France toward the end of 1557

your little Urbino: Vineus was a member of the della Rovere family that ruled Urbino

a noble and virtuous prince: Guidubaldo della Rovere, duke of Urbino from 1538 to 1574

133

It is fun to see, Magny, these magnificent ballocks, their arrogant Arsenal, their vessels, their landing, their Saint Mark's, their palace, their Realto, their port, their exchanges, their profits, their bank, and their commerce.

It is fun to see the beak of their ancient hoods, their large-sleeved robes and their brimless bonnets, their uncouth talk, their seriousness, their bearing, and their wise counsel in public affairs.

It is fun to see their whole senate voting. It is fun to see their gondolas floating everywhere, their wives, their merrymaking, their independent life.

But what must be judged the best of all is when these old cuckolds go out to wed the sea, whose husbands they are and the Turk the adulterous lover.

---

these magnificent ballocks: plays irreverently on the Italian name of the lords of Venice, the *magnifici*

their whole senate: du Bellay's promonarchic, antirepublican prejudices come out here

wed the sea: refers to an annual ritual in which the doge and the other patricians of Venice symbolically wed the sea

the Turk: the Ottoman rivals of the Venetians in the eastern Mediterranean

134

He who has broken the law of friendship seeking the death and disgrace of his friend, he who in a judicial proceeding has ruined his brother or seized for himself the property of a child,

He who has betrayed his country and his king, he who like Oedipus has killed his father, he who like Orestes has killed his mother, he who has renounced his baptism and his faith,

Marseille, as penance for such an unhappily abominable offense it is not necessary that, violently beating his breast night and day,

He go wandering barefoot for six or seven years. It is enough that he do no more than pass in his travels through the Grisons—if, that is, he wants God to owe him a balance.

Marseille: secretary to the French ambassador in Rome

the Grisons: a canton in Switzerland then known for its rough roads and poor inns

133

Il fait bon voir (Magny) ces Coions magnifiques,
Leur superbe Arcenal, leurs vaisseaux, leur abbord,
Leur sainct Marc, leur palais, leur Realte, leur port,
Leurs changes, leurs profitz, leur banque, et leurs trafiques:

Il fait bon voir le bec de leurs chapprons antiques,
Leurs robbes à grand' manche, et leurs bonnetz sans bord,
Leur parler tout grossier, leur gravité, leur port,
Et leurs sages advis aux affaires publiques.

Il fait bon voir de tout leur Senat balloter,
Il fait bon voir par tout leurs gondolles flotter,
Leurs femmes, leurs festins, leur vivre solitere:

Mais ce que lon en doit le meilleur estimer,
C'est quand ces vieux coquz vont espouser la mer,
Dont ilz sont les maris, et le Turc l'adultere.

134

Celuy qui d'amitié a violé la loy,
Cherchant de son amy la mort et vitupere,
Celuy qui en procez a ruiné son frere,
Ou le bien d'un mineur a converty à soy:

Celuy qui a trahy sa patrie et son Roy,
Celuy qui comme Oedipe a fait mourir son pere,
Celuy qui comme Oreste a fait mourir sa mere,
Celuy qui a nié son baptesme et sa foy:

Marseille, il ne fault point que pour la penitence
D'une si malheureuse abominable offense,
Son estomac plombé martelant nuict et jour,

Il voise errant nudz piedz ne six ne sept annees:
Que les Grysons sans plus il passe à ses journees,
J'entens, s'il veult que Dieu luy doibve du retour.

135

La terre y est fertile, amples les edifices,
Les poelles bigarrez, et les chambres de bois,
La police immuable, immuables les loix,
Et le peuple ennemy de forfaitz et de vices. 4

Ilz boivent nuict et jour en Bretons et Suysses,
Ilz sont gras et refaits, et mangent plus que trois:
Voila les compagnons et correcteurs des Roys,
Que le bon Rabelais a surnommez Saulcisses. 8

Ilz n'ont jamais changé leurs habitz et façons,
Ilz hurlent comme chiens leurs barbares chansons,
Ilz comptent à leur mode, et de tout se font croire: 11

Ilz ont force beaux lacz, et force sources d'eau,
Force prez, force bois. J'ay du reste (Belleau)
Perdu le souvenir, tant ilz me firent boire. 14

136

Je les ay veuz (Bizet) et si bien m'en souvient,
J'ay veu dessus leur front la repentance peinte,
Comme on voit ces esprits qui là bas font leur pleinte,
Ayant passé le lac d'où plus on ne revient. 4

Un croire de leger les folz y entretient
Soubz un pretexte faulx de liberté contrainte:
Les coulpables fuitifz y demeurent par crainte,
Les plus fins et rusez honte les y retient. 8

Au demeurant (Bizet) l'avarice et l'envie,
Et tout cela qui plus tormente nostre vie,
Domine en ce lieu là plus qu'en tout autre lieu. 11

Je ne viz onques tant l'un l'autre contre-dire,
Je ne viz onques tant l'un de l'autre mesdire:
Vray est, que, comme icy, lon n'y jure point Dieu. 14

135

The land is fertile there, the buildings are large, the stoves are multicolored, and the bedrooms made of wood, the government is immutable, immutable the laws, and the people enemies of crime and vice.

They drink night and day like Bretons and Swiss. They are fat and full and eat more than enough for three. There you have the companions and chastisers of kings, whom the good Rabelais nicknamed "Sausages."

They have never altered their clothes and customs. They howl out their barbarous songs like dogs. They count in their own way and insist they are right about everything.

They have many beautiful lakes and many springs, many meadows, many woods. I have forgotten the rest, Belleau, they made me drink so much.

---

there: in Switzerland

the companions and chastisers of kings: an allusion to Swiss republican freedom from regal overlordship

the good Rabelais nicknamed "Sausages": allusion to chapter 38 of Rabelais's *Quart Livre*

count in their own way: by saying, for example, *septante* for *soixante-dix.*

136

I have seen them, Bizet, and if I remember well, I saw repentance painted on their brows, as one sees those spirits who, having crossed the lake from which there is no return, wail in the underworld.

Gullibility keeps fools there under the false pretext of involuntary liberty. Guilty fugitives stay there out of fear. The sharpest and craftiest are held there by shame.

Furthermore, Bizet, greed and envy and all that most torments our lives rule over that place more than over anyplace else.

I have never seen people so contradict one another. I have never seen people so slander one another. True it is that they do not, as we do, swear "by God."

---

them: the Calvinists of Geneva

involuntary liberty: the "Christian liberty" touted by the Reformers and contradicted in du Bellay's view by Geneva's authoritarian rule

swear "by God": Geneva had strict laws against blasphemous speech

137

Scève, I found myself like the son of Anchises entering Elysium and leaving Hades when after so many snowcapped peaks I saw this beautiful Lyon, Lyon that I so much admire.

Its narrow length, which the Saône divides, supports a thousand craftsmen and people of all sorts. And let London, Venice, and Antwerp take no offense, for Lyon is not inferior in commerce.

I was astonished to see so many couriers passing by, to see so many bankers, printers, armorers more thickly crowded than flowers in the fields.

But I was more astonished by the strength of the bridges on which they transport so many fine houses and so many estates on their way over the mountains.

Scève: Maurice Scève (1510–1564), poet and Lyonnais, blamed for the difficulty of his poetry in du Bellay's *Defense* 2.2

the son of Anchises: Aeneas

on their way over the mountains: alludes jokingly to the prodigal waste in Italy of so many French fortunes and/or to the papacy's exactions on French wealth

138

Devaulx, the sea receives all the rivers of the world and becomes no larger. Like the great sea is this matchless Paris, where we see all that flows in from every direction engulfed.

In learning, Paris is a fertile Greece. In size, Paris can be called a Rome. In wealth, it can be thought an Asia. And in rare novelties, a second Africa.

In short, Devaulx, seeing this huge city, my eye, which up to then had been accustomed not to marvel at the strangest things,

Was seized with amazement. What I could not like was the wonder of the common idlers, the crowd of wagoners, the lawsuits, and the mud.

Devaulx: has not been identified

137

Sceve, je me trouvay comme le filz d'Anchise
Entrant dans l'Elysee, et sortant des enfers,
Quand apres tant de monts de neige tous couvers,
Je viz ce beau Lyon, Lyon que tant je prise.

Son estroicte longueur, que la Sone divise,
Nourrit mil artisans, et peuples tous divers:
Et n'en desplaise à Londre', à Venise, et Anvers,
Car Lyon n'est pas moindre en fait de marchandise.

Je m'estonnay d'y voir passer tant de courriers,
D'y voir tant de banquiers, d'imprimeurs, d'armuriers,
Plus dru que lon ne voit les fleurs par les prairies.

Mais je m'estonnay plus de la force des pontz,
Dessus lesquelz on passe, allant dela les montz,
Tant de belles maisons, et tant de metairies.

138

De-vaulx, la mer reçoit tous les fleuves du monde,
Et n'en augmente point: semblable à la grand' mer
Est ce Paris sans pair, où lon voit abysmer
Tout ce qui là dedans de toutes parts abonde.

Paris est en sçavoir une Grece feconde,
Une Rome en grandeur Paris on peult nommer,
Une Asie en richesse on le peult estimer,
En rares nouveautez une Afrique seconde.

Bref, en voyant (De-vaulx) ceste grande cité,
Mon œil, qui paravant estoit exercité
A ne s'esmerveiller des choses plus estranges,

Print esbaissement. Ce qui ne me peut plaire,
Ce fut l'estonnement du badaud populaire,
La presse des chartiers, les procez, et les fanges.

139

Si tu veuls vivre en court (Dilliers) souvienne-toy,
De t'accoster tousjours des mignons de ton maistre,
Si tu n'es favori, faire semblant de l'estre,
Et de t'accommoder aux passetemps du Roy. 4

Souvienne-toy encor' de ne prester ta foy
Au parler d'un chacun, mais sur tout sois adextre
A t'aider de la gauche, autant que de la dextre,
Et par les mœurs d'autruy à tes mœurs donne loy. 8

N'avance rien du tien (Dilliers) que ton service,
Ne monstre que tu sois trop ennemy du vice,
Et sois souvent encor' muet, aveugle, et sourd. 11

Ne fay que pour autruy importun on te nomme.
Faisant ce que je dy, tu seras galland homme:
T'en souvienne (Dilliers) si tu veuls vivre en court. 14

140

Si tu veuls seurement en court te maintenir,
Le silence (Ronsard) te soit comme un decret.
Qui baille à son amy la clef de son secret,
Le fait de son amy son maistre devenir. 4

Tu dois encor' (Ronsard) ce me semble, tenir
Aveq' ton ennemy quelque moyen discret,
Et faisant contre luy, monstrer qu'à ton regret
Le seul devoir te fait en ces termes venir. 8

Nous voyons bien souvent une longue amitié
Se changer pour un rien en fiere inimitié,
Et la haine en amour souvent se transformer, 11

Dont (veu le temps qui court) il ne fault s'esbaïr.
Ayme donques (Ronsard) comme pouvant haïr,
Haïs donques (Ronsard) comme pouvant aymer. 14

139

If you want to live at court, Dilliers, remember always to keep your master's mignons on your side. If you are not a favorite, pretend to be one and to fit yourself to the king's pastimes.

Remember, too, not to believe what anyone says, but above all be adroit at using your left hand as much as your right, and rule your manners by the manners of others.

Lend nothing of your own, Dilliers, except your service. Do not show that you are too much the enemy of vice. And also be often mute, blind, and deaf.

Do nothing that would get you labeled as tiresome to others. Doing what I say, you will be a man of honor. Remember it, Dilliers, if you want to live at court.

If you want: the first of a series of sonnets that satirically examine the difficulties of living at the royal court

140

If you want to keep yourself safely at court, let silence, Ronsard, be your law. He who gives his friend the key to his secret makes his friend his master.

You must also, Ronsard, maintain, it seems to me, some discreet contact with your enemy, and in acting against him show that, to your regret, duty alone makes you behave in this way.

We very often see a long friendship change for a trifle into fierce enmity, and hate often change to love.

At this (seeing what the times are like) one must not be amazed. Then love, Ronsard, as though you could hate. Then hate, Ronsard, as though you could love.

141

Friend, I will teach you (though on your own you are wise enough to give yourself advice) how to prevent your poems ever getting you into trouble and what you need most to avoid in your writing.

If you ever speak of God or of the king, make sure to be cautious and sober in your language. Speaking too much of God often brings harm, and princes and kings have a long reach.

Do not attach yourself to anyone who can, if his anger ignites him, avenge with a sword thrust a small stroke of the pen, but press (as they say) your finger to your lips.

Those whom you see fainting with laughter at your witty remarks will be the first to make fun of you if some insulting madman challenges you.

Friend: repeats much of the advice from du Bellay's Latin epigram "Satyram periculosiss. esse genus scribendi, ad Marinum" (*Poemata* 2.21)

142

Cousin, always speak of vices in general and never talk business at dinner. But above all watch out not to be too truthful, especially if you speak of someone in particular.

Do not entrust your secret to the discretion of just anyone. Say nothing that does not at least seem plausible. If you lie, let it be for something profitable and which does not put anyone's honor in question.

Above all keep from being duplicitous in words, and do not, without a good reason, use frivolous wit to acquire a reputation as a good courtier.

Hidden art is true art. The mouse often dies from leaving a trail, and often the artisan goes wrong by showing his art.

Cousin: may be the humanist Gilbert Cousin, the attorney of Anne de Montmorency, Guillaume Cousin, or the artist Jean Cousin, but may also be a simple term of familiarity

141

Amy, je t'apprendray (encores que tu sois
Pour te donner conseil, de toymesme assez sage)
Comme jamais tes vers ne te feront oultrage,
Et ce qu'en tes escriptz plus eviter tu dois. 4

Si de Dieu, ou du Roy tu parles quelquefois,
Fay que tu sois prudent, et sobre en ton langage:
Le trop parler de Dieu porte souvent dommage,
Et longues sont les mains des Princes et des Rois. 8

Ne t'attache à qui peult, si sa fureur l'allume,
Vanger d'un coup d'espee un petit traict de plume,
Mais presse (comme on dit) ta levre avec le doy. 11

Ceulx que de tes bons motz tu vois pasmer de rire,
Si quelque oultrageux fol t'en veult faire desdire,
Ce seront les premiers à se mocquer de toy. 14

142

Cousin, parle tousjours des vices en commun,
Et ne discours jamais d'affaires à la table,
Mais sur tout garde toy d'estre trop veritable,
Si en particulier tu parles de quelqu'un. 4

Ne commets ton secret à la foy d'un chacun,
Ne dy rien qui ne soit pour le moins vray-semblable:
Si tu ments, que ce soit pour chose profitable,
Et qui ne tourne point au deshonneur d'aucun. 8

Sur tout garde toy bien d'estre double en paroles,
Et n'use sans propoz de finesses frivoles,
Pour acquerir le bruit d'estre bon courtisan. 11

L'artifice caché c'est le vray artifice:
La souris bien souvent perit par son indice,
Et souvent par son art se trompe l'artisan. 14

143

Bizet, j'aymerois mieulx faire un bœuf d'un formy,
Ou faire d'une mousche un Indique elephant,
Que le bon heur d'autruy par mes vers estoufant,
Me faire d'un chacun le publiq ennemy.

Souvent pour un bon mot on perd un bon amy,
Et tel par ses bons motz croit (tant il est enfant)
S'estre mis sur la teste un chapeau triomphant,
A qui mieulx eust valu estre bien endormy.

La louange (Bizet) est facile à chacun,
Mais la satyre n'est un ouvrage commun:
C'est, trop plus qu'on ne pense, un œuvre industrieux.

Il n'est rien si fascheux qu'un brocard mal plaisant,
Et fault bien (comme on dit) bien dire en mesdisant,
Veu que le loüer mesme est souvent odieux.

144

Gordes, je sçaurois bien faire un conte à la table,
Et s'il estoit besoing, contrefaire le sourd:
J'en sçaurois bien donner, et faire à quelque lourd,
Le vray ressembler faulx, et le faulx veritable.

Je me sçaurois bien rendre à chacun accointable,
Et façonner mes mœurs aux mœurs du temps qui court,
Je sçaurois bien prester (comme on dit à la court)
Aupres d'un grand seigneur quelque œuvre charitable.

Je sçaurois bien encor, pour me mettre en avant,
Vendre de la fumee à quelque poursuivant,
Et pour estre employé en quelque bon affaire,

Me feindre plus ruzé cent fois que je ne suis:
Mais ne le voulant point (Gordes) je ne le puis,
Et si ne blasme point ceulx qui le sçavent faire.

143

Bizet, I would rather make an ox of an ant or make an Indian elephant of a fly than make myself the public enemy of everyone by stifling other people's happiness with my verse.

Often for a witty word one loses a good friend, and he who childishly thinks that by his witty remarks he has crowned himself with laurel would have been better off had he been sound asleep.

Praise, Bizet, is easy for everyone. But a satire is not an ordinary accomplishment. It is, far more than is thought, a task that demands hard work.

There is nothing as tedious as a taunt that falls flat, and in speaking ill you must (as they say) speak well, seeing that even praise is often loathsome.

---

an ox of an ant/an Indian elephant of a fly: proverbial phrases for excessive praise

144

Gordes, I could easily spin a yarn in company and, if it were necessary, pretend to be deaf. I could easily take someone in and make the truth appear false and falsity true to the eyes of some dull-witted fellow.

I could easily make myself agreeable to everyone and shape my manners after the manners in vogue. I could easily "lend" (as they say at court) some charitable work to a great lord.

I could also easily sell smoke to some suitor to push myself forward and, to be employed in some promising affair,

Pretend to be a hundred times more sly than I am. But since I do not want to do it, Gordes, I cannot. Yet I do not blame those who can.

145

You are deceived, Belleau, if you think that for being learned, learned and virtuous, you are admired. You must (as they say) be an enterprising man if you wish to advance at court.

Those fine names of virtue are nothing but wind. Then, if you are wise, embrace dissembling, ignorance, envy, and covetousness. By these arts, one very often mounts to the heavens.

In company lords prize knowledge, but in their private quarters, Belleau, it makes them laugh. Avoid, if you trust me, getting a reputation for it.

A man who is too virtuous displeases ordinary men. And is he not altogether foolish who, trying to please, seeks a profession that everyone flees?

146

Often we ourselves wrong our own work, even when we are among those who are most able, either by sometimes following the ancients too closely or by too much imitating those of our own time.

We very often discourage princes who would be our benefactors, making ourselves obnoxious either by being too importunate in our demands or by insulting others in praising ourselves too much.

And then we complain to see our efforts deprived of applause, of grace, and of favor and of everything we wish for our work.

In short, let anyone who so wishes praise his art and his craft. But he, Morel, is not a bad workman who, without being mad, can be a good poet.

145

Tu t'abuses (Belleau) si pour estre sçavant,
Sçavant et vertueux, tu penses qu'on te prise:
Il fault (comme lon dit) estre homme d'entreprise,
Si tu veulx qu'à la court on te pousse en avant.

Ces beaux noms de vertu, ce n'est rien que du vent:
Donques, si tu es sage, embrasse la feintise,
L'ignorance, l'envie, avec la couvoitise:
Par ces artz jusqu'au ciel on monte bien souvent.

La science à la table est des seigneurs prisee,
Mais en chambre (Belleau) elle sert de risee:
Garde, si tu m'en crois, d'en acquerir le bruit.

L'homme trop vertueux desplait au populaire:
Et n'est-il pas bien fol, qui s'efforceant de plaire,
Se mesle d'un mestier, que tout le monde fuit?

146

Souvent nous faisons tort nous mesme' à nostre ouvrage,
Encor' que nous soyons de ceulx qui font le mieulx:
Soit par trop quelquefois contrefaire les vieux,
Soit par trop imiter ceulx qui sont de nostre aage.

Nous ostons bien souvent aux princes le courage
De nous faire du bien: nous rendant odieux,
Soit pour en demandant estre trop ennuyeux,
Soit pour trop nous loüant aux autres faire oultrage.

Et puis nous nous plaignons de voir nostre labeur
Veuf d'applaudissement, de grace, et de faveur,
Et de ce que chacun à son œuvre souhette.

Bref, loüe qui vouldra son art, et son mestier,
Mais cestui-là (Morel) n'est pas mauvais ouvrier,
Lequel sans estre fol, peult estre bon poëte.

147

Ne te fasche (Ronsard) si tu vois par la France
Fourmiller tant d'escriptz. Ceulx qui ont merité
D'estre advoüez pour bons de la posterité,
Portent leurt sauf-conduit, et lettre d'asseurance. 4

Tout œuvre qui doit vivre, il a dès sa naissance
Un Demon qui le guide à l'immortalité:
Mais qui n'a rencontré telle nativité,
Comme un fruict abortif, n'a jamais accroissance. 8

Virgile eut ce Demon, et l'eut Horace encor,
Et tous ceulx qui du temps de ce bon siecle d'or
Estoient tenuz pour bons: les autres n'ont plus vie. 11

Qu'eussions-nous leurs escriptz, pour voir de nostre temps
Ce qui aux anciens servoit de passetemps,
Et quelz estoient les vers d'un indocte Mevie. 14

148

Autant comme lon peult en un autre langage
Une langue exprimer, autant que la nature
Par l'art se peult monstrer, et que par la peinture
On peult tirer au vif un naturel visage: 4

Autant exprimes-tu, et encor d'avantage,
Aveques le pinceau de ta docte escriture,
La grace, la façon, le port, et la stature
De celuy, qui d'Enee a descript le voyage. 8

Ceste mesme candeur, ceste grace divine,
Ceste mesme doulceur, et majesté Latine
Qu'en ton Virgile on voit, c'est celle mesme encore, 11

Qui Françoise se rend par ta celeste veine.
Des-Masures sans plus a faulte d'un Mecene,
Et d'un autre Cesar, qui ses vertuz honnore. 14

147

Do not be annoyed, Ronsard, to see such a swarm of writings multiplying in France. Those worthy to be acknowledged as good by posterity carry their safe-conduct and letter of introduction.

Every work destined to live has from its birth a daemon that guides it to immortality. But any that has not enjoyed such a birth, like a stillborn child, never grows.

Virgil had that daemon, and Horace had it too, and all those who were thought good at the time of that good golden age. The others no longer live.

Would that we had their writings so as to see in our own time what served the ancients as diversions and what were the poems of an ignorant Maevius.

Do not be annoyed: response to Ronsard's "Élégie à Chretophle de Choiseul" (1556), where Ronsard complains of the proliferation of bad poetry in France

a daemon: a divinity, guardian spirit, or genius

Maevius: a minor Augustan poet mocked by Virgil and Horace

148

As much as one can express one language in another, as much as nature can be represented by art, and by painting one can bring to life a face from nature,

So much and still more you express with the brush of your learned writing the grace, the manners, the bearing, and the stature of the man who described the voyage of Aeneas.

That same candor, that divine grace, that same Latin sweetness and majesty that we see in your Virgil is exactly that

Which becomes French by means of your heavenly inspiration. Des Masures lacks only a Maecenas and another Caesar to honor his virtues.

Des Masures: Louis des Masures, French translator of Virgil's *Aeneid*

Maecenas and . . . Caesar: the patron and the imperial protector of Virgil

149

You courtiers say, "Poets are mad," and you speak the truth. But I also dare say that, such as you are, you have something of that sweet disposition which is shared by all.

But, gentlemen, the madness that governs you manifests itself differently, in other behavior. We are mad in rhyme, and you in prose. That is the only difference between you and us.

True it is that the court is more favorable to you, but your fame is not so lasting. You have greater honors, and we fewer cares.

If you laugh at us, we do the same. But that which is spoken flies by the ear, and that which is written is not so easily lost.

---

spoken . . . written: echoes the familiar Latin proverb *verba volant, scripta manent*

150

My lord, I could not approve those old court apes who can do nothing but mimic princes in their way of walking and who dress, like them, in magnificent clothes.

If their master scoffs, they will do the same. If he lies, they are not the ones who will say the opposite. Sooner, in order to please him, will they have seen the moon at high noon and at midnight the sun.

If in their presence someone gets a favorable glance, they rush to caress him, though they are bursting with anger. If he gets an unfavorable look, they make fun of him.

But what most vexes me about them is when in the king's presence, with a hypocritical expression, they start laughing and do not know why.

149

Vous dictes (Courtisans) les Poëtes sont fouls,
Et dictes verité: mais aussi dire j'ose,
Que telz que vous soiez, vous tenez quelque chose,
De ceste doulce humeur qui est commune à tous.

Mais celle-là (Messieurs) qui domine sur vous,
En autres actions diversement s'expose:
Nous sommes fouls en rime, et vous l'estes en prose:
C'est le seul different qu'est entre vous et nous.

Vray est que vous avez la court plus favorable,
Mais aussi n'avez vous un renom si durable:
Vous avez plus d'honneurs, et nous moins de souci.

Si vous riez de nous, nous faisons la pareille:
Mais cela qui se dit s'en vole par l'oreille,
Et cela qui s'escript, ne se perd pas ainsi.

150

Seigneur, je ne sçaurois regarder d'un bon œil
Ces vieux Singes de court, qui ne sçavent rien faire,
Sinon en leur marcher les Princes contrefaire,
Et se vestir, comme eulx, d'un pompeux appareil.

Si leur maistre se mocque, ilz feront le pareil,
S'il ment, ce ne sont-eulx, qui diront du contraire,
Plustot auront-ilz veu, à fin de luy complaire,
La Lune en plein midi, à minuict le Soleil.

Si quelqu'un devant eulx reçoit un bon visage,
Ilz le vont caresser, bien qu'ilz crevent de rage,
S'il le reçoit mauvais, ilz le monstrent au doy.

Mais ce qui plus contre eulx quelquefois me despite,
C'est quand devant le Roy, d'un visage hypocrite,
Ilz se prennent à rire, et ne sçavent pourquoy.

151

Je ne te prie pas de lire mes escripts,
Mais je te prie bien qu'ayant fait bonne chere,
Et joué toute nuict aux dez, à la premiere,
Et au jeu que Venus t'a sur tous mieulx appris,

Tu ne viennes icy desfacher tes esprits,
Pour te mocquer des vers que je metz en lumiere,
Et que de mes escripts la leçon coustumiere,
Par faulte d'entretien, ne te serve de riz.

Je te priray encor', quiconques tu puisse' estre,
Qui brave de la langue, et foible de la dextre,
De blesser mon renom te monstres tousjours prest,

Ne mesdire de moy: ou prendre patience,
Si ce que ta bonté me preste en conscience,
Tu te le vois par moy rendre à double interest.

152

Si mes escripts (Ronsard) sont semez de ton loz,
Et si le mien encor tu ne dedaignes dire,
D'estre encloz en mes vers ton honneur ne desire,
Et par là je ne cherche en tes vers estre encloz.

Laissons donc je te pry laissons causer ces sotz,
Et ces petitz gallandz, qui ne sachant que dire,
Disent, voyant Ronsard, et Bellay s'entr'escrire,
Que ce sont deux muletz, qui se grattent le doz.

Noz louanges (Ronsard) ne font tort à personne:
Et quelle loy defend que l'un à l'autre en donne,
Si les amis entre eulx des presens se font bien?

On peult comme l'argent trafiquer la louange,
Et les louanges sont comme lettres de change,
Dont le change et le port (Ronsard) ne couste rien.

151

I do not ask you to read my writings, but I do ask that, having eaten well and played all night at dice, at cards, and at the game Venus has taught you better than any other,

You not come here to relieve the tedium of your mind by making fun of the poems I bring to light and that, through your lack of experience, the simple reading of my writings not give you an excuse to laugh.

I will also ask you, whoever you may be—you who, bold with your tongue and weak with your right arm, are always ready to injure my reputation—

Not to slander me, or else to bear it patiently if you see that I give back with double interest what your goodness so conscientiously bestows on me.

152

If my writings, Ronsard, are strewn with your praise and if you, too, do not disdain to praise me, your reputation does not seek to be enclosed in my poems and I likewise do not seek to be enclosed in yours.

Then let us leave, I pray you, let us leave those fools to prate and those petty gallants who, short of wit, declare, when they see Ronsard and Bellay writing of each other, that we are two mules scratching each other's backs.

Our praises, Ronsard, wrong no one. And what law forbids us to praise one another, if between themselves friends commonly exchange gifts?

One can trade in praise as in money, and praises are like bills of exchange, whose brokerage and transport, Ronsard, cost nothing.

---

two mules scratching each other's backs: from the Latin proverb *asinus asinum fricat*

153

They give degrees to the learned student; they give titles to the man of law; they give courtiers a rich benefice; and to the good commander they give the chain of a knightly order.

They give spoils to the brave adventurer; they give the officeholder the rights of his office; they give the servant the wages of his service; and to the learned poet they give the laurel.

Why then do you make Calliope complain so of the slight reward granted her gentle troop? One must, Jodelle, one must choose other work

Than that of the Muse if one wants to get ahead. For what payment do you expect from your pleasure, since pleasure is itself its own reward?

Calliope: the Muse of heroic poetry

Jodelle: Étienne Jodelle (1532–1573), poet, playwright, and member of the Pléiade

154

If you believe me, Baïf, you will trade Parnassus for the courthouse, Helicon for the bar, your laurel for a lawyer's briefcase, and your lyre for the chattering of those whose hands never tire of grasping.

It is in that profession that one piles up wealth, not in that of verse, where there is less profit than in the calling of a fool or a lackey. Fie on pleasure, Baïf, that brings no profit!

Let us then, I pray you, leave those loquacious sisters, that talkative Apollo, and those vain joys, that have as their only reward nothing but green laurels.

Today the great have their ears wide open to money matters or things that make them laugh. But to poetry their ears are locked shut.

---

those loquacious sisters: the Muses

153

On donne les degrez au sçavant escolier,
On donne les estatz à l'homme de justice,
On donne au courtisan le riche benefice,
Et au bon capitaine on donne le collier:

On donne le butin au brave avanturier,
On donne à l'officier les droits de son office,
On donne au serviteur le gaing de son service,
Et au docte poëte on donne le laurier.

Pourquoy donc fais-tu tant lamenter Calliope
Du peu de bien qu'on fait à sa gentile troppe?
Il fault (Jodelle) il fault autre labeur choisir,

Que celuy de la Muse, à qui veult qu'on l'avance:
Car quel loyer veuls-tu avoir de ton plaisir,
Puis que le plaisir mesme en est la recompense?

154

Si tu m'en crois (Baïf) tu changeras Parnasse
Au palais de Paris, Helicon au parquet,
Ton laurier en un sac, et ta lyre au caquet
De ceulx qui pour serrer, la main n'ont jamais lasse.

C'est à ce mestier là, que les biens on amasse,
Non à celuy des vers: où moins y a d'acquêt,
Qu'au mestier d'un boufon, ou celuy d'un naquet,
Fy du plaisir (Baïf) qui sans profit se passe.

Laissons donq, je te pry, ces babillardes Sœurs,
Ce causeur Apollon, et ces vaines doulceurs,
Qui pour tout leur tresor n'ont que des lauriers verds.

Au choses de profit, ou celles qui font rire,
Les grands ont aujourdhuy les oreilles de cire,
Mais ilz les ont de fer, pour escouter les vers.

155

Thiard, qui as changé en plus grave escritture
Ton doulx stile amoureux, Thiard, qui nous as fait
D'un Petrarque un Platon, et si rien plus parfait
Se trouve que Platon, en la mesme nature:

Qui n'admire du ciel la belle architecture,
Et de tout ce qu'on voit les causes et l'effect,
Celuy vrayement doit estre un homme contrefait,
Lequel n'a rien d'humain, que la seule figure.

Contemplons donq (Thiard) ceste grand' voulte ronde,
Puis que nous sommes faits à l'exemple du monde:
Mais ne tenons les yeux si attachez en hault,

Que pour ne les baisser quelquefois vers la terre,
Nous soions en danger par le hurt d'une pierre
De nous blesser le pied, ou de prendre le sault.

156

Par ses vers Teïens Belleau me fait aymer
Et le vin et l'amour: Baïf, ta challemie
Me fait plus qu'une royne une rustique amie,
Et plus qu'une grand' ville un village estimer.

Le docte Pelletier fait mes flancz emplumer,
Pour voler jusqu'au ciel avec son Uranie:
Et par l'horrible effroy d'une estrange armonie
Ronsard de pié en cap hardy me fait armer.

Mais je ne sçay comment ce Demon de Jodelle
(Demon est-il vrayment, car d'une voix mortelle
Ne sortent point ses vers) tout soudain que je l'oy,

M'aiguillonne, m'espoingt, m'espoüante, m'affolle,
Et comme Apollon fait de sa prestresse folle,
A moymesmes m'ostant, me ravit tout à soy.

155

Thiard, you who have exchanged your sweet amorous style for graver writing; Thiard, you who have made us a Plato of a Petrarch and whatever in that vein may be more perfect than Plato,

He who does not wonder at the beautiful architecture of the heavens and at the causes and the effect of all that we see, must truly be a counterfeit man with nothing human about him but his appearance alone.

Let us then contemplate, Thiard, that great round vault, since we are made in the image of the world. But let us not keep our eyes so fixed on high

That, for not lowering them sometimes toward the earth, we are in danger of stubbing our toe on a stone or taking a tumble.

Thiard: Pontus de Thiard or Tyard (1521–1605), poet, philosopher, and theologian, whose shift to "graver writing" du Bellay imitates by moving from satire to the poetry of praise in this and the remaining poems of the *Regrets*

but let us not: alludes to the story of Thales of Miletus who gazed at the stars and fell into a well

156

With his Teian verses Belleau makes me love both wine and love. Baïf, your rustic song makes me prefer a country love to a queen and a village to a great city.

Learned Peletier makes me sprout wings to fly to the heavens with his Urania, and with the terrible fright of a strange harmony, Ronsard makes me bravely arm myself from head to toe.

But I know not how, as soon as I hear him, that daemon of Jodelle's (a daemon he truly is, for his verse does not spring from a mortal voice),

Goads me, pricks me, terrifies me, maddens me, and, as Apollo does to his mad priestess, stealing me away from myself, makes me all his.

Teian: of Teos, the birthplace of the Greek poet Anacreon, whose work Belleau translated

rustic song: alludes to Baïf's Quatre livres de l'amour de Francine

his Urania: alludes to Peletier's "Urania"

Ronsard: may allude to one of Ronsard's poems of heroic admonition, such as his "Exortation. Au camp du Roy Henry II"

that daemon of Jodelle's: Jodelle claimed that a personal spirit or daemon inspired his verse

his mad priestess: the Cumaean Sibyl in book 6 of Virgil's Aeneid

157

While, Clagny, with a thousand plans that transform the design of the royal edifice, you renew with a bold facade the august grandeur of the oldest monuments,

With other compasses and other instruments, fleeing ambition, envy, and avarice, I construct for the Muses, with a new artfulness, a magnificent palace made up of four apartments.

The Latins will have a Doric work that fits their gravity; the Greeks an Attic one for their naturalness; the French will have

For their grave sweetness an Ionian work; work done in the Corinthian style will complete the quarters where the Tuscans will be.

Clagny: Pierre Lescot (1515–1578), lord of Clagny, the architect of the Louvre

158

In this royal palace that will be built by my hands, if the goodness of the king supplies me material, to make its greatness and beauty more complete the ornaments will be Turkish bows and arrows.

There all our kings will be seen in order side by side. There will be seen many fleeting fauns and nymphs. Over the portal will be the virgin of the woods with her crescent, her bow, and her quiver.

The first apartment will be dedicated to Homer; to Virgil the second; the third to Petrarch; by the name of Ronsard the fourth will be called.

Each will have its own form and architecture, each its own decorations, its elegance, and its painting. And in each, Clagny, your fair name will be read.

---

the virgin of the woods: the goddess Diana, an allusion to Diane de Poitiers (1499–1566), the mistress of King Henry II

157

En-cependant (Clagny) que de mil argumens
Variant le desseing du royal edifice,
Tu vas renouvelant d'un hardy frontispice
La superbe grandeur des plus vieux monumens,

Avec d'autres compaz, et d'autres instrumens
Fuiant l'ambition, l'envie, et l'avarice,
Aux Muses je bastis d'un nouvel artifice
Un palais magnifique à quatre appartemens.

Les Latines auront un ouvrage Dorique
Propre à leur gravité, les Greques un Attique
Pour leur naifveté, les Françoises auront

Pour leur grave doulçeur une œuvre Ionienne,
D'ouvrage elabouré à la Corinthienne
Sera le corps d'hostel, où les Thusques seront.

158

De ce Royal palais, que bastiront mes doigts,
Si la bonté du Roy me fournit de matiere,
Pour rendre sa grandeur et beauté plus entiere,
Les ornemens seront de traicts et d'arcs turquois.

Là d'ordre flanc à flanc se voyront tous noz Roys,
Là se voyra maint Faune, et Nymphe passagere,
Sur le portail sera la Vierge forestiere,
Aveques son croissant, son arc, et son carquois.

L'appartement premier Homere aura pour marque,
Virgile le second, le troisieme Petrarque,
Du surnom de Ronsard le quatrieme on dira.

Chacun aura sa forme et son architecture,
Chacun ses ornemens, sa grace et sa peincture,
Et en chacun (Clagny) ton beau nom se lira.

159

De vostre Dianet (de vostre nom j'apelle
Vostre maison d'Anet) la belle architecture,
Les marbres animez, la vivante peincture,
Qui la font estimer des maisons la plus belle:

Les beaux lambriz dorez, la luisante chappelle,
Les superbes dongeons, la riche couverture,
Le jardin tapissé d'eternelle verdure,
Et la vive fonteine à la source immortelle:

Ces ouvrages (Madame) à qui bien les contemple,
Rapportant de l'antiq' le plus parfait exemple,
Monstrent un artifice, et despence admirable.

Mais ceste grand' doulceur jointe à cette haultesse,
Et cet Astre benin joint à ceste sagesse,
Trop plus que tout cela vous font esmerveillable.

160

Entre tous les honneurs, dont en France est cogneu
Ce renommé Bertran, des moindres n'est celuy
Que luy donne la Muse, et qu'on dise de luy,
Que par luy un Salel soit riche devenu.

Toy donc à qui la France a des-ja retenu
L'un de ses plus beaux lieux, comme seul aujourdhuy
Où les arts ont fondé leur principal appuy,
Quant au lieu qui t'attend tu seras parvenu:

Fay que de ta grandeur ton Magny se resente,
A fin que si Bertran de son Salel se vante,
Tu te puisses aussi de ton Magny vanter.

Tous deux sont Quercinois, tous deux bas de stature,
Et ne seroient pas moins semblables d'escriture,
Si Salel avoit sceu plus doulcement chanter.

159

The beautiful architecture of your Dianet (with your name, I refer to your house in Anet), the lifelike statues, the lively painting, for which it is judged the most beautiful of houses,

The handsome gilded paneling, the radiant chapel, the august towers, the garden carpeted with everlasting greenery, and the living fountain flowing from an undying spring,

These works, madam, which offer him who studies them well the most perfect model of antiquity, show an admirable artfulness and ordering.

But, far more than all this, your great sweetness joined with your eminence, and your propitious star joined with your wisdom make you a wonder.

Dianet: a pun on the name of Diane de Poitiers, to whom this poem is addressed, and her house in Anet (d'Anet)

160

Among all the honors for which the famous Bertrand is known in France, the least is not that which the Muse gives him and that they say that by him a Salel became rich.

You therefore, for whom France has already reserved one of her most eminent places, as he on whom alone the arts today have founded their chief support, when you have reached the place which awaits you,

Let your Magny feel the effects of your greatness, so that if Bertrand boasts of his Salel, you also can boast of your Magny.

Both are from Quercy, both are short, and they would be no less similar in their writing had Salel been able to sing more sweetly.

Bertrand: Jean Bertrand, prelate, future cardinal, and patron of the poet Hugues Salel

You therefore: Jean de Saint-Marcel, lord of Avanson, to whom du Bellay's *Regrets* are dedicated

161

Prelate, to whom the heavens have given the good fortune to be pleasing to kings; prelate, whose prudence in ascending through the degrees of honor has shown that God intended you for the public good;

Prelate, above all prelates wise and fortunate; prelate, keeper of the laws and the seals of France, worthy that on your loyalty rests the confidence of a king, the greatest king ever crowned.

Even before I saw you, I honored your wisdom, your knowledge, your virtue, your greatness, your generosity, and whatever else in this world merits still greater honor.

But now that I have experienced your unequaled goodness, which has often so kindly lent me your ear, I hope one day to worship you.

Prelate: Jean Bertrand
a king: Henry II

162

After building himself an eternal monument on the walls of Carthage, Scipio, angered to see his city ungrateful for his virtue, exiled himself of his own volition to a small village.

You have done, Olivier, what Scipio did in his adversity, but with still greater courage, leaving the court, in the midst of your success, to live on your own the rest of your life.

The fame of Scipio drew many a privateer to gaze on him whom everyone admired, though he had retired to his little Liternum.

People do the same with you, admiring your virtue for leaving the court and that headstrong monster, the vulgar multitude that resembles the Lernaean beast.

Olivier: François Olivier (1487–1560), the former chancellor of France

the Lernaean beast: the Hydra, whose many heads are punningly evoked in du Bellay's *testu* (headstrong)

161

Prelat, à qui les cieulx ce bon heur ont donné
D'estre aggreable aux Roys, Prelat dont la prudence
Par les degrez d'honneur a mis en evidence,
Que pour le bien publiq' Dieu t'avoit ordonné.

Prelat, sur tous prelatz sage, et bien fortuné,
Prelat garde des loix, et des seaulx de la France,
Digne que sur ta foy repose l'asseurance
D'un Roy le plus grand Roy qui fut onq couronné:

Devant que t'avoir veu j'honnorois ta sagesse,
Ton sçavoir, ta vertu, ta grandeur, ta largesse,
Et si rien entre nous se doit plus honnorer:

Mais ayant esprouvé ta bonté nompareille,
Qui souvent m'a presté si doulcement l'oreille,
Je souhaite qu'un jour je te puisse adorer.

162

Apres s'estre basty sus les murs de Carthage
Un sepulchre eternel, Scipion irrité
De voir à sa vertu ingrate sa cité,
Se banit de soymesme en un petit village.

Tu as fait (Olivier) mais d'un plus grand courage,
Ce que fit Scipion en son adversité,
Laissant durant le cours de ta felicité
La court, pour vivre à toy le reste de ton aage.

Le bruit de Scipion maint coursaire attiroit
Pour contempler celuy que chacun admiroit,
Bien qu'il fust retiré en son petit Linterne.

On te fait le semblable: admirant ta vertu,
D'avoir laissé la court, et ce monstre testu,
Ce peuple qui ressemble à la beste de Lerne.

163

Il ne fault point (Duthier) pour mettre en evidence
Tant de belles vertus qui reluisent en toy,
Que je te rende icy l'honneur que je te doy,
Celebrant ton sçavoir, ton sens, et ta prudence,

Le bruit de ta vertu est tel, que l'ignorance
Ne le peult ignorer: et qui loüe le Roy,
Il fault qu'il loüe encor' ta prudence, et ta foy:
Car ta gloire est conjointe à la gloire de France.

Je diray seulement que depuis noz ayeux
La France n'a point veu un plus laborieux
En sa charge que toy, et qu'autre ne se treuve

Plus courtois, plus humain, ne qui ait plus de soing
De secourir l'amy à son plus grand besoing.
J'en parle seurement, car j'en ay fait l'espreuve.

164

Combien que ton Magny ait la plume si bonne,
Si prendrois-je avec luy de tes vertus le soing,
Sachant que Dieu, qui n'a de noz presens besoing,
Demande les presens de plus d'une personne.

Je dirois ton beau nom, qui de luy mesme sonne
Ton bruit parmy la France, en Itale, et plus loing:
Et dirois que Henry est luymesmes tesmoing,
Combien un Avanson avance sa couronne.

Je dirois ta bonté, ta justice, et ta foy,
Et mille autres vertus qui reluisent en toy,
Dignes qu'un seul Ronsard les sacre à la Memoire:

Mais sentant le soucy qui me presse le doz,
Indigne je me sens de toucher à ton loz,
Sachant que Dieu ne veult qu'on prophane sa gloire.

163

To display the many great virtues that shine forth in you, there is no need, Duthier, for me to declare the honor I owe you, celebrating your knowledge, your good sense, and your prudence.

The fame of your virtue is such that ignorance itself cannot ignore it. And whoever praises the king must also praise your prudence and your loyalty, for your glory is linked to the glory of France.

I will say only that from the time of our ancestors France has never seen anyone more devoted in his charge than you and that no other can be found

More courtly, more humane, nor who is more concerned to help a friend in his greatest need. I speak of this with assurance, for I have experienced it at first hand.

164

Though your Magny has an excellent pen, yet would I still join him in the praise of your virtues, knowing that God, who has no need of our gifts, demands gifts from more than one person.

I would pronounce your glorious name, which of itself sounds your fame throughout France, in Italy, and beyond, and would say that Henry is himself witness to how an Avanson advances his crown.

I would speak of your goodness, your justice, and your loyalty, and of a thousand other virtues that shine in you, worthy that none but a Ronsard consecrate them to Memory.

But feeling the care that weighs on my back, I feel myself unworthy to touch on your praise, knowing that God does not want his glory profaned.

165

When I wish to sound the least eminent virtues of my great Avanson, on my lowest string I will speak of his fluency and the dignity of his face and say that he is the dearest nursling of the nine sisters.

When I wish to touch with a higher note on some greater virtue, I will sing his grace, his goodness, his grandeur which embraces justice. But I will not make that the end of my song,

For when I sound his glory with a still higher note, I will say that the daughters of Memory will never speak of one more wise and virtuous than he,

More devoted to his duty, more faithful to his prince, nor who better adapts himself to the reigning powers of today to serve his lord in a foreign land.

---

the daughters of Memory: the Muses

166

Though your virtue, Poulin, is known wherever the fame of the French is known and though your name extends as far abroad as the great sea extends,

It is nevertheless necessary for Bellay to strive as much as the sea to sound your virtue and for him to trumpet about you with his twisted bronze what Triton trumpets with his twisted horn.

I will say that you are the Typhus of Jason, who must depend on you to win the fleece. I will speak of your prudence and your well-known virtue.

I will speak of your power that extends over the sea and say that the marine gods favor you so greatly that the terrestrial gods envy your glory.

Poulin: Escalin Poulin, baron of La Garde, commander of the king's galleys
Typhus: the pilot of Jason's Argonauts

165

Quand je voudray sonner de mon grand Avanson
Les moins grandes vertus, sur ma chorde plus basse
Je diray sa faconde, et l'honneur de sa face,
Et qu'il est des neuf Sœurs le plus cher nourrisson.

Quand je voudray toucher avec un plus hault son
Quelque plus grand' vertu, je chanteray sa grace,
Sa bonté, sa grandeur, qui la justice embrasse,
Mais là je ne mettray le but de ma chanson.

Car quand plus hautement je sonneray sa gloire,
Je diray que jamais les filles de Memoire
Ne diront un plus sage, et vertueux que luy:

Plus prompt à son devoir, plus fidele à son Prince,
Ne qui mieulx s'accommode au regne d'aujourdhuy,
Pour servir son Seigneur en estrange province.

166

Combien que ta vertu (Poulin) soit entendue
Par tout ou des François le bruit est entendu,
Et combien que ton nom soit au large estendu
Autant que la grand' mer est au large estendue:

Si fault il toutefois que Bellay s'esvertue,
Aussi bien que la mer, de bruire ta vertu,
Et qu'il sonne de toy avec' l'ærain tortu
Ce que sonne Triton de sa trompe tortue.

Je diray que tu es le Tiphys du Jason,
Qui doit par ton moyen conquerir la toison,
Je diray ta prudence, et ta vertu notoire:

Je diray ton pouvoir qui sur la mer s'estent,
Et que les Dieux marins te favorisent tant,
Que les terrestres Dieux sont jaloux de ta gloire.

167

Sage De-l'hospital, qui seul de nostre France
Rabaisses aujourdhuy l'orgueil Italien,
Et qui nous monstres seul d'un art Horatien
Comme il fault chastier le vice et l'ignorance:

Si je voulois loüer ton sçavoir, ta prudence,
Ta vertu, ta bonté, et ce qu'est vrayment tien,
A tes perfections je n'adjousterois rien,
Et pauvre me rendroit la trop grand' abondance.

Et qui pourroit, bons dieux! faire plus digne foy
Des rares qualitez qui reluisent en toy,
Que ceste autre Pallas, ornement de nostre aage?

Ainsi jusqu'aujourdhuy, ainsi encor' voit-on
Estre tant renommé le maistre de Platon,
Pour ce qu'il eut d'un Dieu la voix pour tesmoignage.

168

Nature à vostre naistre heureusement feconde,
Prodigue vous donna tout son plus et son mieux,
Soit ceste grand' doulceur qui luit dedans voz yeux,
Soit ceste majesté disertement faconde.

Vostre rare vertu, qui n'a point de seconde,
Et vostre esprit ælé, qui voisine les cieulx,
Vous ont donné le lieu le plus prochain des Dieux,
Et la plus grand' faveur du plus grand Roy du monde.

Bref, vous avez tout seul tout ce qu'on peult avoir
De richesse, d'honneur, de grace, et de sçavoir,
Que voulez-vous donq plus esperer d'avantage?

Le libre jugement de la posterité,
Qui encor' qu'ell' assigne au ciel vostre partage,
Ne vous donnera pas ce qu'avez merité.

167

Wise de l'Hôpital, who alone from our France humbles the Italian pride and who alone shows, with a Horatian art, how one must chastise vice and ignorance.

If I wanted to praise your knowledge, your prudence, your virtue, your goodness, and what is truly yours, I would add nothing to your perfections and yet their great abundance would make me poor.

And who could—good gods!—more worthily testify to the rare qualities that shine in you than that other Pallas, the ornament of our age?

Thus, even up to the present day, Plato's master remains so famous because he had the voice of a god for witness.

---

de l'Hôpital: Michel de l'Hôpital, author of Latin poems, patron of Ronsard and other poets of the Pléiade, and future lord chancellor of France

that other Pallas: Margaret of France, the sister of the king

Plato's master: Socrates, whom the Delphic oracle proclaimed to be the wisest of men

168

Nature, happily fruitful and lavish at your birth, gave you all her finest and best, whether that great sweetness that shines in your eyes or that eloquently fluent majesty.

Your rare virtue, which has no second, and your wingèd spirit, which touches the heavens, have given you the place closest to the gods and the greatest favor of the greatest king in the world.

In short, you have all by yourself all that one can have of riches, of honor, of grace, and of knowledge. What more can you then hope for?

The free judgment of posterity, which, though it acknowledge your place in heaven, will not give you what you have deserved.

---

you: Charles de Guise, cardinal of Lorraine

will not give you: du Bellay's earlier decasyllabic version of this poem reads "will give you" (*Vous donnera*), an apparent reversal in meaning to suit the new meter

169

Fortune, prelate, wanting to demonstrate her sway over us, chose from our age him who with virtue, wit, and courage had best armed himself against her power.

But virtue, which is not accustomed to being moved, any more than a rock is moved by the storm, will overcome fortune, and will know how to supply itself with all it needs against her affliction.

As this virtue remains immutable, so the heavens change in their course from hour to hour. And so, my lord, rely in your need on yourself

And wait joyfully for the happier time that must restore your uncle and your brother to you, for heaven has taken both them and you under its care.

---

prelate: Odet de Coligny, cardinal of Châtillon

your uncle and your brother: Anne de Montmorency and Gaspard de Coligny, who were both taken captive after the battle of Saint-Quentin (1557)

170

It is not without reason that heaven bestowed on you so many beauties of mind and beauties of face, so much royal honor and royal grace, and that still more than this is promised you.

It is not without reason that friendly Fates, to deflate the pride of Spanish impudence, have decreed that, whether by right of marriage or by right of lineage, three great peoples should come under your sway.

They desire that by you France and England change into enduring peace the hereditary war that from father to son has lasted so long.

They desire that by you the beautiful virgin Astraea should return in this iron age and that we should again see the fair golden age.

---

you: Mary Stuart (1542–1587), Queen of Scots, who was to marry the future Francis II of France and was also in the line of inheritance for the English crown

Astraea: the goddess of justice, who fled earth in disgust at the iron age and whose return will restore the age of gold

169

La fortune (Prelat) nous voulant faire voir
Ce qu'elle peult sur nous, a choisi de nostre aage
Celuy qui de vertu, d'esprit, et de courage
S'estoit le mieulx armé encontre son pouvoir.

Mais la vertu qui n'est apprise à s'esmouvoir,
Non plus que le rocher se meut contre l'orage,
Dontera la fortune, et contre son outrage
De tout ce qui luy fault se sçaura bien pourvoir.

Comme ceste vertu immuable demeure,
Ainsi le cours du ciel se change d'heure en heure.
Aidez vous donq (Seigneur) de vous mesme au besoing,

Et joyeux attendez la saison plus prospere,
Qui vous doit ramener vostre oncle et vostre frere:
Car et d'eux et de vous le ciel a pris le soing.

170

Ce n'est pas sans propoz qu'en vous le ciel a mis
Tant de beautez d'esprit, et de beautez de face,
Tant de royal honneur, et de royale grace,
Et que plus que cela vous est encor promis.

Ce n'est pas sans propoz que les Destins amis
Pour rabaisser l'orgueil de l'Espagnole audace,
Soit par droit d'alliance, ou soit par droit de race,
Vous ont par leurs arrestz trois grans peuples soubmis.

Ilz veulent que par vous la France, et l'Angleterre
Changent en longue paix l'hereditaire guerre
Qui a de pere en filz si longuement duré:

Ilz veulent que par vous la belle vierge Astree
En ce Siecle de fer reface encor' entree,
Et qu'on revoye encor le beau Siecle doré.

171

Muse, qui autrefois chantas la verde olive,
Empenne tes deux flancs d'une plume nouvelle,
Et te guindant au ciel aveques plus haulte ælle,
Vole où est d'Apollon la belle plante vive.

Laisse (mon cher souci) la paternelle rive,
Et portant desormais une charge plus belle,
Adore ce hault nom, dont la gloire immortelle
De nostre pole arctiq' à l'autre pole arrive.

Loüe l'esprit divin, le courage indontable,
La courtoise doulceur, la bonté charitable,
Qui soustient la grandeur, et la gloire de France.

Et dy, ceste Princesse et si grande et si bonne,
Porte dessus son chef de France la couronne:
Mais dy cela si hault, qu'on l'entende à Florence.

172

Digne filz de Henry, nostre Hercule Gaulois,
Nostre second espoir, qui portes sus ta face
Retraicte au naturel la maternelle grace,
Et gravee en ton cœur la vertu de Vallois:

Ce pendant que le ciel, qui ja dessous tes loix
Trois peuples a soubmis, armera ton audace
D'une plus grand' vigueur, suy ton pere à la trace,
Et apprens à donter l'Espagnol, et l'Anglois.

Voicy de la vertu la penible montee,
Qui par le seul travail veult estre surmontee:
Voilà de l'autre part le grand chemin battu,

Où au sejour du vice on monte sans eschelle.
Deça (Seigneur) deça, où la vertu t'appelle,
Hercule se fit Dieu par la seule vertu.

171

Muse, you who once sang the green olive, feather your two wings with a new plume and, lofting to heaven with a higher flight, soar where the beautiful living plant of Apollo resides.

Quit, my dear care, the paternal shore and, henceforth charged with a more illustrious task, adore that high name whose undying glory stretches from our arctic pole to the other pole.

Praise the divine spirit, the unconquerable courage, the courtly sweetness, the charitable goodness, which upholds the greatness and glory of France.

And say, "This princess, so great and so good, wears on her head the crown of France." But say it so loudly that they hear it in Florence.

---

olive: the subject of du Bellay's first sonnet sequence, *L'Olive* (1549; expanded in 1550)

the beautiful living plant of Apollo: the laurel

This princess: Catherine de Médicis (1519–1589), the French queen, who came from Florence

172

Worthy son of Henry, our Gallic Hercules, our second hope, you who bear on your face, copied from nature, the grace of your mother and engraved in your heart the virtue of Valois,

While heaven, which has already made three peoples submit to your laws, arms your boldness with increased vigor, follow in the footsteps of your father and learn to tame the Spaniard and the Englishman.

Here is the arduous path of virtue that painful effort alone can climb. There on the other side is the broad and beaten way

By which, without climbing, one reaches the dwelling place of vice. Up this way, my lord, up this way, where virtue summons you, Hercules made himself a god by virtue alone.

---

son of Henry: the future Francis II (1544–1560; king of France, 1559–1560)

your mother: Catherine de Médicis

Here is the arduous path: alludes to the story of Hercules at the crossroads, forced to choose between the arduous path of virtue and the easy path of vice

173

Greek poetry proudly boasts of the praise Alexander gave Homer, and Latin poetry still sings and sings again the verses Caesar wrote about Virgil.

French poetry, which is not as learned as those two, not having its Homer and its Virgil, holds that the laurel that crowned Francis is alone enough to make it live forever.

But the poems that have given it a still greater value are yours, madam, and those divine writings that at her death the queen, your mother, left us.

O fortunate poetry, and well worthy of kings, that can boast of the writings of Navarre, which honor you more than a Virgil or Homer!

Francis: Francis I

madam: Jeanne d'Albret (1528–1572; queen of Navarre, 1555–1572)

the queen, your mother: Margaret of Navarre (1492–1549), author of the *Heptaméron*

174

Bound in the hell of its body (and that hell, madam, was my absence), for four years and more my spirit did penance for all the old transgressions with which it was sullied.

Now, praise be to the gods, now it has been released from that painful hell and, restored by your presence to the original state of its divine being, has unloaded from its back the burden of sin.

Now, with the benefit of your inestimable grace, it enjoys the repose of the beautiful Elysian Fields and has no wish ever to leave them.

Therefore, do not make it drink the water of forgetfulness, madam, for fear that, in drinking, new desire will be kindled to return again to the hell of its body.

---

madam: Margaret of France, the sister of Henry II, to whom this and the next sixteen sonnets are devoted

the water of forgetfulness: from the river Lethe in the classical underworld

173

La Grecque poësie orgueilleuse se vante
Du loz qu'à son Homere Alexandre donna,
Et les vers que Cesar de Virgile sonna,
La Latine aujourdhuy les chante et les rechante.

La Françoise qui n'est tant que ces deux sçavante
Comme qui son Homere et son Virgile n'a,
Maintient que le Laurier qui François couronna,
Baste seul pour la rendre à tout jamais vivante.

Mais les vers qui l'ont mise encor' en plus hault pris,
Sont les vostres (Madame) et ces divins escripts
Que mourant nous laissa la Royne vostre mere.

O poësie heureuse, et bien digne des Roys,
De te pouvoir vanter des escripts Navarrois,
Qui t'honnorent trop plus qu'un Virgile ou Homere!

174

Dans l'enfer de son corps mon esprit attaché
(Et cet enfer, Madame, a esté mon absence)
Quatre ans et d'avantage a fait la penitence
De tous les vieux forfaits dont il fut entaché.

Ores graces aux Dieux, ore' il est relaché
De ce penible enfer, et par vostre presence
Reduit au premier poinct de sa divine essence,
A deschargé son doz du fardeau de peché.

Ores sous la faveur de voz graces prisees,
Il jouït du repoz des beaux champs Elysees,
Et si n'a volunté d'en sortir jamais hors.

Donques, de l'eau d'oubly ne l'abbreuvez Madame,
De peur qu'en la beuvant nouveau desir l'enflamme
De retourner encor dans l'enfer de son corps.

175

Non pource qu'un grand Roy ait esté vostre pere,
Non pour vostre degré, et royale haulteur,
Chacun de vostre nom veult estre le chanteur,
Ni pource qu'un grand Roy soit ores vostre frere. 4

La nature qui est de tous commune mere,
Vous fit naistre (Madame) aveques ce grand heur,
Et ce qui accompagne une telle grandeur,
Ce sont souvent des dons de fortune prospere. 8

Ce qui vous fait ainsi admirer d'un chacun,
C'est ce qui est tout vostre, et qu'avec vous commun
N'ont tous ceulx-là qui ont couronnes sur leurs testes: 11

Ceste grace, et doulceur, et ce je ne sçay quoy,
Que quand vous ne seriez fille, ni sœur de Roy,
Si vous jugeroit-on estre ce que vous estes. 14

176

Esprit royal, qui prens de lumiere eternelle
Ta seule nourriture, et ton accroissement,
Et qui de tes beaux raiz en nostre entendement
Produis ce hault desir, qui au ciel nous r'appelle, 4

N'apperçoy-tu combien par ta vie estincelle
La vertu luit en moy? n'as-tu point sentiment
Par l'œil, l'ouïr, l'odeur, le goust, l'attouchement,
Que sans toy ne reluit chose aucune mortelle? 8

Au seul object divin de ton image pure
Se meut tout mon penser, qui par la souvenance
De ta haulte bonté tellement se r'assure, 11

Que l'ame et le vouloir ont pris mesme assurance
(Chassant tout appetit et toute vile cure)
De retourner au lieu de leur premiere essence. 14

175

Not because a great king was your father, not because of your rank and royal elevation, nor because a great king is now your brother, does everyone wish to be the singer of your name.

Nature, who is the common mother of all, gave you birth, madam, with this great blessing, and the gifts of prosperous fortune often accompany such greatness.

What makes you thus admired by all is what is entirely yours and what none of those who have crowns on their heads share with you:

That grace and sweetness and that indescribable quality that, were you neither the daughter nor the sister of a king, would make one judge you to be what you are.

176

Royal spirit, you who take from eternal light your only food and your growth and who with your glorious rays produce in our understanding that lofty desire that calls us back to heaven,

Do you not see how from your living spark virtue shines in me? Do you not sense by eye, hearing, smell, taste, touch that without you no mortal thing shines?

Toward the single divine object of your pure image all my thought moves, so reassured by the memory of your goodness

That my soul and will have even gained the confidence (banishing all desire and all common care) to return to the place of their first being.

Royal spirit: Margaret of France

177

If virtue, which is by nature immortal as the seeds of the heavens are immortal, showed herself to our eyes as to our minds, and if our dull senses were able to perceive her,

Not only those who imagine her this way and those to whom vice is an odious monster, but even the vicious themselves would be seized by her beauty, of all beauties the most beautiful.

If then virtue would be so desirable to those who could see her, Vineus, are you surprised if I have the image of my princess imprinted on my heart,

If I adore her virtue, and if with fervor I speak so often of her perfection, seeing that virtue itself is painted in her face?

---

my princess: Margaret of France

178

If, sweetly stirred with a sweet fervor, I were sometimes to use in praising my princess the terms *adore, heavenly,* or *goddess* and those titles one grants divinity,

I would not fear, Mellin, that posterity would call my Muse a flatterer, but, in thus praising her royal highness, I would fear offending her great humility.

With such honors ancient vanity used to make idols of princes and lords, but the Christian who uses those terms

Is not an idolater or a flatterer, for in giving the Creator the glory for everything, he praises the workman himself in praising his work.

---

my princess: Margaret of France
ancient vanity: alludes to the deification of Roman emperors

177

Si la vertu qui est de nature immortelle,
Comme immortelles sont les semences des cieulx,
Ainsi qu'à noz esprits, se monstroit à noz yeux,
Et noz sens hebetez estoient capables d'elle,

Non ceulx-là seulement qui l'imaginent telle,
Et ceulx ausquelz le vice est un monstre odieux,
Mais on verroit encor les mesmes vicieux
Epris de sa beauté, des beautez la plus belle.

Si tant aymable donc servoit ceste vertu
A qui la pourroit voir: Vineus, t'esbahis-tu
Si j'ay de ma Princesse au cœur l'image empreinte?

Si sa vertu j'adore, et si d'affection
Je parle si souvent de sa perfection,
Veu que la vertu mesme en son visage est peinte?

178

Quand d'une doulce ardeur doulcement agité
J'userois quelquefois en loüant ma Princesse
Des termes d'adorer, de celeste, ou deesse,
Et ces tiltres qu'on donne à la Divinité,

Je ne craindrois (Melin) que la posterité
Appellast pour cela ma Muse flateresse:
Mais en loüant ainsi sa royale haultesse,
Je craindrois d'offenser sa grande humilité.

L'antique vanité aveques telz honneurs
Souloit idolatrer les Princes et Seigneurs:
Mais le Chrestien qui met ces termes en usage,

Il n'est pas pour cela idolatre ou flateur,
Car en donnant de tout la gloire au Createur,
Il loüe l'ouvrier mesme, en loüant son ouvrage.

179

Voyant l'ambition, l'envie, et l'avarice,
La rancune, l'orgueil, le desir aveuglé,
Dont cet aage de fer de vices tout rouglé
A violé l'honneur de l'antique justice:

Voyant d'une autre part la fraude, la malice,
Le procez immortel, le droit mal conseillé:
Et voyant au milieu du vice dereiglé
Ceste royale fleur, qui ne tient rien du vice,

Il me semble (Dorat) voir au ciel revolez
Des antiques vertuz les escadrons ælez
N'ayans rien delaissé de leur saison doree

Pour reduire le monde à son premier printemps,
Fors ceste Marguerite, honneur de nostre temps,
Qui comme l'esperance, est seule demeuree.

180

De quelque autre subject, que j'escrive, Jodelle,
Je sens mon cœur transi d'une morne froideur,
Et ne sens plus en moy ceste divine ardeur,
Qui t'enflamme l'esprit de sa vive estincelle.

Seulement quand je veulx toucher le loz de celle
Qui est de nostre siecle et la perle, et la fleur,
Je sens revivre en moy ceste antique chaleur,
Et mon esprit lassé prendre force nouvelle.

Bref, je suis tout changé, et si ne sçay comment,
Comme on voit se changer la vierge en un moment,
A l'approcher du Dieu qui telle la fait estre.

D'où vient cela, Jodelle? il vient, comme je croy,
Du subject, qui produict naïvement en moy
Ce que par art contraint les autres y font naistre.

179

Seeing the ambition, the envy, the avarice, the rancor, the pride, the blind desire with which this iron age, all rusted with vices, has violated the honor of ancient justice,

Seeing on the other side the fraud, the malice, the unending trial, the right badly defended, and, in the midst of unbridled vice, that royal flower, which bears no trace of vice,

I think, Dorat, I see the wingèd squadrons of the ancient virtues, flown back to heaven, leaving nothing behind of their golden age

To restore the world to its first springtime, except that Margaret, the honor of our times, who alone remains as a sign of hope.

---

that Margaret: plays on *Marguerite*, which is also the name of a flower, the daisy

180

On whatever other subject I write, Jodelle, I feel my heart numbed with a gloomy chill and no longer feel in myself that divine ardor that inflames your mind with its vital spark.

Only when I seek to touch on the praise of her who is the pearl and the flower of our age, do I feel that ancient warmth live again in me and my weary spirit gather new strength.

In short, I am wholly transformed and do not know how, just as one sees the virgin transformed in an instant at the approach of the god who makes her what she is.

How does that happen, Jodelle? It comes, I believe, from the subject, which naturally produces in me what others bring to life constrained by art.

---

the virgin: the Sibyl
the god: Apollo
the subject: Margaret of France

181

Ronsard, I have seen the glory of the ancient colossi, the amphitheaters open on all sides, the columns, the arches, the high vaulted temples, and the pointed tops of the squared obelisks.

I have seen the emperors' huge public baths. I have seen their monuments that time has conquered. I have seen their beautiful palaces overgrown with grass and the dusty relics of the old Roman walls.

In short, I have seen all Rome has that is extraordinary, rare, excellent, august, and beautiful. But I have never yet seen anything as great

As that Margaret, in whom it seems the heavens, to erase the honor of all ages past, have gathered together the excellence of their most beautiful gifts.

---

that Margaret: again punning on *Marguerite/marguerite*, both princess and flower

182

I am not one of those who conceals praise, unfairly defrauding worthy men, or who, turning black into white, can, as they say, make an angel of a devil.

I do not display, like a rare treasure, what our merchants of honor so loudly proclaim nor do I wish for some great lord to give me goods in exchange for poems.

What I seek, Gournay, from that sister of the king, whom I honor, revere, admire as you do, is that her goodness permit me to praise her,

Seeing that she is the most praiseworthy object of my poems, for in praising, Gournay, such a praiseworthy subject, the praise I acquire is more than enough of a reward for me.

Gournay: unknown

181

Ronsard, j'ay veu l'orgueil des Colosses antiques,
Les theatres en rond ouvers de tous costez,
Les columnes, les arcz, les haults temples voultez,
Et les sommets pointus des carrez obelisques.

J'ay veu des Empereurs les grands thermes publiques,
J'ay veu leurs monuments que le temps a dontez,
J'ay veu leurs beaux palais que l'herbe a surmontez
Et des vieux murs Romains les pouldreuses reliques.

Bref, j'ay veu tout cela que Rome a de nouveau,
De rare, d'excellent, de superbe, et de beau,
Mais je n'y ay point veu encores si grand' chose

Que ceste Marguerite, où semble que les cieux
Pour effacer l'honneur de tous les siecles vieux
De leurs plus beaux presens ont l'excellence enclose.

182

Je ne suis pas de ceulx qui robent la louange,
Fraudant indignement les hommes de valeur,
Ou qui changeant la noire à la blanche couleur
Sçavent, comme lon dit, faire d'un diable un ange.

Je ne fay point valoir, comme un tresor estrange,
Ce que vantent si hault noz marcadants d'honneur,
Et si ne cherche point que quelque grand seigneur
Me baille pour des vers des biens en contr'eschange.

Ce que je quiers (Gournay) de ceste sœur de Roy,
Que j'honnore, revere, admire comme toy,
C'est que de la loüer sa bonté me dispense,

Puis qu'elle est de mes vers le plus loüable object:
Car en loüant (Gournay) si loüable subject,
Le loz que je m'acquiers, m'est trop grand' recompense.

183

Morel, quand quelquefois je perds le temps à lire
Ce que font aujourdhuy noz trafiqueurs d'honneurs,
Je ry de voir ainsi desguiser ces Seigneurs,
Desquelz (comme lon dit) ilz font comme de cire. 4

Et qui pourroit, bons dieux! se contenir de rire
Voyant un corbeau peint de diverses couleurs,
Un pourceau couronné de roses et de fleurs,
Ou le pourtrait d'un asne accordant une lyre? 8

La loüange, à qui n'a rien de loüable en soy,
Ne sert que de le faire à tous monstrer au doy,
Mais elle est le loyer de cil qui la merite. 11

C'est ce qui fait (Morel) que si mal voluntiers
Je diz ceulx dont le nom fait rougir les papiers,
Et que j'ay si frequent celuy de Marguerite. 14

184

Celuy qui de plus près attaint la Deité,
Et qui au ciel (Bouju) vole de plus haulte ælle,
C'est celuy qui suivant la vertu immortelle
Se sent moins du fardeau de nostre humanité. 4

Celuy qui n'a des Dieux si grand felicité,
L'admire toutefois comme une chose belle,
Honnore ceulx qui l'ont, se monstre amoureux d'elle,
Il a le second ranc, ce semble, merité. 8

Comme au premier je tends d'ælle trop foible et basse,
Ainsi je pense avoir au second quelque place:
Et comment puis-je mieulx le second meriter, 11

Qu'en loüant ceste fleur, dont le vol admirable
Pour gaigner du premier le lieu plus honnorable,
Ne laisse rien icy qui la puisse imiter? 14

183

Morel, when I sometimes waste my time reading what our dealers in honors write these days, I laugh to see those lords so disguised whom they shape (as we say) as though they were made of wax.

And who could—good gods!—refrain from laughing seeing a crow painted in a variety of colors, a pig crowned with roses and flowers, or the portrait of an ass tuning a lyre?

Praise of one who has nothing praiseworthy about him serves only to make him a universal laughingstock, but praise is the reward of those who deserve it.

That is why, Morel, I so unwillingly speak of those whose name makes my papers blush and why I so frequently evoke the name of Margaret.

184

He who comes closest to achieving deity and flies toward heaven with the boldest wing, Bouju, is he who, following immortal virtue, feels least the burden of our humanity.

He, to whom the gods have not granted such great happiness, who nevertheless admires it as a glorious thing, who honors those who have it, who shows himself enamored of it, he, it seems, deserves the second rank.

Though I stretch out a wing too weak and humble to be of the first rank, yet I think I have a place in the second. And how can I better deserve the second

Than by praising that flower, whose admirable flight to win the most honorable place in the first, leaves nothing here that can imitate her?

---

that flower: Margaret of France, punning on *Marguerite/ marguerite*

185

When I first saw that beautiful flower who regilds our iron age with her virtues, though I did not yet know her great merit, yet I was ravished with wonder at seeing her.

Since then, having followed the path of Fortune where the twisting Tiber is tinted with yellow, and seeing those great gods whom ignorance worships, vying with one another in ignorance, vice, and cruelty,

Then, Forget, then seeing her again, my eyes were opened to that old mistake of not having properly known your princess and mine.

Then I realized that, unaware of her merit, I had, without knowing her, admired Margaret as one admires the heavens without knowing them.

---

those great gods: popes and cardinals
Forget: secretary to Madame de Savoie

186

Youth, Duval, once made me write of that blind archer who so blinds us. Then, annoyed with Love and with his mother too, I sounded the praises of kings on my lyre.

Now I no longer want to choose such subjects. Instead I want, like you, spurred by a higher concern, to sing of that great king, whose grave brow makes the celestial and infernal realms tremble.

I want to sing of God. But to sing of him well, one must practice his praises with a prelude, praising not the beauty of this round earth

But that flower which holds a still more glorious place. For just as she is, Duval, less perfect than God, so she is more perfect than the rest of the world.

Duval: Pierre Duval, bishop, humanist, and religious poet
that flower: Margaret of France

185

Quand ceste belle fleur premierement je vy,
Qui nostre aage de fer de ses vertuz redore,
Bien que sa grand' valeur je ne cogneusse encore,
Si fus-je en la voyant de merveille ravy.

Depuis ayant le cours de Fortune suivy
Où le Tybre tortu de jaune se colore,
Et voyant ces grands dieux que l'ignorance adore,
Ignorans, vicieux, et meschans à l'envy:

Alors (Forget) alors ceste erreur ancienne
Qui n'avoit bien cogneu ta Princesse et la mienne,
La venant à revoir, se dessilla les yeux:

Alors je m'apperçeu qu'ignorant son merite
J'avois, sans la cognoistre, admiré Marguerite,
Comme, sans les cognoistre, on admire les cieux.

186

La jeunesse (Du-val) jadis me fit escrire
De cet aveugle archer, qui nous aveugle ainsi,
Puis fasché de l'Amour, et de sa mere aussi,
Les louanges des Roys j'accorday sur ma lyre.

Ores je ne veulx plus telz arguments eslire,
Ains je veulx, comme toy, poingt d'un plus hault souci,
Chanter de ce grand Roy, dont le grave sourci
Fait trembler le celeste, et l'infernal empire.

Je veulx chanter de Dieu. Mais pour bien le chanter,
Il fault d'un avant-jeu ses louanges tenter,
Loüant, non la beauté de ceste masse ronde,

Mais ceste fleur, qui tient encor' un plus beau lieu:
Car comme elle est (Du-val) moins parfaitte que Dieu,
Aussi l'est elle plus que le reste du monde.

187

Bucanan, qui d'un vers aux plus vieux comparable
Le surnom de Sauvage ostes à l'Ecossois,
Si j'avois Apollon facile en mon François,
Comme en ton Grec tu l'as, et Latin favorable,

Je ne ferois monter, spectacle miserable,
Dessus un echafault les miseres des Roys,
Mais je rendrois par tout d'une plus doulce voix
Le nom de Marguerite aux peuples admirable:

Je dirois ses vertuz, et dirois que les cieux
L'ayant fait naistre icy d'un temps si vicieux
Pour estre l'ornement, et la fleur de son aage,

N'ont moins en cet endroit demonstré leur sçavoir,
Leur pouvoir, leur vertu, que les Muses d'avoir
Fait naistre un Bucanan de l'Ecosse sauvage.

188

Paschal, je ne veulx point Juppiter assommer,
Ny comme fit Vulcan, luy rompre la cervelle,
Pour en tirer dehors une Pallas nouvelle,
Puis qu'on veult de ce nom ma Princesse nommer.

D'un effroyable armet je ne la veulx armer,
Ny de ce que du nom d'une chevre on appelle,
Et moins pour avoir veu sa Gorgonne cruelle,
Veulx-je en nouveaux cailloux les hommes transformer.

Je ne veulx deguiser ma simple poësie
Sous le masque emprunté d'une fable moisie,
Ny souiller un beau nom de monstres tant hideux:

Mais suivant, comme toy, la veritable histoire,
D'un vers non fabuleux je veulx chanter sa gloire
A nous, à nos enfans, et ceulx qui naistront d'eulx.

187

Buchanan, you who with verse comparable to the most ancient remove the name of savage from the Scots, were I as readily blessed by Apollo in my French as you are in your Greek and Latin,

I would not stage—pitiful spectacle!—the sufferings of kings, but in a sweeter voice I would everywhere make the name of Margaret wonderful to the multitudes.

I would speak of her virtues and would say that the heavens, in bringing her to life here in such corrupt times to be the ornament and flower of her age,

Have shown their knowledge, their power, their virtue no less in this place than the Muses in bringing to life a Buchanan in savage Scotland.

Buchanan: George Buchanan (1506–1582), Scottish humanist and author of Latin tragedies

188

Paschal, I do not want to strike Jupiter on the head nor break open his skull, as Vulcan did, to pull out a new Pallas, just because people want to give her name to my princess.

I do not want to arm her with a dreadful helmet, nor with that which bears the name of a goat, and still less do I want to turn men into stones for looking at her cruel Gorgon.

I do not want to disguise my unadorned verse in a mask borrowed from a musty fable nor defile a beautiful name with such hideous monsters.

But following, as you do, true history, I want, in poetry without fabling, to sing her glory for us, for our children, and for those who will be born of them.

---

my princess: Margaret of France

which bears the name of a goat: Pallas Athena's shield (*aegis*) was made from the skin of a goat (*aex, aegidos*) and bore an image of the Gorgon's head, the sight of which turned men to stones

as you do: Paschal was a noted historian

189

While with your Euclid, Peletier, you demonstrate what the ancients sought so hard in vain and while, in spite of vice and an envious age, you mount to heaven like a second Alcides,

The love of virtue, my only and sure guide, like a new swan leads me toward the heavens, where, in spite of envy and a vicious age, I fill with a glorious name that vast empty space.

Like you, I wanted to abandon poetry so as to give myself to a higher and wiser labor. But seeing that virtue calls me to praise her,

I want to tell of the honors of virtue. With virtue, I want to mount to heaven. Could I mount to heaven with any loftier wing?

---

with your Euclid: Peletier published a commentary on Euclid in 1557
a glorious name: the name of Margaret of France

190

Under that great Francis, whose glorious star shines in the finest place in heaven, France was pregnant with letters and arts and with a blessed troop, to which since then, fruitful under Henry, she has given birth.

But she had no sooner produced such offspring, and this glorious birth had no sooner come to light, than, I know not how, its brightness was extinguished and it saw in the same moment its day and its night.

The Helicon has dried up. Parnassus is a plain. The laurels have withered. And France, once filled with the spirit of Apollo, is now filled only with that of Mars.

Phoebus will flee us, and ancient ignorance under the patronage of Mars will once again return to France, if Pallas does not defend letters and arts.

---

a blessed troop: the Pléiade, whose glory, du Bellays fears, may be eclipsed by the demands of war

Pallas: Margaret of France, here in the guise of Pallas Athena

189

Cependant (Pelletier) que dessus ton Euclide
Tu montres ce qu'en vain ont tant cherché les vieux,
Et qu'en despit du vice, et du siecle envieux
Tu te guindes au ciel comme un second Alcide:

L'amour de la vertu, ma seule et seure guide,
Comme un cygne nouveau me conduit vers les cieux,
Où en despit d'envie, et du temps vicieux,
Je rempliz d'un beau nom ce grand espace vide.

Je voulois comme toy les vers abandonner,
Pour à plus hault labeur plus sage m'addonner:
Mais puis que la vertu à la loüer m'appelle,

Je veulx de la vertu les honneurs raconter:
Aveques la vertu je veulx au ciel monter.
Pourrois-je au ciel monter aveques plus haulte ælle?

190

Dessous ce grand François, dont le bel astre luit
Au plus beau lieu du ciel, la France fut enceincte
Des lettres et des arts, et d'une troppe saincte
Que depuis sous Henry feconde elle a produict:

Mais elle n'eut plus-tost fait monstre d'un tel fruict,
Et plus-tost ce beau part n'eut la lumiere atteincte,
Que je ne sçay comment sa clairte fut esteincte
Et vid en mesme temps et son jour et sa nuict.

Helicon est tary, Parnasse est une plaine,
Les lauriers sont seichez, et France autrefois pleine
De l'esprit d'Apollon, ne l'est plus que de Mars.

Phœbus s'en fuit de nous, et l'antique ignorance
Sous la faveur de Mars retourne encore en France,
Si Pallas ne defend les lettres et les arts.

191

Sire, celuy qui est, a formé toute essence
De ce qui n'estoit rien. C'est l'œuvre du Seigneur:
Aussi tout honneur doit flechir à son honneur,
Et tout autre pouvoir ceder à sa puissance. 4

On voit beaucoup de Roys, qui sont grands d'apparence,
Mais nul, tant soit il grand, n'aura jamais tant d'heur
De pouvoir à la vostre egaler sa grandeur:
Car rien n'est apres Dieu si grand qu'un Roy de France. 8

Puis donc que Dieu peult tout, et ne se trouve lieu
Lequel ne soit encloz sous le pouvoir de Dieu,
Vous, de qui la grandeur de Dieu seul est enclose, 11

Elargissez encor sur moy vostre pouvoir,
Sur moy, qui ne suis rien: à fin de faire voir,
Que de rien un grand Roy peult faire quelque chose. 14

191

Sire, He Who Is made all being from nothing. That is the work of the Lord, and all honor must bow before his honor, and all other power yield to his power.

One sees many kings who are great in appearance. But none, however great he may be, will ever be so fortunate as to equal your greatness, for nothing, after God, is as great as a king of France.

Since then God can do everything and there is no place that is not contained within the power of God, you, whose greatness is contained by God alone,

Expend in turn your power on me—on me who am nothing—so as to show that of nothing a great king can make something.

Sire: King Henry II

He Who Is: God

from nothing: creation *ex nihilo*

for nothing after God: the notion of the unrivaled greatness of the king of France is not mere flattery but rather a legal concept current in early modern France

Le Premier Livre
Des Antiquitez de Rome
contenent une generale description
de sa grandeur,
et comme une deploration de sa ruine
plus un Songe ou Vision
sur le mesme subject

The First Book of
The Antiquities of Rome
containing a general description
of her greatness
and, as it were, a lamentation
on her ruin
with a Dream or Vision
on the same subject

Au Roy

Ne vous pouvant donner ces ouvrages antiques
Pour vostre Sainct-Germain, ou pour Fontainebleau,
Je les vous donne (Sire) en ce petit tableau
Peint, le mieux que j'ay peu, de couleurs poëtiques. 4

Qui mis sous vostre nom devant les yeux publiques,
Si vous le daignez voir en son jour le plus beau,
Se pourra bien vanter d'avoir hors du tumbeau
Tiré des vieux Romains les poudreuses reliques. 8

Que vous puissent les Dieux un jour donner tant d'heur,
De rebastir en France une telle grandeur
Que je la voudrois bien peindre en vostre langage: 11

Et peult estre, qu'à lors vostre grand' Majesté
Repensant à mes vers, diroit qu'ilz ont esté
De vostre Monarchie un bienheureux presage. 14

To the King

Unable to give you these ancient works for your Saint Germain or for Fontainebleau, I give them to you, Sire, in this little picture, painted, as best I could, with poetic colors,

Which, placed before the eyes of the public under your name, if you deign to view it in its best light, will be able to boast of having pulled from the tomb the dusty remains of the ancient Romans.

May the gods one day give you the good fortune to rebuild in France such greatness that I would willingly paint it in your language,

And perhaps then your great majesty, remembering my verses, would say that they have been a blessed omen of your universal dominion.

---

the King: Henry II

Saint Germain and Fontainebleau: royal palaces identified particularly with Henry II (Saint Germain) and his father, Francis I (Fontainebleau)

to rebuild in France: du Bellay seems to be imagining a movement of empire, a *translatio imperii,* from Rome to France

universal dominion: here, as elsewhere, du Bellay's *monarchie* means *empire* in the universal Roman sense

1

Divine Spirits, whose dusty ashes lie under the weight of so many ruined walls (but not your praise, which lives in your fair verses and will never sink beneath the earth),

If a human voice can reach from here to the depths of the underworld, let the abyss open to my cry so that from far below you may hear me.

Thrice devoutly circling your tombs under the veil of the heavens, aloud I thrice call out to you.

I here invoke your ancient inspiration, while with a holy dread I sing your fairest glory.

Divine Spirits: an invocation that suggests the elevated, heroic style of the *Antiquities*

2

The Babylonian will boast of his high walls and hanging gardens; Greece will describe the ancient construction of its Ephesian temple; and the people of the Nile will sing their pyramids.

That same, still vaunting Greece will proclaim the Olympian image of its great Jupiter; the Mausoleum will be the Carian glory; and Crete will not forget its old labyrinth.

The ancient Rhodian will raise the glory of his famous Colossus to the temple of Memory, and if any other work can boast

That it deserves to join this company, someone more eloquent will tell of it. As for me, in place of all these, I wish to sing the Seven Hills of Rome, Seven Wonders of the World.

---

their pyramids: du Bellay's *pointes* could also mean obelisks, but here, as one of the Seven Wonders of the Ancient World, the pyramids of Egypt seem to be intended

1

Divins Esprits, dont la poudreuse cendre
Gist sous le faix de tant de murs couvers,
Non vostre loz, qui vif par voz beaux vers
Ne se verra sous la terre descendre, 4

Si des humains la voix se peult estendre
Depuis icy jusqu'au fond des enfers,
Soient à mon cry les abysmes ouvers,
Tant que d'abas vous me puissiez entendre. 8

Trois fois cernant sous le voile des cieux
De voz tumbeaus le tour devocieux,
A haulte voix trois fois je vous appelle: 11

J'invoque icy vostre antique fureur,
En ce pendant que d'une saincte horreur
Je vays chantant vostre gloire plus belle. 14

2

Le Babylonien ses haults murs vantera,
Et ses vergers en l'air, de son Ephesienne
La Grece descrira la fabrique ancienne,
Et le peuple du Nil ses pointes chantera: 4

La mesme Grece encor vanteuse publira
De son grand Juppiter l'image Olympienne,
Le Mausole sera la gloire Carienne,
Et son vieux labyrinth' la Crete n'oublira: 8

L'antique Rhodien elevera la gloire
De son fameux Colosse, au temple de Memoire:
Et si quelque œuvre encor digne se peult vanter 11

De marcher en ce ranc, quelque plus grand' faconde
Le dira: quant à moy pour tous je veulx chanter
Les sept Costaux Romains, sept miracles du monde. 14

3

Nouveau venu qui cherches Rome en Rome,
Et rien de Rome en Rome n'apperçois,
Ces vieux palais, ces vieux arcz que tu vois,
Et ces vieux murs, c'est ce que Rome on nomme. 4

Voy quel orgueil, quelle ruine: et comme
Celle qui mist le monde sous ses loix
Pour donter tout, se donta quelquefois,
Et devint proye au temps, qui tout consomme. 8

Rome de Rome est le seul monument,
Et Rome Rome a vaincu seulement,
Le Tybre seul, qui vers la mer s'enfuit, 11

Reste de Rome. O mondaine inconstance!
Ce qui est ferme, est par le temps destruit,
Et ce qui fuit, au temps fait resistence. 14

4

Celle qui de son chef les estoilles passoit,
Et d'un pied sur Thetis, l'autre dessous l'Aurore,
D'une main sur le Scythe, et l'autre sur le More,
De la terre, et du ciel, la rondeur compassoit: 4

Juppiter ayant peur, si plus elle croissoit,
Que l'orgueil des Geans se relevast encore,
L'accabla sous ces monts, ces sept monts qui sont ore
Tumbeaux de la grandeur qui le ciel menassoit. 8

Il luy mist sur le chef la croppe Saturnale,
Puis dessus l'estomac assist la Quirinale,
Sur le ventre il planta l'antique Palatin: 11

Mist sur la dextre main la hauteur Celienne,
Sur la senestre assist l'eschine Exquilienne,
Viminal sur un pied, sur l'autre l'Aventin. 14

3

Newcomer, you who seek Rome in Rome and find nothing of Rome in Rome, these old palaces, these old arches that you see, and these old walls, this is what they call Rome.

See what pride, what ruin, and how she who brought the world under her laws, in vanquishing all, at last vanquished herself and became the prey of time, which devours all.

Rome is the only monument to Rome, and only Rome conquered Rome. Only the Tiber, which flees toward the sea,

Remains of Rome. O worldly inconstancy! Whatever stands firm is destroyed by time. And whatever flees resists time.

Newcomer: this sonnet closely follows a Latin epigram by Janus Vitalis, an Italian contemporary of du Bellay

See what pride: compare du Bellay's Latin elegy "Romae descriptio," lines 123–130

4

She whose head passed the stars and who with one foot on Thetis, the other beneath Aurora, one hand on the Scythian, the other on the Moor, encompassed the sphere of earth and sky:

Jupiter fearing that, if she grew still more, the pride of the Giants would rise up again, crushed her under these hills, these seven hills which now entomb the greatness that threatened heaven.

He put on her head the Saturnalian mount, then on her belly seated the Quirinal, on her chest he planted the ancient Palatine,

Put on her right hand the Caelian peak, on her left set the Esquiline spine, Viminal on one foot, on the other the Aventine.

She whose head: compare du Bellay's Latin poem "Romae veteris" (*Poemata* 4.1)

Thetis . . . Aurora . . . the Scythian . . . the Moor: the extremities of west, east, north, and south

the Giants: mythical monsters who sprang from the earth and attacked the Olympian gods

5

Whoever wishes to see all that nature, art, and heaven have been able to do, let him come see you, Rome—if, that is, he can imagine your greatness from what is only your lifeless portrait.

Rome is no more, and if her ruins still show us some shade of Rome, it is like a body raised by magic powers from its sepulchre at night.

The body of Rome has returned to ashes, and her soul has gone to rejoin the great soul of the material universe.

But her writings, which in spite of time wrest her fairest praise from the grave, keep her specter wandering throughout the world.

Whoever wishes: the opening of this sonnet echoes the opening of Petrarch's much-imitated *Rime sparse* 248, "Chi vuol veder quantunque po Natura"

But her writings: compare "Romae descriptio," lines 133–136

6

Like the Berecynthian in her chariot, crowned with towers and overjoyed at having given birth to so many gods, so this ancient city appeared in her happier days,

This city, who bore more children than the Phrygian and whose power was the power of the world; and no greatness equal to her greatness, except her own, will ever be seen again.

Rome alone could resemble Rome. Rome alone could make Rome tremble. Indeed, the decree of Fate had allowed

No other human power, however daring, to boast of equaling her who made her power equal to the earth and her daring to the heavens.

---

the Berecynthian: Cybele, or Rhea, the ancient Greek goddess of the earth and mother of the Olympian gods, the Magna Mater, also known as the Phrygian, here inspired by Virgil's *Aeneid* 6.782–787

5

Qui voudra voir tout ce qu'ont peu nature,
L'art, et le ciel (Rome) te vienne voir:
J'entens s'il peult ta grandeur concevoir
Par ce qui n'est que ta morte peinture.

Rome n'est plus, et si l'architecture
Quelque umbre encor de Rome fait revoir,
C'est comme un corps par magique sçavoir
Tiré de nuict hors de sa sepulture.

Le corps de Rome en cendre est devallé,
Et son esprit rejoindre s'est allé
Au grand esprit de ceste masse ronde.

Mais ses escripts, qui son loz le plus beau
Malgré le temps arrachent du tumbeau,
Font son idole errer parmy le monde.

6

Telle que dans son char la Berecynthienne
Couronnee de tours, et joyeuse d'avoir
Enfanté tant de Dieux, telle se faisoit voir
En ses jours plus heureux ceste ville ancienne:

Ceste ville, qui fut plus que la Phrygienne
Foisonnante en enfans, et de qui le pouvoir
Fut le pouvoir du monde, et ne se peut revoir
Pareille à sa grandeur, grandeur sinon la sienne.

Rome seule pouvoit à Rome ressembler,
Rome seule pouvoit Rome faire trembler:
Aussi n'avoit permis l'ordonnance fatale

Qu'autre pouvoir humain, tant fust audacieux,
Se vantast d'égaler celle qui fit égale
Sa puissance à la terre, et son courage aux cieux.

7

Sacrez costaux, et vous sainctes ruines,
Qui le seul nom de Rome retenez,
Vieux monuments, qui encor soustenez
L'honneur poudreux de tant d'ames divines,

Arcz triomphaux, pointes du ciel voisines,
Qui de vous voir le ciel mesme estonnez,
Las peu à peu cendre vous devenez,
Fable du peuple, et publiques rapines!

Et bien qu'au temps pour un temps facent guerre
Les bastimens, si est-ce que le temps
Oeuvres et noms finablement atterre.

Tristes desirs, vivez donques contents:
Car si le temps finist chose si dure,
Il finira la peine que j'endure.

8

Par armes et vaisseaux Rome donta le monde,
Et pouvoit on juger qu'une seule cité,
Avoit de sa grandeur le terme limité
Par la mesme rondeur de la terre, et de l'onde.

Et tant fut la vertu de ce peuple feconde
En vertueux nepveux, que sa posterité
Surmontant ses ayeux en brave auctorité
Mesura le hault ciel à la terre profonde:

Afin qu'ayant rangé tout pouvoir sous sa main,
Rien ne peust estre borne à l'empire Romain:
Et que si bien le temps destruit les Republiques,

Le temps ne mist si bas la Romaine hauteur,
Que le chef deterré aux fondemens antiques
Qui prindrent nom de luy, fust découvert menteur.

7

Sacred hills and you holy ruins which retain nothing but the name of Rome, ancient monuments which still uphold the dusty honor of so many divine souls,

Triumphal arches, sky-neighboring obelisks at whose sight the heavens themselves are astonished, alas, little by little, you are reduced to ashes, the laughingstock of the crowd and the spoil of all!

And though buildings for a time wage war against time, yet time at last strikes down works and names.

Then, sad desires, live content. For if time puts an end to things so firm, it will put an end to the suffering I endure.

Sacred hills: a translation of an Italian sonnet by Baldesar Castiglione, which accounts for, but does not excuse, the incongruous appearance of the conventional Petrarchan lover in the poem's final tercet

the laughingstock of the crowd: du Bellay's "fable du peuple" echoes, via Castiglione, Petrarch's "al popol tutto/favola fui" in the opening sonnet of the *Rime sparse*

8

By arms and ships, Rome tamed the world, and one could imagine that a single city had her greatness bounded only by the circumference of the earth and the sea.

And such was the virtue of this people, fertile in virtuous offspring, that its descendants, surpassing their ancestors in audacity, extended their empire from high heaven to the depths of the earth.

So that, having gathered all power into her hands, nothing could limit the Roman Empire and that, though time destroys states,

Time would not bring the height of Rome so low that the head discovered in the ancient foundations, which took their name from it, would be proved a liar.

By arms and ships: this sonnet is based on a Latin epigram by the Scottish humanist George Buchanan

the head discovered in the ancient foundations: a head (*caput*) found in the foundations of Rome gave its name to the Capitol and was taken as an omen that Rome would be the head of the world

9

Cruel stars and you inhuman gods, envious heaven and stepmother nature, whether the course of human affairs proceeds by design or by accident,

Why did your hands once labor to fashion this world which is so enduring? Or why were the bold facades of these Roman palaces not made of equally durable matter?

I no longer repeat the commonplace that everything beneath the moon is corruptible and subject to death,

But I do say (with no offense to him who would teach the contrary) that this great All must one day perish.

---

to him who would teach the contrary: Aristotelians, who thought the material world eternal

10

More than the brave son of Aeson, who by enchantment won the rich wool on the Aetean shore, sowing the plain with the teeth of an old dragon, engendered soldiers on the field of the fleece,

This city, who was in her youth a Hydra of warriors, saw herself valiantly filled with valiant offspring, whose high renown spread from the rising to the setting sun,

But who in the end, there being in the world no Hercules to tame such a fertile seed, with horrible fury armed against one another

In a sudden storm, scythed each other down, renewing among themselves the fraternal rage that once blinded the proud soldiers Jason had sown.

---

son of Aeson: Jason
the rich wool: the Golden Fleece

9

Astres cruelz, et vous Dieux inhumains,
Ciel envieux, et marastre Nature,
Soit que par ordre, ou soit qu'à l'aventure
Voyse le cours des affaires humains, 4

Pourquoy jadis ont travaillé voz mains
A façonner ce monde qui tant dure?
Ou que ne fut de matiere aussi dure
Le brave front de ces palais Romains? 8

Je ne dy plus la sentence commune,
Que toute chose au dessous de la Lune
Est corrompable, et sugette à mourir: 11

Mais bien je dy (et n'en veuille desplaire
A qui s'efforce enseigner le contraire)
Que ce grand Tout doit quelquefois perir. 14

10

Plus qu'aux bords Aetëans le brave filz d'Aeson
Qui par enchantement conquist la riche laine,
Des dents d'un vieil serpent ensemençant la plaine
N'engendra de soldatz au champ de la toison, 4

Ceste Ville qui fut en sa jeune saison
Un Hydre de guerriers, se vid bravement pleine
De braves nourrissons, dont la gloire hautaine
A remply du Soleil l'une et l'autre maison. 8

Mais qui finablement, ne se trouvant au monde
Hercule qui dontast semence tant feconde,
D'une horrible fureur l'un contre l'autre armez, 11

Se moissonnarent tous par un soudain orage,
Renouvelant entre eulx la fraternelle rage,
Qui aveugla jadis les fiers soldatz semez. 14

11

Mars vergongneux d'avoir donné tant d'heur
A ses nepveux, que l'impuissance humaine
Enorgueillie en l'audace Romaine
Sembloit fouler la celeste grandeur,

Refroidissant ceste premiere ardeur
Dont le Romain avoit l'ame si pleine,
Soufla son feu, et d'une ardente haleine
Vint eschauffer la Gottique froideur.

Ce peuple adonc, nouveau fils de la terre,
Dardant par tout les fouldres de la guerre,
Ces braves murs accabla sous sa main,

Puis se perdit dans le sein de sa mere,
Afin que nul, fust-ce des Dieux le pere,
Se peust vanter de l'empire Romain.

12

Telz que lon vid jadis les enfans de la Terre
Plantez dessus les monts pour escheller les cieux,
Combattre main à main la puissance des Dieux,
Et Juppiter contre eux qui ses fouldres desserre:

Puis tout soudainement renversez du tonnerre
Tumber deça dela ces squadrons furieux,
La Terre gemissante, et le Ciel glorieux
D'avoir à son honneur achevé ceste guerre:

Tel encor' on a veu par dessus les humains
Le front audacieux des sept costaux Romains
Lever contre le ciel son orgueilleuse face:

Et telz ores on void ces champs deshonnorez
Regretter leur ruine, et les Dieux asseurez
Ne craindre plus là hault si effroyable audace.

11

Mars, ashamed to have given such good fortune to his offspring that human weakness arrogantly grown into Roman pride seemed to trample heavenly greatness underfoot,

Cooling that first ardor which so filled the Roman soul, fanned his fire and with a burning breath inflamed the Gothic cold.

That people then, the new sons of the earth, hurling lightning bolts of war on every side, struck down these brave walls under its hand,

Then was lost in the bosom of its mother, so that no one, not even the father of the gods, could boast of having conquered the Roman Empire.

Mars: here remembered as the father of Romulus and thus the ancestor of the Romans

That people: the Goths, who overran Rome

the new sons of the earth: after the mythical Giants

the father of the gods: Jupiter

12

Just as the children of the earth long ago heaped mountain on mountain to scale the heavens, to fight hand to hand the power of the gods, and Jupiter, who loosed his lightning bolts against them,

Then all at once, thunderstruck, those furious squadrons fell here and there, the earth lamenting, and heaven triumphing at having ended that war to its honor,

So the audacious brow of the seven Roman hills, towering above humanity, raised its proud face against the sky,

And so these dishonored fields now lament their ruin and the secure gods above no longer fear such terrifying audacity.

---

the children of the earth: the Giants, who sprang from the blood of Uranus, which was spilled on the earth when his son Kronos castrated him

13

Neither the fury of raging flame, nor the sharp edge of victorious steel, nor the destruction of the furious soldier, which have so often pillaged you, Rome,

Nor vicissitudes of your changing fortune, nor the destruction of envious time, nor the spite of men and gods, nor your own power turned against yourself,

Nor the shock of impetuous winds, nor the overflowing of that twisting god who has so often flooded you with his waters

Have so lowered your pride that the greatness of the nothing they have left you does not still amaze the world.

---

that twisting god: the Tiber

14

As one crosses without danger in summer the stream that in winter was king of the plain and swept from the fields with its mighty torrent the farmer's hope and the hope of the shepherd,

As cowardly animals brave the courageous lion lying in the sand, bloody their teeth, and with vainglorious daring provoke the enemy who cannot avenge himself,

And as before Troy the least valiant of the Greeks also exulted over the body of Hector, so those who once

Followed with lowered heads the Roman triumph now strut their bravery on these dusty tombs, and the vanquished dare to scorn the vanquishers.

13

Ny la fureur de la flamme enragee,
Ny le trenchant du fer victorieux,
Ny le degast du soldat furieux,
Qui tant de fois (Rome) t'a saccagee,

Ny coup sur coup ta fortune changee,
Ny le ronger des siecles envieux,
Ny le despit des hommes et des Dieux,
Ny contre toy ta puissance rangee,

Ny l'ebranler des vents impetueux,
Ny le débord de ce Dieu tortueux
Qui tant de fois t'a couvert de son onde,

Ont tellement ton orgueil abbaissé,
Que la grandeur du rien, qu'ilz t'ont laissé,
Ne face encor' esmerveiller le monde.

14

Comme on passe en æsté le torrent sans danger,
Qui souloit en hyver estre roy de la plaine,
Et ravir par les champs d'une fuite hautaine
L'espoir du laboureur, et l'espoir du berger:

Comme on void les coüards animaux oultrager
Le courageux lyon gisant dessus l'arene,
Ensanglanter leurs dents, et d'une audace vaine
Provoquer l'ennemy qui ne se peult vanger:

Et comme devant Troye on vid des Grecz encor
Braver les moins vaillans autour du corps d'Hector:
Ainsi ceulx qui jadis souloient, à teste basse,

Du triomphe Romain la gloire accompagner,
Sur ces pouldreux tumbeaux exercent leur audace,
Et osent les vaincuz les vainqueurs desdaigner.

15

Palles Esprits, et vous Umbres pouldreuses,
Qui jouissant de la clarté du jour
Fistes sortir cet orgueilleux sejour,
Dont nous voyons les reliques cendreuses:

Dictes Esprits (ainsi les tenebreuses
Rives de Styx non passable au retour,
Vous enlassant d'un trois fois triple tour,
N'enferment point voz images umbreuses)

Dictes moy donc (car quelqu'une de vous
Possible encor se cache icy dessous)
Ne sentez vous augmenter vostre peine,

Quand quelquefois de ces costaux Romains
Vous contemplez l'ouvrage de voz mains
N'estre plus rien qu'une pouldreuse plaine?

16

Comme lon void de loing sur la mer courroucee
Une montagne d'eau d'un grand branle ondoyant,
Puis trainant mille flotz, d'un gros choc abboyant
Se crever contre un roc, où le vent l'a poussee,

Comme on void la fureur par l'Aquilon chassee
D'un sifflement aigu l'orage tournoyant,
Puis d'une ælle plus large en l'air s'esbanoyant
Arrester tout à coup sa carriere lassee:

Et comme on void la flamme ondoyant en cent lieux
Se rassemblant en un, s'aguiser vers les cieux,
Puis tumber languissante: ainsi parmy le monde

Erra la monarchie: et croissant tout ainsi
Qu'un flot, qu'un vent, qu'un feu, sa course vagabonde
Par un arrest fatal s'est venue perdre icy.

15

Pale Spirits, and you ashen shades, who, while you enjoyed the light of day, brought forth this proud city, whose dusty remains we see,

Tell me, Spirits (and may the dark banks of the Styx, which forbid all return, binding you with a three times triple turn, not confine your shadowy forms),

Tell me then (for one of you may still be hidden here below), do you not feel your pain increase

When you see on these Roman hills the work of your hands reduced to nothing but a dusty plain?

---

three times triple turn: alludes to the nine circles the Styx makes around the underworld in Virgil's *Aeneid* 6.438–439

16

As one sees from afar on the angry sea a mountain of water cresting with violent motion, then, pulling along a thousand waves, crashing with a huge shock, break against a rock on which the wind has flung it,

As one sees the fury driven by Boreas whipping up the storm with a deafening roar, then, with a broader wing sporting in the air, suddenly cease its wearied course,

And as one sees the flame rising from a hundred places, gathering itself in one, flare up toward the heavens, then fall back spent, so throughout the world

Wandered empire and growing like a wave, like the wind, like a flame, its errant course by the decree of fate came to an end here.

Boreas: du Bellay's *Aquilon*, the Greek god of the north wind

Wandered empire: another allusion to the notion of *translatio imperii*, the westward movement that brought empire to Rome and might one day bring it to France

17

So long as the bird of Jupiter still flew, carrying the fire with which heaven threatens us, heaven had no fear of the dreadful audacity that drove the Giants to madness.

But as soon as the sun burned the wing that soared too high above the earth, the earth sent forth from its heavy mass the ancient horror that ravished right.

Then the German crow disguised itself to resemble the Roman eagle, and these bold hills, formerly reduced to dust,

Rose up once again toward heaven, for they no longer saw that great bird, the minister of Jove's lightning, flying over their heads.

---

the bird of Jupiter: the eagle, the symbol of the Roman Empire

the ancient horror: the Gothic invaders as new Giants, new sons of the earth

the German crow: the Holy Roman Empire, which du Bellay here denies is the rightful descendant of Rome—not, that is, deserving of the eagle which in imitation of Rome it had adopted as its imperial sign

18

These great stony piles, these old walls that you see, at first enclosed country fields, and these brave palaces, which time has overthrown, were once the cottages of shepherds.

Then the shepherds assumed the ornaments of kings, and the rough plowman armed his right hand with steel. Then the year-long power became greatest, and still greater was the power of six months,

Which, made perpetual, grew to such strength that from it the imperial eagle was born. But heaven, opposing such increase,

Placed that power in the hands of the successor of Peter, who, under name of pastor, a name linked by fate to that land, shows that everything returns to its beginning.

---

year-long power: consuls

power of six months: dictators

made perpetual: emperors

the successor of Peter: popes, who by the spurious Donation of Constantine claimed to be the heirs of the Roman emperors

a name linked by fate to that land: because *pastor* means both "shepherd" and "priest"

17

Tant que l'oyseau de Juppiter vola,
Portant le feu, dont le ciel nous menace,
Le ciel n'eut peur de l'effroyable audace
Qui des Geans le courage affolla:

Mais aussi tost que le Soleil brusla
L'ælle qui trop se fit la terre basse,
La terre mist hors de sa lourde masse
L'antique horreur qui le droit viola.

Alors on vid la corneille Germaine
Se deguisant feindre l'aigle Romaine,
Et vers le ciel s'eslever de rechef

Ces braves monts autrefois mis en pouldre,
Ne voyant plus voler dessus leur chef
Ce grand oyseau ministre de la fouldre.

18

Ces grands monceaux pierreux, ces vieux murs que tu vois,
Furent premierement le cloz d'un lieu champestre:
Et ces braves palais dont le temps s'est fait maistre,
Cassines de pasteurs ont esté quelquefois.

Lors prindrent les bergers les ornemens des Roys,
Et le dur laboureur de fer arma sa dextre:
Puis l'annuel pouvoir le plus grand se vid estre,
Et fut encor plus grand le pouvoir de six mois:

Qui, fait perpetuel, creut en telle puissance,
Que l'aigle Imperial de luy print sa naissance:
Mais le Ciel s'opposant à tel accroissement,

Mist ce pouvoir es mains du successeur de Pierre,
Qui sous nom de pasteur, fatal à ceste terre,
Monstre que tout retourne à son commencement.

19

Tout le parfait dont le ciel nous honnore,
Tout l'imperfait qui naist dessous les cieux,
Tout ce qui paist noz esprits et noz yeux,
Et tout cela qui noz plaisirs devore:

Tout le malheur qui nostre aage dedore,
Tout le bonheur des siecles les plus vieux,
Rome du temps de ses premiers ayeux
Le tenoit clos, ainsi qu'une Pandore.

Mais le destin debrouillant ce Caos,
Où tout le bien et le mal fut enclos,
A fait depuis que les vertus divines

Volant au ciel ont laissé les pechez,
Qui jusqu'icy se sont tenus cachez
Sous les monceaux de ces vieilles ruines.

20

Non autrement qu'on void la pluvieuse nüe
Des vapeurs de la terre en l'air se soulever,
Puis se courbant en arc, à fin de s'abrever,
Se plonger dans le sein de Thetis la chenue,

Et montant derechef d'où elle estoit venue,
Sous un grand ventre obscur tout le monde couver,
Tant que finablement on la void se crever
Or' en pluie, or' en neige, or' en gresle menue:

Ceste ville qui fut l'ouvrage d'un pasteur
S'élevant peu à peu, creut en telle hauteur,
Que Royne elle se vid de la terre et de l'onde:

Tant que ne pouvant plus si grand faix soustenir,
Son pouvoir dissipé s'écarta par le monde,
Monstrant que tout en rien doit un jour devenir.

19

All the perfection with which heaven honors us, all the imperfection that is born beneath the heavens, all that feeds our minds and our eyes, and all that devours our pleasures,

All the misfortune that takes the gilding from our age, all the good fortune of the most ancient times, Rome, like a Pandora, held in store from the time of her first ancestors.

But destiny, sorting out this chaos in which all good and ill were contained, has since arranged that the divine virtues,

Mounting to heaven, have left behind the sins which were hidden until now under the heaps of these ancient ruins.

---

takes the gilding from our age: that is, makes this an iron rather than a golden age

the divine virtues: like the goddess Astraea, who left the world in disgust at the injustices of the Iron Age

20

Just as the rain-filled cloud rises in the air from earth's vapors, then bending in an arc, to slake its thirst plunges into the bosom of gray-haired Thetis,

And, rising once again to the place from which she had fallen, covers the whole world under her great dark belly, until at last she bursts open, now in rain, now in snow, now in fine hail,

This city, which was the work of a shepherd, raising herself little by little, grew to such height that she became queen of earth and sea,

Until, unable to bear such great weight any longer, her spent force was scattered throughout the world, showing that all must one day come to nothing.

---

gray-haired Thetis: du Bellay may be confusing Thetis, the mother of Achilles, and Tethys, the wife of Oceanus, who was called "gray-haired"

covers the whole world: as a bird covers her eggs, brooding them

21

She whom Pyrrhus and the Libyan Mars could not tame, this brave city, which, with a heart armed against misfortune, withstood the shock of universal envy,

As long as her ship, tossed by so many waves, had the whole world roused against her, the rock of adversity never broke her happy course.

But when her virtue went unopposed, her power defeated itself, like the man whom the fierce storm

Has long kept from reaching shore, if too great a wind drives him into port, in the port itself his ship goes down.

Pyrrhus: king of Epirus, who defeated the Romans at Heraclea and Asculum

the Libyan Mars: Hannibal, the great Carthaginian general and enemy of Rome

22

When this brave city, the honor of the Latin name, which extended her greatness from Africa to the north wind, from the people that lives on the banks of the Thames to that which sees the morning dawn,

Incited her own nurslings with mutinous rage against themselves, her conquered spoils, which she had acquired over so many years from the whole world, suddenly became the world's booty.

So when the course of the great All has turned back on itself, or when thirty-six thousand years have measured their flight, the natural harmony of the elements will be broken,

The seeds, which are the mothers of all things, will return once again to their primal discord, closed forever in the womb of Chaos.

---

thirty-six thousand years: the length of the Great Year whose end will bring the end of all things

21

Celle que Pyrrhe et le Mars de Libye
N'ont sceu donter, celle brave cité
Qui d'un courage au mal exercité
Soustint le choc de la commune envie,

Tant que sa nef par tant d'ondes ravie
Eut contre soy tout le monde incité,
On n'a point veu le roc d'adversité
Rompre sa course heureusement suivie:

Mais defaillant l'object de sa vertu,
Son pouvoir s'est de luymesme abbatu,
Comme celuy, que le cruel orage

A longuement gardé de faire abbord,
Si trop grand vent le chasse sur le port,
Dessus le port se void faire naufrage.

22

Quand ce brave sejour, honneur du nom Latin
Qui borna sa grandeur d'Afrique, et de la Bize,
De ce peuple qui tient les bords de la Tamize,
Et de celuy qui void esclore le matin,

Anima contre soy d'un courage mutin
Ses propres nourrissons, sa despouille conquise,
Qu'il avoit par tant d'ans sur tout le monde acquise,
Devint soudainement du monde le butin:

Ainsi quand du grand Tout la fuite retournee
Où trentesix mil' ans ont sa course bornee,
Rompra des elemens le naturel accord,

Les semences qui sont meres de toutes choses,
Retourneront encor' à leur premier discord,
Au ventre du Caos eternellement closes.

23

O que celuy estoit cautement sage,
Qui conseilloit pour ne laisser moisir
Ses citoiens en paresseux loisir,
De pardonner aux rampars de Cartage!

Il prevoyoit que le Romain courage
Impatient du languissant plaisir,
Par le repos se laisseroit saisir
A la fureur de la civile rage.

Aussi void-on qu'en un peuple ocieux,
Comme l'humeur en un corps vicieux,
L'ambition facilement s'engendre.

Ce qui advint, quand l'envieux orgueil
De ne vouloir ny plus grand, ny pareil,
Rompit l'accord du beaupere et du gendre.

24

Si l'aveugle fureur, qui cause les batailles,
Des pareilz animaux n'a les cœurs allumez,
Soient ceulx qui vont courant, ou soient les emplumez,
Ceulx-là qui vont rampant, ou les armez d'escailles:

Quelle ardente Erinnys de ses rouges tenailles
Vous pinsetoit les cœurs de rage envenimez,
Quand si cruellement l'un sur l'autre animez
Vous destrempiez le fer en voz propres entrailles?

Estoit-ce point (Romains) vostre cruel destin,
Ou quelque vieil peché qui d'un discord mutin
Exerçoit contre vous sa vengeance eternelle?

Ne permettant des Dieux le juste jugement,
Voz murs ensanglantez par la main fraternelle
Se pouvoir asseurer d'un ferme fondement.

23

O cunningly wise was he who counseled, so that his fellow citizens would not grow soft in idleness, that the walls of Carthage be spared!

He foresaw that Roman vigor, unable to bear insipid pleasure, in rest would let itself be seized by the fury of civil rage.

Thus in a nation with too much leisure, ambition is easily born, like illness in an unhealthy body,

Which happened when the jealous pride that would not abide anyone greater or equal broke the truce between the father-in-law and the son-in-law.

---

he who counseled: Scipio Nasica Corculum, who argued against the destruction of Carthage

the father-in-law and the son-in-law: Pompey and Julius Caesar

24

If the blind fury, which causes battles, does not inflame the hearts of animals against their own kind, whether they run or are feathered or creep or are armed with scales,

What fiery Erinyes gripped your hearts with her red pincers envenomed with rage, when so cruelly provoked against one another, you buried your swords in your own entrails?

Was it, Romans, your cruel destiny, or was it some ancient sin that with mutinous discord wrought everlasting vengeance upon you,

The just decree of the gods denying your walls, bloodied by a brother's hand, a firm foundation?

If the blind fury: this sonnet is based on Horace's *Epodes* 7.11–20

Erinyes: the Furies or Eumenides

bloodied by a brother's hand: the murder of Remus by Romulus, an echo of Lucan's *Pharsalia* 1.95

25

Would that I had the Thracian harp to wake from the slothful underworld those old Caesars and the shades of those who built this ancient city?

Or would that I had Amphion's harp to rouse with a happier harmony the stony remains of these old walls and restore the Ausonian glory?

Would that I could at least with a more agile brush fashion the portraits of these palaces after the model of some great Virgil,

I would, with the ardor that inflames me, undertake to rebuild with the pen what hands cannot construct in stone.

---

the Thracian harp: the harp of Orpheus, which he used to bring his wife Eurydice at least partway back from the underworld

Amphion's harp: Amphion rebuilt the wall of Thebes with stones moved by the enchanting force of his harp

26

He who would measure the greatness of Rome in all its dimensions would not have to seek out with line or lead or compass or square its length and width, height and depth.

He would have to gird in a perfect sphere all that the ocean embraces in its long arms, from where the yearly star most warms the earth to where Boreas blows with greatest cold.

Rome was the whole world, and the whole world is Rome. And if we call the same things by the same names, just as we could do without the name of Rome,

Calling her by the name of the earth and the sea, so we can measure the world by measuring Rome, for the map of Rome is the map of the world.

---

the yearly star: the sun

map . . . map: du Bellay plays on the difference in French between *plan*, the map of a town or city, and *carte*, the map of a larger territory

25

Que n'ay-je encore la harpe Thracienne,
Pour réveiller de l'enfer paresseux
Ces vieux Cesars, et les Umbres de ceux
Qui ont basty ceste ville ancienne? 4

Ou que je n'ay celle Amphionienne,
Pour animer d'un accord plus heureux
De ces vieux murs les ossemens pierreux,
Et restaurer la gloire Ausonienne? 8

Peusse-je aumoins d'un pinceau plus agile
Sur le patron de quelque grand Virgile
De ces palais les protraits façonner: 11

J'entreprendrois, veu l'ardeur qui m'allume,
De rebastir au compas de la plume
Ce que les mains ne peuvent maçonner. 14

26

Qui voudroit figurer la Romaine grandeur
En ses dimensions, il ne luy faudroit querre
A la ligne, et au plomb, au compas, à l'equerre
Sa longueur et largeur, hautesse et profondeur: 4

Il luy faudroit cerner d'une egale rondeur
Tout ce que l'Ocean de ses longs bras enserre,
Soit où l'Astre annuel eschauffe plus la terre,
Soit où soufle Aquilon sa plus grande froideur. 8

Rome fut tout le monde, et tout le monde est Rome.
Et si par mesmes noms mesmes choses on nomme,
Comme du nom de Rome on se pourroit passer, 11

La nommant par le nom de la terre et de l'onde:
Ainsi le monde on peult sur Rome compasser,
Puis que le plan de Rome est la carte du monde. 14

27

Toy qui de Rome emerveillé contemples
L'antique orgueil, qui menassoit les cieux,
Ces vieux palais, ces monts audacieux,
Ces murs, ces arcs, ces thermes, et ces temples,

Juge, en voyant ces ruines si amples,
Ce qu'a rongé le temps injurieux,
Puis qu'aux ouvriers les plus industrieux
Ces vieux fragmens encor servent d'exemples.

Regarde apres, comme de jour en jour
Rome fouillant son antique sejour,
Se rebatist de tant d'œuvres divines:

Tu jugeras, que le demon Romain
S'efforce encore d'une fatale main
Ressusciter ces pouldreuses ruines.

28

Qui a veu quelquefois un grand chesne asseiché,
Qui pour son ornement quelque trophee porte,
Lever encor' au ciel sa vieille teste morte,
Dont le pied fermement n'est en terre fiché,

Mais qui dessus le champ plus qu'à demy panché
Monstre ses bras tous nuds, et sa racine torte,
Et sans fueille umbrageux, de son poix se supporte
Sur son tronc noüailleux en cent lieux esbranché:

Et bien qu'au premier vent il doive sa ruine,
Et maint jeune à l'entour ait ferme la racine,
Du devot populaire estre seul reveré.

Qui tel chesne a peu voir, qu'il imagine encores
Comme entre les citez, qui plus florissent ores,
Ce vieil honneur pouldreux est le plus honnoré.

27

You who look with wonder on the ancient pride of Rome, which threatened the heavens, these old palaces, these audacious hills, these walls, these arches, these baths, and these temples,

Judge, in seeing these so ample ruins, what injurious time has gnawed away, since these old fragments still serve as models for the most ambitious artisans.

Then observe how from day to day Rome, excavating her ancient abode, rebuilds herself with so many divine works.

You will judge that the spirit of Rome still strives with a fated hand to resurrect these dusty ruins.

---

to resurrect these dusty ruins: alludes to the reuse of ancient materials in the sixteenth-century rebuilding of Rome

28

He who has seen a huge dry oak which bears some trophy as ornament, still lifting its old lifeless head to the sky, whose foot is not firmly planted in the earth,

But which, leaning more than halfway over to the ground, shows its naked arms and its twisted root, and without shady leaves, holds itself up by its own weight on a knotted trunk stripped of branches in a hundred places,

And though it seems ready to crash down at the first wind, and many a young tree around it is firmly rooted, by the devout populace it alone is revered.

He who has seen such an oak, let him think too how, among the cities which most flourish now, the ancient and dusty honor of this city is the most honored.

He who has seen: this sonnet is based on Lucan's *Pharsalia* 1.136–143, where the fallen oak is compared not to Rome but rather to the defeated Pompey

29

All the obelisks that Egypt built, all that Greece constructed in the Corinthian, Ionic, Attic, or Dorian style to embellish its temples,

All that the art of Lysippus, the hand of Apelles, or the Phidian hand produced, used to decorate this ancient city whose greatness astonished heaven itself.

All the wisdom Athens once had, all the wealth Asia once had, all the novelty Africa once had

Was seen here. O surpassing wonder! Alive Rome was the ornament of the world, and dead she is the world's tomb.

Lysippus: Greek sculptor
Apelles: the best known Greek painter
the Phidian hand: the hand of Phidias, the greatest Greek sculptor

30

As the seeded field abounds in greenery, from the greenery springs a green stalk, from the stalk bristles a flourishing ear, from the ear yellows the grain, which warm weather ripens,

And as in due season the farmer harvests the waving locks from the golden furrow, lays them out in loose bundles, and from the yellowing wheat makes a thousand sheaves on the denuded field,

So the Roman Empire grew little by little until it was cut down by a barbarian's hand which left behind only these ancient ruins

That everyone pillages, like the gleaner who, walking step by step, gathers the remains of what falls behind the harvester.

As the seeded field: the opening two quatrains echo Mark 4.26–29, where the comparison is not to the fall of the Roman Empire, which had not yet fallen, but rather to the richness of the kingdom of God

29

Tout ce qu'Egypte en poincte façonna,
Tout ce que Grece à la Corinthienne,
A l'Ionique, Attique, ou Dorienne
Pour l'ornement des temples maçonna: 4

Tout ce que l'art de Lysippe donna,
La main d'Apelle, ou la main Phidienne,
Souloit orner ceste Ville ancienne,
Dont la grandeur le ciel mesme estonna. 8

Tout ce qu'Athene' eut onques de sagesse,
Tout ce qu'Asie eut onques de richesse,
Tout ce qu'Afrique eut onques de nouveau, 11

S'est veu icy. Ô merveille profonde!
Rome vivant fut l'ornement du monde,
Et morte elle est du monde le tumbeau. 14

30

Comme le champ semé en verdure foisonne,
De verdure se haulse en tuyau verdissant,
Du tuyau se herisse en epic florissant,
D'epic jaunit en grain que le chauld assaisonne: 4

Et comme en la saison le rustique moissonne
Les undoyans cheveux du sillon blondissant,
Les met d'ordre en javelle, et du blé jaunissant
Sur le champ despouillé mille gerbes façonne: 8

Ainsi de peu à peu creut l'Empire Romain,
Tant qu'il fut despouillé par la Barbare main,
Qui ne laissa de luy que ces marques antiques, 11

Que chacun va pillant: comme on void le gleneur
Cheminant pas à pas recueillir les reliques
De ce qui va tumbant apres le moissonneur. 14

31

De ce qu'on ne void plus qu'une vague campagne
Où tout l'orgueil du monde on a veu quelquefois,
Tu n'en n'es pas coupable, ô quiconques tu sois
Que le Tygre, et le Nil, Gange, et Euphrate baigne: 4

Coupables n'en sont pas l'Afrique ny l'Espaigne,
Ny ce peuple qui tient les rivages Anglois,
Ny ce brave soldat qui boit le Rhin Gaulois,
Ny cet autre guerrier, nourrisson d'Alemaigne. 8

Tu en es seule cause, ô civile fureur,
Qui semant par les champs l'Emathienne horreur,
Armas le propre gendre encontre son beaupere: 11

Afin qu'estant venue à son degré plus hault,
La Romaine grandeur trop longuement prospere,
Se vist ruer à bas d'un plus horrible sault. 14

32

Esperez vous que la posterité
Doive (mes vers) pour tout jamais vous lire?
Esperez vous que l'œuvre d'une lyre
Puisse acquerir telle immortalité? 4

Si sous le ciel fust quelque eternité,
Les monuments que je vous ay fait dire,
Non en papier, mais en marbre et porphyre,
Eussent gardé leur vive antiquité. 8

Ne laisse pas toutefois de sonner
Luth, qu'Apollon m'a bien daigné donner:
Car si le temps ta gloire ne desrobbe, 11

Vanter te peuls, quelque bas que tu sois,
D'avoir chanté le premier des François,
L'antique honneur du peuple à longue robbe. 14

31

O whoever you may be who bathe in the Tigris or the Nile, the Ganges or the Euphrates, it is not your fault that we no longer see anything but empty fields where we once saw the pride of the whole world.

Nor is it the fault of Africa or Spain, nor of the people that lives on the English shores, nor of the brave soldier who drinks from the Gallic Rhine, nor of that other warrior, the offspring of Germany.

You alone are responsible, O civil war, which sowing the fields with the Emathian horror, armed the son-in-law against his own father-in-law,

So that, having risen to its highest degree, Roman greatness, prosperous for too long, might see itself thrown down with a more terrible fall.

O whoever you may be: note that this and the following sonnet reverse the pattern that characterizes every other page of the *Antiquities* and of the *Dream* in that the poem in alexandrine verse is at the top of the page and the poem in the shorter decasyllabic verse is at the bottom

the Emathian horror: Pompey was defeated by his son-in-law, Julius Caesar, at Pharsalus in Emathia, a province of Macedonia

32

Do you hope, my poems, that posterity will read you forever? Do you hope that the work of a lyre can win such immortality?

Were there any eternity under heaven, the ancient monuments of which I have made you speak would have survived intact not on paper but in marble and porphyry.

Do not for all that cease playing, lute, which Apollo has deigned to give me, for if time does not steal away your glory

You can boast, however lowly you are, that you have sung, first among the French, the ancient honor of the long-robed people.

---

first among the French: echoes Horace's claim in *Odes* 3.30 to have been the first to adapt Aolian song to Italian—that is, Latin—verses, as the sonnet as a whole echoes Horace's aspiration to immortality

the long-robed people: the ancient Romans, the *gens togata,* as Virgil calls them in *Aeneid* 1.282, a line that begins, as du Bellay would have remembered, by referring to the Romans as "lords of the world" and that is preceded by Jove's promise, highly ironic in the context of the *Antiquities,* to give the Romans "empire without end" (*imperium sine fine*)

Dream

1

It was when the gift of the gods most gently flows in the eyes of man, drowning in the forgetfulness of sleep all the care of the toilsome day,

That a spirit appeared before my eyes on the bank of the great river of Rome, who, calling me by the name with which I name myself, ordered me to look toward the heavens,

Then cried out to me, "See," said he, "and reflect on all that is encompassed under this great temple. See how all is nothing but vanity.

"Then, understanding the inconstancy of worldly things, since God alone resists time, hope for nothing save from the divine."

It was when: echoes Virgil's *Aeneid* 2.268–269, where Hector appears in a dream to Aeneas, warning of the destruction of Troy

all is nothing but vanity: echoes Ecclesiastes 1.2

2

On the top of a hill I saw a building one hundred fathoms high. One hundred round columns, all made of diamond, ornamented the bold facade, and the style of the work was Doric.

The wall was neither of marble nor of brick but of a shining crystal, which from top to bottom shot out a thousand rays from its deep interior on a hundred stairs gilt with the finest gold of Africa.

The ceiling was of gold and the roof also shone shingled with great sheets of gold. The paving stone was jasper and fine emerald.

O vanity of the world! A sudden earthquake, collapsing the deepest roots of the hill, brought this beautiful structure crashing down from its foundation.

Songe

1

C'estoit alors que le present des Dieux
Plus doulcement s'écoule aux yeux de l'homme,
Faisant noyer dedans l'oubly du somme
Tout le soucy du jour laborieux, 4

Quand un Demon apparut à mes yeux
Dessus le bord du grand fleuve de Rome,
Qui m'appelant du nom dont je me nomme,
Me commanda regarder vers les cieux: 8

Puis m'escria, Voy (dit-il) et contemple
Tout ce qui est compris sous ce grand temple,
Voy comme tout n'est rien que vanité. 11

Lors cognoissant la mondaine inconstance,
Puis que Dieu seul au temps fait resistence,
N'espere rien qu'en la divinité. 14

2

Sur la croppe d'un mont je vis une Fabrique
De cent brasses de hault. Cent columnes d'un rond
Toutes de diamant ornoient le brave front:
Et la façon de l'œuvre estoit à la Dorique. 4

La muraille n'estoit de marbre ny de brique,
Mais d'un luisant crystal, qui du sommet au fond
Elançoit mille rayz de son ventre profond
Sur cent degrez dorez du plus fin or d'Afrique. 8

D'or estoit le lambriz, et le sommet encor
Reluisoit escaillé de grandes lames d'or:
Le pavé fut de jaspe, et d'esmeraulde fine. 11

O vanité du monde! un soudain tremblement
Faisant crouler du mont la plus basse racine,
Renversa ce beau lieu depuis le fondement. 14

3

Puis m'apparut une Poincte aguisee
D'un diamant de dix piedz en carré,
A sa hauteur justement mesuré,
Tant qu'un archer pourroit prendre visee. 4

Sur ceste Poincte une urne fut posee
De ce metal sur tous plus honnoré:
Et reposoit en ce vase doré
D'un grand Cæsar la cendre composee. 8

Aux quatre coings estoient couchez encor
Pour pedestal quatre grands lyons d'or,
Digne tumbeau d'une si digne cendre. 11

Las rien ne dure au monde que torment!
Je vy du ciel la tempeste descendre,
Et fouldroyer ce brave monument. 14

4

Je vy hault eslevé sur columnes d'ivoire,
Dont les bases estoient du plus riche metal,
A chapiteaux d'albastre, et frizes de crystal,
Le double front d'un arc dressé pour la memoire. 4

A chaque face estoit protraicte une victoire,
Portant ælles au doz, avec habit Nymphal,
Et hault assise y fut sur un char triomphal
Des Empereurs Romains la plus antique gloire. 8

L'ouvrage ne monstroit un artifice humain,
Mais sembloit estre fait de celle propre main
Qui forge en aguisant la paternelle fouldre. 11

Las je ne veulx plus voir rien de beau sous les cieux,
Puis qu'un œuvre si beau j'ay veu devant mes yeux,
D'une soudaine cheute estre reduict en pouldre. 14

3

Then appeared before me a pointed obelisk made of a diamond ten feet square, as high, justly measured, as an archer could shoot.

On top of that obelisk was set an urn made of that metal which is honored above all others, and in that golden vase were exposed the ashes of a great Caesar.

At the four corners, as a pedestal, lay four huge crouching lions made of gold—a worthy tomb for such worthy ashes.

Alas, nothing lasts in this world but suffering! I saw a storm descend from heaven and blast with a lightning bolt that brave monument.

Alas, nothing lasts: translated from Petrarch's *Rime sparse* 323.72

4

I saw raised high on columns of ivory, whose bases were made of the richest metal, with alabaster capitals and crystal friezes, the double facade of a memorial arch.

On each side was portrayed a victory, with wings on her back and dressed like a nymph, and she was seated high on a triumphal chariot, the most ancient glory of the Roman emperors.

The work revealed no human artifice but seemed to have been made by that same hand that forges and sharpens the paternal thunderbolt.

Alas, I no longer wish to see any beautiful thing under the heavens, since I saw before my eyes such a beautiful work with a sudden fall reduced to dust.

---

that same hand: the hand of Vulcan

5

And then I saw the Dodonaean tree spreading its shade over seven hills and conquerors adorned with its foliage on the bank of the Ausonian river.

There many ancient trophies were displayed, many spoils, and many glorious testimonies to the greatness of that bold race that descended from Dardanian blood.

I was enraptured to see a thing so rare, when a barbarous troop of peasants came to desecrate the honor of those boughs.

I heard the trunk groan under the axe, and then, later, I saw the scorned stump sprout two twin trees.

---

the Dodonaean tree: an oak dedicated to Jupiter

the Ausonian river: the Tiber

Dardanian blood: Trojan blood

a barbarous troop of peasants: the Goths

two twin trees: the empires of the east and west or the papacy and the Holy Roman Empire

6

A she-wolf I saw in a den under a rock nursing twins. I saw those twins playing prettily at her teat and with her neck extended the she-wolf licking them.

I saw her go out to seek food and, running through the fields with a new fury, bloody her tooth and her cruel paw on the small flocks to quench her thirst.

I saw a thousand huntsmen come down from the mountains that border the Lombard plains on one side and saw them stab her in the flank with a hundred spears.

I saw her lie outstretched on the plain, wailing out a thousand sobs, wallow in her blood, and her skin hung from an old tree trunk.

---

twins: Romulus and Remus

a thousand huntsmen: the Goths

5

Et puis je vy l'Arbre Dodonien
Sur sept costaux espandre son umbrage,
Et les vainqueurs ornez de son fueillage
Dessus le bord du fleuve Ausonien.

Là fut dressé maint trophee ancien,
Mainte despouille, et maint beau tesmoignage
De la grandeur de ce brave lignage
Qui descendit du sang Dardanien.

J'estois ravy de voir chose si rare,
Quand de paisans une troppe barbare
Vint oultrager l'honneur de ces rameaux.

J'ouy le tronc gemir sous la congnee,
Et vy depuis la souche desdaignee
Se reverdir en deux arbres jumeaux.

6

Une Louve je vy sous l'antre d'un rocher
Allaictant deux bessons. Je vis à sa mamelle
Mignardement joüer ceste couple jumelle,
Et d'un col allongé la Louve les lecher.

Je la vy hors de là sa pasture chercher,
Et courant par les champs, d'une fureur nouvelle
Ensanglanter la dent et la patte cruelle
Sur les menus troppeaux pour sa soif estancher.

Je vy mille veneurs descendre des montagnes,
Qui bornent d'un costé les Lombardes campagnes,
Et vy de cent espieux luy donner dans le flanc.

Je la vy de son long sur la plaine estendue
Poussant mille sanglotz, se veautrer en son sang,
Et dessus un vieux tronc la despouille pendue.

7

Je vy l'Oyseau, qui le soleil contemple,
D'un foible vol au ciel s'avanturer,
Et peu à peu ses ælles asseurer,
Suivant encor le maternel exemple. 4

Je le vy croistre, et d'un voler plus ample
Des plus hauts monts la hauteur mesurer,
Percer la nuë, et ses ælles tirer
Jusques au lieu, où des Dieux est le temple. 8

Là se perdit. Puis soudain je l'ay veu
Rouant par l'air en tourbillon de feu,
Tout enflammé sur la plaine descendre. 11

Je vy son corps en poudre tout reduit,
Et vy l'oyseau, qui la lumiere fuit,
Comme un vermet renaistre de sa cendre. 14

8

Je vis un fier Torrent, dont les flots escumeux
Rongeoient les fondemens d'une vieille ruine:
Je le vy tout couvert d'une obscure bruine,
Qui s'eslevoit par l'air en tourbillons fumeux: 4

Dont se formoit un corps à sept chefz merveilleux,
Qui villes et chasteaux couvoit sous sa poittrine,
Et sembloit devorer d'une egale rapine
Les plus doulx animaux, et les plus orgueilleux. 8

J'estois esmerveillé de voir ce monstre enorme
Changer en cent façons son effroyable forme,
Lors que je vy sortir d'un antre Scythien 11

Ce vent impetueux, qui soufle la froidure,
Dissiper ces nuaux, et en si peu que rien
S'esvanouïr par l'air ceste horrible figure. 14

7

I saw the bird who gazes on the sun venture toward heaven with a weak flight and, still following the example of his mother, little by little gain confidence in his wings.

I saw him grow and with more ample flight measure the height of the tallest mountains, pierce through the cloud, and soar to the site of the temple of the gods.

There he disappeared. Then suddenly I saw him, wheeling in the air in a fiery whirlwind, fall to the plain all in flames.

I saw his body reduced to dust and saw the bird who flees light reborn like a worm from his ashes.

---

the bird who gazes on the sun: the eagle, the symbol of the Roman Empire

the bird who flees light: the owl, which, like the crow in *Antiquities* 17, may stand for the Holy Roman Empire

8

I saw a raging torrent whose foaming waves were eating away the foundations of an old ruin. I saw it all covered by a dark mist which rose through the air in hazy swirls

From which a body with seven wondrous heads was formed, which hatched cities and castles under its breast and seemed to devour with equal rapacity the gentlest animals and the most ferocious.

I was amazed to see that huge monster alter its dreadful form in a hundred ways, when I saw emerging from a Scythian cave

That impetuous wind that blows cold scatter those clouds and in an instant I saw that horrible form dissolve in the air.

---

a body with seven wondrous heads: Rome and its seven hills represented as both the classical Hydra and the biblical seven-headed beast of Revelation 13 and 17

That impetuous wind that blows cold: the north wind, an allusion to the barbarians who invaded Rome

9

Terrified by that nocturnal portent, I saw a hideously sinewy body with a long beard, with long flowing hair, with wrinkled brow and the face of Saturn

Which, leaning on the belly of an urn, poured out water whose flowing course bathed the whole winding shore where the Trojan fought Turnus.

Under his feet a she-wolf nursed two infants. His right hand held the tree of peace; the other, the sturdy palm.

His head was crowned with laurel. And then the palm and olive fell from his hands, and the laurel branch died.

---

a hideously sinewy body: a personification of the Tiber

the Trojan: Aeneas, who fought Turnus on the banks of the Tiber in Virgil's *Aeneid* 12.30ff.

the tree of peace: the olive

the sturdy palm: the sign of military victory

crowned with laurel: the poetic glory of Rome

10

On the bank of a river a weeping nymph, lifting her arms to heaven with a thousand sobs, tuned her complaint to the murmur of the stream, clawing her beautiful skin and tearing her golden tresses.

"Alas, where now is that honored face, where is that greatness and that ancient praise, in which all the fortune and the honor of the world were contained when I was adored by men and gods?

"Was it not enough that mutinous discord had made me the common booty of the whole world, but that this new Hydra, worthy of a hundred Hercules,

"Multiplying with monstrous vices in seven heads, also engendered on these twisting banks so many cruel Neros and so many Caligulas?"

---

a weeping nymph: the Roman republic or simply ancient Rome

this new Hydra: imperial Rome or, more likely, modern papal Rome, in which case the popes would themselves be Neros and Caligulas

these twisting banks: of the Tiber

9

Tout effroyé de ce monstre nocturne,
Je vis un Corps hydeusement nerveux,
A longue barbe, à long flottans cheveux,
A front ridé, et face de Saturne:

Qui s'accoudant sur le ventre d'une urne,
Versoit une eau, dont le cours fluctueux
Alloit baignant tout ce bord sinueux,
Où le Troyen combattit contre Turne.

Dessous ses piedz une Louve allaictoit
Deux enfançons: sa main dextre portoit
L'arbre de paix, l'autre la palme forte:

Son chef estoit couronné de laurier:
Adonc luy cheut la palme, et l'olivier,
Et du laurier la branche devint morte.

10

Sur la rive d'un fleuve une Nymphe esploree
Croisant les bras au ciel avec mille sanglotz
Accordoit ceste plainte au murmure des flotz,
Oultrageant son beau teinct, et sa tresse doree:

Las où est maintenant ceste face honoree,
Où est ceste grandeur, et cet antique los,
Où tout l'heur et l'honneur du monde fut enclos,
Quand des hommes j'estois, et des Dieux adoree?

N'estoit-ce pas assez que le discord mutin
M'eut fait de tout le monde un publique butin,
Si cet Hydre nouveau digne de cent Hercules,

Foisonnant en sept chefz de vices monstrueux
Ne m'engendroit encor à ces bords tortueux
Tant de cruelz Nerons, et tant de Caligules?

11

Dessus un mont une Flamme allumee
A triple pointe ondoyoit vers les cieux,
Qui de l'encens d'un cedre precieux
Parfumoit l'air d'une odeur embasmee:

D'un blanc oyseau l'ælle bien emplumee
Sembloit voler jusqu'au sejour des Dieux,
Et dégoisant un chant melodieux
Montoit au ciel avecques la fumee:

De ce beau feu les rayons escartez,
Lançoient partout mille et mille clartez,
Quand le degout d'une pluie doree

Le vint esteindre. Ô triste changement!
Ce qui sentoit si bon premierement,
Fut corrompu d'une odeur sulphuree.

12

Je vy sourdre d'un roc une vive Fonteine,
Claire comme crystal aux rayons du soleil,
Et jaunissant au fond d'un sablon tout pareil
A celuy que Pactol' roule parmy la plaine.

Là sembloit que nature et l'art eussent pris peine
D'assembler en un lieu tous les plaisirs de l'œil:
Et là s'oyoit un bruit incitant au sommeil,
De cent accords plus doulx que ceulx d'une Sirene.

Les sieges et relaiz luisoient d'ivoire blanc,
Et cent Nymphes autour se tenoient flanc à flanc,
Quand des monts plus prochains de Faunes une suyte

En effroyables criz sur le lieu s'assembla,
Qui de ses villains piedz la belle onde troubla,
Mist les sieges par terre, et les Nymphes en fuyte.

11

On a hilltop a lighted flame with a triple tip rippled toward the heavens and with incense of precious cedar perfumed the air with a balmy fragrance.

The well-feathered wing of a white bird seemed to soar to the abode of the gods and singing out a melodious song rose to heaven with the smoke.

The scattered rays of this fair fire threw off thousands and thousands of beams on every side, when the drops of a golden shower

Extinguished it. O sad change! What first smelled so sweet was corrupted with a sulfurous odor.

---

a triple tip: a possible allusion to the papal tiara
a golden shower: the material corruption of the papacy

12

I saw a living fountain gushing from a rock, clear as crystal in the rays of the sun, and yellow-hued in its depths with sand like that which the Pactolus carries through the plain.

There it seemed that nature and art had labored to gather in one place all the pleasures of the eye, and there a sound was heard lulling to sleep with a hundred harmonies sweeter than those of a Siren.

The seats and benches shone with white ivory, and a hundred nymphs stood around it side by side, when from the nearest hills a troop of fauns

Gathered in the place with dreadful cries, who muddied the fair stream with their ugly feet, threw down the seats, and chased off the nymphs.

I saw a living fountain: adapted from Petrarch's *Rime sparse* 323.37–39
the Pactolus: the Libyan river whose sand was turned to gold by the touch of King Midas

13

Casting my eyes on the Latin shore, I saw from afar a skiff come into view still richer than the one that appeared to the sad Florentine.

But all of a sudden the fierce tempest, envious of such a rich prize, with a mutinous north wind assailed the beautiful boat, the most beautiful of all.

At last, the impetuous storm wrecked in a churning abyss the great wealth second to none.

I saw the fair treasure, the beautiful boat and the sailors too, lost beneath the water. Then I saw the boat reemerge on the wave.

---

the sad Florentine: Petrarch, whose *Rime sparse* 323.13–24 supplied the inspiration for this sonnet

I saw the boat reemerge: papal Rome, the Holy Roman Empire, or the French *monarchie* of the dedicatory sonnet to King Henry II

14

Having groaned for so many miseries, I saw a city much like the one the herald of good news saw, but its foundation was built on sand.

Its head seemed to touch the heavens, and its form was no less proud than beautiful—worthy, if anything was ever worthy, to be immortal, if under the heavens anything could claim a firm foundation.

I was astonished to see such a beautiful work, when from the north came a fierce storm, which, blowing the fury of its spiteful heart

On all that stood in its way, at once overturned in a cloud of dust the weak foundations of the great city.

---

the one the herald of goods news saw: the heavenly Jerusalem seen by Saint John in Revelation 21.2

its foundation was built on sand: echoes Matthew 7.26

13

Plus riche assez que ne se monstroit celle
Qui apparut au triste Florentin,
Jettant ma veüe au rivage Latin
Je vy de loing surgir une Nasselle: 4

Mais tout soudain la tempeste cruelle,
Portant envie à si riche butin,
Vint assaillir d'un Aquilon mutin
La belle Nef des autres la plus belle. 8

Finablement l'orage impetueux
Fit abysmer d'un gouphre tortueux
La grand' richesse à nulle autre seconde. 11

Je vy sous l'eau perdre le beau thresor,
La belle Nef, et les Nochers encor,
Puis vy la Nef se ressourdre sur l'onde. 14

14

Ayant tant de malheurs gemy profondement,
Je vis une Cité quasi semblable à celle
Que vit le messager de la bonne nouvelle,
Mais basty sur le sable estoit son fondement. 4

Il sembloit que son chef touchast au firmament,
Et sa forme n'estoit moins superbe que belle:
Digne, s'il en fut onc, digne d'estre immortelle,
Si rien dessous le ciel se fondoit fermement. 8

J'estois esmerveillé de voir si bel ouvrage,
Quand du costé du Nort vint le cruel orage,
Qui souflant la fureur de son cœur despité 11

Sur tout ce qui s'oppose encontre sa venüe,
Renversa sur le champ, d'une pouldreuse nüe,
Les foibles fondemens de la grande Cité. 14

15

Finablement sur le poinct que Morphee
Plus veritable apparoit à noz yeux,
Fasché de voir l'inconstance des cieux,
Je voy venir la sœur du grand Typhee: 4

Qui bravement d'un morion cœffee
En majesté sembloit egale aux Dieux,
Et sur le bord d'un fleuve audacieux
De tout le monde erigeoit un trophee. 8

Cent Roys vaincuz gemissoient à ses piedz,
Les bras aux doz honteusement liez:
Lors effroyé de voir telle merveille, 11

Le ciel encor je luy voy guerroyer,
Puis tout à coup je la voy fouldroyer,
Et du grand bruit en sursault je m'esveille. 14

15

Finally, at that moment when Morpheus appears with greater truth before our eyes, weary from seeing the inconstancy of the heavens, I see the sister of the great Typhoeus come,

Who, boldly helmeted, seemed in majesty the equal of the gods, and on the bank of a proud river raised a trophy over the whole world.

A hundred defeated kings were groaning at her feet, their arms shamefully tied behind their backs. Then frightened to see such a marvel,

I see her wage war against heaven as well. Then all at once I see her struck down by lightning and, at the great noise, with a start I awake.

Morpheus: the god of sleep, who grants truer dreams near dawn

I see: note the shift to the present tense in this last of the fifteen sonnets in the *Dream*

the sister of the great Typhoeus: Rome, who here and elsewhere in the *Dream* may recall the Whore of Babylon in Revelation 17

Three Latin Elegies

Description of Rome

Let not cruel Mars excite my heart, nor the rage of litigation; let not the harsh storm toss me about. Let me not desire to suffer endlessly the mad labors of the court, but let a wreath of laurel crown my head.

Sometimes I delight to lead the troop of dancing virgins down from the holy peak of lofty Pindhos along the high ridges. Sometimes I delight to stretch out lazily under the cover of shady caves and to sing, while strumming with a plectrum, a long melody, whether it pleases me to sound in the meter of a Tuscan lyre tender flames for a blessed Olive, or rather to compose to the glory of my great king, or to speak your praises, Divine Margaret, or those of the great man—the glory of the family of the du Bellays—who now, in Rome, raises to the stars his head crowned with purple.

Under the auspices of this hero, we crossed the harsh Alps and saw the plains of beautiful Hesperia. We saw the whirling currents of the golden Tiber and the walls of the descendants of Romulus scattered across the plains: those walls, though overthrown in vast ruins everywhere, domineering, still breathe out ancient threats. We saw him who holds the keys to highest Olympus, august in his miter, and the fathers garbed in purple. Why mention the towering dome dedicated to great Peter? There exists no more beautiful work in Ausonia. Why recall the golden coffered

---

Description of Rome: this is the second elegy in du Bellay's *Poemata* (1558) and was probably written shortly after his arrival in Rome in 1553

Let not cruel Mars: du Bellay here rejects the professions of soldier, lawyer, sailor (or merchant), and courtier in favor of that of poet

the troop of dancing virgins: the Muses

lofty Pindhos: mountain in Thrace consecrated to Apollo and the Muses

in the meter of the Tuscan lyre: in the manner of Petrarch

blessed Olive: the object of du Bellay's adoration in his Petrarchan sonnet sequence *Olive*

my great king: Henry II

Divine Margaret: Margaret of France, the sister of Henry II and du Bellay's chief patron

the great man: Cardinal Jean du Bellay, du Bellay's kinsman and employer during his years in Rome

Hesperia: Italy, the promised end of Aeneas's wanderings

the descendants of Romulus: the Romans

him who holds the keys: Julius III, who was pope when du Bellay arrived in Rome

the fathers garbed in purple: the cardinals

the towering dome: du Bellay's *pendentia* may suggest both the great height and the unfinished state of Michelangelo's dome of Saint Peter's

Ausonia: Italy

Romae descriptio

Non mea sollicitet saevus praecordia Mavors,
Nec rabies litis, durave iactet hyems.
Nec cupiam insanos Aulae perferre labores,
Sed cingant nostras laurea serta comas.
Nunc iuvat aerii sacro de vertice Pindi
Ducere virgineos per iuga celsa choros.
Nunc iuvat umbrosis lentum iacuisse sub antris,
Et longum plectro concinuisse melos,
Seu libuit molles flammas foelicis Olivae
Hetruscae ad numeros personuisse lyrae,
Seu potius magni laudes contexere Regis,
Dicere vel laudes, Margari Diva, tuas,
Vel qui nunc Romae, Bellaiae gloria gentis,
Purpureum magnus tollit ad astra caput.
Illius auspiciis duras superavimus Alpeis,
Et pulchrae campos vidimus Hesperiae.
Vidimus et flavi contortas Tybridis undas,
Sparsaque per campos moenia Romulidum:
Moenia quae vastis passim convulsa ruinis
Antiquas spirant imperiosa minas.
Vidimus excelsi claveis qui gestat Olympi,
Augustum mitra, purpureosque Patres.
Quid referam magni pendentia culmina Petri?
Quo nullum Ausonia pulchrius extat opus.

panels for the painted ceilings, and the exalted doorways of the pontifical galleries? Add, too, so many august residences, so many long reception rooms, and the villa, beautiful to the eye and in its name. Add so many lofty structures and the massive sepulchre, and the houses of gold, and the painted temples of the gods. I omit the broad bridges and their high arches beneath which the Albula flows with its swift waters. I omit the vast temple with its wide dome, where greatest Rome honored all her gods. I leave aside the marble statues which adorn the Virginal fountain, consecrated by the will of the supreme pontiff, and many other marvels of ancient Rome that everywhere now return to life from the upturned earth.

Here too—if I may be permitted to run through the whole subject—let us speak of your manners and customs, illustrious Rome. If you should aspire to triumph by the arts of Pallas, sweet Attic honey flows for the Romans. If you enjoy armed combat and horse races, this city will give you many Tyndarides. If you should wish to hear of the various tumults of kings, here Rumor, whether true or false, flies. If you delight in the spectacle of Fortune's power, nowhere does she reign with more ample sway. If Venus attracts you, everything here is charged with Venus; she was the origin of the Roman people. Here is the realm of winks and innuendos, of noisy voices, of meaningful whistles, of gaiety mixed with loud joking. Here they delight in dancing indiscriminately all kinds of dances or in singing Tuscan songs to the accompaniment of a lyre. In a closed carriage, by the side of his lovely mother, Cupid with his tuneful plectrum plays harmoniously on his ivory instrument. Bejeweled diadems adorn a marble forehead, and faces are made up with the deceptive red of ground mollusk shells. Pendants of gold grace milk-white necks; sparkling jewels decorate hands of snow. Pearls hang from ears, and curled hair causes a thousand heads to bow, subjected to a pleasant yoke. Belts of gold bind clothes of Tyrian purple, and a long gown flows down to delicate feet. By art, cothurn-shod feet step gracefully; by art, amorous glances dart; by art, fingers flirt.

---

the villa: possibly the Belvedere, with a pun on its name

the massive sepulchre: the Mausoleum of Hadrian

the Albula: the Tiber

the vast temple: the Pantheon

the Virginal fountain: the Aqua Virgo, attributed to Agrippa

Pallas: Athena

Tyndarides: Castor and Pollux, the sons of Tyndarus

the origin of the Roman people: as the mother and guide of Aeneas, Venus could be considered a founder of Rome

Aurea quid memorem pictis laquearia tectis,
Altaque porticibus limina Pontificum?
Adde tot augustas aedes, totque atria longa,
Quaeque oculis villa est nomine pulchra suo.
Adde tot aerias arceis, molemque sepulchri,
Auratasque domos, pictaque templa Deum.
Praetereo longos excelso fornice ponteis,
Quos subter rapidis Albula fertur aquis.
Praetereo vastum lata testudine templum,
Quo cunctos coluit maxima Roma Deos.
Mitto Virginei surgentia marmora fontis,
Qui sacer est summi numine Pontificis,
Multaque praeterea veteris miracula Romae,
Undique defosso nunc rediviva solo.
Hic quoque (nam liceat toto decurrere campo)
Dicamus mores, inclyta Roma, tuos.
Si quis Palladias optet regnare per arteis,
Dulcia Romanis Attica mella fluunt.
Si placet armorum lusus, si cursus equorum,
Tyndaridas multos urbs dabit ista tibi.
Si varios Regum cupias audire tumultus,
Hic veri et falsi nuntia fama volat.
Si spectare iuvat Fortunae iura potentis
Non alio regnat latius illa loco.
Si Venus oblectat, Veneris sunt omnia plena:
Romani auspicium sanguinis illa fuit.
Hic signa, hic strepitus vocesque, et nota vocantum
Sibila, nec tacitis gaudia mixta iocis.
Hic iuvat aut varias passim saltare choreas,
Aut Thuscos cithara concinuisse modos.
Carpento invectus pulchra cum matre Cupido
Arguto resonum pectine pulsat ebur.
Gemmea marmoream cingunt redimicula frontem,
Oraque fallaci murice tincta rubent.
Aurea lacteolo pendentque monilia collo,
Et niveas ornat gemma corusca manus.
Et baccae auriculis pendent, tortique capilli
Mille trahunt dulci colla subacta iugo.
Sidonias vestes limbus complectitur aureus,
Defluit in teneros et stola longa pedes.
Arte cothurnati librant vestigia gressus,
Arte oculi spectant, arte micant digiti.

Whatever yielding Arabia and Egypt, whatever the Indians or Tyrians bring blest Rome possesses. Why mention the wealth of the fields and the gifts of Lyaeus? Why your woods and pastures, your rustic throng? Why the cool fountains, the meadows refreshed by streams, and all the colors that paint the earth with the coming of spring? Though such riches are to be seen in abundance in the land of Ausonia, still greater is the pleasure of seeing them in the midst of the city.

Why recall the marble statues that breathe in august dwellings, the artists' skillful hand that has made them live? Or that about the limbs of that father are entwined scale-covered whorls, and that his sons are entangled in the same knots? Or Phoebus and Venus, statues of Parian marble, stone so cunningly fashioned into ancient gods? Here Rome, known by her helmet and menacing look, steps victoriously on the bowed necks of kings. Here the twins play, grasping at the obliging teats of the she-wolf, their nurse. Here, with his eyes and his whole body fixed on it, a boy living in bronze plucks a thorn from the sole of his foot. Terrible with his club, the son of Amphitryon stands naked in tawny gold, breathing forth Herculean spirit. Here a warlike steed, bearing a rider on his back, breathes forth Mars from breast, nostrils, and eyes. And who would not admire the heads of the Caesars and so many striking busts everywhere in Rome? And who would ignore the Tiber, known by the she-wolf and the twins? And the seven-mouthed god? With snakes twisted about her, reclining on her elbow, lies the wife of Antony, bravely daring to die. Here with Mars Cypris

---

ground mollusk shells: murex, used for rouge

delicate feet: girls' feet but also metrical ones, particularly the "delicate" feet of Roman love poetry

Lyaeus: Bacchus, the god of wine

that father: Laocoön, the subject of one of the celebrated ancient statues du Bellay saw in Rome, statues he describes in this and the following lines

Phoebus and Venus: the *Apollo Belvedere* and the *Venus of Cnidos*

the twins: Romulus and Remus, refers to a bronze statue known as the *Capitoline Wolf*

a boy: the *Spinario,* or *Thorn-puller,* a bronze statue of the first century BCE

the son of Amphitryon: Hercules, refers to the colossal gilt bronze statue of *Hercules Standing*

a warlike steed: the equestrian statue of Marcus Aurelius

the seven-mouthed god: the Nile, a river god represented, like the Tiber, in a colossal marble statue

the wife of Antony: Cleopatra, whose suicide du Bellay, like his contemporaries, supposed was represented in a statue now identified as the sleeping Ariadne

Cypris: Venus

Quicquid mollis Arabs, Aegyptus, quicquid et Indi
Aut portant Tyrii, Roma beata tulit.
Quid referam laetas segetes ac dona Lyaei?
Quid nemora et saltus, rustica turba, tuos?
Quid gelidos fonteis, quid prata recentia rivis,
Et quicquid pingit vere ineunte solum?
Quae licet Ausonia spectentur plurima terra,
Spectare in media plus tamen urbe iuvat.
Quid memorem augustis spirantia marmora tectis,
Artificum docta vivere iussa manu?
An patris implexos squamosis orbibus artus,
Et natos iisdem nexibus implicitos?
An Phoebum et Venerem, Pario de marmore signa,
Saxaque in antiquos tam bene ficta Deos?
Hic Roma, insignis galea vultuque minaci,
Victorum Regum colla subacta premit.
Hic ludunt gemini prensantes ubera Nati,
Ubera nutricis officiosa Lupae.
Hic plantae affixis oculis et corpore toto
Evellit spinam vivus in aere Puer.
Terribilis clava fulvo stat nudus in auro,
Herculeum spirans Amphitryoniades.
Hic bellator Equus, tergum sessore premente,
Pectore flat Martem, naribus atque oculis.
Caesareos vultus quis non miretur et ora
Tam multis Romae conspicienda locis?
Quis Tybrim notumque Lupa notumque gemellis,
Quis septemgemini nesciat ora Dei?
Anguibus intortis, cubitoque innixa recumbit
Antoni Coniux, fortiter ausa mori.

talks; turning toward him eyes bathed in tears, she tames a savage heart. Here two chargers which twin colossi restrain; they lift their heads and, rearing, whinny for battle. Here a satyr tries to seduce a boy with his face and a gift; gifts are no doubt pleasing, but the beast lacks all appeal. In a vein of marble, Adonis shows his wound, a wound, from the tusk of a wild boar, by which he was felled.

But why attempt to tally the blue waves of the sea or desire to number the stars of the night? If I should wish briefly to describe these wonders one by one, my pen would fail me, a day would be too little. Shall I speak of the height of the obelisks, the ruined colossi, the theaters, now gloomy and silent, their enclosures empty? Behold how a luxuriant growth of weeds and decay cover these piles of stones and these walls that once threatened the gods. Here, where pinnacles of stone break off and topple from the sky, was greatest Rome. Now I delight to see everywhere columns gnawed away and everywhere buried temples of the ancient gods, now the Field of Mars, the Baths, the Circus, and the Forum, now the Seven Hills and the monuments to great men. Here conquerors went by on their way up to the Capitol. Here were the twin fasces, symbol of the consuls' power. Here was the place of the Rostra, here great Tully was accustomed to reign, here was assembled the vast plebeian throng. Alas, such a great empire, whose pride ruled over lands and seas, has by steel and flames been reduced to ashes. This city, which once rivaled the gods of heaven, was made to bow her neck under a barbarian yoke. She who had plundered the whole world became the world's prey, and all that belonged to this city belongs now to the world. Devouring time buries the rest under long ages, and Rome dead is now her own tomb.

Learn from this what faith one can put in human things. So brief is the course of such power. Enormous Rome has perished. Learned Virgil lives everywhere, and the harmonious chords of the Latin lyre live on. The flames of Ovid live, living still are those of Tibullus, and your verses live, learned Catullus.

Hail, O ashes, hail, sacred poets, whom glorious Rome counts as her prophets. Would that I, Frenchman that I am, might make your fountains flow once again, while I enjoy the more bountiful genius of this clime.

---

twin colossi: the *Dioscuri*, a colossal marble pair in the Piazza Quirinale

the twin fasces: bundled rods with a projecting axe blade that represented the authority of Roman magistrates

the Rostra: platforms for speakers in the Roman Forum

great Tully: Cicero

This city: compare *Antiquities* 3.5–8

Learned Virgil: compare *Antiquities* 5.12–14

Hic Martem alloquitur Cypris, lacrymisque madentes
Inflectens oculos, effera corda domat.
Hic geminus Sonipes, gemino cohibente Colosso,
Cervicem attollens arduus arma fremit.
Hic Puerum Satyrus vultuque et munere tentat:
Munera grata quidem, non ferus ille placet.
Marmorea in vena vulnus demonstrat Adonis,
Vulnus, quo iacuit dente ferocis apri.
Sed quid caeruleos tento percurrere fluctus,
Nocturnasque volo connumerare faceis?
Singula si cupiam brevibus describere chartis,
Scribentem calamus destituatque dies,
Ardua Pyramidum dicam, truncosque Colossos,
Maestaque nunc vacuo muta theatra sinu?
Aspice ut has moleis, quondamque minantia Divis
Moenia luxurians herba situsque tegant.
Hic, ubi praeruptis nutantia culmina saxis
Descendunt caelo, maxima Roma fuit.
Nunc iuvat exesas passim spectare columnas,
Et passim veterum templa sepulta Deum.
Nunc Martis campum, Thermas, Circumque Forumque,
Nunc septem Colleis et monumenta virum.
Hac se victores Capitolia ad alta ferebant,
Hic gemini fasces, Consulis imperium.
Hic Rostris locus, hic magnus regnare solebat
Tullius, hic plebis maxima turba fuit.
Heu tantum imperium, terrisque undisque superbum,
Et ferro et flamma corruit in cineres.
Quaeque fuit quondam summis Urbs aemula Divis,
Barbarico potuit subdere colla iugo.
Orbis praeda fuit, totum quae exhauserat orbem,
Quaeque Urbis fuerant, nunc habet Orbis opes.
Caetera tempus edax longis tegit obruta seclis,
Ipsaque nunc tumulus mortua Roma sui est.
Disce hinc humanis quae sit fiducia rebus:
Hic tanti cursus tam brevis imperii.
Roma ingens periit, vivit Maro doctus ubique,
Et vivunt Latiae fila canora lyrae.
Nasonis vivunt, vivunt flammaeque Tibulli,
Et vivunt numeri, docte Catulle, tui.
Salvete o cineres, sancti salvete Poetae,
Quos numerat vates inclyta Roma suos.
Sit mihi fas, Gallo, vestros recludere fonteis,
Dum caeli Genio liberiore fruor,

Would that I might utter verses still unknown to our Muses, and wield the plectrum with an unfamiliar sound. To my ambition, Latin Camenae, grant your indulgence, join with the Muses of my fatherland, and here may a second harvest of my talent spring forth. Perhaps the monuments of our labor will indeed live on, while all the rest will perish with its master.

Virtue alone lifts a man above the heights of heaven, and only the Muse blesses virtue with heaven's joys.

To P. de Ronsard, Prince of the French Lyre

Ronsard, you who by merit hold the highest place in the Aonian troop, you who were once half my soul, you to whom the French lyre, when struck with a Dircean note, confesses owing its plectrum and its strings, now France, the mother of the Muses, now the court of your invincible prince keeps you: there where learned Carle, your friend, thunders forth your verses, Carle, the glory of ancient Bordeaux, Carle, the priest of the Muses, whose nature luminous Pallas fashioned with honorable traits. It is he who wins you the favor of the nobles and of our powerful king. No longer does devouring envy injure your songs.

Happy the man who in his lifetime has, to the applause of the whole theater of the nation, trampled dire envy. This monster, Ronsard, you, enjoying the favor of people and kings alike, have overcome with Herculean strength. Well done! Already the victory is assuredly yours, and a sacred crown encircles your head. Already the whole cohort of Phoebus, already Phoebus himself rises up in your honor and grants you a place in the midst of the chorus. Thus in Elysium the thick crowd of souls that comes from all sides look up admiringly at Orpheus. Who then, Ronsard, enjoys a life more blessed than you? Or to whom do the gods extend so many delights?

Camenae: the Muses

Virtue: *virtus* in the untranslatable Latin sense of those qualities ideally belonging to a man (*vir*), merit, excellence, capacity, worth, goodness, virtue

To P. de Ronsard: elegy 6 in the *Poemata* (1558), translated into French and published as "À Pierre de Ronsard" in du Bellay's posthumous *Divers poemes* (1568)

the Aonian troop: the Muses

Dircean note: Pindaric odes, a form Ronsard had introduced in France

learned Carle: Lancelot de Carle, bishop of Riez, who read parts of Ronsard's unfinished epic poem, the *Franciade*, to the French court

thunder forth: *tonare* (to thunder) was a verb Roman elegiac poets used with reference to epic poetry

Happy the man: compare *Regrets* 20

Hactenus et nostris incognita carmina Musis
Dicere, et insolito plectra movere sono.
Hoc mihi cum patriis Latiae indulgete Camoenae,
Alteraque ingenii sit seges ista mei.
Forte etiam vivent nostri monumenta laboris,
Caetera cum domino sunt peritura suo.
Sola virum virtus caeli super ardua tollit,
Virtutem caelo solaque Musa beat.

Ad P. Ronsardum, lyrae Gallicae principem

Ronsarde, Aoniae merito pars maxima turbae,
Pars animae quondam dimidiata meae,
Cui plectra et nervos sese debere fatetur
Gallica Dircaeo pectine pulsa chelys,
Musarum nunc alma parens te Gallia, nunc te
Detinet invicti Principis Aula tui,
Doctus ubi tonat ore tuus tua carmina Carlus,
Antiquae Carlus gloria Burdigalae,
Musarum Antistes Carlus, cui candida Pallas
Ingenuis finxit moribus ingenium.
Hic tibi conciliat proceres Regemque potentem,
Nec tua iam laedit carmina livor edax.
Foelix qui, populi toto plaudente Theatro,
Vivus adhuc diram contudit invidiam.
Hoc tu, Ronsarde, et populis et Regibus aequis,
Vicisti monstrum viribus Herculeis.
Macte animo, iam certa tibi victoria parta est,
Praecingitque tuum sacra corona caput.
Iam tibi tota cohors Phoebi, iam Phoebus et ipse
Assurgit, medio constituitque choro,
Elysiis qualem mirantes Orphea campis
Hinc atque hinc densae suspiciunt animae.
Quis te igitur vivit, Ronsarde, beatior uno,
Aut cui tot praestant numina delicias?

Now the well-tended vineyards of lofty Sabut claim you, and the verdant Braye and the Gastine forest. Now the nymphs of the Loir echo your songs, and the Bellerian stream bounds to the rhythm of your verses. Happy the nymphs who can hear such a poet and perform to his song their sacred dances by night. He honors your woods, O guardian spirits, he honors your caves, your rivers, and your crags.

All the while, miserable we, tossed about in a fierce southern wind, flee poverty by sea and by land, but we do not escape the care that night and day follows us on land and pursues us at sea. Alas! Where is now that disdain for fortune, where is that once unvanquished courage, and that love for a long posterity? Then, with Phoebus showing the way above the heights of the Cyrrhean peak, I sailed swiftly through the lofty clouds. Undaunted, I spurned base cares and all the hubbub of life, led by the love of a glory like yours. Now I do not know what languor numbs my mind, and a Lethean dullness oppresses my eyes. Cyrrha no longer pleases me, nor the Permessian stream. All such desire has melted from my heart. What delight can it be to pass one's whole life in foolish cares, to torment one's mind with vain apprehensions?

Once we were happy, when, filled with joy, in the rural retreats of our fatherland, Calliope gently caressed us and held us to her breast. It is she who at your birth took you tenderly in her arms and fondly smilingly said, "Be my son." It is she, too, who taught you to scorn the deceptive rewards of the vulgar throng and run toward the stars by an untraveled way. Under her guidance, you made the Pierian Muses come down from the double-domed mount to your little Loir river. There, now aflame with a great love for Cassandre, you triumph when you sing in the Tuscan manner. Now, with a graver song, you celebrate men and gods, you who can learnedly sound the strings of Pindar's lyre. Nor have you disdained to lower your

---

Sabut . . . the verdant Braye . . . the Gastine forest: places memorialized in his poems by Ronsard

Loir: river in Limousin near which Ronsard was born

the Bellerian stream: the Bellerie, a small river associated with Ronsard

Happy the nymphs: compare *Regrets* 6.5–8, where du Bellay pictures himself in a similar scene

All the while: compare *Regrets* 24.9–14

a fierce southern wind: the Auster

Alas!: compare *Regrets* 6

the Cyrrhean peak: Parnassus, the seat of Apollo and the Muses

the Permessian stream: the Helicon, the stream of Apollo and the Muses

Calliope: the Muse of epic poetry

the Pierian Muses: from Pieria, a region of Thrace associated with the Muses

the double-domed mount: Parnassus

Nunc te culta tenent celsi vineta Sabuti,
Nunc virides Braiae, Gastineumque nemus.
Et tua Ledinae respondent carmina Nymphae,
Et salit ad numeros Belleris unda tuos.
Foelices Nymphae, queis talem audire poetam
Et licuit sacros ducere nocte choros.
Ille colit vestras, tutissima numina, sylvas,
Ille antra et fluvios saxaque vestra colit.
Nos miseri interea, rapidis iactantibus Austris,
Per mare, per terras pauperiem fugimus.
Sed non effugimus curam, quae nocte dieque
Nos sequitur terra persequiturque mari.
Heus ubi contemptus fortunae invictaque quondam
Vis animi et longae posteritatis amor?
Cum, Phoebo monstrante viam super ardua Cyrrhae,
Tranabam celeri nubila celsa fuga,
Atque humiles curas strepitusque, interritus, omnes
Spernebam, laudis ductus amore tuae.
Nunc mihi nescio quo torpet mens ipsa veterno,
Lethaeusque urget lumina nostra sopor.
Nec iam Cyrrha placet, nec iam Permessidos unda:
Hic totus nostro e pectore fluxit amor.
Quid iuvat insanis vitam traducere curis,
Atque animum vano sollicitare metu?
Fortunati olim, patrio dum rure beatos
Nos fouit molli Calliope in gremio.
Haec te nascentem teneris excepit in ulnis,
Et blandum arridens: sis mihi natus, ait.
Haec te eadem docuit fallacis praemia vulgi
Spernere, et insolita currere ad astra via.
Hac duce, Pierias gemino de vertice Musas
Deduxti ad Ledi parva fluenta tui.
Nunc ubi Cassandrae magno inflammatus amore,
Hetruscos superas ore canente modos,
Nunc plectro graviore sonas hominesque Deosque,
Pindaricae doctus tangere fila lyrae.

verse to a more tender mode, whether yours, Catullus, or yours, Tibullus. Whatever you do (for we must suppose that you will never cease), all that you sing is worthy of divine Virgil. Whether you compose Bacchic verses or pastoral songs, grace sits always on the lips of Ronsard. I speak of small things, but already the whole court joyfully resounds with the name of your Francus; all France sings Francus. Here too (and even the waters of the golden Tiber sing you) the triumphant fame of your *Franciade* echoes.

Up then, while beauteous Apollo reaches out his lyre to you, while the divine spirits aid with your songs. Write, be bold, and let France boast at last of a work to which Greece gives way and Italy as well.

Longing for His Fatherland

Whoever spends with indifference his leisure in unknown lands and, roving, seeks a home in a foreign world, whom neither sweet love, nor attachment to parents, nor a still more tender tie, if any there be, could summon back—he is a man of iron, worthy, when he emerged from his mother's womb, to have been suckled by Hyrcanian tigresses.

I do not have a heart of stone, nor a heart stiffened with unyielding iron; neither a tigress nor a bear was my mother, so that in my hardness I would not be touched by sweet love of my fatherland, so that I would wish to be exiled far away for so many months. What indeed is exile but to have left behind your familiar stars, your fatherland, and your household gods? Thrice has the inexorable sun completed his annual course since I was compelled to begin a journey on such long roads, to live far from home, a stranger, under unknown roofs—only with difficulty can I recall my dear Liré—obliged to learn other customs and other manners, and to form alien words with an unfamiliar sound.

Cassandre: Ronsard's beloved in his Petrarchan (thus "Tuscan") sonnet sequence, the *Amours de Cassandre*

a graver song: Ronsard's Pindaric odes

Francus: the hero of Ronsard's unfinished epic poem, the *Franciade*

Longing for His Fatherland: elegy 7 in du Bellay's *Poemata* (1558)

Whoever spends: compare *Regrets* 30

Nec piguit molli versus deducere filo,
Sive Catulle tuos, sive Tibulle tuos.
Quicquid agis (nam te nunquam cessare putandum est)
Omnia divino digna Marone sonas.
Seu Bacchi numeros, seu rustica carmina pangis,
Gratia Ronsardi semper in ore sedet.
Parva loquor: iam tota tuum, iam Regia Francum
Laeta sonat, Francum Gallia tota canit.
Hic quoque (et ipsa canit flavi te Tybridis unda)
Franciados resonat fama superba tuae.
Ergo age, dum Citharam pulcher tibi tendit Apollo,
Dumque tuis adsunt numina carminibus
Scribe, aude, atque aliquid iam tandem Gallia iactet,
Graecia cui cedat, cedat et Ausonia.

Patriae desiderium

Quicunque ignotis lentus terit ocia terris,
Et vagus externo quaerit in orbe domum,
.Quem non dulcis amor, quem non revocare parentes,
Nec potuit si quid dulcius esse potest,
Ferreus est, dignusque olim cui matris ab alvo
Hyrcanae tigres ubera praebuerint.
Non mihi saxea sunt durove rigentia ferro
Pectora, nec tigris, nec fuit ursa parens,
Ut dulci patriae durus non tangar amore,
Totque procul menses exul ut esse velim.
Quid nanque exilium est aliud quam sidera nota,
Quam patriam et proprios deseruisse lares?
Annua ter rapidi circum acta est orbita Solis,
Ex quo tam longas cogor inire vias,
Ignotisque procul peregrinus degere tectis,
Et Lyrii tantum vix meminisse mei,
Atque alios ritus, aliosque ediscere mores,
Fingere et insolito verba aliena sono.

But (you will say) what is more splendid than the Roman court and what place in all the world is more beautiful? Rome is the fatherland of the world, and he who dwells within the walls of high Rome lives—he, too—on his own soil. Perhaps living in Rome (which is not, after all, the lot of every foreigner) pleases me as well. My paternal uncle holds a high place in the purple-robed Senate, and a high place, too, in the Aonian chorus. His goodness favors my Muses and fosters them, and he keeps poverty from our door.

But as often as I remember how I left my studies of old and my old friends and my dear home, where I had once learned to despise the anxiety-producing riches of Persia and to live happily on little, so often the image of my fatherland presses itself on me, and so often fresh cares torment me through and through. And though I lack nothing, I lack everything while unhappily I am not allowed to enjoy a familiar world. I cannot see the banks of the Loire, the pastures, the leafy woods, the rich products of the Angevin soil, which for milk, for wine, and for the fertility of its golden fields rivals the praises of ancient Italy. But the Ithacan, though the land of Laertes was sterile and bore neither the gifts of Bacchus nor those of Ceres, came back to his fatherland. Neither beautiful Calypso nor the beautiful daughter of Alcinous kept him from returning. Happy the man who has known the manners and the cities of many people and has been able to grow old in his own home. Everyone wishes to return to his birthplace; few foreign things please for long; and even wild beasts seek out their lair.

When will I see the smoke rise from the chimney of my own country house and when will I see the few acres of my own estate? No, the seven hills do not touch my heart, nor do the waters of the Tiber lay claim to my feelings. The monuments of the ancient Quirites are nothing to me. The statues and paintings bring me no joy. Nor do the Laurentian nymphs or the green woods or the flowering fields please me as once they did. Even

---

My paternal uncle: Cardinal Jean du Bellay, Joachim's father's cousin

the purple-robed Senate: the College of Cardinals

the Aonian chorus: alludes to Cardinal du Bellay's own skill as a poet

the Loire: the river that runs by du Bellay's home in Anjou (compare *Regrets* 19)

the Ithacan: Ulysses, the son of Laertes (compare *Regrets* 40)

Happy the man: compare *Regrets* 30 and 31

the ancient Quirites: the ancient Romans

Laurentian: refers to a town near Rome

At quid Romana (dices) speciosius Aula,
  Aut quisnam toto pulchrior orbe locus?
Roma orbis patria est, quique altae moenia Romae
  Incolit, in proprio degit et ille solo.
Forsan et est Romae (quod non contingere cuiuis
  Hic solet externo) vivere dulce mihi,
Est cui purpurei patruus pars magna Senatus,
  Atque idem Aonii pars quoque magna chori,
Qui nostras ornetque bonus, foveatque Camoenas,
  Arceat a nostro pauperiemque lare.
At quoties studia antiqua antiquosque sodales,
  Et memini charam deseruisse domum,
Quondam ubi sollicitas Persarum temnere gazas,
  Et foelix parvo vivere doctus eram,
Ipsa mihi patriae toties occurrit imago,
  Et toties curis torqueor usque novis.
Utque nihil desit, nobis tamen omnia desunt,
  Dum miseris noto non licet orbe frui.
Nec Ligeris ripas, saltus, sylvasque comantes
  Cernere et Andini pinguia culta soli,
Quae lacte et Baccho flaventis et ubere campi
  Antiquae certant laudibus Italiae.
Ast Ithacus, licet ipsa foret Laertia tellus
  Et Bacchi et Cereris muneribus sterilis,
In patriam rediit, reditum nec pulchra Calypso,
  Nec pulchra Alcinoi detinuit soboles.
Foelix qui mores multorum vidit et urbes,
  Sedibus et potuit consenuisse suis.
Ortus quaeque suos cupiunt, externa placentque
  Pauca diu, repetunt et sua lustra ferae.
Quando erit ut notae fumantia culmina villae,
  Et videam regni iugera parva mei?
Non septemgemini tangunt mea pectora Colles,
  Nec retinet sensus Tybridis unda meos.
Non mihi sunt cordi veterum monumenta Quiritum,
  Nec statuae, nec me picta tabella iuvat.
Non mihi Laurentes Nymphae sylvaeque virentes,
  Nec mihi, quae quondam, florida rura placent.

the Muses, who in my earliest youth taught me to bend the words of my native tongue to the sound of the lyre—alas!—they flee from me, and Apollo turns his back and flees, and the sweet-sounding plectrum flees from my fingers.

When my little books circulated among the crowd of courtiers and my poems were worn smooth in their hands and when the sister of the king, she, she, that illustrious virgin, inspired my little verses with a sacred majesty—Margaret, the sister of our invincible king, she who by her golden virtue is a goddess among mortals—then was I privileged to be wholly united with Phoebus, who made fruitful my mind, and to open my sails fully to the wind.

Now, miserable, we are blindly tossed on unknown seas and we entrust our sails to Latin straits. Latium demands it. It is the service owed to the language of Rome. The genius of this place himself compelled me to it. Thus the poet who once taught the art of tender love, when he lived in exile far from his fatherland, composed (without shame) songs in a barbarous tongue to the sound of a foreign lyre, preferring them to his Latin Muses.

Poetry delights in the acclaim of princes and the applause of the theater. He who pleases few, displeases even himself.

Even the Muses: compare *Regrets* 6

When my little books: compare *Regrets* 7

Latium: Roman Italy

the poet who once taught the art of love: Ovid (compare *Regrets* 10)

Poetry delights: compare *Regrets* 7.12–14

Ipsae etiam quae me primis docuere sub annis
  Ad citharam patrio flectere verba sono,
Heu fugiunt Musae, refugitque aversus Apollo,
  Et fugiunt digitos mollia plectra meos.
Aulica dum nostros gestaret turba libellos,
  Et tereret manibus carmina nostra suis,
Dumque meos Regis soror, illa, illa inclyta virgo
  Afflaret sancto numine versiculos,
Margaris, invicti Regis soror, aurea virtus
  Inter mortales cui dedit esse Deam,
Tunc licuit totum foecundo pectore Phoebum
  Concipere, et pleno pandere vela sinu.
Nunc miseri ignotis caeci iactamur in undis,
  Credimus et Latio lintea nostra freto.
Hoc Latium poscit; Romanae haec debita linguae
  Est opera; huc Genius compulit ipse loci.
Sic teneri quondam vates praeceptor Amoris,
  Dum procul a patriis finibus exul agit,
Barbara (nec puduit) Latiis praelata Camoenis
  Carmina non propriam condidit ad citharam.
Carmina Principibus gaudent plausuque theatri,
  Quique placet paucis, displicet ipse sibi.

La Deffence et Illustration de la Langue Françoyse

The Defense and Enrichment of the French Language

To My Lord the Most Reverend Cardinal du Bellay, Greetings.

Given the role you play in the spectacle of all Europe, indeed of the whole world, in that great Roman theater, given the many and great affairs you uphold almost alone—O honor of the Sacred College!—would I not sin (as the Latin Pindar says) against the public good if with lengthy speech I infringed on the time you give to the service of your prince, to the benefit of your fatherland, and to the increase of your immortal fame? Thus spying out an hour in the midst of the little rest you take to breathe under the heavy burden of French affairs (a charge truly worthy of such robust shoulders, no less than the heavens are worthy of those of the great Hercules), my Muse has had the temerity to enter the sacred confines of your holy and studious occupations, and there, among so many rich and excellent votive offerings dedicated daily to the image of your greatness, to make a gift of her own, humble and small, but still fortunate if it encounter some favor in the eyes of your goodness, which, like those of the immortal gods, show no less regard for the poor presents of a rich desire than for those proud and ambitious offerings.

It is, in fact, *The Defense and Enrichment of our French Language*, which nothing has prompted me to undertake but natural affection for my fatherland, and to dedicate to you but the greatness of your name, so that it may hide (as under the shield of Ajax) from the envenomed darts of that ancient enemy of virtue under the shadow of your wings. Of you, I say, whose incomparable knowledge, virtue, and conduct—all the greatest of things—have for so long been experienced by everyone that I could not more vividly express them than by covering them (imitating the trick of that noble painter Timanthes) under the veil of silence. For of anything so

---

Cardinal du Bellay: Jean du Bellay (1492–1560), Joachim's kinsman, an eminent churchman, diplomat, and man of letters, whom Joachim was later to serve as secretary and household intendant in Rome

Sacred College: the College of Cardinals in Rome

Latin Pindar: Horace, whose *Epistles* 2.1.1–4 du Bellay paraphrases

fatherland: in translating du Bellay's *patrie* with *fatherland* I mean to catch both the slight foreignness of du Bellay's term, which was then still new in French, and its masculine gender marking, though even *fatherland* misses the distinctly Roman feel of *patrie*

the great Hercules: to give Atlas a rest, Hercules bore on his shoulders the weight of the heavens

that noble painter Timanthes: Timanthes was said to have veiled the face of Agamemnon in his painting of the sacrifice of Iphigenia

A Monseigneur le Reverendissime Cardinal du Bellay, Salut.

Veu le personnaige que tu joues au spectacle de toute l'Europe, voyre de tout le monde, en ce grand theatre Romain, veu tant d'affaires, et telz, que seul quasi tu soutiens: ô l'honneur du sacré College! pecheroy'-je pas (comme dit le Pindare Latin) contre le bien publicq', si par longues paroles j'empeschoy' le tens que tu donnes au service de ton Prince, au profit de la patrie, et à l'accroissement de ton immortelle renommée? Epiant donques quelque heure de ce peu de relaiz que tu prens pour respirer soubz le pesant faiz des affaires Françoyses (charge vrayement digne de si robustes epaules, non moins que le ciel de celles du grand Hercule), ma Muse a pris la hardiesse d'entrer au sacré cabinet de tes sainctes et studieuses occupations: et là, entre tant de riches et excellens vœux de jour en jour dediez à l'image de ta grandeur, pendre le sien humble et petit: mais toutesfois bien heureux s'il rencontre quelque faveur devant les yeux de ta bonté, semblable à celle des Dieux immortelz, qui n'ont moins agreables les pauvres presentz d'un bien riche vouloir que ces superbes et ambicieuses offrandes.

C'est en effect la *Deffence et Illustration de nostre Langue Françoyse,* à l'entreprise de laquele rien ne m'a induyt, que l'affection naturelle envers ma patrie, et à te la dédier, que la grandeur de ton nom: afin qu'elle se cache (comme soubz le bouclier d'Ajax) contre les traictz envenimez de ceste antique ennemye de vertu, soubz l'umbre de tes esles. De toy dy-je, dont l'incomparable sçavoir, vertu et conduyte, toutes les plus grandes choses, de si long tens de tout le monde sont experimentées, que je ne les sçauroy' plus au vif exprimer, que les couvrant (suyvant la ruse de ce noble peintre Tymante) soubz le voyle de silence. Pour ce que d'une si grande chose il

great, it is much better (as Livy said of Carthage) to say nothing than to say little. Then accept with that customary goodness, which renders you no less obliging toward the least than your virtue and authority make you venerated by the greatest, the first fruits or, to put it better, the first flowers of spring of him who with all reverence and humility kisses the hands of Your Very Reverend Lordship, praying heaven to grant you as happy and long life and to be as favorable to your high undertakings as it has been liberal, indeed prodigal, in bestowing its graces on you.

Farewell. From Paris this 15th of February 1549.

The author begs the readers to suspend their judgment until the end of the book and not to condemn it without having first thoroughly seen and examined its arguments.

Jean Dorat

in support of *The Defense of the French Language.*

"There is no better omen than to fight for one's country," said the sweet eloquence of the Homeric Muse. But in echoing the poet I affirm, "There is no greater glory than to fight for the language of one's country." Bellay, just as your ancestors have incontestably won the reputation of good patriots in fighting for the land of our country, so you too, who plead on behalf of our country's language, will win forever the reputation of a good patriot.

---

as Livy said of Carthage: the quotation du Bellay recalls actually comes from Sallust, *Jugurtha* 19.2

The author begs: echoes the similar request in Étienne Dolet's *La Maniere de bien traduire d'une langue en autre* [The Way to Translate Well from One Language to Another] (1540), a book that was dedicated to Jean du Bellay's brother Guillaume and had a considerable influence on Joachim's *Defense*

Jean Dorat: (1508–1588) humanist and teacher of du Bellay, Ronsard, and Baïf at the College of Coqueret in Paris

the Homeric Muse: *Iliad* 12.243

vault trop myeux (comme de Carthage disoit Tite Live) se taire du tout que d'en dire peu. Recoy donques avecques ceste accoutumée bonté, qui ne te rend moins aymable entre les plus petiz que ta vertu et auctorité venerable entre les plus grands, les premiers fruictz, ou pour myeulx dire, les premieres fleurs du printens de celuy qui en toute reverence et humilité bayse les mains de ta Reverendissime Seigneurie. Priant le Ciel te departir autant de heureuse et longue vie, et à tes haultes entreprises estre autant favorable, comme envers toy il a eté liberal, voyre prodigue de ses graces.

A Dieu. De Paris ce 15 de Fevrier 1549.

L'autheur prye les Lecteurs differer leur jugement jusques à la fin du livre, et ne le condamner sans avoir premierement bien veu et examiné ses raisons.

'Ιωάννης 'Αυρατὸς
εἰς κελτικῆς γλώσσης 'Απολογίαν

Εἷς οἰωνὸς ἄριστος ἀμύνεσθαι περὶ πάτρης,
  Εἶπεν ὁμηρείωη εὐεπίη χαρίτων.
Ἓν δὲ κλέος μέγ' ἄριστον ἀμύνεσθαι περὶ γλώττης
  Τῆς πατρίης, κἀγώ φημὶ παρῳδιάων.
Βελλάϊ', ὡς γοῦν σεῦ πρόγονοι φιλοπάτριδες ἄνδρες
  Ἤκουσαν, πατρίης γῆς πὲρι μαρνάμενοι,
Οὕτως καὶ πατρίης σὺ συνηγορέων περὶ γλώττης
  Κληδόν' ἀεὶ σχήσεις, ὡς φιλόπατρις ἀνήρ.

The Defense and Enrichment of the French Language First Book

Chapter 1
The Origin of Languages

If Nature (of whom a person of great renown has, not without reason, wondered whether we should call her mother or stepmother) had given all men the same desire and inclination, besides the innumerable benefits that would have resulted, human inconstancy would not have had to forge for itself so many ways of speaking. This diversity and confusion can rightly be called the Tower of Babel. For languages are not born of themselves like herbs, roots, and trees, some of them sickly and weak in their kind, others healthy and robust and more capable of bearing the weight of human conceptions, but all their strength is born of the desire and will of mortals. That, it seems to me, is a great reason why we should not praise one language and blame another, since they all come from a single source and origin—that is, from the imagination of men—and have been shaped by the same judgment and for a single end—that is, to express among us the conceptions and apprehensions of the mind. It is true that with the passage of time some, from having been more carefully ordered, have become richer than others. But that should not be attributed to the natural superiority of those languages, but only to the artifice and industry of men. And therefore all things Nature has created, all the arts and learned disciplines in the four quarters of the world, are in themselves the same, but since men differ in their desires, they speak and write differently. Accordingly, I cannot sufficiently blame the foolish arrogance and temerity of some of our fellow countrymen who, taking themselves for nothing less than Greeks or Romans, despise and reject with a more than Stoic haughtiness everything written in French. And I cannot sufficiently wonder at the strange opinion

---

Chapter 1: the opening sentences of this chapter are the first of du Bellay's nearly thirty borrowings scattered through some nine chapters of the *Defense* from Sperone Speroni's *Dialogo delle Lingue* [Dialogue on Languages] (1542)

a person of great renown: Pliny the Elder in his *Natural History* 7.1.1

La Deffence et Illustration de la Langue Françoise Livre Premier

Chapitre 1
L'Origine des Langues

Si la Nature (dont quelque personnaige de grand' renommée non sans rayson a douté si on la devoit appeller mere ou maratre) eust donné aux hommes un commun vouloir et consentement, outre les innumerables commoditez qui en feussent procedées, l'inconstance humaine n'eust eu besoing de se forger tant de manieres de parler. Laquéle diversité et confusion se peut à bon droict appeller la Tour de Babel. Donques les langues ne sont nées d'elles mesmes en façon d'herbes, racines, et arbres: les unes infirmes et debiles en leurs espéces: les autres saines et robustes, et plus aptes à porter le faiz des conceptions humaines: mais toute leur vertu est née au monde du vouloir et arbitre des mortelz. Cela (ce me semble) est une grande rayson pourquoy on ne doit ainsi louer une langue et blamer l'autre: veu qu'elles viennent toutes d'une mesme source et origine: c'est la fantasie des hommes: et ont été formées d'un mesme jugement à une mesme fin: c'est pour signifier entre nous les conceptions et intelligences de l'esprit. Il est vray que par succession de tens les unes, pour avoir eté plus curieusement reiglées, sont devenues plus riches que les autres: mais cela ne se doit attribuer à la félicité desdites langues, ains au seul artifice et industrie des hommes. Ainsi donques toutes les choses que la Nature a crées, tous les ars et sciences en toutes les quatre parties du monde, sont chacune endroict soy une mesme chose: mais pour ce que les hommes sont de divers vouloir, ilz en parlent et ecrivent diversement. A ce propos, je ne puis assez blamer la sotte arrogance et temerité d'aucuns de notre nation, qui n'etans riens moins que Grecz ou Latins, deprisent et rejetent d'un sourcil plus que stoïque toutes choses ecrites en François: et ne me puys assez emerveiller de l'etrange opinion d'aucuns sçavans, qui pensent

of some learned men, who think that our vulgar tongue is incapable of all good letters and erudition, as if an idea should be judged good or bad for its language alone. I do not aim to satisfy the first sort. I do wish (if I can do it) to change the opinion of the second with some arguments I hope briefly to develop, not that I feel myself more clear-sighted in this or in other things than they are, but because the affection they bear toward foreign languages does not allow them to reach a sound and impartial judgment concerning their vulgar tongue.

Chapter 2
That the French Language should not be called barbarous

To begin, then, to broach the subject, as to the meaning of this word *barbarous*: in antiquity they were called barbarous who spoke Greek badly. For as foreigners coming to Athens attempted to speak Greek, they often fell into this absurd sound *Barbaras.* Afterwards the Greeks transferred this term to brutal and cruel customs, calling all nations but Greece barbarous. This should in no way lessen the excellence of our language, seeing that this Greek arrogance, admiring only its own inventions, had neither the right nor the privilege thus to legitimate its nation and bastardize others. As Anacharsis said, the Scythians were barbarians among the Athenians, but so were the Athenians among the Scythians. And even if the barbarity of the manners of our ancestors did rightly move them to call us barbarians, I do not see why we should be thought so now, since in civility of manners, equity of laws, greatness of courage, in short, in all forms and ways of living that are no less praiseworthy than beneficial, we are in nothing inferior to them, but rather superior, seeing that they are now such that we can justly call them by the name they gave others. That the Romans called us barbarians is of still less concern, given their ambition and insatiable hunger for glory, which strove not only to subjugate but to render all other nations vile and abject in comparison with them, especially the Gauls from whom they suffered more shame and injury than from the others.

On this subject, often wondering how it happens that the deeds of the Roman people are so celebrated by everyone, indeed for so long preferred over those of all other nations together, I find no greater reason than this: it is because the Romans had such a great multitude of writers that most of

---

vulgar tongue: here and elsewhere I translate du Bellay's *vulgaire* as *vulgar tongue* rather than *vernacular* to retain the status marking that is of such concern in his attempt to make French illustrious

Anacharsis: a Scythian philosopher of the sixth century BCE, known to the Renaissance through the works of Plutarch and Lucian

que nostre vulgaire soit incapable de toutes bonnes lettres et erudition: comme si une invention pour le languaige seulement devoit estre jugée bonne ou mauvaises. A ceux là je n'ay entrepris de satisfaire. A ceux cy je veux bien (s'il m'est possible) faire changer d'opinion par quelques raisons que brefvement j'espere deduyre: non que je me sente plus cler voyant en cela, ou autres choses, qu'ilz ne sont, mais pour ce que l'affection qu'ilz portent aux langues estrangieres ne permet qu'ilz veillent faire sain et entier jugement de leur vulgaire.

Chapitre 2
Que la Langue Françoyse ne doit estre nommée barbare

Pour commencer donques à entrer en matiere, quand à la signification de ce mot *barbare*: barbares anciennement etoint nommez ceux qui ineptement parloint Grec. Car comme les etrangers venans à Athenes s'efforcoint de parler Grec, ilz tumboint souvent en ceste voix absurde βάρβαρας. Depuis les Grecz transportarent ce nom aux meurs brutaux et cruelz, appellant toutes nations, hors la Grece, barbares. Ce qui ne doit en rien diminuer l'excellence de notre langue: veu que ceste arrogance Greque, admiratrice seulement de ses inventions, n'avoit loy ny privilege de legitimer ainsi sa nation et abatardir les autres: comme Anacharsis disoit que les Scythes etoint barbares entre les Atheniens, mais les Atheniens aussi entre les Scythes. Et quand la barbarie des meurs de notz ancéstres eust deu les mouvoir à nous apeller barbares, si est ce que je ne voy point pourquoy on nous doive maintenant estimer telz: veu qu'en civilité de meurs, equité de loix, magnanimité de couraiges, bref en toutes formes et manieres de vivre non moins louables que profitables, nous ne sommes rien moins qu'eux: mais bien plus, veu qu'ilz sont telz maintenant, que nous les pouvons justement apeller par le nom qu'ilz ont donné aux autres. Encores moins doit avoir lieu, de ce que les Romains nous ont appellez barbares, veu leur ambition et insatiable faim de gloyre: qui tachoint non seulement à subjuguer, mais à rendre toutes autres nations viles et abjectes aupres d'eux: principalement les Gauloys, dont ilz ont receu plus de honte et dommaige que des autres.

A ce propos, songeant beaucoup de foys d'ou vient que les gestes du peuple Romain sont tant celebrés de tout le monde, voyre de si long intervale preferés à ceux de toutes les autres nations ensemble, je ne treuve point plus grande raison que ceste cy: c'est que les Romains ont eu si grande

their deeds (to say no worse) through the space of so many years—their eagerness in battle, their devastation of Italy, their foreign invasions—have been conserved intact to our times. The deeds of other nations, particularly of the Gauls before they fell to the power of the French, and the deeds of the French themselves from the time they gave their name to the Gauls, have, on the contrary, been so poorly preserved, that we have nearly lost not only the glory of them but their very memory. This loss has been aggravated by the envy of the Romans, who, as if joined together to conspire against us, have diminished in every way they could our warlike praises, whose brilliance they could not endure. And not only have they wronged us in that, but to render us still more odious and contemptible, they have called us brutal, cruel, and barbarous. Someone will say, "Why did they spare the Greeks this name?" Because they would have done themselves still greater injury than to the Greeks, from whom they had borrowed everything good they had, at least with regard to the learned disciplines and the enrichment of their language. These reasons seem to me sufficient to make any equitable judge of things understand that our language (though we have been called barbarous either by our enemies or by those who had no right to give us this name) should not be scorned, especially by those to whom it belongs and is natural and who are in nothing inferior to the Greeks and Romans.

Chapter 3
Why the French Language is not as rich as Greek and Latin

And if our language is not as copious and rich as Greek or Latin, that should not be imputed to any defect in it, as though of itself it could never be other than poor and sterile, but should rather be attributed to the ignorance of our ancestors, who, holding (as someone said, speaking of the ancient Romans) well-doing in higher esteem than fair speaking and preferring to leave to their posterity examples of virtue rather than precepts, denied themselves the glory of their high deeds and us the benefit of imitating them, and by the same means left us our language so poor and naked that it needs the ornaments and (so to speak) the feathers of others. But who would dare say that Greek and Latin were always at the level of excellence they attained at the time of Homer and of Demosthenes, of Virgil and of Cicero? And had those authors judged that, whatever diligence and

copious: du Bellay's frequent use of this term echoes a major preoccupation of Renaissance rhetorical theory, expressed most famously in Erasmus's *De duplici copia verborum et rerum* [On the Copiousness of Both Words and Things] (1512)

as someone said: Sallust, *Catilina* 8.5

multitude d'ecrivains, que la plus part de leur gestes (pour ne dire pis) par l'espace de tant d'années, ardeur de batailles, vastité d'Italie, incursions d'estrangers, s'est conservée entiere jusques à nostre tens. Au contraire les faiz des autres nations, singulierement des Gauloys, avant qu'ilz tumbassent en la puyssance des Françoys, et les faiz des Françoys mesmes depuis qu'ilz ont donné leur nom aux Gaules, ont eté si mal recueilliz, que nous en avons quasi perdu non seulement la gloyre, mais la memoyre. A quoy a bien aydé l'envie des Romains, qui comme par une certaine conjuration conspirant contre nous, ont extenué en tout ce qu'ilz ont peu notz louanges belliques, dont ilz ne pouvoint endurer la clarté: et non seulement nous ont fait tort en cela, mais pour nous rendre encor' plus odieux et contemptibles, nous ont apellez brutaux, cruelz, et barbares. Quelqu'un dira, pourquoy ont ilz exempté les Grecz de ce nom? Pource qu'ilz se feussent fait plus grand tort qu'aux Grecz mesmes, dont ilz avoint emprunté tout ce qu'ilz avoint de bon, au moins quand aux sciences et illustration de leur langue. Ces raysons me semblent suffisantes de faire entendre à tout equitable estimateur des choses, que nostre langue (pour avoir été nommés barbares ou de noz ennemys ou de ceux qui n'avoint loy de nous bailler ce nom) ne doit pourtant estre deprisée, mesmes de ceux aux quelz elle est propre et naturelle, et qui en rien ne sont moindres que les Grecz ou Romains.

Chapitre 3
Pourquoy la Langue Françoyse n'est si riche que la Greque et Latine

Et si nostre langue n'est si copieuse et riche que la Greque ou Latine, cela ne doit estre imputé au default d'icelle, comme si d'elle mesme elle ne pouvoit jamais estre si non pauvre et sterile: mais bien on le doit attribuer à l'ignorance de notz majeurs, qui ayans (comme dict quelqu'un, parlant des anciens Romains) en plus grande recommendation le bien faire que le bien dire, et mieux aymans laisser à leur posterité les exemples de vertu que les preceptes, se sont privez de la gloyre de leurs bien faitz, et nous du fruict de l'immitation d'iceux: et par mesme moyen nous ont laissé nostre langue si pauvre et nue, qu'elle a besoing des ornementz et (s'il fault ainsi parler) des plumes d'autruy. Mais qui voudroit dire que la Greque et Romaine eussent tousjours eté en l'excellence qu'on les a vues du tens d'Homere et de Demosthene, de Virgile et de Ciceron? Et si ces

cultivation were applied to those languages, they would never be able to produce greater fruit, would they have made such great efforts to bring them to the height at which we now see them?

I can say as much of our language, which is just beginning to flower without bearing fruit, or rather, like a seedling and fresh shoot, has not yet flowered, much less yielded all the fruit it is capable of producing. That comes certainly not from any defect in its nature, as apt to engender as others, but through the fault of those who have had it in their care and have not sufficiently tended it; but like a wild plant in that same uncultivated place where it was born, they have let it grow old and nearly die, without ever watering it, pruning it, or protecting it from the bramble and thorns that shaded it. Had the ancient Romans been as negligent in the cultivation of their language when it first began to sprout, it would certainly not have become so great in such a brief time. But they, like good farmers, first transplanted it from a wild to a cultivated site. Then, so that it might yield fruit better and more quickly, pruning away the useless branches, they replaced them with fine and cultivated branches, taken in masterly fashion from the Greek language, which were rapidly so well grafted to their trunk and made to resemble it that from that time on they have no longer appeared adopted but natural. From this were born in the Latin language those flowers and those fruits colored with great eloquence, along with meter and the skillful blending of sound with sense, all of which every language produces not by its own nature but by art. Thus if the Greeks and Romans, more diligent in the cultivation of their languages than we are in that of ours, could not find in theirs, save as the result of great labor and industry, either grace or meter or indeed any eloquence, should we be surprised if our vulgar tongue is not as rich as it might be and take that as a reason to despise it as vile and worthless?

The time will perhaps come—and with the help of the good fortune of France, I have high hopes for it—when this noble and powerful kingdom will in its turn seize the reins of universal dominion and when our language (if with Francis the French language has not been wholly buried), which is just beginning to put down roots, will spring from the ground and grow to such height and girth that it will equal the Greeks and Romans themselves, producing, like them, Homers, Demosthenes, Virgils, and Ciceros, just as France has sometimes produced Pericles, Nicias, Alcibiades, Themistocles, Caesars, and Scipios.

---

the skillful blending of sound with sense: du Bellay's *lyaison* translates the Latin *conjunctio,* used for the poetic union of sound and meaning

universal dominion: du Bellay's *monarchie* does not mean *monarchy* in our modern sense but rather expresses the dream of universal empire inspired by the example of Rome

aucteurs eussent jugé que jamais, pour quelque diligence et culture qu'on y eust peu faire, elles n'eussent sceu produyre plus grand fruict, se feussent ilz tant eforcez de les mettre au point où nous les voyons maintenant?

Ainsi puys-je dire de nostre langue, qui commence encores à fleurir sans fructifier, ou plus tost, comme une plante et vergette, n'a point encores fleury, tant se fault qu'elle ait apporté tout le fruict qu'elle pouroit bien produyre. Cela certainement non pour le default de la nature d'elle, aussi apte à engendrer que les autres: mais pour la coulpe de ceux qui l'ont euë en garde, et ne l'ont cultivée à suffisance: ains comme une plante sauvaige, en celuy mesmes desert ou elle avoit commencé à naitre, sans jamais l'arrouser, la tailler, ny defendre des ronces et epines qui luy faisoint umbre, l'ont laissée envieillir et quasi mourir. Que si les anciens Romains eussent eté aussi negligens à la culture de leur langue, quand premierement elle commenca à pululer, pour certain en si peu de tens elle ne feust devenue si grande. Mais eux, en guise de bons agriculteurs, l'ont premierement transmuée d'un lieu sauvaige en un domestique: puis affin que plus tost et mieux elle peust fructifier, coupant à l'entour les inutiles rameaux, l'ont pour échange d'iceux restaurée de rameaux francz et domestiques, magistralement tirez de la langue Greque, les quelz soudainement se sont si bien entez et faiz semblables à leur tronc, que desormais n'apparoissent plus adoptifz, mais naturelz. De là sont nées en la langue Latine ces fleurs, et ces fruictz colorez de cete grande eloquence, avecques ces nombres et cete lyaison si artificielle, toutes les quelles choses, non tant de sa propre nature que par artifice, toute langue a coutume de produyre. Donques si les Grecz et Romains, plus diligens à la culture de leurs langues que nous à celle de la nostre, n'ont peu trouver en icelles, si non avecques grand labeur et industrie, ny grace, ny nombre, ny finablement aucune eloquence, nous devons nous emerveiller si nostre vulgaire n'est si riche comme il pourra bien estre, et de la prendre occasion de le mepriser comme chose vile et de petit prix?

Le tens viendra (peut estre), et je l'espere moyennant la bonne destinée Françoyse, que ce noble et puyssant Royaume obtiendra à son tour les resnes de la monarchie, et que nostre langue (si avecques Françoys n'est du tout ensevelie la langue Françoyse) qui commence encor' à jeter ses racines, sortira de terre, et s'elevera en telle hauteur et grosseur, qu'elle se poura egaler aux mesmes Grecz et Romains, produysant comme eux des Homeres, Demosthenes, Virgiles et Cicerons aussi bien que la France a quelquesfois produit des Pericles, Nicies, Alcibiades, Themistocles, Cesars et Scipions.

Chapter 4
That the French Language is not as poor as many judge it

I do not, however, consider our vulgar tongue, as it is now, to be as vile and abject as do those ambitious admirers of the Greek and Latin languages, who would not think, were they Pitho herself, goddess of persuasion, that they could say anything of worth except in a foreign language not understood by the common people. And whoever wishes to look closely into the matter will find that our French language is not so poor that it cannot render faithfully what it borrows from others or so barren that it cannot produce on its own some fruit of good invention by means of the industry and diligence of its cultivators, if any are found who are such friends to their country and to themselves that they would apply themselves to it. But to whom, after God, shall we give thanks for such a benefit if not to our late good king and father Francis, the first of that name and first in all virtues? I say "first" inasmuch as he first in his noble kingdom restored all the good arts and learned disciplines to their former dignity and thus made our language, which was previously rude and unpolished, elegant and, if not as copious as it might be, at least a faithful interpreter of all others. And because of this, philosophers, historians, physicians, poets, Greek and Latin orators have learned to speak French. As, I might add, have the Hebrews: the Holy Scriptures bear ample witness to what I say.

I will here leave aside the superstitious arguments of those who maintain that the mysteries of theology must not be laid bare and, as it were, profaned in a vulgar tongue, as well as what they allege who hold the contrary opinion. For that controversy does not belong to what I have undertaken, which is only to show that our language did not at its birth have the gods and the stars so set against it that it could not one day achieve a level of excellence and perfection as well as any other, since all branches of learning can be faithfully and copiously treated in it, as may be seen from such a great number of Greek and Latin books, as well as Italian, Spanish, and others, translated into French by many excellent pens of our times.

Francis: Francis I (1494–1547; king of France, 1515–1547), who did much to foster humanist studies in France, as du Bellay points out in the following chapter

the Holy Scriptures: alludes to biblical translations by, among others, Jacques Lefèvre d'Étaples in 1530 and Pierre-Robert Olivetan in 1535, to which objections of the sort du Bellay mentions in the following sentence were raised, especially by the theology faculty of the Sorbonne

Chapitre 4
Que la Langue Françoyse n'est si pauvre que beaucoup l'estiment

Je n'estime pourtant nostre vulgaire, tel qu'il est maintenant, estre si vil et abject, comme le font ces ambicieux admirateurs des langues Greque et Latine, qui ne penseroint, et feussent ilz la mesme Pythô, déesse de persuasion, pouvoir rien dire de bon, si n'etoit en langaige etranger et non entendu du vulgaire. Et qui voudra de bien près y regarder, trouvera que nostre langue Françoyse n'est si pauvre, qu'elle ne puysse rendre fidelement ce qu'elle emprunte des autres, si infertile, qu'elle ne puysse produyre de soy quelque fruict de bonne invention, au moyen de l'industrie et diligence des cultiveurs d'icelle, si quelques uns se treuvent tant amys de leur païz et d'eux mesmes, qu'ilz s'y veillent employer. Mais à qui, apres Dieu, rendrons nous graces d'un tel benefice, si non à nostre feu bon Roy et pere Françoys, premier de ce nom et de toutes vertuz? Je dy premier, d'autant qu'il a en son noble Royaume premierement restitué tous les bons ars et sciences en leur ancienne dignité: et si à nostre langaige, au paravant scabreux et mal poly, rendu elegant, et si non tant copieux qu'il poura bien estre, pour le moins fidele interprete de tous les autres. Et qu'ainsi soit, philosophes, historiens, medicins, poëtes, orateurs Grecz et Latins ont apris à parler François. Que diray-je des Hebreux? Les Saintes Lettres donnent ample temoingnaige de ce que je dy.

Je laisseray en cest endroict les superstitieuses raisons de ceux qui soutiennent que les mysteres de la theologie ne doivent estre decouvers et quasi comme prophanez en langaige vulgaire, et ce que vont allegant ceux qui sont d'opinion contraire. Car ceste disputation n'est propre à ce que j'ay entrepris, qui est seulement de montrer que nostre langue n'ha point eu à sa naissance les Dieux et les Astres si ennemis, qu'elle ne puisse un jour parvenir au point d'excellence et de perfection, aussi bien que les autres, entendu que toutes sciences se peuvent fidelement et copieusement traicter en icelle, comme on peut voir en si grand nombre de livres Grecz et Latins, voyre bien Italiens, Espaignolz, et autres, traduictz en Françoys par maintes excellentes plumes de nostre tens.

Chapter 5
That Translations are not sufficient to give perfection to the French Language

Nevertheless this very praiseworthy labor of translation does not seem to me the only or sufficient means to raise our vulgar tongue to be the equal—and the rival—of other more famous languages. I intend to prove this so clearly that no one (I believe) will wish to say the opposite, unless he is a manifest slanderer of truth. And first it is an accepted fact among all the best authors on rhetoric that there are five parts of speaking well: invention, elocution, disposition, memory, and pronunciation. Now inasmuch as these last two are not so much learned by the benefit of languages as they are given to each person according to his innate talent, augmented and maintained by studious exercise and continual diligence, and inasmuch as disposition resides more in the discrimination and good judgment of the orator than in particular rules and precepts—since events of time, circumstances of place, conditions of persons, and diversity of occasions are innumerable—I will content myself with speaking of the first two: namely, invention and elocution.

The duty of the orator is then to speak elegantly and copiously on whatever topic is proposed. Now, the ability to speak in this way of all things can only be acquired by a perfect knowledge of all branches of learning, which were first treated by the Greeks and then by their imitators, the Romans. It is thus necessary that those two languages be understood by anyone who wishes to attain that copiousness and richness of invention, which is the first and principal piece in the orator's armor. And with regard to this point, faithful translators can greatly aid and support those who have not the unique opportunity to devote themselves to foreign languages. But as for elocution, certainly the most difficult part of rhetoric and that without which all others remain useless, like a sword still enclosed in its sheath: elocution (I say), by which an orator is principally judged more excellent and one way of speaking thought better than another, being that from which eloquence is itself named, and whose virtue resides in appropriate words, familiar and not estranged from their common use, in metaphors, allegories, comparisons, similes, vivid descriptions, and so many other figures

The duty of the orator: recalls Cicero, *De oratore* 1.6.20

vivid descriptions: du Bellay's *energies* comes from the Greek *enargeia* or *energeia*, rhetorical terms for vivid description or description of things in motion

Chapitre 5
Que les Traductions ne sont suffisantes pour donner perfection à la Langue Françoyse

Toutesfois ce tant louable labeur de traduyre ne me semble moyen unique et suffisant, pour elever nostre vulgaire à l'egal et parangon des autres plus fameuses langues. Ce que je pretens prouver si clerement, que nul n'y vouldra (ce croy je) contredire, s'il n'est manifeste calumniateur de la verité. Et premier, c'est une chose accordée entre tous les meilleurs aucteurs de rethorique, qu'il y a cinq parties de bien dire, l'invention, l'eloquution, la disposition, la memoire, et la pronuntiation. Or pour autant que ces deux dernieres ne se aprennent tant par le benefice des langues, comme elles sont données à chacun selon la felicité de sa nature, augmentées et entretenues par studieux exercice et continuelle diligence: pour autant aussi que la disposition gist plus en la discretion et bon jugement de l'orateur qu'en certaines reigles et preceptes: veu que les evenementz du tens, la circunstance des lieux, la condition des personnes et la diversité des occasions sont innumerables: je me contenteray de parler des deux premieres, sçavoir de l'invention et de l'eloquution.

L'office donques de l'orateur est de chacune chose proposée elegamment et copieusement parler. Or ceste faculté de parler ainsi de toutes choses ne se peut acquerir que par l'intelligence parfaite des sciences, les queles ont eté premierement traitées par les Grecz, et puis par les Romains imitateurs d'iceux. Il fault donques necessairement que ces deux langues soint entendues de celuy qui veut acquerir cete copie et richesse d'invention, premiere et principale piece du harnoys de l'orateur. Et quand à ce poinct, les fideles traducteurs peuvent grandement servir et soulaiger ceux qui n'ont le moyen unique de vacquer aux langues estrangeres. Mais quand à l'eloquution, partie certes la plus difficile, et sans la quelle toutes autres choses restent comme inutiles et semblables à un glayve encores couvert de sa gayne: eloquution (dy je) par la quelle principalement un orateur est jugé plus excellent, et un genre de dire meilleur que l'autre: comme celle dont est apellée la mesme eloquence: et dont la vertu gist aux motz propres, usitez, et non aliénes du commun usaige de parler, aux methaphores, alegories, comparaisons, similitudes, energies, et tant d'autres figures et ornemens, sans les quelz tout oraison et poëme sont

and ornaments without which any writing in prose or verse is bare, maimed, and weak; I will never believe that one can learn all that from translators, for it is impossible to render a work with the same grace the author put into it, inasmuch as each language has an indescribable something that belongs to it alone, so that if you strive to express its inborn quality in another language, abiding by the law of translation, which is never to stray beyond the bounds of the author, your diction will be constrained, cold, and graceless. And as proof, just read a Latin Demosthenes and Homer, a French Cicero and Virgil, to see if they will beget such emotions in you—will, indeed, transform you like a Proteus into differing kinds—as you feel reading those authors in their own languages. Going from the original to the translation, you will seem to pass from the burning mountain of Etna to the cold summit of the Caucasus. And what I say of the Latin and Greek languages can be equally said of all the vulgar tongues, of which I will cite only Petrarch, of whom I dare say that if a reborn Homer and Virgil undertook to translate him, they could not render him with the same grace and freshness that he has in his native Tuscan. Yet some in our time have tried to make him speak French.

These, in brief, are the reasons that have made me think that the diligent service of translators, otherwise very useful in instructing those ignorant of foreign languages in the knowledge of things, is not sufficient to give our language that perfection and, as painters do with their paintings, that final touch we desire. And if the reasons I have provided do not appear strong enough, I will produce as my guarantors and defenders the ancient Roman authors, principally poets and orators, who (although Cicero translated several books of Xenophon and Aratus and Horace offers precepts on good translating) devoted themselves to this activity more for their study and individual benefit than to publish it for the amplification of their language, for their own glory, and for the use of others. If any have seen works of that time under the title of translations—I mean works of Cicero, of Virgil, and of the happy age of Augustus—they can contradict what I say.

Chapter 6
Of bad Translators and of not translating Poets

But what shall I say of some who truly deserve rather to be called traitors than translators? For they betray those they undertake to reveal, denying

---

deserve rather to be called traitors than translators: from the Italian proverb traduttore traditore

nudz, manques et débiles: je ne croyray jamais qu'on puisse bien apprendre tout cela des traducteurs, pour ce qu'il est impossible de le rendre avecques la mesme grace dont l'autheur en a usé: d'autant que chacune langue a je ne sçay quoy propre seulement à elle, dont si vous efforcez exprimer le naif en une autre langue, observant la loy de traduyre, qui est n'espacier point hors des limites de l'aucteur, vostre diction sera contrainte, froide, et de mauvaise grace. Et qu'ainsi soit, qu'on me lyse un Demosthene et Homere Latins, un Ciceron et Vergile Françoys, pour voir s'ilz vous engendreront telles affections, voyre ainsi qu'un Prothée vous transformeront en diverses sortes, comme vous sentez, lysant ces aucteurs en leurs langues. Il vous semblera passer de l'ardente montaigne d'Aethne sur le froid sommet de Caucase. Et ce que je dy des langues Latine et Greque se doit reciproquement dire de tous les vulgaires, dont j'allegueray seulement un Petrarque, du quel j'ose bien dire, que si Homere et Virgile renaissans avoint entrepris de le traduyre, ilz ne le pouroint rendre avecques la mesme grace et nayfveté qu'il est en son vulgaire Toscan. Toutesfois, quelques uns de notre tens ont entrepris de le faire parler Françoys.

Voyla en bref les raisons qui m'ont fait penser que l'office et diligence des traducteurs, autrement fort utile pour instruyre les ingnorans des langues etrangeres en la congnoissance des choses, n'est suffisante pour donner à la nostre ceste perfections, et comme font les peintres à leurs tableaux, ceste derniere main que nous desirons. Et si les raisons que j'ay alleguées ne semblent assez fortes, je produiray pour mes garans et deffenseurs les anciens aucteurs Romains, poëtes principalement et orateurs, les quelz (combien que Ciceron ait traduyt quelques livres de Xenophon et d'Arate, et qu' Horace baille les preceptes de bien traduyre) ont vacqué à ceste partie plus pour leur etude et profit particulier, que pour le publier, à l'amplification de leur langue, à leur gloire, et commodité d'autruy. Si aucuns ont veu quelques œuvres de ce tens là soubz tiltre de traduction, j'entens de Ciceron, de Virgile, et de ce bienheureux siecle d'Auguste, ilz me pourroint dementir de ce que je dy.

Chapitre 6
Des mauvais Traducteurs, et de ne traduyre les Poëtes

Mais que diray-je d'aucuns, vrayement mieux dignes d'estre appellés traditeurs que traducteurs? Veu qu'ilz trahissent ceux qu'ilz entreprennent

them their glory and by the same means seduce ignorant readers, showing them white for black. To gain the name of learned men, they translate on credit languages, like Hebrew and Greek, of which they have never understood the first elements and to raise their standing still further, take on poets, a race of authors that, if I could or would translate, I would address as little as possible because of that divinity of invention they have more than others, that greatness of style, magnificence of words, gravity of thoughts, boldness and variety of figures, and a thousand other adornments of poetry; in short, that energy and indefinable spirit in their writings which the Latins would call *genius.* All these things can be no more rendered in translation than a painter can represent the soul along with the body of the person he undertakes to portray from life.

What I say is not directed at those who by the order of princes and great lords translate the most famous Greek and Latin poets, for the obedience one owes such figures admits no excuse in this regard, but I mean rather to speak to those who from gaiety of heart (as they say) lightly undertake such things and accomplish them in the same way. O Apollo! O Muses! Thus to profane the sacred remains of antiquity! But I will say no more. Let him then who wishes to produce a work worthy to be valued in his own vulgar tongue leave the work of translating, especially of poets, to those who from a laborious task of little profit—one, I dare say again, useless and even harmful to the growth of their language—rightly earn more vexation than glory.

Chapter 7
How the Romans enriched their Language

If the Romans (someone will say) did not devote themselves to this labor of translation, then by what means were they able so to enrich their language, indeed to make it almost the equal of Greek? By imitating the best Greek authors, transforming themselves into them, devouring them, and, after having thoroughly digested them, converting them into blood and nourishment, selecting, each according to his own nature and the topic he wished to choose, the best author, all of whose rarest and most exquisite strengths they diligently observed and, like shoots, grafted them, as I said earlier, and adapted them to their own language. In doing this (I say) the Romans constructed all those fine writings we so ardently praise and admire, judging some to be the equal of the Greeks, preferring some as superior to them.

exposer, les frustrant de leur gloire, et par mesme moyen seduysent les lecteurs ignorans, leur montrant le blanc pour le noyr: qui, pour acquerir le nom de sçavans, traduysent à credict les langues, dont jamais ilz n'ont entendu les premiers elementz, comme l'Hebraique et la Grecque: et encor' pour myeux se faire valoir, se prennent aux poëtes, genre d'aucteurs certes auquel, si je sçavoy' ou vouloy' traduyre, je m'adroisseroy' aussi peu, à cause de ceste divinité d'invention qu'ilz ont plus que les autres, de ceste grandeur de style, magnificence de motz, gravité de sentences, audace et varieté de figures, et mil' autres lumieres de poësie: bref ceste energie, et ne sçay quel esprit, qui est en leurs ecriz, que les Latins appelleroient *genius.* Toutes les quelles choses se peuvent autant exprimer en traduisant, comme un peintre peut representer l'ame avecques le cors de celuy qu'il entreprent tyrer apres le naturel.

Ce que je dy ne s'adroisse pas à ceux qui, par le commandement des Princes et grands Seigneurs, traduysent les plus fameux poëtes Grecz et Latins: pour ce que l'obeïssance qu'on doit à telz personnaiges ne reçoit aucune excuse en cet endroit: mais bien j'entens parler à ceux qui de gayeté de coeur (comme on dict) entreprennent telles choses legerement, et s'en aquitent de mesmes. O Apolon! O Muses! prophaner ainsi les sacrées reliques de l'Antiquité! Mais je n'en diray autre chose. Celuy donques qui voudra faire œuvre digne de prix en son vulgaire, laisse ce labeur de traduyre, principalement les poëtes, à ceux qui de chose laborieuse et peu profitable, j'ose dire encor' inutile, voyre pernicieuse à l'acroissement de leur langue, emportent à bon droict plus de molestie que de gloyre.

Chapitre 7
Comment les Romains ont enrichy leur Langue

Si les Romains (dira quelqu'un) n'ont vaqué à ce labeur de traduction, par quelz moyens donques ont ilz peu ainsi enrichir leur langue, voyre jusques à l'egaller quasi à la Greque? Immitant les meilleurs aucteurs Grecz, se transformant en eux, les devorant, et apres les avoir bien digerez, les convertissant en sang et nouriture, se proposant, chacun selon son naturel, et l'argument qu'il vouloit elire, le meilleur aucteur, dont ilz observoint diligemment toutes les plus rares et exquises vertuz, et icelles comme grephes, ainsi que j'ay dict devant, entoint et apliquoint à leur langue. Cela faisant (dy-je) les Romains ont baty tous ces beaux ecriz, que nous louons et admirons si fort: egalant ores quelqu'un d'iceux, ores le preferant aux Grecz.

And of what I say Cicero and Virgil, whom willingly and with honor I always cite from the Latin language, provide good proof. The one gave himself entirely to the imitation of the Greeks, counterfeited and so vividly expressed the copiousness of Plato, the vehemence of Demosthenes, and the joyful sweetness of Isocrates that Molo of Rhodes, once hearing him declaim, cried that he was bringing Greek eloquence to Rome. The other so well imitated Homer, Hesiod, and Theocritus that since then it has been said of him that of those three he surpassed one, equaled one, and came so close to the other that, if the felicity of the subjects they treated had been the same, the prize would have been in doubt. Thus I ask you, you who undertake only translations, if these famous authors had diverted themselves in translating, would they have raised their language to the excellence and height where we now see it? Then do not think, whatever diligence and industry you may expend in that pursuit, that you can do enough for our language, which still crawls on all fours, for it to lift its head and get on its feet.

Chapter 8
Of amplifying the French Language by the imitation of ancient Greek and Roman Authors

Thus let him who would enrich his language devote himself to the imitation of the best Greek and Latin authors and aim, as at a sure target, the point of his stylus at all their greatest strengths. For there is no doubt that the largest part of artfulness is encompassed in imitation, and just as it was most praiseworthy in the ancients to invent well, so is it most useful to imitate well, especially for those whose language is not yet very copious and rich. But let him who would imitate understand that it is not an easy thing faithfully to follow the strengths of a good author and, as it were, transform oneself into him, seeing that Nature herself, even with things that appear most similar, has not managed to prevent their being distinguished by some mark and difference. I say this because there are many in all languages who, without delving into the most hidden and inward parts of the author they have chosen, adapt themselves only to what they see at first and, diverting themselves with the beauty of words, miss the force of things.

And certainly, since it is no vice, but greatly praiseworthy, to borrow from a foreign language ideas and words and to claim them as one's own, so is it greatly to be blamed and is indeed odious to any reader of liberal charac-

---

Molo of Rhodes: Apollonius Molon, a Greek rhetorician of the first century BCE

Et de ce que je dy font bonne preuve Ciceron et Virgile, que voluntiers et par honneur je nomme tousjours en la langue Latine, des quelz comme l'un se feut entierement adonné à l'immitation des Grecz, contrefist et exprima si au vif la copie de Platon, la vehemence de Demosthene et la joyeuse douceur d'Isocrate, que Molon Rhodien l'oyant quelquefois declamer, s'ecria qu'il emportoit l'eloquence Grecque à Rome. L'autre immita si bien Homere, Hesiode, et Thëocrit, que depuis on a dict de luy, que de ces troys il a surmonté l'un, egalé l'autre, et aproché si pres de l'autre, que si la felicité des argumens qu'ilz ont traitez eust esté pareille, la palme seroit bien douteuse. Je vous demande donq', vous autres, qui ne vous employez qu'aux translations, si ces tant fameux aucteurs se fussent amusez à traduyre, eussent ilz elevé leur langue à l'excellence et hauteur où nous la voyons maintenant? Ne pensez donques, quelque diligence et industrie que vous puissez mettre en cest endroict, faire tant que nostre langue, encores rampante à terre, puisse hausser la teste et s'élever sur piedz.

Chapitre 8
D'amplifier la Langue Françoyse par l'immitation des anciens Aucteurs Grecz et Romains

Se compose donq' celuy qui voudra enrichir sa langue, à l'immitation des meilleurs aucteurs Grecz et Latins: et à toutes leurs plus grandes vertuz, comme à un certain but, dirrige la pointe de son style. Car il n'y a point de doute que la plus grand' part de l'artifice ne soit contenue en l'immitation, et tout ainsi que ce feut le plus louable aux Anciens de bien inventer, aussi est ce le plus utile de bien immiter, mesmes à ceux dont la langue n'est encor' bien copieuse et riche. Mais entende celuy qui voudra immiter, que ce n'est chose facile de bien suyvre les vertuz d'un bon aucteur, et quasi comme se transformer en luy, veu que la Nature mesmes aux choses qui paroissent tressemblables, n'a sceu tant faire, que par quelque notte et difference elles ne puissent estre discernées. Je dy cecy, pour ce qu'il y en a beaucoup en toutes langues, qui sans penetrer aux plus cachées et interieures parties de l'aucteur qu'ilz se sont proposé, s'adaptent seulement au premier regard, et s'amusant à la beauté des motz, perdent la force des choses.

Et certes, comme ce n'est point chose vicieuse, mais grandement louable, emprunter d'une langue etrangere les sentences et les motz, et les approprier à la sienne: aussi est ce chose grandement à reprendre, voyre

ter to see such imitation within the same language, like that of even some learned men who judge themselves to be among the best when they most resemble a Héroët or a Marot. I thus admonish you (O you who desire the growth of your language and wish to excel in it) not to imitate lightly, as someone recently said, its most famous authors, as the greater number of our French poets commonly do, a thing surely as reprehensible as it is worthless to our vulgar tongue, since it amounts to no more (O great generosity!) than to give it what it already has. I wish our language were so rich in homegrown models that we had no need to have recourse to foreign ones. But if Virgil and Cicero had been content to imitate those of their own language, what would the Latins have beyond Ennius or Lucretius, beyond Crassus or Anthony?

Chapter 9
Reply to some objections

After having opened, as succinctly as I could, the way to those who desire the amplification of our language, it seems to me good and necessary to answer those who judge it barbarous and irregular, incapable of that elegance and abundance that are found in Greek and Latin, all the more (they say) since it lacks the declensions, the feet, and the meter of those two other languages. I do not wish here (though I could do it without shame) to make an excuse of the simplicity of our ancestors who were con-

---

Héroët: Antoine Héroët (1492–1568), French poet and author of *La Parfaicte Amye* [The Perfect Beloved] (1542)

Marot: Clément Marot (1496–1544), the leading French poet of the generation preceding du Bellay's

as someone recently said: Thomas Sébillet (1512–1589) in his *Art Poetique François* (1548), 2.6, the book that helped prompt du Bellay to write his *Defense* and whose admiration for Marot du Bellay opposes

Ennius or Lucretius: Latin poets who preceded Virgil

Crassus or Anthony: Lucius Licinius Crassus and Marcus Antonius, the leading Roman orators in the generation before Cicero and the principal speakers in Cicero's *De oratore*

the declensions: as du Bellay uses the term, *declination* (declension) refers both to suffixes added to Greek and Latin nouns, pronouns, and adjectives to indicate their grammatical function—our *declension*—and to those added to verbs to indicate mode, tense, and person—our *conjugation*

the feet, and the meter: feet (*piez*) are the basic units into which lines of Greek and Latin verse are divided; meter (*nombres*), the larger pattern of long and short syllables—neither of which were to be found in French verse

odieuse à tout lecteur de liberale nature, voir en une mesme langue une telle immitation, comme celle d'aucuns sçavans mesmes, qui s'estiment estre des meilleurs, quand plus ilz ressemblent un Heroet ou un Marot. Je t'amonneste donques (ô toy, qui desires l'accroissement de ta langue, et veux exceller en icelle) de non immiter à pié levé, comme n'agueres a dict quelqu'un, les plus fameux aucteurs d'icelle, ainsi que font ordinairement la plus part de notz poëtes Françoys, chose certes autant vicieuse, comme de nul profict à nostre vulgaire: veu que ce n'est autre chose (ô grande liberalité!) si non luy donner ce qui estoit à luy. Je voudroy' bien que nostre langue feust si riche d'exemples domestiques, que n'eussions besoing d'avoir recours aux etrangers. Mais si Virgile et Ciceron se feussent contentez d'immiter ceux de leur langue, qu'auront les Latins outre Ennie ou Lucrece, outre Crasse ou Antoyne?

Chapitre 9
Response à quelques objections

Apres avoir le plus succintement qu'il m'a eté possible ouvert le chemin à ceux qui desirent l'amplification de notre langue, il me semble bon et necessaire de repondre à ceux qui l'estiment barbare et irreguliere, incapable de cete elegance et copie, qui est en la Greque et Romaine: d'autant (disent ilz) qu'elle n'a ses declinations, ses piez et ses nombres comme ces deux autres langues. Je ne veux alleguer en cet endroict (bien que je le peusse faire sans honte) la simplicité de notz majeurs, qui se sont con-

tent to express their ideas with plain words, without art and ornament, not imitating the curious diligence of the Greeks to whom the Muse had given (as someone said) a round mouth—perfect, that is, in all elegance and grace of expression—as since then to the Romans, the imitators of the Greeks. But I will say that our language is not as irregular as some would claim, given that it is declined, if not by nouns, pronouns, and participles, at least by verbs, in all their tenses, modes, and persons. And if it is not as elaborately ordered—or rather tied up and tortured—in its other parts, it also does not have as many irregularities and anomalies, strange monsters of Greek and Latin. As for feet and meter, I will explain in the second book how we make up for them.

And certainly (as a great author on rhetoric says, in speaking of the felicity of the Greeks in the composition of their words) I do not think such things occur as a result of the nature of the said languages, but we always favor foreigners. Who would have prevented our ancestors from varying all the declinable parts of speech, from stretching out one syllable and shortening another, and making of them feet or hands? And who will prevent our successors from observing such things if a few learned and no less ingenious men of this age undertake to reduce them to art, as Cicero promised to do for the civil law, a thing that appeared impossible to some, to others not? We must not here claim the superiority of antiquity and say, as Homer did when he complained that bodies in his time were too small, that modern minds cannot be compared to ancient ones. Architecture, the art of navigation, and other ancient inventions are certainly admirable. Yet if one takes necessity, the mother of the arts, into consideration, they are not so great that one must suppose that the heavens and Nature spent on them all their strength, vigor, and industry. I will call forth as witnesses of what I say only printing, the sister of the Muses and the tenth of them, and that no less admirable than pernicious thunderbolt of artillery, with so many other nonancient inventions, which truly show that through the long passage of the ages the minds of men have not been as debased as some would claim. I say only that it is not impossible that our language can one day acquire ornament and artifice as elaborate as in Greek and Latin.

---

as someone said: Horace in the *Ars poetica* (*Epistles* 2.3.323)

irregularities and anomalies: in fact, as Barthélemy Aneau pointed out in his attack on the *Defense*, his *Quintil Horatian* (1550), French itself has an ample share of grammatical irregularities

as a great author on rhetoric says: Quintilian in the *Institutio oratorio* 1.5.70

Who would have prevented our ancestors: like other Renaissance humanists, du Bellay seems to have thought that the highly inflected grammatical structure and the characteristic sound patterns of Greek and Latin were imposed on those languages by art rather than being the products of their natural development

tentez d'exprimer leurs conceptions avecques paroles nues, sans art et ornement: non immitans la curieuse diligence des Grecz, aux quelz la Muse avoit donné la bouche ronde (comme dict quelqu'un) c'est à dire parfaite en toute elegance et venusté de paroles: comme depuis aux Romains immitateurs des Grecz. Mais je diray bien que nostre langue n'est tant irreguliere qu'on voudroit bien dire: veu qu'elle se decline, si non par les noms, pronoms, et participes, pour le moins par les verbes, en tous leurs tens, modes, et personnes. Et si elle n'est si curieusement reiglée, ou plus tost liée et gehinnée en ses autres parties, aussi n'ha elle point tant d'hetheroclites et anomaux, monstres etranges de la Grecque et de la Latine. Quand aux piedz et aux nombres, je diray au second livre en quoy nous les recompensons.

Et certes (comme dict un grand aucteur de rethorique, parlant de la felicité qu'ont les Grecz en la composition de leurs motz), je ne pense que telles choses se facent par la nature desdites langues, mais nous favorisons tousjours les etrangers. Qui eust gardé notz ancestres de varier toutes les parties declinables, d'allonger une syllabe et accoursir l'autre, et en faire des piedz ou des mains? Et qui gardera notz successeurs d'observer telles choses, si quelques sçavans et non moins ingenieux de cest aage entreprennent de les reduyre en art? comme Ciceron promettoit de faire au droict civil: chose qui à quelques uns a semblé impossible, aux autres non. Il ne fault point icy alleguer l'excellence de l'antiquité, et comme Homere se plaignoit que de son tens les cors estoient trop petiz, dire que les espris modernes ne sont à comparer aux anciens. L'architecture, l'art du navigaige, et autres inventions antiques, certainement sont admirables: non toutesfois, si on regarde à la necessité mere des Ars, du tout si grandes, qu'on doyve estimer les Cieux et la Nature y avoir dependu toute leur vertu, vigueur, et industrie. Je ne produiray pour temoings de ce que je dy l'imprimerie, seur des Muses et dixieme d'elles, et ceste non moins admirable que pernicieuse foudre d'artillerie, avecques tant d'autres non antiques inventions, qui montrent veritablement que par le long cours des siecles les espris des hommes ne sont point si abatardiz qu'on voudroit bien dire. Je dy seulement qu'il n'est pas impossible que nostre langue puisse recevoir quelquefoys cest ornement et artifice aussi curieux qu'il est aux Grecz et Romains.

As for the sound and the indescribable natural sweetness (as they say) which is in their languages, I do not see that we have any less in the judgment of the most delicate ears. It is true that we follow the dictates of Nature which has given us only the tongue for speaking. We do not vomit our words from the stomach like drunkards; we do not strangle them in our throats like frogs; we do not cut them up in the palate like birds; we do not whistle them from our lips like snakes. If the sweetness of languages resides in such ways of speaking, I confess that ours is rude and ill-sounding. But we also have the advantage of not twisting our mouths in a hundred thousand ways like monkeys—indeed like many, not remembering Minerva, who, once playing the flute and seeing in a mirror the deformity of her lips, threw her flute far away: an ill omen for the presumptuous Marsyas who was later flayed alive for playing it.

So then (someone will say) do you, following the example of Marsyas, who dared compare his rustic flute to the sweet lyre of Apollo, wish to liken your language to Greek and Latin? I confess that their authors have surpassed us in knowledge and fluency, in which things it was very easy for them to vanquish those who did not fight back. But I will not say that by long and diligent imitation of those who first claimed that which Nature has nevertheless not denied to others we cannot follow them as well in this as we have already done in the greater part of their mechanical arts and at times in their universal rule, for such an insult would touch not only the minds of men but also God, who gave as an inviolable law to all created things that they cannot endure forever but must pass ceaselessly from one state to another, the end and corruption of one being the beginning and generation of another. Some stubborn person will still reply, "Your language has waited too long to achieve such perfection." And I say that this delay does not prove that it cannot achieve perfection, but I say that having acquired perfection with such prolonged effort, it may be sure to keep it for a long time, in accordance with the law of Nature, which has decreed that each tree that is born, flowers, and bears fruit quickly also grows old and dies quickly and that, on the contrary, the one that has long toiled to put down roots lasts for many years.

---

and at times their universal rule: du Bellay may here be thinking of Charlemagne who restored "Roman" imperial rule—*monarchie* in du Bellay's sense—in western Europe

Quand au son, et je ne sçay quelle naturelle douceur (comme ilz disent) qui est en leurs langues, je ne voy point que nous l'ayons moindre, au jugement des plus delicates oreilles. Il est bien vray que nous usons du prescript de Nature, qui pour parler nous a seulement donné la langue. Nous ne vomissons pas notz paroles de l'estommac, comme les yvroingnes: nous ne les etranglons pas de la gorge, comme les grenoilles: nous ne les decoupons pas dedans le palat, comme les oyzeaux: nous ne les siflons pas des levres, comme les serpens. Si en telles manieres de parler gist la douceur des langues, je confesse que la nostre est rude et mal sonnante. Mais aussi avons nous cest avantaige de ne tordre point la bouche en cent mile sortes, comme les singes, voyre comme beaucoup mal se souvenans de Minerve, qui jouant quelquefois de la fluste, et voyant en un myroir la deformité de ses levres, la jeta bien loing, malheureuse rencontre au presumptueux Marsye, qui depuis en feut ecorché.

Quoy donques (dira quelqu'un) veux tu à l'exemple de ce Marsye, qui osa comparer sa fluste rustique à la douce lyre d'Apolon, egaler ta langue à la Grecque et Latine? Je confesse que les aucteurs d'icelles nous ont surmontez en sçavoir et facunde: és quelles choses leur a eté bien facile de vaincre ceux qui ne repugnoint point. Mais que par longue et diligente immitation de ceux qui ont occupé les premiers ce que Nature n'ha pourtant denié aux autres, nous ne puissions leur succeder aussi bien en cela que nous avons deja fait en la plus grand' part de leurs ars mecaniques, et quelquefois en leur monarchie, je ne le diray pas: car telle injure ne s'etendroit seulement contre les espris des hommes, mais contre Dieu, qui a donné pour loy inviolable à toute chose crée de ne durer perpetuellement, mais passer sans fin d'un etat en l'autre, etant la fin et corruption de l'un, le commencement et generation de l'autre. Quelque opiniatre repliquera encores: Ta langue tarde trop à recevoir ceste perfection. Et je dy que ce retardement ne prouve point qu'elle ne puisse la recevoir: aincoys je dy qu'elle se poura tenir certaine de la garder longuement l'ayant acquise avecques si longue peine, suyvant la loy de Nature, qui a voulu que tout arbre qui naist, florist et fructifie bien tost, bien tost aussi envieillisse et meure, et au contraire, celuy durer par longues années, qui a longuement travaillé à jeter ses racines.

Chapter 10
That the French Language is not incapable of Philosophy and why the Ancients were more Learned than the Men of our Age

Everything I have said for the defense and enrichment of our language concerns principally those who make a profession of speaking well, such as poets and orators. As for other kinds of writing and that cycle of learned disciplines the Greeks called the "encyclopedia," I touched in the beginning on what I think in that regard: namely, that the efforts of faithful translators are in this area very useful and necessary. And they should not be held back if they sometimes encounter words that have no equivalent in the French family, for the Latins did not feel compelled to translate every Greek word, like *rhetoric, music, arithmetic, geometry, philosophy*, and almost all the names of the learned disciplines, the names of rhetorical figures, of herbs, of illnesses, the sphere and its parts, and generally the greater part of the terms used in the natural sciences and mathematics. Those words will then be like foreigners in a city, for whom paraphrases will nonetheless serve as interpreters. Indeed, I would be of the opinion that the learned translator should perform rather the role of a paraphraser than of word-for-word translator, striving to give to all the disciplines that he wishes to treat the ornament and light of his language, as Cicero boasts of having done in philosophy, and following the example of the Italians who have converted nearly all of it into their vulgar tongue, especially Platonic philosophy.

And if any would say that philosophy is a burden for other shoulders than those of our language, I said at the beginning of this work and I say it again that all languages are of equal value and are formed by mortals to the same end by the same judgment. For which reason, without changing customs or nation, the Frenchman, and the German, not only the Greek or Roman, can devote himself to philosophy, and so I believe that to each his own language can competently communicate any teaching. Thus if the philosophy sown by Aristotle and Plato in the fertile Attic field were transplanted in our French plain, it would not be casting it among brambles and thorns where it would prove sterile, but it would be making it near

Chapitre 10
Que la Langue Françoyse n'est incapable de la Philosophie, et pourquoy les Anciens estoint plus Sçavans que les Hommes de notre Aage

Tout ce que j'ay dict pour la defence et illustration de notre langue, apartient principalement à ceux qui font profession de bien dire, comme les poëtes et les orateurs. Quand aux autres parties de literature, et ce rond de sciences que les Grecz ont nommé enyclopedie, j'en ay touché au commencement une partie de ce que m'en semble: c'est que l'industrie des fideles traducteurs est en cet endroict fort utile et necessaire: et ne les doit retarder, s'ilz rencontrent quelquefois des motz qui ne peuvent estre receuz en la famille Françoyse: veu que les Latins ne se sont point eforcez de traduyre tous les vocables Grecz, comme *rhetorique, musique, arithmetique, gëometrie, phylosophie*, et quasi tous les noms des sciences, les noms des figures, des herbes, des maladies, la sphere et ses parties, et generallement la plus grand' part des termes usitez aux sciences naturelles et mathematiques. Ces motz là donques seront en notre langue comme etrangers en une cité: aux quelz toutesfois les periphrazes serviront de truchementz. Encores seroy' je bien d'opinion que le sçavant translateur fist plus tost l'office de paraphraste que de traducteur, s'efforceant donner à toutes les sciences qu'il voudra traiter l'ornement et lumiere de sa langue, comme Ciceron se vante d'avoir fait en la phylosophie, et à l'exemple des Italiens, qui l'ont quasi toute convertie en leur vulgaire, principalement la Platonique.

Et si on veut dire que la phylosophie est un faiz d'autres epaules que de celles de notre langue, j'ay dict au commencement de cet œuvre, et le dy encores, que toutes langues sont d'une mesme valeur, et des mortelz à une mesme fin d'un mesme jugement formées. Parquoy ainsi comme sans muer des coutumes ou de nation, le Françoys, et l'Alement, non seulement le Grec ou Romain, se peut donner à phylosopher, aussi je croy qu'à un chacun sa langue puysse competemment communiquer toute doctrine. Donques si la phylosophie semée par Aristote et Platon au fertile champ Atique etoit replantée en notre pleine Françoyse, ce ne seroit la jeter entre les ronses et epines, où elle devint sterile: mais ce seroit la faire de loing-

rather than distant and, instead of a foreigner, a citizen of our own republic. And perhaps just as the spices and other eastern riches that India sends us are better known and treated by us and held in higher esteem than in the land of those who sow and harvest them, similarly philosophic speculations would become more familiar than they are now and would be more easily understood by us, had some learned man brought them over from Greek and Latin into our vulgar tongue, than by those who gather them (if one must put it this way) in the places where they grow.

And should one object that different languages are fit to signify different conceptions, some the conceptions of the learned, others those of the unlearned, and that Greek, in particular, is so well suited to the teachings of philosophy that it seems to have been formed by Nature herself, and not by human ingenuity, to express them—by that Nature, I say, which in every age, in every region, in every culture is always the same and willingly exercises her art throughout the world, no less on earth than in heaven. And although she concerns herself with the production of rational creatures, she does not for all that forget the irrational, but with an equal artfulness begets one and the other. So is she worthy to be known and praised by all people and in all languages. Birds, fish, and land animals in whatever way, now with one sound, now with another, with no distinguishing of words, signify their emotions. Much more should we humans do the same, each in his own language, without having recourse to others. Writing and languages were invented not for the preservation of Nature, who—being divine—has no need of our aid, but only for our good and utility so that present and absent, living and dead, revealing to one another the secret of our hearts, we may more easily attain our true happiness, which resides in the understanding of all branches of learning and not in the sound of words. And as a result, those languages and those ways of writing should be most in use which would be most easily learned.

Alas, how much better would it be were there only one natural language in the world, rather than spending so many years learning words! And this very often to an age where we no longer have either the means or the leisure to devote to greater things. And certainly, often wondering how it happens that men of our time are generally less learned in all disciplines and of less worth than the ancients, among many reasons I find this one, which I would dare say is the most important: it is the study of the Greek

taine prochaine, et d'etrangere citadine de notre republique. Et paravanture ainsi que les episseries et autres richesses orientales que l'Inde nous envoye, sont mieulx congnues et traitées de nous, et en plus grand prix, qu'en l'endroict de ceux qui les sement ou recueillent: semblablement les speculations phylosophiques deviendroient plus familieres qu'elles ne sont ores, et plus facilement seroient entendues de nous, si quelque sçavant homme les avoit transportées de Grec et Latin en notre vulgaire, que de ceux qui les vont (s'il fault ainsi parler) cueillir aux lieux ou elles croissent.

Et si on veut dire que diverses langues sont aptes à signifier diverses conceptions, aucunes les conceptions des doctes, autres celles des indoctes, et que la Grecque principalement convient si bien avecques les doctrines, que pour les exprimer il semble qu'elle ait eté formée de la mesme Nature, non de l'humaine providence: je dy qu'icelle Nature, qui en tout aage, en toute province, en toute habitude est tousjours une mesme chose, ainsi comme voluntiers elle s'exerce son art par tout le monde, non moins en la terre qu'au ciel, et pour estre ententive à la production des creatures raisonnables, n'oublie pourtant les iraisonnables, mais avecques un egal artifice engendre cetes cy et celles là: aussi est elle digne d'estre congneue et louée de toutes personnes, et en toutes langues. Les oyzeaux, les poissons, et les bestes terrestres de quelquonque maniere, ores avecques un son, ores avecques l'autre, sans distinction de paroles signifient leurs affections. Beaucoup plus tost nous hommes devrions faire le semblable, chacun avecques sa langue, sans avoir recours aux autres. Les ecritures et langaiges ont eté trouvez, non pour la conservation de la Nature, la quelle (comme divine qu'elle est) n'a mestier de nostre ayde: mais seulement à nostre bien et utilité: affin que presens, absens, vyfz et mors, manifestans l'un à l'autre le secret de notz cœurs, plus facilement parvenions à notre propre felicité, qui gist en l'intelligence des Sciences, non point au son des paroles: et par consequent celles langues et celles ecritures devroint plus estre en usaige, les queles on apprendroit plus facilement.

Las et combien seroit meilleur qu'il y eust au monde un seul langaige naturel, que d'employer tant d'années pour apprendre des motz! et ce jusques à l'aage bien souvent, que n'avons plus ny le moyen ny le loysir de vaquer à plus grandes choses. Et certes songeant beaucoup de foys, d'ou provient que les hommes de ce siecle generalement sont moins sçavans en toutes sciences, et de moindre prix que les Anciens, entre beaucoup de raysons je treuve cete cy, que j'oseroy' dire la principale: c'est l'étude des

and Latin languages. For were the time we spend in learning those languages spent in the study of the disciplines, Nature has surely not become so barren that she would not give birth in our time to some Platos and some Aristotles. But we, who ordinarily strive more to appear learned than to be learned, consume not only our youth in this vain exercise but, as if repenting that we have left the cradle and become men, return again to childhood and over the space of twenty or thirty years do nothing but learn to speak, some of us Greek, some Latin, some Hebrew. Which years once past—and gone with them that vigor and quickness that naturally reign in the minds of young men—we then seek to become philosophers, at a time when, due to illnesses, troubles of household business, and other hindrances that age brings, we are no longer fit for speculation on things. And very often, astonished by the difficulty and length of learning only words, we abandon everything out of despair and hate letters before we have tasted them or begun to love them.

Must we then give up the study of languages? No, inasmuch as the arts and learned disciplines are for now in the hands of the Greeks and Latins. But for the future, one should be able to speak of all things throughout the world in every language. I well understand that language professors will not share my opinion and still less those venerable druids who, from the ambitious desire they have to be among us what the philosopher Anacharsis was among the Scythians, fear nothing so much as that the secret of their mysteries, which must be learned from them alone as the days once were from the Chaldeans, should be revealed to the vulgar multitude and that we undermine their monopoly or (as Cicero says) "poke out the eyes of crows." In this regard, I recall having often heard some of their academy say that King Francis—I mean that Francis to whom France owes no less than Rome to Augustus—had dishonored knowledge and left the learned in contempt. O times! O manners! O rude ignorance! Not to understand that just as an evil is more pernicious the further it spreads, so a good is more beneficial the more common it is! And if they mean (as they also say) that as a consequence such a good is less highly regarded and wondered at by men, I will answer that such a great appetite for glory and such envy should not reign among the pillars of a Christian republic, but rather in that ambitious king who complained to his tutor because the tutor had

---

those venerable druids: professors of theology, especially at the Sorbonne

as the days once were from the Chaldeans: the Chaldeans were thought to have held a monopoly on calendrical knowledge

"poke out the eyes of crows": to overcome the advantage of strong oppressors, from Cicero's *Pro Murena* 11.25

that ambitious king: Alexander, whose tutor was Aristotle

langues Greque et Latine. Car si le tens que nous consumons à apprendre les dites langues estoit employé à l'etude des sciences, la Nature certes n'est point devenue si brehaigne, qu'elle n'enfentast de nostre tens des Platons et des Aristotes. Mais nous, qui ordinairement affectons plus d'estre veuz sçavans que de l'estre, ne consumons pas seulement nostre jeunesse en ce vain exercice: mais comme nous repentans d'avoir laissé le berseau et d'estre devenuz hommes, retournons encor' en enfance, et par l'espace de vingt ou trente ans ne faisons autre chose qu'apprendre à parler, qui Grec, qui Latin, qui Hebreu. Les quelz ans finiz, et finie avecques eux ceste vigueur et promptitude qui naturellement regne en l'esprit des jeunes hommes, alors nous procurons estre faictz phylosophes, quand pour les maladies, troubles d'afaires domestiques, et autres empeschementz qu'ameine le tens, nous ne sommes plus aptes à la speculation des choses. Et bien souvent etonnez de la difficulté et longueur d'apprendre des motz seulement, nous laissons tout par desespoir, et hayons les Lettres premier que les ayons goutées ou commencé à les aymer.

Fault il donques laisser l'etude des langues? Non, d'autant que les ars et sciences sont pour le present entre les mains des Grecz et Latins. Mais il se devroit faire à l'avenir qu'on peust parler de toute chose, par tout le monde, et en toute langue. J'entens bien que les proffesseurs des langues ne seront pas de mon opinion: encores moins ces venerables Druydes, qui pour l'ambicieux desir qu'ilz ont d'estre entre nous ce qu'estoit le philosophe Anacharsis entre les Scythes, ne craignent rien tant, que le secret de leurs mysteres, qu'il fault apprendre d'eux, non autrement que jadis les jours des Chaldëes, soit decouvert au vulgaire, et qu'on ne creve (comme dict Ciceron) les yeulx des corneilles. A ce propos, il me souvient avoir ouy dire maintesfois à quelques uns de leur academie, que le Roy Françoys, je dy celuy Françoys à qui la France ne doit moins qu'à Auguste Romme, avoit deshonnoré les sciences et laissé les doctes en mespris. O tens! ò meurs! ò crasse ignorance! n'entendre point que tout ainsi qu'un mal, quand il s'etent plus loing, est d'autant plus pernicieux, aussi est un bien plus profitable, quand plus il est commun! Et s'ilz veulent dire (comme aussi disent ilz) que d'autant est un tel bien moins excellent et admirable entre les hommes, je repondray qu'un si grand appetit de gloire et une telle envie ne devroit regner aux coulonnes de la Republique Chrestienne, mais bien en ce Roy ambicieux qui se plaignoit à son maitre, pour ce

made known the acroamatic disciplines—that is, those which can only be learned from the mouth of a teacher. What then? Do these giants, the enemies of heaven, wish to limit the power of the gods and restrain and shut up in the hands of those who do not know how to keep good watch over it that which the gods have, by a singular favor, given to men? I am reminded of those relics that one can see only through a small window and that one is forbidden to touch with one's hand. That is what they would to do to all the learned disciplines, which they keep shut up in Greek and Latin books, not allowing them to be seen in any other way or to be translated from those dead words into words that are alive and fly commonly through the lips of men.

I must have (it seems to me) sufficiently answered those who say that our vulgar tongue is too vile and barbarous to deal with such lofty subjects as philosophy. And if they are still not satisfied, I will ask them, "Why then did the ancient Greeks travel through so many countries and dangers, some to the Indies to see the gymnosophists, others to Egypt to borrow from old priests and prophets those great riches of which Greece is now so proud?" And yet those nations where philosophy has so willingly lived produced (I believe) people as barbarous and inhumane as we are and words as strange as ours. I would care little for the elegance of style which can be found in Plato and Aristotle were their books not written with reason. Truly, Philosophy adopted them as her sons, not because they were born in Greece, but because with great judgment they spoke well and wrote well of her. The truth they so ably sought out, their arrangement and ordering of things, the sententious brevity of the one and the divine copiousness of the other belong to them alone and not to others. But Nature, of whom they have spoken so well, is also the mother of everyone else and does not disdain to make herself known to those who strive with all diligence to understand her secrets, not in order to become Greeks but to become philosophers.

True it is that, because the arts and learned disciplines were always under the dominion of the Greeks and Romans, who were more devoted than others to whatever can make men immortal, we believe that by them alone they can and must be treated. But the time will perhaps come (and I beg of God, the most good and great, that it be in our age) that some good person, no less courageous than ingenious and learned, neither ambitious nor

---

these giants: again referring to theologians, here as the giants who warred against the gods

the gymnosophists: ascetics in ancient India much admired by the Greeks

qu'il avoit divulgué les sciences acroamatiques, c'est à dire, qui ne se peuvent apprendre que par l'audition du precepteur. Mais quoy? ces geans ennemis du Ciel veulent ilz limiter la puissance des Dieux, et ce qu'ilz ont par un singulier benefice donné aux hommes, restreindre et enserrer en la main de ceux qui n'en sçauroient faire bonne garde? Il me souvient de ces reliques, qu'on voit seulement par une petite vitre, et qu'il n'est permis toucher avecques la main. Ainsi veullent ilz faire de toutes les disciplines, qu'ilz tiennent enfermées dedans les livres Grecz et Latins, ne permettant qu'on les puisse voir autrement, ou les transporter de ces paroles mortes en celles qui sont vives et volent ordinairement par les bouches des hommes.

J'ay (ce me semble) deu assez contenter ceux qui disent que nostre vulgaire est trop vil et barbare, pour traiter si hautes matieres que la philosophie. Et s'ilz n'en sont encores bien satisfaiz, je leur demanderay: Pourquoy donques ont voyaigé les anciens Grecz par tant de païz et dangers, les uns aux Indes, pour voir les gymnosophistes, les autres en Egypte, pour emprunter de ces vieux prestres et prophetes ces grandes richesses, dont la Grece est maintenant si superbe? Et toutefoys ces nations, ou la phylosophie a si voluntiers habité, produysoint (ce croy-je) des personnes aussi barbares et inhumaines que nous sommes, et des paroles aussi etranges que les nostres. Bien peu me soucyroy'-je de l'elegance d'oraison qui est en Platon et en Aristote, si leurs livres sans rayson etoint ecriz. La phylosophie vrayement les a adoptez pour ses filz, non pour estre nez en Grece, mais pour avoir d'un hault sens bien parlé et bien écrit d'elle. La vérité si bien par eux cherchée, la disposition et l'ordre des choses, la sentencieuse breveté de l'un et la divine copie de l'autre est propre à eux, et non à autres: mais la Nature, dont ilz ont si bien parlé, est mere de tous les autres, et ne dedaigne point se faire congnoitre à ceux qui procurent avecques toute industrie entendre ses secrez, non pour devenir Grecz, mais pour estre faictz phylosophes.

Vray est que pour avoir les ars et sciences tousjours eté en la puissance des Grecz et Romains, plus studieux de ce qui peut rendre les hommes immortelz que les autres, nous croyons que par eux seulement elles puyssent et doyvent estre traictées. Mais le tens viendra paravanture (et je suplye au Dieu tresbon et tresgrand que ce soit de nostre aage) que quelque bonne personne, non moins hardie qu'ingenieuse et sçavante, non ambicieuse,

fearing the envy or hatred of any, will free us from that false opinion, giving our language the flower and the fruit of good letters. Otherwise, if the affection we bear toward foreign languages (whatever excellence they may have) were to prevent this great good fortune of ours, they would truly deserve not envy but hatred, not application but anger. They would, finally, deserve not to be learned but to be taken away from those who need rather a living understanding of the spirit than the sound of dead words.

So much then for learned disciplines. I come back to poets and orators, the main subjects of the matter I am treating, which is the adornment and enrichment of our language.

Chapter 11
That it is impossible to equal the Ancients in their Languages

Everyone of any intelligence will easily understand that what I say in defense of our language is not meant to discourage any from Greek or Latin, for I am so far from being of that opinion that I confess and maintain that he who is ignorant of those two languages, or who does not at least understand Latin, cannot accomplish an excellent work in his vulgar tongue. But I would be strongly of the opinion that, after having learned them, one should not despise one's own and that he who by a natural inclination (which we can see in comparing the Latin and Tuscan works of Petrarch and Boccaccio and, indeed, of some learned men of our time) feels himself better suited to write in his own language than in Greek or Latin should work rather to attain immortality among his own people by writing well in his vulgar tongue than to disgrace himself in the eyes of the learned and unlearned alike by writing badly in those two other languages.

But were there still to be found any of those who make all their art and learning of mere words, so that to name Greek or Latin seems to them to speak of a divine language and to speak of the vulgar tongue, to name an inhuman language, incapable of all erudition, were there (I say) to be found any such who would puff themselves up and despise everything written in French, I would gladly ask them this: What then do they think they

non craignant l'envie ou hayne d'aucun, nous otera cete faulse persuasion, donnant à notre langue la fleur et le fruict des bonnes lettres: autrement si l'àffection que nous portons aux langues etrangeres (quelque excellence qui soit en elles) empeschoit cete notre si grande felicité, elles seroint dignes veritablement non d'envie, mais de hayne, non de fatigue, mais de facherie: elles seroint dignes finablement d'estre non apprises, mais reprises de ceux qui ont plus de besoing du vif intellect de l'esprit que du son des paroles mortes.

Voyla quand aux disciplines. Je reviens aux poëtes et orateurs, principal object de la matiere que je traite, qui est l'ornement et illustration de notre langue.

Chapitre 11
Qu'il est impossible d'egaler les Anciens en leurs Langues

Toutes personnes de bon esprit entendront assez que cela que j'ay dict pour la deffence de notre langue, n'est pour decouraiger aucun de la Greque et Latine: car tant s'en fault que je soye de cete opinion, que je confesse et soutiens celuy ne pouvoir faire œuvre excellent en son vulgaire, qui soit ignorant de ces deux langues, ou qui n'entende la Latine pour le moins. Mais je seroy' bien d'avis qu'apres les avoir apprises, on ne deprisast la sienne et que celuy qui par une inclination naturelle (ce qu'on peut juger par les œuvres Latines et Thoscanes de Petrarque et Boccace, voire d'aucuns sçavans hommes de nostre tens) se sentiroit plus propre à ecrire en sa langue qu'en Grec ou en Latin, s'etudiast plus tost à se rendre immortel entre les siens, ecrivant bien en son vulgaire, que mal ecrivant en ces deux autres langues, estre vil aux doctes pareillement et aux indoctes.

Mais s'il s'en trouvoit encores quelques uns de ceux qui de simples paroles font tout leur art et science, en sorte que nommer la langue Greque et Latine leur semble parler d'une langue divine, et parler de la vulgaire, nommer une langue inhumaine, incapable de toute erudition: s'il s'en trouvoit de telz (dy je) qui voulussent faire des braves, et depriser toutes choses ecrites en Françoys, je leur demanderoy' voluntiers en ceste

are doing, these whitewashers, who rack their brains day and night to imitate—do I say imitate?—nay, to transcribe a Virgil and a Cicero? They build their poems from half-lines of the one and swear fealty in their prose writings to the words and phrases of the other, dreaming (as someone said) of senators, of consuls, of tribunes, of plebeian assemblies, and of all ancient Rome, not unlike Homer, who in his *Batrachomyomachia* applies to rats and frogs the magnificent titles of gods and goddesses. They surely merit the punishment of him who, brought before the tribunal of the Great Judge, confessed that he was a Ciceronian. Do they then expect not, I say, to equal, but even to come close to those authors in their own languages? They gather from this orator and from that poet now a noun, now a verb, now a line of verse, and now a phrase, as though, in the way one reconstructs an old building, they hoped with those gathered stones to restore to the ruined edifice of these languages their original grandeur and excellence. But you will never be such good masons (you who so zealously admire the Greek and Latin languages) that you will be able to restore them to the form those good and excellent architects first gave them. And if you hope that with those gathered fragments they can be brought back to life (as Aesculapius did with the limbs of Hippolytus), you are fooling yourselves, not realizing that at the fall of such proud structures, together with the predestined ruin of those two powerful empires, one part was reduced to dust and the rest must be in many pieces which it would be impossible to reassemble. Besides, many other parts have remained in the foundations of old walls or, scattered in the long course of the ages, can no longer be found. As a result, in undertaking to rebuild that edifice you will be far from restoring its original grandeur, when in the place where the great hall once stood you may perhaps put the bedrooms, the stables, or the kitchen, confusing doors and windows, changing, in short, the whole form of the building.

I would, finally, think art had the power to express the life-giving energy of Nature, could you make that restored building resemble the ancient one, seeing that you lack the very Idea from which you would have to derive the model for its reconstruction. And this (to set forth more clearly what I am saying) is all the more so in that the ancients used languages

---

these whitewashers: a term used in du Bellay's time of translators, which he here applies to modern writers in Latin and Greek

his *Batrachomyomachia*: a mock-heroic poem no longer attributed to Homer

of him who . . . confessed he was a Ciceronian: Saint Jerome

as Aesculapius did with the limbs of Hippolytus: the mythic physician Aesculapius brought Hippolytus, the son of Theseus, back to life after he had been dismembered through the malice of his stepmother Phaedra

you lack the very Idea: du Bellay here uses *Idea* in the Platonic sense as the transcendent entity from which existing things derive

sorte: Que pensent doncq' faire ces reblanchisseurs de murailles, qui jour et nuyt se rompent la teste à immiter? que dy je immiter? mais transcrire un Virgile et un Ciceron? batissant leur poëmes des hemystyches de l'un, et jurant en leurs proses aux motz et sentences de l'autre: songeant (comme a dict quelqu'un) des Peres conscriptz, des Consulz, des Tribuns, des Commices, et toute l'antique Rome, non autrement qu'Homere, qui en sa *Batracomyomachie* adapte aux raz et grenoilles les magnifiques tiltres des Dieux et Déesses. Ceux là certes meritent bien la punition de celuy qui ravy au tribunal du grand Juge, repondit qu'il etoit Ciceronien. Pensent ilz donques, je ne dy egaler, mais aprocher seulement de ces aucteurs en leurs langues? recuillant de cet orateur et de ce poëte ores un nom, ores un verbe, ores un vers, et ores une sentence: comme si en la façon qu'on rebatist un vieil edifice, ilz s'attendoint rendre par ces pierres ramassées à la ruynée fabrique de ces langues sa premiere grandeur et excellence. Mais vous ne serez ja si bons massons (vous, qui estes si grands zelateurs des langues Greque et Latine) que leur puissiez rendre celle forme que leur donnarent premierement ces bons et excellens architectes: et si vous esperez (comme fist Esculape des membres d'Hippolyte) que par ces fragmentz recuilliz elles puyssent estre resuscitées, vous vous abusez, ne pensant point qu'à la cheute de si superbes edifices conjointe à la ruyne fatale de ces deux puissantes monarchies, une partie devint poudre, et l'autre doit estre en beaucoup de pieces, les queles vouloir reduire en un seroit chose impossible: outre que beaucoup d'autres parties sont demeurées aux fondementz des vieilles murailles, ou egarées par le long cours des siecles ne se peuvent trouver d'aucun. Parquoy venant à redifier cete fabrique, vous serez bien loing de luy restituer sa premiere grandeur, quand, où souloit estre la sale, vous ferez paravanture les chambres, les etables ou la cuysine, confundant les portes et les fenestres, bref changeant toute la forme de l'édifice.

Finablement j'estimeroy' l'art pouvoir exprimer la vive energie de la Nature, si vous pouviez rendre cete fabrique renouvelée semblable à l'antique, etant manque l'Idée de la quele faudroit tyrer l'exemple pour la redifier. Et ce (afin d'exposer plus clerement ce que j'ay dict) d'autant que les Anciens usoint des langues, qu'ilz avoint succées avecques le laict de la

they had sucked in with their nurses' milk and that were spoken by the unlearned as well as by the learned, save that the latter studied academic disciplines and the art of speaking well, thus making themselves more eloquent than the others. That is why their happy ages were so fertile in good poets and orators. That is why even women aspired to the glory of eloquence and erudition, like Sappho, Corinna, Cornelia, and a thousand others, whose names are joined with the memory of the Greeks and Romans. Then do not think, you imitators, you servile flock, that you will achieve the summit of their excellence, since you have learned their words with great effort and the better part of your life is already past. You despise our vulgar tongue perhaps for no other reason than because we learn it from childhood and without study, and the others with great effort and diligence. Had our language died, like Greek and Latin, and been put in the reliquary of books, I do not doubt that it would be as difficult or almost as difficult to learn as they are. I wanted to make this remark because human curiosity admires excessively things rare and difficult to find, even though they are less suitable for the uses of daily life, like perfumes and gems, than those that are common and necessary, like bread and wine. I do not, however, see why we must judge one language better than another simply because it is more difficult, unless we were to say that Lycophron is better than Homer because he is more obscure and Lucretius better than Virgil for the same reason.

Chapter 12
Defense of the Author

Let those who may think I am too great an admirer of my own language consult the first book of the *Ends of Goods and Evils*, written by that father of Latin eloquence Cicero, who at the beginning of the said book, among other things, answers those who despise things written in Latin and prefer to read Greek. The conclusion of the argument is that he judges the Latin language not only not poor, as the Romans then thought, but even richer than Greek. "What ornament," he says, "of abundant or elegant speech has been lacking, I will say to us, or to good orators, or to poets, since they have had someone they can imitate?" I would not give such high praise to our language, for it does not yet have its Ciceros and Virgils. But I do dare to assert that if the learned men of our nation deigned to esteem it as highly as the Romans did theirs, it would someday—and soon—climb to the rank of the most famous.

Ends of Goods and Evils: *De finibus bonorum et malorum* from which du Bellay takes something of his heroic stance in defense of his native language

nourice, et aussi bien parloint les indoctes comme les doctes, si non que ceux cy aprenoint les disciplines et l'art de bien dire, se rendant par ce moyen plus eloquens que les autres. Voyla pourquoy leurs bienheureux siecles etoint si fertiles de bons poëtes et orateurs. Voyla pourquoy les femmes mesmes aspiroint à ceste gloire d'eloquence et erudition, comme Sapho, Corynne, Cornelie, et un milier d'autres, dont les noms sont conjoings avecques la memoire des Grecz et Romains. Ne pensez donques, immitateurs, troupeau servil, parvenir au point de leur excellence: veu qu'à grand' peine avez vous appris leurs motz, et voyla le meilleur de votre aage passé. Vous deprisez nostre vulgaire, paravanture non pour autre raison, sinon que des enfance et sans etude nous l'apprenons, les autres avecques grand peine et industrie. Que s'il etoit comme la Greque et Latine pery et mis en reliquaire de livres, je ne doute point qu'il ne feust (ou peu s'en faudroit) aussi dificile à apprendre comme elles sont. J'ay bien voulu dire ce mot, pour ce que la curiosité humaine admire trop plus les choses rares et difficiles à trouver, bien qu'elles ne soint si commodes pour l'usaige de la vie, comme les odeurs et les gemmes, que les communes et necessaires, comme le pain et le vin. Je ne voy pourtant qu'on doyve estimer une langue plus excellente que l'autre, seulement pour estre plus difficile, si on ne vouloit dire que Lycophron feust plus excellent qu'Homere, pour estre plus obscur, et Lucrece que Virgile, pour ceste mesme raison.

Chapitre 12
Deffence de l'Aucteur

Ceux qui penseront que je soye trop grand admirateur de ma langue, aillent voir le premier livre des *Fins des Biens et des Maulx*, fait par ce pere d'eloquence Latine Ciceron, qui au commencement dudict livre, entre autres choses, repond à ceux qui deprisoint les choses ecrites en Latin, et les aymoint myeux lire en Grec. La conclusion du propos est qu'il estime la langue Latine non seulement n'estre pauvre, comme les Romains estimoint lors, mais encor' estre plus riche que la Greque. Quel ornement (dit il) d'orayson copieuse ou elegante a defailly, je diray à nous, ou aux bons orateurs, ou aux poëtes, depuis qu'ilz ont eu quelqu'un qu'ilz peussent immiter? Je ne veux pas donner si hault loz notre langue, pour ce qu'elle n'a point encores ses Cicerons et Virgiles: mais j'ose bien àsseurer que si les sçavans hommes de notre nation la daignoint autant estimer que les Romains faisoint la leur, elle pouroit quelquesfoys et bien tost se mettre au ranc des plus fameuses.

It is time to conclude this discussion, so as to touch in particular on the main points of the amplification and adornment of our language. In this, Reader, do not be surprised if I neglect the orator in favor of the poet. For in addition to the fact that the strengths of the one are, for the most part, common to the other, I am not ignorant that Étienne Dolet, a man of good judgment in our vulgar tongue, has written *The French Orator*, which perhaps someone, a friend to the memory of the author and to France, will soon and faithfully bring to light.

End of the First Book of *The Defense and Enrichment of the French Language.*

Étienne Dolet: (1509–1546), a leading humanist and printer who was burned at the stake for his supposed heresy and atheism three years before du Bellay wrote these admiring words of him

Il est tens de clore ce pas, afin de toucher particulierement les principaux poinctz de l'amplification et ornement de notre langue. En quoy (Lecteur) ne t'ebahis, si je ne parle de l'orateur comme du poëte. Car outre que les vertuz de l'un sont pour la plus grand' part communes à l'autre, je n'ignore point qu'Etienne Dolet, homme de bon jugement en notre vulgaire, a formé l'*Orateur Françoys,* que quelqu'un (peut estre) amy de la memoire de l'aucteur et de la France, mettra de bref et fidelement en lumiere.

Fin du premier Livre de la *Deffence et Illustration de la Langue Françoyse.*

The Second Book of The Defense and Enrichment of the French Language

Chapter 1
The intention of the Author

Since the poet and the orator are like the two pillars that support the edifice of each language, leaving aside the one that I understand has been built by others, I wanted, out of the duty I owe my fatherland, to sketch as well as I can the one that remained, hoping that it may be brought to perfection by me or by some more learned hand. Now in doing this I do not wish to feign, as it were, an image of the poet that can be perceived neither with the eyes, nor ears, nor any other sense, but that can be understood only by reasoning and thought, like those Ideas that Plato made the essence of all things, to which, as to a model conceived by the imagination, all that can be seen refers. That would surely demand far greater knowledge and leisure than mine. And I will think I have deserved well of my fellow countrymen if I only point out the path they must follow to attain the excellence of the ancients, where someone else, perhaps prompted by our little work, will lead them by the hand.

Let us then take as a starting point what (it seems to me) we have sufficiently proved in the first book: namely, that without imitating the Greeks and Romans we cannot give our language the excellence and light of other more famous ones. I know that many will criticize me, who, first among the French, have dared to introduce what is virtually a new poetry, or will not be fully satisfied, whether because of the brevity I have used or because of the diversity of minds that make some think good what others think bad. Marot pleases me (someone says) because he is easy and never strays from

---

the one that I understand has been built by others: the orator, discussed, as du Bellay points out at the end of book 1, by Étienne Dolet in his unpublished *Orateur Françoys*

can be perceived neither with the eyes: this phrase and the remainder of the sentence are translated from Cicero's *Orator,* from which du Bellay also borrows later in this chapter

Le Second Livre de la Deffence et Illustration de la Langue Françoyse

Chapitre 1
L'intention de l'Aucteur

Pour ce que le poëte et l'orateur sont comme les deux piliers qui soutiennent l'edifice de chacune langue, laissant celuy que j'entens avoir eté baty par les autres, j'ay bien voulu, pour le devoir en quoy je suys obligé à la patrie, tellement quellement ebaucher celuy qui restoit, esperant que par moy, ou par une plus docte main, il poura recevoir sa perfection. Or ne veux-je en ce faisant feindre comme une certaine figure de poëte, qu'on ne puysse ny des yeux, ny des oreilles, ny d'aucun sens apercevoir, mais comprendre seulement de la cogitation et de la pensée: comme ces Idées que Platon constituoit en toutes choses, aux queles, ainsi qu'à une certaine espece imaginative, se refere tout ce qu'on peut voir. Cela certainement est de trop plus grand sçavoir et loysir que le mien: et penseray avoir beaucoup merité des miens, si je leur montre seulement avecques le doy le chemin qu'ilz doyvent suyvre pour attaindre à l'excellence des Anciens, où quelque autre (peut estre) incité par nostre petit labeur les conduyra avecques la main.

Mettons donques pour le commencement ce que nous avons (ce me semble) assez prouvé au premier Livre: c'est que sans l'immitation des Grecz et Romains nous ne pouvons donner à notre langue l'excellence et lumiere des autres plus fameuses. Je sçay que beaucoup me reprendront, qui ay osé le premier des Françoys introduyre quasi comme une nouvelle poësie: ou ne se tiendront plainement satisfaictz, tant pour la breveté dont j'ay voulu user, que pour la diversité des espris, dont les uns treuvent bon ce que les autres treuvent mauvais. Marot me plaist (dit quelqu'un) pour ce qu'il est facile, et ne s'eloingne point de la commune maniere de parler.

the common way of speaking; I like Héroët (says another) because all his poems are learned, grave, and labored; others delight in some other. As for me, no such ill-founded attachment has kept me from my undertaking, for I have always thought our French poetry capable of some higher and better style than that with which we have for so long satisfied ourselves. Let us then say briefly what we think of our French poets.

Chapter 2
Of the French Poets

Of all the old French poets only one, Guillaume de Lorris and Jean de Meung, deserve to be read, not so much because there is much in them that moderns should imitate, but in order to see something like a first image of the French language, venerable for its antiquity. I have no doubt that all graybeards would cry that shame is lost if I dared to criticize or amend anything in those they learned when they were young, which I have no intention of doing. But I do maintain that he is too great an admirer of everything old who would rob the young of the glory they merit, esteeming nothing, as Horace says, unless death has sanctified it, as though time improved poems like wines. The more recent poets, including those who were named by Clément Marot in an epigram to Salel, are sufficiently known by their works. I refer readers to them to make their own judgment. Still, I will say that Jean Lemaire de Belges seems to me to have been the first to render illustrious both the Gauls and the French language, giving it many poetic words and ways of speaking which have been useful even to the best of our time.

As for the moderns, they will one day be sufficiently named. And were I to speak of them, it would only be to change the opinion of some, either too unjust or too severe in their judgment, who everyday find something to

---

Guillaume de Lorris and Jean de Meung: the authors of the two parts of the thirteenth-century *Roman de la Rose* in speaking of whom Du Bellay mixes singular and plural forms

all graybeards would cry: an echo of Horace's *Epistles* 2.1.79–85

as Horace says: *Epistles* 2.1.48–49 and 34

those who were named by Clément Marot: the poets named by Marot in his *Epigram* 175, "Des poëtes Françoys, à Salel," are Jean de Meung, Alain Chartier, Octavien de Saint-Gelais, Jean Molinet, Jean Lemaire de Belges, Georges Chastellain, François Villon, Guillaume Crotin, Arnoul and Simon Greban, Jean Merchinot, Guillaume Coquillart, Hugues Salel, and Marot himself

Jean Lemaire de Belges: (1473–c. 1515), one of the generation of poets known as *les grands rhétoriqueurs* (the great rhetoricians)

Heroët (dit quelque autre) pour ce que tous ses vers sont doctes, graves, et elabourez. Les autres d'un autre se delectent. Quand à moy, telle superstition ne m'a point retiré de mon entreprinse, pour ce que j'ay tousjours estimé notre poësie Françoyse estre capable de quelque plus hault et meilleur style que celuy dont nous sommes si longuement contentez. Disons donques brevement ce que nous semble de notz poëtes Françoys.

Chapitre 2
Des Poëtes Françoys

De tous les anciens poëtes Françoys, quasi un seul, Guillaume du Lauris et Jan de Meun, sont dignes d'estre leuz, non tant pour ce qu'il y ait en eux beaucoup de choses qui se doyvent immiter des modernes, comme pour y voir quasi comme une premiere imaige de la langue Françoyse, venerable pour son antiquité. Je ne doute point que tous les peres cryroint la honte estre perdue, si j'osoy' reprendre ou emender quelque chose en ceux que jeunes ilz ont appris: ce que je ne veux faire aussi, mais bien soutiens-je que celuy est trop grand admirateur de l'ancienneté, qui veut defrauder les jeunes de leur gloire meritée, n'estimant rien, comme dict Horace, si non ce que la mort a sacré, comme si le tens, ainsi que les vins, rendoit les poësies meilleures. Les plus recens, mesmes ceux qui ont esté nommez par Clement Marot en un certain epygramme à Salel, sont assez congneuz par leurs œuvres. J'y renvoye les lecteurs pour en faire jugement. Bien diray-je que Jan le Maire de Belges me semble avoir premier illustré et les Gaules et la langue Françoyse, luy donnant beaucoup de motz et manieres de parler poëtiques, qui ont bien servy mesmes aux plus excellens de notre tens.

Quand aux modernes, ilz seront quelquesfoys assez nommez: et si j'en vouloy' parler, ce seroit seulement pour faire changer d'opinion à quelques uns ou trop iniques ou trop severes estimateurs des choses, qui

criticize in three or four of the best, saying that one lacks what is the foundation of good writing—that is, knowledge—and would have doubled his glory had he cut his book in half. Another, aside from his rhyme, which is not everywhere sufficiently rich, is so lacking in all poetic delights and ornaments that he deserves rather to be called a philosopher than a poet. Another, because he has yet to bring anything to light under his own name, does not deserve to be given the first place, and it appears (say some) that he wants to immortalize his name through the writings of others of his time, just as Demades was ennobled by his rivalry with Demosthenes and Hortensius by his with Cicero. And were one's judgment of him based only on reputation, his faults would be thought to equal—indeed, to exceed—his strengths, inasmuch as every day new writings circulate under his name, which are, in my opinion, as unlike anything I have sometimes been assured is by him as they are lacking in grace or learning. Another, wishing to distance himself too far from the commonplace, has fallen into an obscurity in his writings that the most learned found as difficult to elucidate as did the most ignorant.

So there you have a part of what I have heard said in many places concerning the best poets in our language. Would to God everyone were by nature as candid in praising the strengths as they are diligent in marking the faults of others! The crowd of those (except five or six) who follow the most important poets, as one follows standard-bearers, is so ill informed in everything that through them our vulgar tongue takes little care to extend very far the limits of its empire. And were I one of those ancient critics, who were judges of poems, such as an Aristarchus and Aristophanes, or (if one must speak this way) a battle sergeant of our French language, I would drive from the field many who are so badly armed that, were we to rely on them, we would be very far from achieving the victory toward which we must aspire.

I do not doubt that many, especially those who have embraced commonplace opinions and whose tender ears cannot stand to hear anything against those they have already accepted as oracles, will object that I dare to speak so freely and to pronounce, almost like a sovereign judge, upon our French poets. But as to whether I am right or wrong, I appeal to those

---

one lacks what is the foundation of good writing: Clément Marot

Another, aside from his rhyme: Antoine Héroët

Another, because he has yet to bring anything to light: Mellin de Saint-Gelais (1487–1558), little of whose work had appeared in print in 1549

Another, wishing to distance himself: Maurice Scève (1510–1564), author of *Délie* (1544), a sequence of ten-line love poems noted for their obscurity

Aristarchus and Aristophanes: Aristarchus of Samothrace and Aristophanes of Byzantium, Alexandrian scholars and critics of the third and second centuries BCE

tous les jours treuvent à reprendre en troys ou quatre des meilleurs: disant qu'en l'un default ce qui est le commencement de bien ecrire, c'est le sçavoir, et auroit augmenté sa gloire de la moitié, si de la moitié il eust diminué son livre. L'autre, outre sa ryme, qui n'est par tout bien riche, est tant denué de tous ces delices et ornementz poëtiques, qu'il merite plus le nom de phylosophe que de poëte. Un autre, pour n'avoir encores rien mis en lumiere soubz son nom, ne merite qu'on luy donne le premier lieu: et semble (disent aucuns) que par les ecriz de ceux de son tens, il veille eternizer son nom, non autrement que Demade est ennobly par la contention de Demosthene, et Hortense de Ciceron. Que si on en vouloit faire jugement au seul rapport de la renommée, on rendroit les vices d'iceluy egaulx, voyre plus grands que ses vertuz, d'autant que tous les jours se lysent nouveaux ecriz soubz son nom, à mon avis aussi eloignez d'aucunes choses qu'on m'a quelquesfois asseuré estre de luy, comme en eux n'y a ny grace ny erudition. Quelque autre, voulant trop s'eloingner du vulgaire, est tumbé en obscurité aussi difficile à eclersir en ses ecriz aux plus sçavans comme aux plus ignares.

Voyla une partie de ce que j'oy dire en beaucoup de lieux des meilleurs de notre langue. Que pleust à Dieu le naturel d'un chacun estre aussi candide à louer les vertuz, comme diligent à observer les vices d'autruy! La tourbe de ceux (hors mis cinq ou six) qui suyvent les principaux, comme port'enseignes, est si mal instruicte de toutes choses, que par leur moyen nostre vulgaire n'a garde d'etendre gueres loing les bornes de son empire. Et si j'étoy' du nombre de ces anciens critiques juges des poëmes, comme un Aristarque et Aristophane, ou (s'il fault ainsi parler) un sergent de bande en notre langue Françoyse, j'en mettroy' beaucoup hors de la bataille si mal armez, que se fiant en eux, nous serions trop eloingnez de la victoire où nous devons aspirer.

Je ne doute point que beaucoup, principalement de ceux qui sont accommodez à l'opinion vulgaire, et dont les tendres oreilles ne peuvent rien souffrir au desavantaige de ceux qu'ilz ont desja receuz comme oracles, trouverront mauvais de ce que j'ose si librement parler, et quasi comme juge souverain pronuncer de notz poëtes Françoys: mais si j'ay dict

who are more friends of truth than of Plato or Socrates and do not take after the Pythagoreans whose only argument is: "Such a one said so." As for me, if I were asked what I think of our best French poets, I would answer in the manner of the Stoics, who, when asked whether Zeno, Cleanthes, and Chrysippus were wise, answered that they were certainly great and venerable, yet they did not possess what is most excellent in the nature of man. I would (I say) answer that our French poets have written well, that they have given greater luster to our language, that France is in their debt, but I would also say that one could find in our language (if some learned man would put his hand to it) a far more exquisite form of poetry, which would have to be sought in those old Greeks and Latins and not in French authors. For from the latter very little can be taken, no more than skin and coloring, while from the former one can take flesh, bones, sinews, and blood. And if someone hard to please were not satisfied with these arguments, I will say (so as not to seem to judge things so severely without cause) that in other arts and learned disciplines mediocrity may deserve some praise, but to poets neither gods, nor men, nor booksellers have granted the right to be mediocre, according to the opinion of Horace, whom I cannot name often enough, for with regard to the subjects I am addressing, he seems to me to have a better-purged brain and a better nose than others. Furthermore, as Demosthenes once replied to Aeschines, who had criticized him for using bitter and harsh words, the fortunes of Greece do not depend on such things. So, if anyone becomes angry that I have spoken so freely, I will say that the victories of King Henry, to whom may God give the fortune of Augustus and the goodness of Trajan, do not depend on my words.

I have, Reader devoted to the French language, chosen to dwell at length on this topic, which may perhaps appear to you contrary to what I have promised, since I, who have undertaken to praise and defend our vulgar tongue, do not greatly prize those who occupy the first rank in it. Yet I think you will not find it odd if you consider that I cannot better defend it

---

the Pythagoreans: the disciples of the Greek philosopher Pythagorus were noted for their unwavering devotion to the teachings of their master

in the manner of the Stoics: a story borrowed from Quintilian's *Institutio oratorio* 12.1.18

nor booksellers: du Bellay's *coulonnes* comes from Horace's *columnae* in the *Ars poetica* (*Epistles* 2.3.373), where it stands metonymically for the Roman booksellers who advertised their wares on columns in front of their shops

as Demosthenes once replied to Aeschines: story taken from Cicero's *Orator* 8.27

bien ou mal, je m'en rapporte à ceux qui sont plus amis de la verité que de Platon ou Socrate, et ne sont imitateurs des Pythagoriques, qui pour toutes raisons n'alleguoint si non: Cetuy là l'a dit. Quand à moy, si j'etoy' enquis de ce que me semble de notz meilleurs poëtes Françoys, je diroy' à l'exemple des Stoïques, qui interroguez si Zenon, si Clëante, si Chrysippe sont saiges, repondent ceulx là certainement avoir eté grands et venerables, n'avoir eu toutefois ce qui est le plus excellent en la nature de l'homme: je repondroy' (dy-je) qu'ilz ont bien ecrit, qu'ilz ont illustré notre langue, que la France leur est obligée: mais aussi diroy-je bien qu'on pouroit trouver en notre langue (si quelque sçavant homme y vouloit mettre la main) une forme de poësie beaucoup plus exquise, la quele il faudroit chercher en ces vieux Grecz et Latins, non point és aucteurs Françoys: pour ce qu'en ceux cy on ne sçauroit prendre que bien peu, comme la peau et la couleur: en ceux là on peut prendre la chair, les oz, les nerfz, et le sang. Et si quelqu'un mal aysé à contenter ne vouloit prendre ces raisons en payement, je diray (afin de n'estre veu examiner les choses si rigoreusement sans cause) qu'aux autres ars et sciences la mediocrité peut meriter quelque louange: mais aux poëtes ny les Dieux, ny les hommes, ny les coulonnes n'ont point concedé estre mediocres, suyvant l'opinion d'Horace, que je ne puis assez souvent nommer: pour ce qu'és choses que je traicte, il me semble avoir le cerveau myeux purgé et le nez meilleur que les autres. Au fort, comme Demosthene repondit quelquesfois à Echines, qui l'avoit repris de ce qu'il usoit de motz apres et rudes, de telles choses ne dependre les fortunes de Grece: aussi diray-je, si quelqu'un se fache de quoy je parle si librement, que de la ne dependent les victoires du Roy Henry, à qui Dieu veille donner la felicité d'Auguste et la bonté de Trajan.

J'ay bien voulu (Lecteur studieux de la langue Françoyse) demeurer longuement en cete partie, qui te semblera (peut estre) contraire à ce que j'ay promis: veu que je ne prise assez haultement ceux qui tiennent le premier lieu en nostre vulgaire, qui avoy' entrepris de le louer et deffendre. Toutesfoys je croy que tu ne le trouveras point etrange, si tu consideres que

than by attributing its poverty not to its own natural character but to the negligence of those who have taken it in charge and cannot better persuade you to write in it than by showing you how to enrich it and render it illustrious, which is by imitation of the Greeks and Romans.

Chapter 3
That Natural Talent is not enough for him who in Poetry would produce a work worthy of immortality

But since there are good and bad models in all languages, I do not, Reader, want you to attach yourself without choice and judgment to the first comer. It would be far better to write without imitation than to resemble a bad author, seeing that even the most learned agree that natural talent without the rules of art does more than rules without talent. Nevertheless, inasmuch as the amplification of our language (which is the subject I am addressing) cannot be accomplished without rules and erudition, I do want to warn those who aspire to that glory to imitate good Greek and Roman authors—indeed, even Italians, Spaniards, and others—or not to write at all, unless for yourself (as we say) and your Muses. Let no one answer me here by citing some of our writers who without any rules of art, or at most with no more than mediocre ones, have acquired great renown in our vulgar tongue. Those who willingly admire petty things and disdain whatever exceeds their capacity will make as much of them as they want. But I know that the learned will put them in no other rank than that of those who speak French well and who have (as Cicero said of the earliest Roman authors) good wits but very little art. Nor let anyone claim that poets are born, for that can be assumed from the ardor and alacrity of mind which naturally motivates poets and without which all the rules of art would be lost on them and useless. Certainly it would be all too easy, and for that very reason contemptible, to win everlasting fame, if the felicity of nature that is granted even to the most ignorant were enough to do something worthy of immortality. He who wishes to fly through the hands and

---

the most learned: Cicero in *Pro Archia* 7.15 and *De oratore* 1.25.113 and Quintilian in *Institutio Oratorio* 2.19.2

some of our writers: aimed at Clément Marot, whom du Bellay has already blamed in the previous chapter for his want of learning, and his followers, the Marotiques

as Cicero said: Cicero reported by Quintilian, *Institutio pratorio* 10.1.40

poets are born: alludes to the familiar saying, cited by Sébillet in his *Art Poetique François* (1.3), "Fiunt oratores, poetae nascuntur" (Orators are made, poets are born)

je ne le puis mieux defendre, qu'atribuant la pauvreté d'iceluy, non à son propre et naturel, mais à la négligence de ceux qui en ont pris le gouvernement: et ne te puis mieux persuader d'y ecrire, qu'en te montrant le moyen de l'enrichir et illustrer, qui est l'imitation des Grecz et Romains.

Chapitre 3
Que le Naturel n'est suffisant à celuy qui en Poësie veult faire œuvre digne de l'immortalité

Mais pource qu'en toutes langues y en a de bons et de mauvais, je ne veux pas (Lecteur) que sans election et jugement tu te prennes au premier venu. Il vauldroit beaucoup mieux ecrire sans immitation que ressembler un mauvais aucteur: veu mesmes que c'est chose accordée entre les plus sçavans, le naturel faire plus sans la doctrine que la doctrine sans le naturel. Toutesfois, d'autant que l'amplification de nostre langue (qui est ce que je traite) ne se peut faire sans doctrine et sans erudition, je veux bien avertir ceux qui aspirent à ceste gloire, d'immiter les bons aucteurs Grecz et Romains, voyre bien Italiens, Hespagnolz, et autres, ou du tout n'ecrire point, si non à soy (comme on dit) et à ses Muses. Qu'on ne m'allegue point icy quelques uns des nostres, qui sans doctrine, à tout le moins non autre que mediocre, ont acquis grand bruyt en nostre vulgaire. Ceux qui admirent voluntiers les petites choses, et deprisent ce qui excede leur jugement, en feront tel cas qu'ilz voudront: mais je sçay bien que les sçavans ne les mettront en autre ranc, que de ceux qui parlent bien Françoys, et qui ont (comme disoit Ciceron des anciens aucteurs Romains) bon esprit, mais bien peu d'artifice. Qu'on ne m'allegue point aussi que les poëtes naissent, car cela s'entend de ceste ardeur et allegresse d'esprit qui naturellement excite les poëtes, et sans la quele toute doctrine leur seroit manque et inutile. Certainement ce seroit chose trop facile, et pourtant contemptible, se faire eternel par renommée, si la felicité de nature donnée mesmes aux plus indoctes etoit suffisante pour faire chose digne de l'immortalité. Qui veut voler par les mains et bouches des hommes, doit

lips of men must long dwell in his study. And he who desires to live in the memory of posterity must, as though dead unto himself, often sweat and tremble and, just as our courtier poets drink, eat, and sleep at their ease, endure hunger, thirst, and long vigils. These are the wings by which the writings of men soar to heaven.

But to return to the beginning of this topic, let our imitator first consider those he would imitate and what in them can and should be imitated, so as not to do as those who, wanting to resemble some great lord, will imitate rather a petty gesture of his or a vicious mode of behavior than his virtues and good graces. Above all, our imitator must have the judgment to know his own strength and to weigh how much his shoulders can bear. Let him diligently sound his own nature and adapt himself to the imitation of him to whom he feels closest. Otherwise his imitation will resemble that of an ape.

Chapter 4
What kinds of Poems the French Poet should choose

First then, O future Poet, read and reread. With nightly and daily hand, turn over the pages of Greek and Roman models. Then do me the favor of leaving to the Floral Games of Toulouse and the Confraternity of Rouen all those old French poetic forms, such as rondels, ballads, virelays, royal airs, songs, and other such spices, which corrupt the taste of our language and serve only as evidence of our ignorance. Give yourself over to those amusing epigrams, not as a host of new tale-tellers do today, who in a poem of ten lines are happy to have said nothing of worth in the first nine lines so long as there is a little joke in the tenth. But if lasciviousness does not please you, in imitation of a Martial or some other of good reputation mix profit with pleasure. Distill in a flowing and not harsh style those touching

---

Floral Games of Toulouse: a poetic society founded in Toulouse in 1323

Confraternity of Rouen: one of many semireligious, semiliterary confraternities (*puys*) that from the twelfth century on were established in various places in northern and western France

those old French poetic forms: du Bellay's disdain for the customary forms of French poetry and his desire to see them replaced with forms borrowed from Greek, Latin, and Italian provoked an immediate outcry from such critics as Barthélemy Aneau and Guillaume des Autels

mix profit and pleasure: a recollection of Horace's famous dictum in the *Ars poetica* (*Epistles* 2.3.343), "Omne tulit punctum, qui miscuit utile dulce" (He wins every vote, who combines the useful and the sweet)

longuement demeurer en sa chambre: et qui desire vivre en la memoire de la posterité, doit comme mort en soymesmes suer et trembler maintesfois, et autant que notz poëtes courtizans boyvent, mangent, et dorment à leur oyse, endurer de faim, de soif, et de longues vigiles. Ce sont les esles dont les ecriz des hommes volent au Ciel.

Mais afin que je retourne au commencement de ce propos, regarde nostre immitateur premierement ceux qu'il voudra immiter, et ce qu'en eux il poura, et qui se doit immiter, pour ne faire comme ceux qui, voulans aparoitre semblables à quelque grand Seigneur, immiteront plus tost un petit geste et façon de faire vicieuse de luy, que ses vertuz et bonnes graces. Avant toutes choses, fault qu'il ait ce jugement de cognoitre ses forces et tenter combien ses epaules peuvent porter: qu'il sonde diligemment son naturel, et se compose à l'immitation de celuy dont il se sentira approcher de plus pres. Autrement son immitation ressembleroit celle du singe.

Chapitre 4
Quelz genres de Poëmes doit elire le Poëte Françoys

Ly donques et rely premierement (ô Poëte futur), fueillete de main nocturne et journelle les exemplaires Grecz et Latins: puis me laisse toutes ces vieilles poësies Françoyses aux Jeuz Floraux de Thoulouze et au Puy de Rouan: comme rondeaux, ballades, vyrelaiz, chantz royaulx, chansons, et autres telles episseries, qui corrumpent le goust de nostre langue, et ne servent si non à porter temoingnaige de notre ignorance. Jéte toy à ces plaisans epigrammes, non point comme font au jourd'huy un tas de faiseurs de comtes nouveaux, qui en un dizain sont contens n'avoir rien dict qui vaille aux neuf premiers vers, pourveu qu'au dixiesme il y ait le petit mot pour rire: mais à l'immitation d'un Martial, ou de quelque autre bien approuvé, si la lascivité ne te plaist, mesle le profitable avecques le doulz. Distile avecques un style coulant et non scabreux ces pitoyables ele-

elegies, modeled after an Ovid, a Tibullus, and a Propertius, weaving in from time to time some of those ancient myths, no small adornment of poetry. Sing me those odes, still unknown to the French Muse, on a lute well tuned to the sound of the Greek and Roman lyre, and let there be no line in which some vestige of rare and ancient learning fails to appear. And for this, the praises of the gods and of virtuous men, the destined course of worldly things, the preoccupations of young men, such as love, free-flowing wine, and all good living, will supply you with matter. Above all, take care that this kind of poem be removed from the commonplace, enriched and illuminated with fit words and lively epithets, adorned with grave reflections, and varied with all sorts of poetic colors and ornaments, not like a "Laissez la verte couleur," "Amour avec Psyches," "O combien est heureuse," and other such works, worthier to be called vulgar songs than odes or lyric poems. As for epistles, this is not a kind of poem that can greatly enrich our vulgar tongue, since they are normally about familiar and domestic matters, unless you wanted to write them in imitation of elegies, like Ovid, or make them sententious and grave, like Horace. I say much the same of satires, which the French, for I know not what reason, have called *coqs-à-l'âne,* and which I advise you to practice just as infrequently, since I want you to avoid slander, unless, after the example of the ancients, you would spare the names of vicious persons and reprehend with moderation the vices of your time in heroic lines (that is, lines of ten or eleven syllables and not of eight or nine) under the name of *satire* and not that inept title of *coq-à-l'âne.* For this, you have the example of Horace, who, according to Quintilian, holds first place among the satirists. Ring out for me those beautiful sonnets, a no less learned than pleasant Italian invention which agrees in name with the ode and differs from it only in that the sonnet has a certain number of lines of a fixed length, while the ode can run through

---

Sing me those odes: the ode was the form in which du Bellay's friend Pierre de Ronsard first distinguished himself with the publication in 1550, a little less than a year after the *Defense,* of his *First Four Books of Odes*

"Laissez la verte couleur": the first and third of the three poems du Bellay mentions here are by Mellin de Saint-Gelais; the second is by Pernette du Guillet, a close friend of Maurice Scève

worthier to be called vulgar songs: in his *Art Poetique François* (2.6), Sébillet had identified the ode with the traditional French song (*chanson*)

according to Quintilian: *Institutio oratorio* 10.1.94

Ring out for me those beautiful sonnets: the form in which du Bellay hoped to make his own mark with the almost simultaneous publication of his first sonnet sequence, *Olive* (1549)

gies, à l'exemple d'un Ovide, d'un Tibule, et d'un Properce, y entremeslant quelquesfois de ces fables anciennes, non petit ornement de poësie. Chante moy ces odes incongnues encor' de la Muse Françoyse, d'un luc bien accordé au son de la lyre Greque et Romaine: et qu'il n'y ait vers, ou n'aparoisse quelque vestige de rare et antique erudition. Et quand à ce, te fourniront de matiere les louanges des Dieux et des hommes vertueux, le discours fatal des choses mondaines, la solicitude des jeunes hommes, comme l'amour, les vins libres, et toute bonne chere. Sur toutes choses, prens garde que ce genre de poëme soit eloingné du vulgaire, enrichy et illustré de motz propres et epithetes non oysifz, orné de graves sentences, et varié de toutes manieres de couleurs et ornementz poëtiques, non comme un *Laissez la verde couleur, Amour avecques Psyches, O combien est heureuse,* et autres telz ouvraiges, mieux dignes d'estre nommez chansons vulgaires qu'odes ou vers lyriques. Quand aux epistres, ce n'est un poëme qui puisse grandement enrichir nostre vulgaire, pource qu'elles sont voluntiers de choses familieres et domestiques, si tu ne les voulois faire à l'immitation d'elegies, comme Ovide, ou sentencieuses et graves, comme Horace. Autant te dy-je des satyres, que les François, je ne sçay comment, ont apellées *coqz à l'asne*: es quelz je te conseille aussi peu t'exercer, comme je te veux entre aliene de mal dire, si tu ne voulois, à l'exemple des Anciens, en vers heroiques (c'est à dire de dix à onze, et non seulement de huit à neuf), soubz le nom de *satyre,* et non de cete inepte appellation de *coq à l'asne,* taxer modestement les vices de ton tens, et pardonner aux noms des personnes vicieuses. Tu has pour cecy Horace, qui, selon Quintilian, tient le premier lieu entre les satyriques. Sonne moy ces beaux sonnetz, non moins docte que plaisante invention Italienne, conforme de nom à l'ode, et differente d'elle seulement pource que le sonnet a certains vers reiglez

all sorts of lines freely—can, indeed, invent them at will, after the example of Horace, who sang odes in nineteen kinds of lines, as the grammarians say. For the sonnet then, you have Petrarch and several modern Italians. With a resounding pipe and a well-joined flute, sing me those pleasant rustic eclogues after the example of Theocritus and Virgil or seafaring ones after the example of Sannazaro, a Neapolitan gentleman.

May it please the Muses that in all the kinds of poetry I have named we have many imitations like that eclogue on the birth of the son of Monseigneur the Dauphin, in my opinion one of the best little works that Marot ever wrote. Adopt, too, into the French family those flowing and dainty hendecasyllabics, after the example of a Catullus, a Pontanus, and a Secundus, which you could do, though not in quantitative meter, at least with regard to the number of syllables. As for comedies and tragedies, if kings and commonwealths would restore them to their ancient dignity, which farces and morality plays have usurped, I would surely think you should set yourself to them, and if you wished to do so for the adornment of your language, you know where you must find the models for them.

Chapter 5
Of the long French Poem

Therefore, O you, who are blessed with excellent gifts of Nature, instructed in all good arts and learned disciplines, particularly the natural and mathematical sciences, versed in all kinds of good Greek and Latin authors, not ignorant of the obligations and duties of human life, not of too high condition or called to public service, also not abject and poor, not troubled with domestic affairs, but in repose and tranquillity of mind, moved first by your greatness of heart, then maintained by your prudence

---

Petrarch: despite du Bellay's emphasis on Greek and Latin models, the *Rime sparse* of Francis Petrarch (1304–1374) did more to shape the work of du Bellay and the other "new" poets of sixteenth-century Europe than any other poetic work

Sannazaro: Jacopo Sannazaro (1458–1530), known especially for his Italian pastoral romance, the *Arcadia*, and for his neo-Latin *Piscatory Eclogues*, where the speakers are fishermen rather than shepherds

that eclogue on the birth of the son: a rare favorable comment on Clément Marot, who, whether explicitly or implicitly, is the target of du Bellay's disdain through much of the *Defense*

hendecasyllabics: in his *Quintil Horatian*, Barthélemy Aneau objects that verses of eleven syllables were already common in French

a Pontanus, and a Secundus: Giovanni Pontano (1426–1503) and Joannes Secundus (1511–1536), well-known neo-Latin poets

et limitez, et l'ode peut courir par toutes manieres de vers librement, voyre en inventer à plaisir, à l'exemple d'Horace, qui a chanté en dix-neuf sortes de vers, comme disent les grammariens. Pour le sonnet donques tu as Petrarque et quelques modernes Italiens. Chante moy d'une musette bien resonnante et d'une fluste bien jointe ces plaisantes ecclogues rustiques, à l'exemple de Thëocrit et de Virgile: marines à l'exemple de Sennazar, gentilhomme Nëapolitain.

Que pleust aux Muses, qu'en toutes les especes de poësie que j'ay nommées, nous eussions beaucoup de telles immitations, qu'est cete ecclogue sur la naissance du filz de Monseigneur le Dauphin, à mon gré un des meilleurs petiz ouvraiges que fist onques Marot. Adopte moy aussi en la famille Françoyse ces coulans et mignars hendecasyllabes, à l'exemple d'un Catulle, d'un Pontan, et d'un Second: ce que tu pouras faire, si non en quantité, pour le moins en nombre de syllabes. Quand aux comedies et tragedies, si les Roys et les Republiques les vouloint restituer en leur ancienne dignité, qu'ont usurpée les farces et moralitez, je seroy' bien d'opinion que tu t'y employasses, et si tu le veux faire pour l'ornement de ta langue, tu sçais où tu en doibs trouver les archetypes.

Chapitre 5
Du long Poëme Françoys

Donques, ò toy, qui doué d'une excellente felicité de nature, instruict de tous bons ars et sciences, principalement naturelles et mathematiques, versé en tous genres de bons aucteurs Grecz et Latins, non ignorant des parties et offices de la vie humaine, non de trop haulte condition, ou appellé au regime publiq', non aussi abject et pauvre, non troublé d'afaires domestiques, mais en repoz et tranquilité d'esprit, acquise premierement par la magnanimité de ton couraige, puis entretenue par ta prudence et

and wise conduct, O you (I say), who are adorned with so many graces and perfections, if you at times pity your poor language, if you deign to enrich it with your treasures, it will truly be you who will make it lift its head and with a gallant brow match those proud Greek and Latin languages, as in our time an Italian Ariosto has done in his vulgar tongue, whom I would dare (were it not for the sanctity of the old poems) compare to a Homer and Virgil. Then like him, who borrowed from our language the names and the story for his poem, choose some one of those fine old French romances, such as a *Lancelot,* a *Tristan,* or others, and from it bring to life again in the world an admirable *Iliad* and laborious *Aeneid.*

I would, in passing, say a word to those who busy themselves only to adorn and amplify our romances and who make from them books, certainly in fine and fluent language, but far better suited to entertain young ladies than to write learnedly. I would (I say) advise them to use that great eloquence to gather the fragments of old French chronicles and, as Livy did with the annals and other ancient Roman chronicles, to build from them the whole body of a fine history, mixing in where appropriate fine speeches and harangues in imitation of him whom I just named, of Thucydides, of Sallust, or some other notable historian, according to the kind of writing to which they feel themselves suited. Such a work would surely be to their everlasting glory, the honor of France, and the great enrichment of our language.

To return to the topic I left, someone will perhaps find it strange that I require such a thoroughgoing perfection in him who would like to write a long poem, seeing that it would be hard enough, even were he possessed of all those attributes, to find anyone who would be willing to undertake a work of such laborious length, demanding almost the lifetime of a man. To someone else it will appear that, intending to furnish the means to enrich our language, I am doing the opposite in that I impede and cool the zeal of those who were well inclined toward their vulgar tongue rather than encourage them, for, disabled by despair, they will not wish to attempt what they cannot hope to accomplish. But it is appropriate that everything be tried by those who aim to attain a high level of excellence and uncommon glory. And if someone does not have in full measure that great vigor of

---

an Italian Ariosto: Ludovico Ariosto (1474–1533), whose *Orlando furioso* was easily the most popular poem of sixteenth-century Europe

who borrowed from our language the names: Ariosto's poem features such figures from French history and legend as Roland (Orlando) and Charlemagne

a *Lancelot,* a *Tristan*: Arthurian romances of the sort associated particularly with the twelfth-century poet Chrétien de Troyes

To someone else it will appear: much of this sentence and the remainder of this paragraph is translated from Cicero's *Orator* 1.4 and 2.5

saige gouvernement, ò toy (dy-je) orné de tant de graces et perfections, si tu as quelquefois pitié de ton pauvre langaige, si tu daignes l'enrichir de tes thesors, ce sera toy veritablement qui luy feras hausser la teste, et d'un brave sourcil s'egaler aux superbes langues Greque et Latine, comme a faict de nostre tens en son vulgaire un Arioste Italien, que j'oseroy' (n'estoit la saincteté des vieulx poëmes) comparer à un Homere et Virgile. Comme luy donq', qui a bien voulu emprunter de nostre langue les noms et l'hystoire de son poëme, choysi moy quelque un de ces beaux vieulx romans Françoys, comme un *Lancelot*, un *Tristan*, ou autres: et en fay renaitre au monde un admirable *Iliade* et laborieuse *Eneïde*.

Je veux bien en passant dire un mot à ceulx qui ne s'employent qu'à orner et amplifier notz romans, et en font des livres, certainement en beau et fluide langaige, mais beaucoup plus propre à bien entretenir damoizelles qu'à doctement ecrire: je voudroy' bien (dy-je) les avertir d'employer cete grande eloquence à recuillir ces fragmentz de vieilles chroniques Françoyses, et comme a fait Tite Live des annales et autres anciennes chroniques Romaines, en batir le cors entier d'une belle histoire, y entremeslant à propos ces belles concions et harangues à l'immitation de celuy que je viens de nommer, de Thucidide, Saluste, ou quelque autre bien approuvé, selon le genre d'ecrire ou ilz se sentiroint propres. Tel œuvre certainement seroit à leur immortelle gloire, honneur de la France, et grande illustration de nostre langue.

Pour reprendre le propos que j'avoy' laissé, quelqu'un (peut estre) trouverra etrange que je requiere une si exacte perfection en celuy qui voudra faire un long poëme, veu aussi qu'à peine se trouverroint, encores qu'ilz feussent instruictz de toutes ces choses, qui voulussent entreprendre un œuvre de si laborieuse longueur, et quasi de la vie d'un homme. Il semblera à quelque autre, que voulant bailler les moyens d'enrichir nostre langue, je face le contraire, d'autant que je retarde plus tost et refroidis l'etude de ceux qui etoint bien affectionnez à leur vulgaire, que je ne les incite, pource que, debilitez par desespoir, ne voudront point essayer ce à quoy ne s'attendront de pouvoir parvenir. Mais c'est chose convenable, que toutes choses soint experimentées de tous ceux qui desirent attaindre à quelque hault point d'excellence et gloire non vulgaire. Que si quelqu'un n'a du tout cete grande vigueur d'esprit, cete parfaite intelli-

mind, that perfect command of the various branches of learning, and all those other qualities that I have mentioned, let him nevertheless proceed as far as he can. For it is an honorable thing for him who aspires to the first rank to reach the second or even the third. Not only Homer among the Greeks nor Virgil among the Latins won praise and reputation, but so great was the merit of many others, each in his kind, that the praise of lower things was not neglected because of admiration for the high.

Surely had we any Maecenases and Augustuses, the heavens and Nature are not so hostile to our age that we would not also have some Virgils. Honor nourishes the arts. Glory inflames us all to the pursuit of learning. And those things despised by all never rise. Kings and princes should (it seems to me) remember that great emperor who preferred that the venerable power of the law be broken than that the works of Virgil, condemned to fire by the last will and testament of their author, be burned. What shall I say of that other great monarch who more desired the rebirth of Homer than victory in a great battle and who once at the tomb of Achilles loudly cried out, "O blessed youth who found such a trumpeter of your praises!" And, in truth, without the divine Muse of Homer, the same tomb that covered the body of Achilles would also have buried his renown. That is what happens to all those who put their assurance of immortality in marble, in brass, in huge statues, in pyramids, in laborious buildings, and other things that are no less subject to the injuries of heaven and of time, of fire and of steel, than to excessive costs and perpetual care.

The delights of Venus, gluttony, and feather-bedded sloth have driven from men all desire for immortality. But it is a still viler thing that those who glory most in ignorance and all sorts of vices ridicule those who devote to this so praiseworthy poetic labor the hours that others waste in gaming, at baths, in banquets, and in other such petty pleasures. Now, despite the several misfortunes of the age in which we live, you to whom the gods and the Muses have been as favorable as I have said, though you may lack the favor of men, do not for all that neglect to undertake a work worthy of you, but not granted to those who, just as they do nothing praiseworthy, also take no interest in being praised. Expect the fruit of your labor from incorruptible and

---

Maecenases and Augustuses: the great Roman patron and the Emperor Augustus, the supporters of Virgil and Horace, represented for Renaissance poets an ideal they were constantly striving to replicate in their own time

Honor nourishes the arts: from Cicero's *Tusculan Disputations* 1.2.4

that great emperor: Augustus, who was said to have saved the manuscript of the *Aeneid* from being burned, as Virgil had willed

that other great monarch: Alexander, of whom this story is told in Cicero's *Pro Archia* 10.24 and famously retold in Petrarch's *Rime sparse* 187

gluttony, and feather-bedded sloth: from Petrarch's *Rime sparse* 7

gence des disciplines, et toutes ces autres commoditez que j'ay nommées, tienne pourtant le cours tel qu'il poura. Car c'est chose honneste à celuy qui aspire au premier ranc, demeurer au second, voire au troizieme. Non Homere seul entre les Grecz, non Virgile entre les Latins, ont aquis loz et reputation. Mais telle a été la louange de beaucoup d'autres, chacun en son genre, que pour admirer les choses haultes, on ne laissoit pourtant de louer les inferieures.

Certainement si nous avions des Mecenes et des Augustes, les Cieux et la Nature ne sont point si ennemis de nostre siecle, que n'eussions encores des Virgiles. L'honneur nourist les ars, nous sommes tous par la gloire enflammez à l'etude des sciences, et ne s'elevent jamais les choses qu'on voit estre deprisées de tous. Les Roys et les Princes devroint (ce me semble) avoir memoire de ce grand Empereur qui vouloit plus tost la venerable puissance des loix estre rompue, que les œuvres de Virgile, condamnées au feu par le testament de l'aucteur, feussent brulées. Que diray-je de cet autre grand Monarque, qui desiroit plus le renaitre d'Homere que le gaing d'une grosse battaille? et quelquefoys etant près du tumbeau d'Achile, s'ecria haultement: O bienheureux adolescent, qui as trouvé un tel buccinateur de tes louanges! Et à la verité, sans la divine Muse d'Homere, le mesme tumbeau qui couvroit le corps d'Achille, eust aussi accablé son renom. Ce qu'avient à tous ceux qui mettent l'asseurance de leur immortalité au marbre, au cuyvre, aux collosses, aux pyramides, aux laborieux edifices, et autres choses non moins subjectes aux injures du Ciel et du tens, de la flamme, et du fer, que de fraiz excessifz et perpetuelle sollicitude.

Les allechementz de Venus, la gueule et les ocieuses plumes ont chassé d'entre les hommes tout desir de l'immortalité: mais encores est ce chose plus indigne, que ceux qui d'ignorance et toutes especes de vices font leur plus grande gloire, se moquent de ceux qui en ce tant louable labeur poëtique employent les heures que les autres consument aux jeuz, aux baings, aux banquez, et autres telz menuz plaisirs. Or neantmoins quelque infelicité de siecle ou nous soyons, toy à qui les Dieux et les Muses auront eté si favorables comme j'ay dit, bien que tu soyes depourveu de la faveur des hommes, ne laisse pourtant à entreprendre un œuvre digne de toy, mais non deu à ceux, qui tout ainsi qu'ilz ne font choses louables, aussi ne font ilz cas d'estre louez. Espere le fruict de ton labeur de l'incorruptible et

envy-free posterity. Glory is the only ladder by whose steps mortals mount with light foot to heaven and make themselves the companions of the gods.

Chapter 6
Of inventing Words and some other things the French Poet must observe

But for fear lest the wind of affection drive my ship so far into that sea that I am in danger of shipwreck, returning to the course I had left, I want to advise him who would undertake a great work that he should not be afraid to invent, adopt, and create in imitation of the Greeks some French words, as Cicero boasts of having done in his language. But had the Greeks and Latins been excessively cautious in this regard, what would they now have to justify the high praise for the copiousness of their languages? And if Horace allows that in a long poem one can sometimes nod, does he forbid the use of any new words, even when necessity demands it? No one, unless he is thoroughly ignorant—lacking, indeed, all common sense—doubts that first there were things and then later words were invented to name them and that, consequently, new things need new words, especially in those arts whose practice is not yet common and widespread. This can often happen to our poet, who will find it necessary to borrow many things not yet treated in our language. Workmen (to say nothing of the liberal professions), including even common laborers and craftsmen of all kinds, could not maintain their trades if they used no words familiar to them but unknown to us. I share the opinion that procurators and lawyers should use terms proper to their profession without any innovation. But to take from a man of learning who wishes to enrich his language the freedom occasionally to lay claim to words that are not widely known would be to bind our language, which is not yet sufficiently rich, with a far stricter law than the Greeks and Romans gave themselves. Though they were beyond all comparison richer and better furnished than we, they nevertheless allowed learned men often to use unfamiliar words for unfamiliar things. Then do not fear, future poet, to use some new terms, especially in a long poem, always with moderation, fitness, and the judgment of your ear, and do not worry who thinks it good or bad, but hope for the approval of posterity, as that which gives faith to doubtful things, light to dark ones, newness to old ones, familiarity to unaccustomed ones, and sweetness to those that are bitter and harsh.

And if Horace allows: *Ars poetica* (*Epistles* 2.3.360), where Horace says that Homer sometimes nods

new things need new words: the first of several borrowings in this paragraph from Cicero's *De finibus bonorum et malorum*

non envieuse posterité: c'est la gloire, seule echelle par les degrez de la quele les mortelz d'un pié leger montent au Ciel et se font compaignons des Dieux.

Chapitre 6
D'inventer des Motz, et quelques autres choses que doit observer le Poëte Françoys

Mais de peur que le vent d'affection ne pousse mon navire si avant en cete mer, que je soye en danger du nauffrage, reprennant la route que j'avoy' laissée, je veux bien avertir celuy qui entreprendra un grand œuvre, qu'il ne craigne point d'inventer, adopter, et composer à l'immitation des Grecz quelques motz Françoys, comme Ciceron se vante d'avoir fait en sa langue. Mais si les Grecz et Latins eussent esté supersticieux en cet endroit, qu'auroint-ilz ores de quoy magnifier si haultement cete copie qui est en leurs langues? Et si Horace permet qu'on puysse en un long poëme dormir quelquesfois, est-il deffendu en ce mesme endroict user de quelques motz nouveaux, mesmes quand la necessité nous y contraint? Nul, s'il n'est vrayment du tout ignare, voire privé de sens commun, ne doute point que les choses n'ayent premierement eté: puis apres, les motz avoit eté inventez pour les signifier: et par consequent aux nouvelles choses estre necessaire imposer nouveaux motz, principalement és ars, dont l'usaige n'est point encores commun et vulgaire, ce qui peut arriver souvent à nostre poëte, au quel sera necessaire emprunter beaucoup de choses non encor' traitées en nostre langue. Les ouvriers (afin que je ne parle des sciences liberales) jusques aux laboureurs mesmes, et toutes sortes de gens mecaniques, ne pouroint conserver leurs metiers, s'ilz n'usoint de motz à eux usitez et à nous incongneuz. Je suis bien d'opinion que les procureurs et avocatz usent des termes propres à leur profession sans rien innover: mais vouloir oter la liberté à un sçavant homme, qui voudra enrichir sa langue, d'usurper quelquefois des vocables non vulgaires, ce seroit retraindre notre langaige, non encor' assez riche, soubz une trop plus rigoreuse loy, que celle que les Grecz et Romains se sont donnée. Les quelz, combien qu'ilz feussent sans comparaison plus que nous copieux et riches, neantmoins ont concedé aux doctes hommes user souvent de motz non acoutumés és choses non acoutumées. Ne crains donques, Poëte futur, d'innover quelques termes, en un long poëme principalement, avecques modestie toutesfois, analogie et jugement de l'oreille, et ne te soucie qui le treuve bon ou mauvais: esperant que la posterité l'approuvera, comme celle qui donne foy aux choses douteuses, lumiere aux obscures, nouveauté aux antiques, usaige aux non accoutumées, et douceur aux apres et rudes.

Among other things, our poet should keep from using Latin or Greek proper nouns, a thing truly as absurd as if you were to sew a piece of green velvet on a red velvet gown. For would it not be laughable to use in a Latin work the name of a man or some other thing in French, like *Jean currit, Loire fluit,* and others of the same sort? Adapt then such proper nouns from whatever language to the usage of your vulgar tongue, following the Latins who for *Heraklēs* said *Hercules,* for *Thēseus, Theseus,* and in French say *Hercule, Thésée, Achille, Ulysse, Virgile, Cicéron, Horace.* In this you must, however, use judgment and discretion, for there are many such nouns that cannot be accommodated to French, some of them monosyllables like *Mars,* others disyllables like *Venus,* some of several syllables like *Jupiter* (unless you chose to say *Jove*), and an infinite number of others for which I can give no certain rule. For these, I refer you to the judgment of your ear.

For the rest, use words that are purely French, although not too common nor too unfamiliar, unless you sometimes wish to adopt and, as it were, enshrine, like a rare and precious stone, a few antique words in your poem, following the example of Virgil, who used the word *olli* for *illi, aulaï* for *aulae,* and others. To do this, you would have to look through all those old romances and French poets, where you will find an *ajourner* for *faire jour* (which men of the law have made their own), *anuiter* for *faire nuit, assener* for *frapper où on visait* (and fittingly for a blow given with the hand), *isnel* for *léger,* and a thousand other good words that we have lost through our negligence. Do not doubt that the moderate use of such terms gives great majesty to verse as to prose, just as relics of saints do to crosses and other sacred jewels consecrated to the use of churches.

---

a few antique words: de Bellay's most fervent disciple in this regard was the English poet Edmund Spenser (1552–1599), whose poetic diction in works like *The Shepheardes Calender* and *The Faerie Queene* is marked by the inclusion of large numbers of archaic English words

it should be rich: a technical term for a rhyme that falls on at least two syllables

Entre autres choses, se garde bien nostre poëte d'user de noms propres Latins ou Grecz, chose vrayment aussi absurde, que si tu appliquois lune piece de velours verd à une robe de velours rouge. Mais seroit-ce pas une chose bien plaisante, user en un ouvraige Latin d'un nom propre d'homme ou d'autre chose en Françoys? comme *Jan currit, Loyre fluit,* et autres semblables. Accommode donques telz noms propres, de quelque langue que ce soit, à l'usaige de ton vulgaire: suyvant les Latins, qui pour 'Ηρακλῆς ont dict *Hercules,* pour Θησεὺς, *Theseus*: et dy *Hercule, Thesée, Achile, Ulysse, Virgile, Ciceron, Horace.* Tu doibz pourtant user en cela de jugement et discretion, car il y a beaucoup de telz noms, qui ne se peuvent approprier en Françoys: les uns monosyllabes, comme *Mars*: les autres dissyllabes, comme *Venus*: aucuns de plusieurs syllabes, comme *Jupiter,* si tu ne voulois dire *Jove*: et autres infinitz, dont je ne te sçauroy bailler certaine reigle. Parquoy je renvoye tout au jugement de ton oreille.

Quand au reste, use de motz purement Françoys, non toutesfois trop communs, non point aussi trop inusitez, si tu ne voulois quelquefois usurper, et quasi comme enchasser, ainsi qu'une pierre precieuse et rare, quelques motz antiques en ton poëme, à l'exemple de Virgile, qui a usé de ce mot *olli* pour *illi, aulaï* pour *aulæ,* et autres. Pour ce faire, te faudroit voir tous ces vieux romans et poëtes Françoys, où tu trouverras un *ajourner* pour *faire jour* (que les praticiens se sont fait propre), *anuyter* pour *faire nuyt, assener* pour *frapper où on visoit,* et proprement d'un coup de main, *isnel* pour *leger,* et mil' autres bons motz, que nous avons perduz par notre negligence. Ne doute point que le moderé usaige de telz vocables ne donne grande majesté tant au vers comme à la prose: ainsi que font les reliques des sainctz aux croix et autres sacrez joyaux dediez aux temples.

Chapter 7
Of Rhyme and of Poems without Rhyme

As for rhyme, I am altogether of the opinion that it should be rich, since it is for us what quantitative meter is for the Greeks and Latins. And though we do not have the use of metrical feet as they do, we do nevertheless have a defined number of syllables for each kind of poem, by which, as by fetters, the French verse line, bound and chained, is forced to yield itself to the narrow prison of rhyme, most often under the guard of a feminine caesura, a vexatious and rude jailer, unknown to other vulgar tongues. When I say the rhyme must be rich, I do not mean that it should be forced and like that of some who think they have produced a great masterpiece in French when they have rhymed *imminent* and *éminent*, *miséricordieusement* and *mélodieusement*, and others of the same grain, even though there is neither sense nor reason of any worth. But the rhyme of our poet will be willing, not forced; received, not conscripted; proper, not alien; natural, not adopted. It will, in short, be such that the verse, falling into it, will please the ear no less than thoroughly harmonious music when it falls into a good and perfect accord. Therefore let those puns and those root words rhymed with their compounds, like a *baiser* and *abaiser* (unless the compound alters or greatly augments the meaning of the root), be driven far from me. Otherwise, he who declines to rule his rhymes as I have said would do much better not to rhyme at all but to write blank verse, as Petrarch did in some places and as in our time the Lord Luigi Alamanni does in his no less learned than pleasing *Agriculture*. But just as painters and sculptors work harder to make beautiful and well proportioned naked bodies than others, so these unrhymed verses must be especially well fleshed out and sinewy so as to compensate in this way for the lack of rhyme.

I am not unaware that some have distinguished two categories of rhyme, one based on sound, the other on spelling, because of those diphthongs *ai*,

---

quantitative meter: the regular pattern of long and short syllables in Greek and Latin verse whose lack in the vernacular languages, including French, was of great concern to sixteenth-century poets

a defined number of syllables: lacking the accentual pattern of other European vernaculars, French verse is defined metrically by the number of syllables in each line

a feminine caesura: the requirement in French verse that a mute *e* preceding a caesura must be followed by a word beginning with a vowel to permit an elision

Lord Luigi Alamanni: (1495–1556), exiled Florentine poet whose blank-verse *Coltivazione* [Agriculture] was published in Paris in 1546

Chapitre 7
De la Rythme et des Vers sans Rythme

Quand à la rythme, je suy' bien d'opinion qu'elle soit riche, pour ce qu'elle nous est ce qu'est la quantité aux Grecz et Latins. Et bien que n'ayons cet usaige de piez comme eux, si est ce que nous avons un certain nombre de syllabes en chacun genre de poëme, par les quelles, comme par chesnons, le vers François lié et enchainé est contraint de se rendre en cete etroite prison de rythme, soubz la garde le plus souvent d'une couppe feminine, facheux et rude gëolier, et incongnu des autres vulgaires. Quand je dy que la rythme doit estre riche, je n'entens qu'elle soit contrainte, et semblable à celle d'aucuns, qui pensent avoir fait un grand chef d'œuvre en Françoys, quand ilz ont rymé un *imminent* et un *eminent*, un *misericordieusement* et un *melodieusement*, et autres de semblable farine, encores qu'il n'y ait sens ou raison qui vaille. Mais la rythme de notre poëte sera voluntaire, non forcée: receüe, non appellée: propre, non aliene: naturelle, non adoptive: bref, elle sera telle, que le vers tumbant en icelle ne contentera moins l'oreille, qu'une bien armonieuse musique tumbante en un bon et parfait accord. Ces equivoques donq' et ces simples rymez avecques leurs composez, comme un *baisser* et *abaisser*, s'ilz ne changent ou augmentent grandement la signification de leurs simples, me soint chassez bien loing: autrement, qui ne voudroit reigler sa rythme comme j'ay dit, il vaudroit beaucoup mieux ne rymer point, mais faire des vers libres, comme a fait Petrarque en quelque endroit, et de notre tens le Seigneur Loys Aleman, en sa non moins docte que plaisante *Agriculture.* Mais tout ainsi que les peintres et statuaires mettent plus grand' industrie à faire beaux et bien proportionnez les corps qui sont nuds, que les autres: aussi faudroit-il bien que ces vers non rymez feussent bien charnuz et nerveux, afin de compenser par ce moyen le default de la rythme.

Je n'ignore point que quelques uns ont fait une division de rythme, l'une en son et l'autre en écriture, à cause de ces dyphthongues *ai, ei, oi,*

ei, oi, making it a point of conscience not to rhyme *maître* and *prêtre, fontaines* and *Athènes, connoître* and *naître.* But I do not want our poet to be so scrupulously concerned with these petty matters. It should be enough for him that the two last syllables have the same sound, which would almost always appear in writing as one hears it in speech had French spelling not been corrupted by lawyers. And since Louis Meigret has no less amply than learnedly treated this issue, Reader, I refer you to his book and will bring this topic to a close with only this word of advice in passing: namely, that you avoid rhyming words containing obviously long vowels with words containing obviously short ones, such as *passe* and *trace, maître* and *mettre, chevelure* and *hure, bât* and *bat,* and so with others.

Chapter 8
Of this word *Rhyme,* of the invention of rhymed Verses, and of some other Ancient Practices used in our Language

Everything that falls under any measurement and judgment of the ear (says Cicero) is called *numerus* in Latin and *rhythmos* in Greek, not only with regard to poetry but also to prose. From this our ancestors improperly took the name of the genus for the species, calling *rhyme* that consonance of syllables at the end of lines of verse which should instead be called *homoioteleuton,* that is, "ending the same," one of the species of rhyme. Thus verses, even when they do not end with the same sound, can in general be called "rhymes," inasmuch as the meaning of the word *rhythmos* is very broad and encompasses many other terms, such as *kanōn, metron, melos, euphōnon, akolouthia, taxis, synkrisis*: rule, measure, melodious consonance of voice, interlacing, order, and comparison.

Now as for the antiquity of those verses we call rhymed and that the other vulgar tongues have borrowed from us: if one believes Jean Lemaire de Belges, a diligent student of antiquity, Bardus V, king of the Gauls, was their inventor and introduced a sect of poets called bards, who melodiously sang their rhymes with musical instruments, praising some and blaming others, and were (as Diodorus the Sicilian testifies in his sixth book) so greatly esteemed among the Gauls that if two opposed armies were about

---

Louis Meigret: grammarian whose *Traité touchant le commun usage de l'Escriture Françoise* [Treatise on the Usual Manner of Writing French] (1542) deals with spelling, a matter of keen concern in all the sixteenth-century vernacular languages

says Cicero: *Orator* 20.67

if one believes Jean Lemaire de Belges: the passage is taken from Lemaire's *Illustrations de Gaule et Singularitez de Troye* (1509), 1.10

Diodorus the Sicilian: Diodorus Siculus, who testifies to this in the fifth book (not the sixth, as Lemaire led du Bellay to think) of his world history, the *Bibliotheca historica*

faisant conscience de rymer *maitre* et *prestre, fontaines* et *Athenes, connoitre* et *naitre.* Mais je ne veulx que notre poëte regarde si supersticieusement à ces petites choses: et luy doit suffire que les deux dernieres syllabes soint unisones, ce qui arriveroit en la plus grand' part, tant en voix qu'en ecriture, si l'orthographe Françoyse n'eust point eté depravée par les praticiens. Et pour ce que Loys Mégret non moins amplement que doctement a traité cete partie, Lecteur, je te renvoye à son livre: et feray fin à ce propos, t'ayant sans plus averti de ce mot en passant, c'est que tu gardes de rythmer les motz manifestement longs avecques les brefz aussi manifestement brefz, comme un *pásse* et *trace,* un *máitre* et *mettre,* un *chevelúre* et *hure,* un *bast* et *bat,* et ainsi des autres.

Chapitre 8
De ce mot *Rythme,* de l'invention des Vers rymez, et de quelques autres Antiquitez usitées en notre Langue

Tout ce qui tumbe soubz quelque mesure et jugement de l'oreille (dit Ciceron) en Latin s'appelle *numerus,* en Grec ῥυθμὸς, non point seulement au vers, mais à l'oraison. Parquoy improprement notz anciens ont astrainct le nom du genre soubz l'espece, appellant *rythme* cete consonance de syllabes à la fin des vers, qui se devroit plus tost nommer ὁμοιοτέλευτον, c'est à dire finissant de mesmes, l'une des especes du rythme. Ainsi les vers, encores qu'ilz ne finissent point en un mesme son, generalement se peuvent apeller rythme: d'autant que la signification de ce mot ῥυθμὸς est fort ample, et emporte beaucoup d'autres termes, comme καηὼν, μέτρον, μέλος, εὔφῶνον, ἀκολουθία, τάξις, σύγκρισις, *reigle, mesure, melodieuse consonance de voix, consequution, ordre,* et *comparaison.*

Or quand à l'antiquité de ces vers que nous appellons rymez, et que les autres vulgaires ont empruntez de nous, si on adjoute foy à Jan le Maire de Belges, diligent rechercheur de l'antiquité, Bardus V Roy des Gaules en feut inventeur: et introduysit une secte de poëtes nommez bardes, les quelz chantoint melodieusement leurs rymes avecques instrumentz, louant les uns et blamant les autres, et etoint (comme temoingne Dyodore Sicilien en son sixieme livre) de si grand' estime entre les Gaullois, que si deux armées ennemies etoint prestes à combattre, et les ditz poëtes se mis-

to fight and the said poets put themselves between them, the battle ceased and each calmed his anger. I could cite many other ancient practices by which our language is today ennobled and which show that the histories were not false that said that the Gauls long ago flourished not only in arms but in all kinds of learning and good letters. But that would take a whole book and would, after so many excellent pens have written on this topic, even in our time, be only to weave once again (as they say) Penelope's cloth.

I wish only to show—and it seems to me not inappropriate—the antiquity of two things that are very widespread in our language and no less ancient among the Greeks. One is that scrambling of the letters in a name which produces a device suitable to the person, as in François de Valois, *De façon suis royal* [I am kingly in manner]; Henri de Valois, *Roi es de nul haï* [King you are hated by none]. The other is a certain choice of capital letters in an epigram or some other poem disposed in such a way that they produce either the name of the author or some saying. As for the scrambling of letters, which the Greeks call *anagrammatismos*, the interpreter of Lycophron says in his *Life*, "At that time Lycophron flourished, not so much for poetry as because he made anagrams." An example from the name of the king Ptolemy: *Ptolomaios, apo melitos*, that is, "honeyed" or "of honey." Of the queen Arsinoë, who was the wife of the said Ptolemy: *Arsinoē, Hēras ion*, that is, "the violet of Juno." Artemidorus the Stoic also left us a chapter on anagrams in his book of *Dreams*, where he shows that one can decipher dreams by scrambling letters. As for the disposition of capital letters, Eusebius in the book of *Evangelical Preparation* says that the Erythraean sibyl had prophesied concerning Jesus Christ, beginning each of her lines of verse with certain letters which announced the last coming of Christ. The said letters produced these words: JESUS. CHRISTUS. SERVATOR. CRUX. The lines were translated by Saint Augustine, and they are what are called the fifteen signs of the Judgment, which are still sung in some places. The Greeks call this placement of letters at the beginning of lines of verse *akrostichis*. Cicero speaks of it in his book *On Divination*, with the intent to prove by reference to that painstaking practice that the poems of the sibyls were made by artifice and not by divine inspiration. That same

---

the interpreter of Lycophron: the twelfth-century Byzantine grammarian Joannes Tzetzes

Artemidorus the Stoic: Artemidorus Daldianus, second-century student of dreams

Eusebius: third-century bishop of Caesarea, whose *Praeparatio evangelica* argued for the superiority of Christianity over Greek philosophy

Cicero speaks of it: *De divinatione* 2.54.110–112

sent entre deux, la bataille cessoit, et moderoit chacun son ire. Je pourroy' alleguer assez d'autres antiquitez, dont notre langue aujourd'huy est ennoblie, et qui montrent les histoires n'estre faulses, qui ont dit les Gaulles anciennement avoir eté florissantes, non seulement en armes, mais en toutes sortes de sciences et bonnes lettres. Mais cela requiert bien un œuvre entier: et ne seroit apres tant d'excellentes plumes qui en ont ecrit, mesmes de notre tens, que retixtre (comme on dit) la toile de Penelope.

Seulement j'ay bien voulu, et ne me semble mal à propos, montrer l'antiquité de deux choses fort vulgaires en notre langue, et non moins anciennes entre les Grecz. L'une est cete inversion de lettres en un propre nom, qui porte quelque devise convenable à la personne: comme en FRANÇOYS DE VALOYS, *De façon suys royal*, HENRY DE VALOYS, *Roy es de nul hay.* L'autre est en un epigramme, ou quelque autre œuvre poëtique, une certaine election des lettres capitales, disposées en sorte qu'elles portent ou le nom de l'autheur ou quelque sentence. Quand à l'inversion de lettres, que les Grecz appellent ἀναγραμματισμὸς, l'interprete de Lycophron dit en sa vie: En ce tens la florissoit Lycophron, non tant pour la poësie, que pour ce qu'il faisoit des anagrammatismes. Exemple du nom du Roy Ptolomée, Πτολεμαῖος, ἀπὸ μέλιτος, c'est à dire *emmiellé* ou *de miel.* De la Royne Arsinoë, qui feut femme dudit Ptolomée 'Αρσινόη, Ἥρας ἴον, c'est à dire *la violette de Juno.* Artemidore aussi le Stoïque a laissé en son livre des *Songes* un chapitre de l'anagrammatisme, où il montre que par l'inversion des lettres on peut exposer les songes. Quand à la disposition des lettres capitales, Eusebe, au livre de la *Preparation Evangelique,* dit que la Sybille Erythrée avoit prophetizé de JESUCHRIST, preposant à chacun de ses vers certaines lettres qui declaroint le dernier advenement de Christ. Les dites lettres portoint ces motz: JESUS. CHRISTUS. SERVATOR. CRUX. Les vers feurent translatez par Saint Augustin (et c'est ce qu'on nomme les quinze signes du Jugement) les quelz se chantent encor' en quelques lieux. Les Grecz appellent cete preposition de lettres, au commencement des vers, ἀκροστιχὶς. Ciceron en parle au livre de *Divination,* voulant prouver par cete curieuse diligence que les vers des Sybilles etoint faictz par artifice, et

ancient device can be seen in all the arguments prefaced to the plays of Plautus, each of which bears in its capital letters the name of the comedy.

Chapter 9
Observation on some French ways of speaking

I have set forth in few words what had not yet (so far as I know) been touched on by our French rhetoricians. As for feminine caesuras, apostrophes, accents, the masculine *é* and the feminine *e*, and other such well-known things, our poet will learn them from those who have written about them. As for the kinds of verse, which the rhetoricians would limit, they are as diverse as the fantasy of men and as Nature herself. As for the strengths and weaknesses of poetry, so diligently treated by the ancients, such as Aristotle, Horace, and, after them, Girolamo Vida, as for the figures of thought and of words and all other parts of elocution, the commonplaces of commiseration, of joy, of sadness, of anger, of wonder, and of all other emotions of the soul: I say nothing of them after such a great number of excellent philosophers and orators who have treated them, whom I would have well read and reread by our poet before he undertakes any high and excellent work. And just as among the Latin authors those are thought best who most closely imitated the Greeks, I would also have you strive to render as close to their native manner as you can the Latin turn of phrase and way of speaking, to the extent that the particular nature of both languages will permit. I say as much regarding Greek, whose ways of speaking closely approach those of our vulgar tongue, which can be told even by the articles, unknown in the Latin language. Thus make bold use of the infinitive as a noun, like *l'aller, le chanter, le vivre, le mourir,* of the substantive adjective, like *le liquide des eaux, le vide de l'air, le frais des ombres, l'épais des forêts, l'enroué des cymbales,* so long as such a way of speaking adds some grace and vehemence, and not *le chaud du feu, le froid de la glace, le dur du fer,* and their like; of verbs and participles which by their nature have no infinitive after them with infinitives, like *tremblant de mourir* and *volant d'y aller* for *craignant de mourir* and *se hâtant d'y aller,* of adjectives for adverbs, like *ils*

---

our French rhetoricians: either the poets known as the *grands rhétoriqueurs* or, more probably, rhetorical theorists

from those who have written about them: Thomas Sébillet, Étienne Dolet, and Louis Meigret

Girolamo Vida: Marco Girolamo Vida (1480–1566), neo-Latin poet, author of an art of poetry, his *De arte poetica* (1527)

non par inspiration divine. Cete mesme antiquité se peut voir en tous les argumens de Plaute, dont chacun en ses lettres capitales porte le nom de la comedie.

Chapitre 9
Observation de quelques manieres de parler Françoyses

J'ay declaré en peu de paroles ce qui n'avoit encor' eté (que je saiche) touché de notz rhetoriqueurs Françoys. Quand aux couppes feminines, apostrophes, accens, l'*é* masculin et l'*e* feminin, et autres telles choses vulgaires, notre poëte les apprendra de ceux qui en ont ecrit. Quand aux especes de vers, qu'ilz veulent limiter, elles sont aussi diverses que la fantasie des hommes et que la mesme Nature. Quand aux vertuz et vices du poëme, si diligemment traités par les Anciens, comme Aristote, Horace, et apres eux Hieronyme Vide: quand aux figures des sentences et des motz, et toutes les autres parties de l'eloquution, les lieux de commiseration, de joye, de tristesse, d'ire, d'admiration, et toutes autres commotions de l'ame: je n'en parle point apres si grand nombre d'excellens phylosophes et orateurs qui en ont traicté, que je veux avoir eté bien leuz et releuz de nostre poëte, premier qu'il entreprenne quelque hault et excellent ouvraige. Et tout ainsi qu'entre les aucteurs Latins, les meilleurs sont estimez ceux qui de plus pres ont immité les Grecz, je veux aussi que tu t'eforces de rendre, au plus pres du naturel que tu pouras, la phrase et maniere de parler Latine, en tant que la proprieté de l'une et l'autre langue le voudra permettre. Autant te dy je de la Greque, dont les façons de parler sont fort approchantes de notre vulgaire, ce que mesmes on peut congnoitre par les articles, incongneuz de la langue Latine. Uses donques hardiment de l'infinitif pour le nom, comme *l'aller, le chanter, le vivre, le mourir.* De l'adjectif substantivé, comme *le liquide des eaux, le vuide de l'air, le fraiz des umbres, l'epes des forestz, l'enroué des cimballes,* pourveu que telle maniere de parler adjoute quelque grace et vehemence: et non pas, *le chault du feu, le froid de la glace, le dur du fer,* et leurs semblables. Des verbes et participes, qui de leur nature n'ont point d'infinitifz apres eux, avecques des infinitifz, comme *tremblant de mourir* et *volant d'y aller,* pour *craignant de mourir* et *se hatant d'y aller.* Des noms pour les adverbes, comme *ilz combattent obstinez,* pour *obstinéement, il*

combattent obstinés for *obstinément, il vole léger* for *légèrement*; and a thousand other ways of speaking that you will be better able to observe by frequent and attentive reading than I could explain to you.

Among other things, I advise you to make frequent use of the figure antonomasia, which is as common in the ancient poets as it is little used—indeed, unknown—among the French. Its grace comes from replacing the name of something by that which is characteristic of it, such as *the thundering father* for *Jupiter, the twice-born god* for *Bacchus, the chaste huntress* for *Diana.* This figure has many other species, which you will find in the rhetoricians, and lends very good grace especially to descriptions, like *from those who first see Aurora blush to where Thetis receives in her waves the son of Hyperion* for *from the east to the west.* You have many other examples in the Greeks and Latins, especially in those divine inventions of Virgil, such as those on an icy river, on the twelve signs of the zodiac, on Iris, on the twelve labors of Hercules, and others. As for epithets, which in our French poets are for the most part cold or trite or inappropriate, I would have you use them in such a way that without them what you say would be greatly diminished, like *the devouring flame, gnawing cares, torturing anxiety,* and take care that they fit not only their substantive but also what you wish to describe, so that you do not say *rippling water* when you mean to describe it as *impetuous* or *the ardent flame* when you want to show it *languishing.* Among the Latins, you have Horace who is very good at this, as at all things. Be careful, too, not to fall into a fault that is common even among the best in our language, that is, the omission of articles. You have examples of this fault in innumerable places in those little French ditties. I had nearly forgotten another very common fault, and one that is particularly awkward: namely, when in the construction of a decasyllabic line the caesura falls too abruptly, such as *Sinon que tu | en montres un plus sûr.*

There you have what I wanted briefly to tell you concerning what you must observe both in versification and in certain ways of speaking, which are infrequently or not yet used by the French. There are some who very scrupulously alternate masculine and feminine rhymes, as you can see in the Psalms translated by Marot. He did this (or so I believe) so that they could be sung more easily without changing the music to fit the variety of meters that would oth-

---

the son of Hyperion: the sun (Helios)

those divine inventions of Virgil: du Bellay borrows this passage from Erasmus (*De copia* 1.2), who finds these examples in Virgil's *Georgics* and *Aeneid*

the caesura falls too abruptly: that is, where there is no natural syntactic break, as in the line du Bellay quotes from the sonnet that introduces Sébillet's *Art Poetique François*

scrupulously alternate masculine and feminine rhymes: du Bellay himself observes this alternation in all but a very few poems of both the *Regrets* and the *Antiquities*

vole leger, pour *legerement*, et mil' autres manieres de parler, que tu pouras mieux observer par frequente et curieuse lecture, que je ne te les sçauroy' dire.

Entre autres choses, je t'averty' user souvent de la figure ANTONOMASIE, aussi frequente aux anciens poëtes, comme peu usitée, voire incongnue des Françoys. La grace d'elle est quand on designe le nom de quelque chose par ce qui luy est propre, comme *le Pere foudroyant* pour *Jupiter, le Dieu deux fois né* pour *Bacchus, la Vierge chasseresse* pour *Dyane*. Cete figure a beaucoup d'autres especes, que tu trouverras chés les rhetoriciens, et a fort bonne grace principalement aux descriptions, comme: *Depuis ceux qui voyent premiers rougir l'Aurore, jusques là où Thetis reçoit en ses undes le filz d'Hyperion* pour *Depuis l'Orient jusques à l'Occident*. Tu en as assez d'autres exemples és Grecz et Latins, mesmes en ces divines experiences de Virgile, comme du fleuve glacé, des douze signes du Zodiaque, d'Iris, des douze labeurs d'Hercule, et autres. Quand aux epithetes, qui sont en notz poëtes Françoys la plus grand' part ou froids ou ocieux ou mal à propos, je veux que tu en uses de sorte que sans eux ce que tu diras seroit beaucoup moindre, comme *la flamme devorante, les souciz mordans, la gehinnante sollicitude*: et regarde bien qu'ilz soint convenables, non seulement à leurs substantifz, mais aussi à ce que tu decriras, afin que tu ne dies *l'eau' undoyante*, quand tu la veux decrire *impetueuse*, ou la *flamme ardente*, quand tu la veux montrer *languissante*. Tu as Horace entre les Latins fort heureux en cecy, comme en toutes choses. Garde toy aussi de tumber en un vice commun, mesmes aux plus excellens de nostre langue, c'est l'omission des articles. Tu as exemple de ce vice en infiniz endroictz de ces petites poësies Françoyses. J'ay quasi oublié un autre default bien usité, et de tres mauvaise grace. C'est quand en la quadrature des vers heroïques la sentence est trop abruptement coupée, comme: *Si non que tu en montres un plus seur*.

Voyla ce que je te vouloy' dire brevement de ce que tu doibz observer tant au vers, comme à certaines manieres de parler, peu ou point encor' usitées des Françoys. Il y en a qui fort supersticieusement entremeslent les vers masculins avecques les feminins, comme on peut voir aux *Psalmes* traduictz par Marot. Ce qu'il a observé (comme je croy') afin que plus facilement on les peust chanter sans varier la musique, pour la diversité des

erwise be found at the end of the lines. I strongly approve that diligence so long as you do not make such a religion of it as to constrain your diction in order to observe such things. Most important, be sure that in your verse there is nothing harsh, choppy, or redundant. Let the periods be well joined, rhythmic, satisfying to the ear, and such that they do not overstep that limit and end we naturally feel whether in reading or listening.

Chapter 10
Of reciting Verse well

This does not seem to me an inappropriate place to say a word on recitation, which the Greeks called *hypokrisis,* so that if you sometimes have occasion to present your poems in public, you recite them with a sound that is clear and not confused, virile and not effeminate, with a voice adapted to all the emotions you wish to express in them. And surely, as declamation and gestures fitted to the matter one is treating are, according to the opinion of Demosthenes himself, the principal concern of the orator, so it is no small thing to recite one's poems with good grace. For poetry (as Cicero says) was invented by the observation of careful speakers and measurement by the ears, whose judgment is extraordinarily fine, as with those ears which reject everything harsh and rude, not only in the composition and structure of words but also in the modulation of the voice. We read that Virgil greatly excelled in graceful recitation, so much so that a poet of his time said that his verses spoken by him were sonorous and grave, but by others, slack and effeminate.

Chapter 11
Of some observations concerning matters other than the Rules of Art with an Invective against bad French Poets

I will not dwell long on what follows, for our poet, as I imagine him, will understand these things well enough by his own good judgment without any rules being passed on. Thus of the time and place he should choose for reflection, I will not give him other precepts than those which his pleasure and inclination will command. Some love cool forest shades, clear brooks sweetly

---

the periods: the sentences and other grammatical units, which, in du Bellay's view, should be harmoniously related to the metrical structure of the poem

Of reciting Verse well: du Bellay's *prononcer* has the sense of the Latin *pronuntio,* "to declaim," "to recite," or "to deliver"

the opinion of Demosthenes: as reported by both Cicero (*De oratore* 3.56.213) and Quintilian (*Institutio oratorio* 11.3.6)

as Cicero says: *Orator* 53.178

meseures qui se trouverroint à la fin des vers. Je treuve cete diligence fort bonne, pourveu que tu n'en faces point de religion jusques à contreindre ta diction pour observer telles choses. Regarde principalement qu'en ton vers n'y ait rien dur, hyulque ou redundant. Que les periodes soint bien joinctz, numereux, bien remplissans l'oreille, et telz qu'ilz n'excedent point ce terme et but, que naturellement nous sentons, soit en lisant ou ecoutant.

Chapitre 10
De bien prononcer les Vers

Ce lieu ne me semble mal à propos, dire un mot de la pronunciation, que les Grecz appellent ὑπόκρισις, afin que s'il t'avient de reciter quelquesfois tes vers, tu les pronunces d'un son distinct, non confuz: viril, non effeminé: avecques une voix accommodée à toutes les affections que tu voudras exprimer en tes vers. Et certes comme icelle pronunciation et geste approprié à la matiere que lon traite, voyre par le jugement de Demosthene, est le principal de l'orateur: aussi n'est-ce peu de chose que de pronuncer ses vers de bonne grace: veu que la poësie (comme dit Ciceron) a eté inventée par observation de prudence et mesure des oreilles: dont le jugement est tressuperbe, comme de celles qui repudient toutes choses apres et rudes, non seulement en composition et structure de motz, mais aussi en modulation de voix. Nous lisons cete grace de pronuncer avoir eté fort excellente en Virgile, et telle qu'un poëte de son tens disoit que les vers de luy, par luy pronuncez, etoint sonoreux et graves: par autres, flacques et effeminez.

Chapitre 11
De quelques observations oultre l'Artifice, avecques une Invective contre les mauvais Poëtes Françoys

Je ne demeureray longuement en ce que s'ensuit, pource que nostre poëte, tel que je le veux, le poura assez entendre par son bon jugement, sans aucunes traditions de reigles. Du tens donques et du lieu qu'il fault elire pour la cogitation, je ne luy en bailleray autres preceptes, que ceux que son plaisir et sa disposition luy ordonneront. Les uns ayment les fresches umbres des forestz, les clers ruisselez doucement murmurans parmy

murmuring through fields adorned and carpeted with greenery. Others delight in the privacy of chambers and learned studies. One must accommodate oneself to the season and the place. I would, however, advise you to seek solitude and silence, friend of the Muses, who also (so as not to let slip away that divine inspiration which sometimes excites and heats poetic spirits and without which no one can hope to accomplish anything lasting) never open the door of their sacred study except to those who knock rudely.

I do not want to forget revision, surely the most useful part of our studies. Its role is to add, remove, or change at leisure, which the initial impetuosity and ardor in writing did not permit you to do. That is why it is necessary, so that our writings, like newborn children, do not flatter us, to set them aside, to revise them often, and, like bears, by licking them to give their limbs form and fashion, not imitating those importunate versifiers, called by the Greeks *mousopatagoi,* who at all hours offend the ears of their miserable listeners with their new poems. Yet you must not be too scrupulous or, like elephants with their young, take ten years to give birth to your poems. Above all, it is good to have some learned and faithful companion or a very familiar friend—indeed, three or four—who watch over us and can see our faults and are not afraid to wound our paper with their fingernails. I would also advise you sometimes to frequent not only the learned but also all sorts of workmen and craftsmen, such as sailors, foundrymen, painters, engravers, and others, to know their inventions, the names of materials, of tools, and the terms used in their arts and crafts, to take from them those fine comparisons and lively descriptions of all things.

Does it not seem to you, Gentlemen, you who are such enemies of your language, that so armed our poet can enter into battle and show himself in the ranks with the brave Greek and Roman squadrons? And you others who are so badly equipped, whose ignorance has given our language the ridiculous name of *rhymesters* (as the Latins call their bad poets *versificators*), will you dare to endure the sun, the dust, and the dangerous labor of this combat? I am of the opinion that you would withdraw to the baggage with the pages and lackeys or (for I have pity on you) under the cool shades at the sumptuous palaces of great lords and the magnificent courts of princes, among the ladies and maidens, where your fair and dainty works, no longer lasting than your life, will be received, admired, and adored—not to the scholarly studies and rich libraries of the learned.

---

with their fingernails: that is, erase faults by scratching them out, as might be done on parchment

the magnificent courts of princes: du Bellay here expresses his disdain for court poets

les prez ornez et tapissez de verdure. Les autres se delectent du secret des chambres et doctes etudes. Il fault s'accommoder à la saison et au lieu. Bien te veux-je avertir de chercher la solitude et le silence amy des Muses, qui aussi (affin que ne laisses passer cete fureur divine, qui quelquesfois agite et echaufe les espris poëtiques, et sans la quele ne fault point que nul espere faire chose qui dure) n'ouvrent jamais la porte de leur sacré cabinet, si non à ceux qui hurtent rudement.

Je ne veux oublier l'emendation, partie certes la plus utile de notz etudes. L'office d'elle est ajouter, oter, ou muer à loysir ce que cete premiere impetuosité et ardeur d'ecrire n'avoit permis de faire. Pourtant est il necessaire, afin que noz ecriz, comme enfans nouveaux nez, ne nous flattent, les remettre à part, les revoir souvent, et en la maniere des ours, à force de lecher, leur donner forme et façon de membres, non immitant ces importuns versificateurs, nommez des Grecz μουσοπάταγοι, qui rompent à toutes heures les oreilles des miserables auditeurs par leurs nouveaux poëmes. Il ne fault pourtant y estre trop supersticieux, ou (comme les elephans leurs petiz) estre dix ans à enfanter ses vers. Sur tout nous convient avoir quelque sçavant et fidele compaignon, ou un amy bien familier, voire trois ou quatre, qui veillent et puissent congnoitre noz fautes, et ne craignent point blesser nostre papier avecques les ungles. Encores te veux-je advertir de hanter quelquesfois, non seulement les sçavans, mais aussi toutes sortes d'ouvriers et gens mecaniques, comme mariniers, fondeurs, peintres, engraveurs, et autres, sçavoir leurs inventions, les noms des matieres, des outilz, et les termes usitez en leurs ars et metiers, pour tyrer de la ces belles comparaisons et vives descriptions de toutes choses.

Vous semble point, Messieurs, qui etes si ennemis de vostre langue, que nostre poëte ainsi armé puisse sortir à la campaigne, et se montrer sur les rancz, avecques les braves scadrons Grecz et Romains? Et vous autres si mal equipez, dont l'ignorance a donné le ridicule nom de *rymeurs* à nostre langue (comme les Latins appellent leurs mauvais poëtes *versificateurs*), oserez vous bien endurer le soleil, la poudre, et le dangereux labeur de ce combat? Je suis d'opinion que vous retiriés au bagaige avecques les paiges et laquais, ou bien (car j'ay pitié de vous) soubz les fraiz umbraiges, aux sumptueux palaiz des grands Seigneurs et cours magnifiques des Princes, entre les dames et damoizelles, ou votz beaux et mignons ecriz, non de plus longue durée que vostre vie, seront receuz, admirés et adorés: non point aux doctes etudes et riches byblyotheques des sçavans.

Might it please the Muses, for the good I desire for our language, that your inept works should be banished not only from those studies and libraries (as they are) but from all of France! I would that, following the example of that great monarch who forbade that any portray him in a painting but Apelles or in a statue but Lysippus, all kings and princes who love their language would forbid, by express decree, their subjects to bring to light any work and printers to print it if it had not first endured the file of some learned man as little inclined to adulation as was that Quintilius of whom Horace speaks in his *Art of Poetry*, where, as in many places in the said Horace, one can see the faults of modern poets expressed so vividly that he seems to have written not of the time of Augustus but of that of Francis and Henry. Physicians (he says) promise to do what pertains to physicians; blacksmiths treat what pertains to blacksmiths; but among us the unlearned commonly write poems as much as the learned. That is why it is no wonder if today many learned men do not deign to write in our language and if foreigners do not prize it as we do theirs, inasmuch as they see in it so many ignorant new authors, which makes them think that it is incapable of bearing greater adornment and erudition. O how I desire to see those *Springtimes* wither, those little *Youths* punished, those *Essays* pulled down, those *Fountains* run dry—in short, to see all those fine titles abolished that are enough to disgust any learned reader and keep him from reading further! I wish no less that those Deprived Ones, those Humble Hopeful Ones, those Exiles from Joy, those Slaves, those Travelers be sent back to the Round Table, and those pretty little devices back to the gentlemen and ladies from whom they were borrowed.

What more shall I say? I beg Phoebus Apollo that France, after having been barren so long, pregnant by him, will soon give birth to a poet whose resonant lute will silence those hoarse bagpipes, not unlike frogs when you throw a stone in their swamp. And if, despite that, the burning fever to

---

that great monarch: Alexander, of whom this story is told by Horace, *Epistles* 2.1.239–241

Quintilius of whom Horace speaks: *Ars poetica* (*Epistles* 2.3.438–444), a passage Aneau seizes on in calling his attack on du Bellay the *Quintil Horatian*

Physicians (he says): Horace, *Epistles* 2.1.115–117

those *Springtimes*: these titles belong to works by Jean le Blond, François Habert, François Sagan, and Charles Fontaine

those *Deprived Ones*: these pseudonyms were used by Marot, le Blond, Habert, Michel d'Amboise, and Jean Bouchet

those pretty little devices: Marot and his followers adopted mottos—Marot's was "La mort n'y mord" (Death does not bite)—to identify them

Que pleust aux Muses, pour le bien que je veux à nostre langue, que votz ineptes œuvres feussent bannys, non seulement de là (comme ilz sont) mais de toute la France! Je voudroys bien qu'à l'exemple de ce grand Monarque, qui defendit que nul n'entreprist de le tirer en tableau, si non Apelle, ou en statue, si non Lysippe, tous Roys et Princes amateurs de leur langue deffendissent, par edict expres, à leurs subjectz de non mettre en lumiere œuvre aucun, et aux imprimeurs de non l'imprimer, si premierement il n'avoit enduré la lyme de quelque sçavant homme, aussi peu adulateur qu'etoit ce Quintilie, dont parle Horace en son *Art Poëtique*, où, et en infiniz autres endroictz dudict Horace, on peut voir les vices des poëtes modernes exprimés si au vif, qu'il semble avoir ecrit, non du tens d'Auguste, mais de Françoys et de Henry. Les medicins (dict il) promettent ce qui appartient aux medicins, les feuvres traictent ce qui appartient aux feuvres: mais nous ecrivons ordinairement des poëmes autant les indoctes comme les doctes. Voyla pourquoy ne se fault emerveiller, si beaucoup de sçavans ne daignent au jourd'huy ecrire en nostre langue, et si les etrangers ne la prisent comme nous faisons les leur, d'autant qu'ilz voyent en icelle tant de nouveaux aucteurs ignorans, ce qui leur fait penser qu'elle n'est capable de plus grand ornement et erudition. O combien je desire voir secher ces *Printems*, chatier ces petites *Jeunesses*, rabbattre ces *Coups d'essay*, tarir ces *Fontaines*, bref, abolir tous ces beaux tiltres assez suffisans pour degouter tout lecteur sçavant d'en lire d'avantaige! Je ne souhaite moins que ces Depourveuz, ces Humbles esperans, ces Banniz de lyesse, ces Esclaves, ces Traverseurs soient renvoyés à la Table ronde: et ces belles petites devises aux gentilzhommes et damoyzelles, d'où on les a empruntées.

Que diray plus? Je supplie à Phebus Apollon que la France, apres avoir eté si longuement sterile, grosse de luy enfante bien tost un poëte, dont le luc bien resonnant face taire ces enrouées cornemuses, non autrement que les grenoilles, quand on jette une pierre en leur maraiz. Et si non obstant cela, cete fiévre chaude d'ecrire les tormentoit encores, je leur con-

write torments them still, I would counsel them either to go take medicine in Anticyra or, better, to take up their studies again and to do it without shame, following the example of Cato, who learned Greek in his old age. I am well aware that in speaking in this way of our rhymesters I will seem too biting and satiric to many but truthful to those who have knowledge and judgment and who desire the good health of our language, where that ulcer and rotten flesh of bad poetry is so ingrown that it can be removed only with a knife and cauterizing iron.

To conclude this matter, know, Reader, that he will truly be the poet I seek in our language who will make me angry, calm me, fill me with joy, make me grieve, love, hate, admire, wonder—who will, in short, hold the reins of my emotions, turning me this way and that as he pleases. That is the true touchstone by which you must try all poems in all languages. I expect there will be many, who judge nothing good unless they understand it and think they can imitate it, to whom our poet will not appeal, who will say there is no pleasure and less profit in reading such writings, that they are only poetical fictions, that Marot never wrote like that. To these, since of poetry they understand only the name, I do not intend to respond, producing as my only defense so many excellent Greek, Latin, and Italian poetic works that are as foreign to the kind of writing they so approve as they are themselves far removed from all good erudition. I wish only to admonish him who aspires to an uncommon glory to distance himself from these inept admirers, to flee this ignorant race, these enemies of all rare and ancient knowledge, to be content with few readers, following the example of him who for listeners asked only for Plato, and of Horace who wished that his works would be read only by three or four, Augustus among them.

You have, Reader, my judgment concerning our French poet, which you will follow if you think it good or hold onto your own if you have some other. For I am not unaware how men's judgments differ, as in all things, especially in poetry, which is like a painting and no less subject to the opinion of the vulgar. The principal target I aim at is the defense of our lan-

---

take medicine in Anticyra: that is, take hellebore, which was produced in Anticyra and was thought to cure madness

the example of Cato: Cato the Elder

the example of him: Antimachus of Colophon, Greek poet and scholar, of whom this story is told by Cicero (*Brutus* 51.191)

and of Horace: *Satires* 1.10.72ff., where the Octavius Horace mentions is not, as du Bellay thought, the Emperor Augustus but rather a historian and friend of Virgil

which is like a painting: recalls Horace's enormously influential dictum in the *Ars poetica* (*Epistles* 2.3.361), "Ut pictura poesis" (A poem is like a painting)

seilleroy' ou d'aller prendre medicine en Antycire, ou, pour le mieux, se remettre à l'étude, et sans honte, à l'exemple de Caton, qui en sa vieillesse apprist les lettres Greques. Je pense bien qu'en parlant ainsi de notz rymeurs, je sembleray à beaucoup trop mordant et satyrique, mais veritable à ceux qui ont sçavoir et jugement, et qui desirent la santé de nostre langue, où cet ulcere et chair corrumpue de mauvaises poësies est si inveterée, qu'elle ne se peut oter qu'avecques le fer et le cautere.

Pour conclure ce propos, saiches, Lecteur, que celuy sera veritablement le poëte que je cherche en nostre langue, qui me fera indigner, apayser, ejouyr, douloir, aymer, hayr, admirer, etonner, bref, qui tiendra la bride de mes affections, me tournant ça et là à son plaisir. Voyla la vraye pierre de touche, où il fault que tu epreuves tous poëmes, et en toutes langues. Je m'attens bien qu'il s'en trouverra beaucoup de ceux qui ne treuvent rien bon, si non ce qu'ilz entendent et pensent pouvoir immiter, aux quelz nostre poëte ne sera pas agreable: qui diront qu'il n'i a aucun plaisir, et moins de profit, à lire telz ecriz, que ce ne sont que fictions poëtiques, que Marot n'a point ainsi ecrit. A telz, pour ce qu'ilz n'entendent la poësie que de nom, je ne suis deliberé de repondre, produysant pour deffence tant d'excellens ouvraiges poëtiques Grecz, Latins, et Italiens, aussi alienes de ce genre d'ecrire, qu'ilz approuvent tant, comme ilz sont eux mesmes eloingnez de toute bonne erudition. Seulement veux-je admonnester celuy qui aspire à une gloyre non vulgaire, s'eloingner de ces ineptes admirateurs, fuyr ce peuple ignorant, peuple ennemy de tout rare et antique sçavoir, se contenter de peu de lecteurs, à l'exemple de celuy qui pour tous auditeurs ne demandoit que Platon, et d'Horace, qui veult ses œuvres estre leuz de trois ou quatre seulement, entre les quelz est Auguste.

Tu as, Lecteur, mon jugement de nostre poëte Françoys, le quel tu suyvras, si tu le treuves bon, ou te tiendras au tien, si tu en as quelque autre. Car je n'ignore point combien les jugementz des hommes sont divers, comme en toutes choses, principalement en la poësie, la quelle est comme une peinture, et non moins qu'elle subjecte à l'opinion du vulgaire. Le principal but où je vise, c'est la deffence de notre langue, l'orne-

guage, its ornamentation and amplification, in which if I have not greatly eased the efforts and labor of those who aspire to that glory, or if I have not helped them at all, I will at least think I have done much if I have made them more willing.

Chapter 12
Exhortation to the French to write in their Language: with Praises of France

If then it is true that in our time the stars, as if by common accord, have through fortunate influence conspired for the honor and growth of our language, who among the learned will not want to put his hand to the task, spreading on all sides the flowers and fruits from those rich Greek and Latin horns of plenty? Or who, at the least, will not praise and approve the effort of others? And who will be the one to blame it? No one, unless he is truly an enemy of the name of France. When he condemned to death a herald of the King of Persia only for having used the Attic tongue for the commands of the barbarian, that prudent and virtuous Themistocles the Athenian clearly showed that the same natural law that commands each to defend his native land also obliges us to maintain the dignity of our language. The glory of the Roman people derives no less (as someone said) from the amplification of their language than from the extension of their borders. For even in the time of Augustus, the highest achievements of their commonwealth—its Capitol, its baths, and magnificent palaces—were not sufficient to ward off the ravages of time without the benefit of their language, for which alone we praise them, we admire them, we worship them.

Themistocles the Athenian: a story told by Plutarch, *Themistocles* 6.3–4

as someone said: Lazaro says something very much like this in Speroni's *Dialogo delle Lingue,* and similar views can be found in Pliny the Elder (*Natural History* 7.31.117) and Lorenzo Valla (*Elegantiae de lingua latina,* preface)

the ravages of time: this sentence summarizes the argument du Bellay would later develop in his *Antiquities*

ment et amplification d'icelle, en quoy si je n'ay grandement soulaigé l'industrie et labeur de ceux qui aspirent à cete gloire, ou si du tout je ne leur ay point aydé, pour le moins je penseray avoir beaucoup fait, si je leur ay donné bonne volonté.

Chapitre 12
Exhortation aux Françoys d'ecrire en leur Langue: avecques les Louanges de la France

Donques, s'il est ainsi que de nostre tens les Astres, comme d'un accord, ont par une heureuse influence conspiré en l'honneur et accroissement de notre langue, qui sera celuy des sçavans qui n'y voudra mettre la main, y rependant de tous cotez les fleurs et fruictz de ces riches cornes d'abundance Greque et Latine? ou, à tout le moins, qui ne louëra et approuvera l'industrie des autres? Mais qui sera celuy qui la voudra blâmer? Nul, s'il n'est vrayment ennemy du nom Françoys. Ce prudent et vertueux Themistocle Athenien montra bien que la mesme loy naturelle, qui commande à chacun defendre le lieu de sa naissance, nous oblige aussi de garder la dignité de notre langue, quand il condamna à mort un herault du Roy de Perse, seulement pour avoir employé la langue Attique aux commendemens du barbare. La gloire du peuple Romain n'est moindre (comme a dit quelqu'un) en l'amplification de son langaige que de ses limites. Car la plus haulte excellence de leur republique, voire du tens d'Auguste, n'etoit assez forte pour se deffendre contre l'injure du tens, par le moyen de son Capitole, de ses thermes et magnifiques palaiz, sans le benefice de leur langue, pour la quele seulement nous les louons, nous les admirons, nous les adorons.

Are we then inferior to the Greeks or Romans, we who take so little care of our own? I have not attempted to compare us to the former, in order not to wrong French virtue by setting it against Greek vanity; and still less to the latter, because of the excessively tedious length it would take to rehearse the origin of the two nations, their deeds, their laws, customs, and ways of life, the consuls, dictators, and emperors of the one, the kings, dukes, and princes of the other. I confess that Fortune may at times have been more favorable to them than to us, but I will also say (without reopening the old wounds of Rome and recalling from what height to what universal disdain she fell by her own doing) that France, whether in peace or in war, is by far to be preferred over Italy, now the slave and mercenary of those she used to command.

I will not speak here of the temperateness of the air, the fertility of the soil, the abundance of every kind of fruit needed for the ease and maintenance of human life, and other innumerable benefits that heaven, rather prodigally than liberally, has bestowed on France. I will not recount the many great rivers, the many beautiful forests, the many cities, no less opulent than strong and provided with all the munitions of war. Finally, I will not speak of the many trades, arts, and learned disciplines—such as music, painting, sculpture, architecture, and others—that flourish among us scarcely less than they once did among the Greeks and Romans. And if with iron we do not rip through the sacred entrails of our ancient mother to find gold and silver, if avaricious merchants do not seek here gems, perfumes, and other corruptions of the primal goodness of Nature toward men, so too are the raging tiger, the cruel breed of lions, poisonous herbs, and so many other plagues of human life far from us.

I am pleased that we have these benefits in common with other nations, particularly Italy. But as for piety, religion, integrity of morals, greatness of courage, and all those rare and ancient virtues (from which come true and solid praise), France has always won without controversy the first place. Why then are we such great admirers of others? Why are we so unjust to ourselves? Why do we beg from foreign languages, as though we were ashamed to use our own? Cato the Elder (I mean that Cato whose grave

---

the old wounds of Rome: the civil wars and the decadence that were credited with the fall of the Roman Empire

now the slave and mercenary: alludes to the French and Hispanic-Imperial invasions of Italy and occupation of large parts of the Italian peninsula from 1494 on

I will not recount: du Bellay's praise of France is copied from praise of Italy he found in Virgil (*Georgics* 2.136–176) and Pliny the Elder (*Natural History* 3.6.39–42)

Cato the Elder: a story told by Plutarch in his *Life of Cato the Elder* 12.7

Sommes nous donques moindres que les Grecz ou Romains, qui faisons si peu de cas de la nostre? Je n'ay entrepris de faire comparaison de nous à ceulx là, pour ne faire tort à la vertu Françoyse, la conferant à la vanité Gregeoyse: et moins à ceux cy, pour la trop ennuyeuse longueur que ce seroit de repeter l'origine des deux nations, leurs faictz, leurs loix, meurs, et manieres de vivre, les Consulz, Dictateurs et Empereurs de l'une, les Roys, Ducz, et Princes de l'autre. Je confesse que la fortune leur ait quelquesfoys eté plus favorable qu'à nous: mais aussi diray-je bien (sans renouveler les vieilles playes de Romme, et de quele excellence en quel meprix de tout le monde, par ses forces mesmes elle a eté precipitée) que la France, soit en repos ou en guerre, est de long intervale à preferer à l'Italie, serve maintenant et mercenaire de ceux aux quelz elle souloit commander.

Je ne parleray icy de la temperie de l'air, fertilité de la terre, abundance de tous genres de fruictz necessaires pour l'ayse et entretien de la vie humaine, et autres irnnumerables commoditez, que le Ciel, plus prodigalement que liberalement, a elargy à la France. Je ne conteray tant de grosses rivieres, tant de belles forestz, tant de villes, non moins opulentes que fortes, et pourveuës de toutes munitions de guerre. Finablement je ne parleray de tant de metiers, arz, et sciences, qui florissent entre nous, comme la musique, peinture, statuaire, architecture, et autres, non gueres moins que jadis entre les Grecz et Romains. Et si pour trouver l'or et l'argent, le fer n'y viole point les sacrées entrailles de nostre antique mere: si les gemmes, les odeurs, et autres corruptions de la premiere generosité des hommes n'y sont point cherchées du marchant avare: aussi le tigre enraigé, la cruelle semence des lyons, les herbes empoisonneresses, et tant d'autres pestes de la vie humaine, en sont bien eloignées.

Je suis content que ces felicitez nous soient communes avecques autres nations, principalement l'Italie: mais quand à la pieté, religion, integrité de meurs, magnanimité de couraiges, et toutes ces vertuz rares et antiques (qui est la vraye et solide louange), la France a tousjours obtenu sans controverse le premier lieu. Pourquoy donques sommes nous si grands admirateurs d'autruy? Pourquoy sommes nous tant iniques à nous mesmes? Pourquoy mandions nous les langues etrangeres, comme si nous avions honte d'user de la nostre? Caton l'Aisné (je dy celuy Caton, dont la grave

judgment was so many times approved by the senate and people of Rome) said to Posthumus Albinus, when Posthumus excused himself for having, as a Roman, written a history in Greek, "It is true that it would have been necessary to pardon you if by the decree of the Amphyctionic Council you had been compelled to write in Greek." He thus mocked the ambitious effort of him who preferred to write in a foreign language than in his own. Horace said that in a dream Romulus admonished him, when he wrote poems in Greek, not to carry wood to the forest, which ordinarily they do who write in Greek or Latin. And even if glory alone and not the love of virtue leads us to virtuous acts, yet I do not see that less of it awaits him who excels in his vulgar tongue than him who writes only in Greek or Latin. True it is that the latter's name (inasmuch as those two languages are more famous) spreads to more places, but it is very often lost, like smoke, which comes out thick in the beginning then little by little fades away in the great expanse of air, or it remains as if in silence and obscurity from being overwhelmed by the infinite multitude of others more renowned. But the glory of the former, inasmuch as it is contained within limits and is not divided among as many places as the other, lasts longer from having a fixed seat and dwelling.

When Cicero and Virgil began to write in Latin, eloquence and poetry were still in their infancy among the Romans and at the height of their excellence among the Greeks. If then those I have named, disdaining their own language, had written in Greek, is it to be believed that they would have equaled Homer and Demosthenes? At the least, they would not have been among the Greeks what they are among the Latins. Similarly for Petrarch and Boccaccio. Although they wrote much in Latin, yet that would not have been enough to give them that great honor they have acquired, if they had not written in their own language. Knowing this well, many good wits of our time, though they had already acquired uncommon renown among the Latins, nevertheless switched to their mother tongue—even Italians, who have much greater reason to adore the Latin language than we do. I will limit myself to naming that learned Cardinal Pietro Bembo, than whom I doubt that any man has ever imitated Cicero more assiduously, unless it is perhaps Christophe de Longueil. In any case, because he wrote in Italian, as much in verse as in prose, Bembo made both his language and his own name far more illustrious than either had been before.

Horace said: *Satires* 1.10.31–35

Cardinal Pietro Bembo: (1470–1547), a neo-Latin Ciceronian whose conversion to Italian in his *Prose della volgar lingua* (1525) and whose Petrarchan poems in Italian were a major inspiration to vernacular poets all over Europe

Christophe de Longueil: (1488–1522), a French Ciceronian whose excesses helped inspire Erasmus's anti-Ciceronian *Ciceronianus* (1528)

sentence a été tant de foys approuvée du Senat et peuple Romain) dist à Posthumie Albin, s'excusant de ce que luy, homme Romain, avoit ecrit une hystoire en Grec: Il est vray qu'il t'eust faillu pardonner, si par le decret des Amphyctioniens tu eusses eté contraint d'ecrire en Grec: se moquant de l'ambicieuse curiosité de celuy qui aymoit mieulx ecrire en une langue etrangere qu'en la sienne. Horace dit que Romule en songe l'amonnesta, lors qu'il faisoit des vers Grecz, de ne porter du boys en la forest. Ce que font ordinairement ceux qui ecrivent en Grec et en Latin. Et quand la gloire seule, non l'amour de la vertu, nous devroit induire aux actes vertueux, si ne voy-je pour tant qu'elle soit moindre à celuy qui est excellent en son vulgaire, qu'à celuy qui n'ecrit qu'en Grec ou en Latin. Vray est que le nom de cetuy cy (pour autant que ces deux langues sont plus fameuses) s'etent en plus de lieux: mais bien souvent, comme la fumée, qui sort grosse au commencement, peu à peu s'evanouist parmy le grand espace de l'air, il se perd, ou pour estre opprimé de l'infinie multitude des autres plus renommez, il demeure quasi en silence et obscurité. Mais la gloire de cetuy là, d'autant qu'elle se contient en ses limites, et n'est divisée en tant de lieux que l'autre, est de plus longue durée, comme ayant son siege et demeure certaine.

Quand Ciceron et Virgile se misrent à ecrire en Latin, l'eloquence et la poësie etoint encor' en enfance entre les Romains, et au plus haut de leur excellence entre les Grecz. Si donques ceux que j'ay nommez, dedaignans leur langue, eussent ecrit en Grec, est-il croyable qu'ilz eussent egalé Homere et Demosthene? Pour le moins n'eussent ilz eté entre les Grecz ce qu'ilz sont entre les Latins. Petrarque semblablement et Boccace, combien qu'ilz aient beaucoup ecrit en Latin, si est-ce que cela n'eust eté suffisant pour leur donner ce grand honneur qu'ilz ont acquis, s'ilz n'eussent ecrit en leur langue. Ce que bien congnoissans maintz bons espris de notre tens, combien qu'ilz eussent ja acquis un bruyt non vulgaire entre les Latins, se sont neantmoins convertiz à leur langue maternelle, mesmes Italiens, qui ont beaucoup plus grande raison d'adorer la langue Latine que nous n'avons. Je me contenteray de nommer ce docte Cardinal Pierre Bembe, duquel je doute si onques homme immita plus curieusement Ciceron, si ce n'est paraventure un Christofle Longueil. Toutesfois par ce qu'il a ecrit en Italien, tant en vers comme en prose, il a illustré et sa langue et son nom trop plus qu'ilz n'estoint au paravant.

Perhaps someone, already persuaded by the arguments I have made, would willingly switch to his vulgar tongue if he had a few domestic examples. And I say he should begin all the more quickly in order to be the first to occupy the place where others have been lacking. The broad fields of Greek and Latin are already so full that very little empty space remains. With fleet foot many have already reached the goal that is so greatly desired. The prize was won long ago. But, O God, how much sea yet remains before we reach the port! How far off is still the end of our race! Yet I do want to point out that all the learned men of France have not despised their vulgar tongue. He who brings Aristophanes back to life and so well imitates the fine wit of Lucian bears good witness to this. Would that many others would do the same in different kinds of writing and not amuse themselves by stripping the bark from the one of whom I speak to cover with it the worm-eaten wood of I know not what dull-witted jokes, which are so lacking in humor that no other recipe would be needed to take from Democritus all desire to laugh. In place of all the others, I will not hesitate to mention those two French lights, Guillaume Budé and Lazare de Baïf. The first wrote, no less amply than learnedly, the *Institution of the Prince,* a work that is sufficiently recommended by the name alone of its maker. The other has not only translated Sophocles' *Electra* almost line for line, a laborious task, as those who have tried anything similar understand, but has, still more, given our language the name of *epigrams* and of *elegies* with that fine composite word *aigredoux* [bittersweet], lest the honor of these things be attributed to anyone else. And of what I say I have the assurance of a gentleman and friend of mine, a man surely no less trustworthy than possessed of singular erudition and uncommon judgment. It seems to me (Reader, friend of the French Muses) that after those I have named, you must not be ashamed to write in your language, but rather that you must, if you are a friend of France (indeed, of yourself), give yourself over to it altogether with that generous opinion that it is better to be an Achilles among his own people than a Diomedes—indeed, often a Thersites—among others.

He who brings Aristophanes back to life: François Rabelais (1483–1553), whose comic genius recalled that of Aristophanes and Lucian

that many others: du Bellay here mocks dull-witted imitators of Rabelais

Democritus: Democritus of Abdera, known as "the laughing philosopher"

Guillaume Budé: (1468–1540), a leading French humanist, whose *Institution du Prince* was published posthumously in 1547

Lazare de Baïf: (1496–1547), a humanist and counselor to King Francis I, whose translation of Sophocles' *Electra* was published in 1537

a gentleman and friend of mine: possibly Lazare's son, Jean-Antoine de Baïf, du Bellay's classmate, friend, and fellow poet

a Diomedes . . . a Thersites: Homeric figures, Diomedes ended his life living among foreigners and Thersites was known as a fool among the Greeks

Quelqu'un (peut estre) deja persuadé par les raisons que j'ay alléguées, se convertiroit voluntiers à son vulgaire, s'il avoit quelques exemples domestiques. Et je dy que d'autant s'y doit-il plus tost mettre, pour occuper le premier ce à quoy les autres ont failly. Les larges campaignes Greques et Latines sont déja si pleines, que bien peu reste d'espace vide. Ja beaucoup d'une course legere ont attaint le but tant desiré. Long temps y a que le prix est gaigné. Mais, ô bon Dieu, combien de mer nous reste encores, avant que soyons parvenuz au port! combien le terme de nostre course est encores loing! Toutesfoys je te veux bien avertir que tous les sçavans hommes de France n'ont point meprisé leur vulgaire. Celuy qui fait renaitre Aristophane, et faint si bien le nez de Lucian, en porte bon temoignage. A ma volunté que beaucoup en divers genres d'écrire volussent faire le semblable, non point s'amuser à derober l'ecorce de celuy dont je parle, pour en couvrir le boys tout vermoulu de je ne sçay queles lourderies si mal plaisantes, qu'il ne faudroit autre recepte pour faire passer l'envie de ryre à Democrite. Je ne craindray point d'aleguer encores pour tous les autres ces deux lumieres Françoyses, Guillaume Budé et Lazare de Bayf. Dont le premier a ecrit, non moins amplement que doctement, l'*Institution du Prince,* œuvre certes assez recommandé par le seul nom de l'ouvrier. L'autre n'a pas seulement traduict l'*Electre* de Sophocle quasi vers pour vers, chose laborieuse, comme entendent ceux qui ont essayé le semblable: mais davantaige a donné à nostre langue le nom d'*epigrammes* et d'*elegies,* avecques ce beau mot composé *aigredoulx*: afin qu'on n'attribue l'honneur de ces choses à quelque autre. Et de ce que je dy, m'a asseuré un gentilhomme mien amy, homme certes non moins digne de foy, que de singuliere erudition et jugement non vulgaire. Il me semble (Lecteur amy des Muses Françoyses) qu'apres ceux que j'ay nommez, tu ne doys avoir honte d'ecrire en ta langue: mais encores doibstu, si tu es amy de la France, voyre de toymesmes, t'y donner du tout, avecques ceste genereuse opinion, qu'il vault mieux estre un Achille entre les siens, qu'un Diomede, voyre bien souvent un Thersite, entre les autres.

Conclusion to the Whole Work

Now, by the grace of God, through many perils and foreign seas, we have safely reached the port. We have escaped from the midst of the Greeks and through the Roman squadrons have penetrated to the bosom of much-desired France. Up then, Frenchmen! March courageously on that proud Roman city and from her captured spoils (as you have done more than once) adorn your temples and altars. Fear no more those shrill geese, that proud Manlius, and that traitor Camillus, who under cover of good faith would surprise you wholly unarmed as you count the ransom for the Capitol. Attack that lying Greece and sow there once again the famous nation of Gallo-Greeks. Pillage without scruple the sacred treasures of that Delphic temple, as you did in the past, and fear no more that mute Apollo, his false oracles, nor his blunted arrows. Remember your ancient Marseilles, the second Athens, and your Gallic Hercules, who drew the nations after him by their ears with a chain attached to his tongue.

End of *The Defense and Enrichment of the French Language*

---

those shrill geese: the sacred geese that alerted Manlius to the Gauls' invasion of Rome in 390 BCE, an invasion that was ultimately thwarted by Camillus, who led a massacre of the unarmed Gauls

sow there once again: alludes to an invasion of Greece and a sack of the temple of the Delphic oracle by the Gauls in the third century BCE

your ancient Marseilles: recalls the cultural efflorescence of Marseilles under the Roman Empire, when it was a center for Greek studies

your Gallic Hercules: a figure for French eloquence taken from Lucian and much favored by sixteenth-century French humanists

Conclusion de tout l'Oeuvre

Or sommes nous, la grace à Dieu, par beaucoup de perilz et de flotz etrangers, renduz au port à seureté. Nous avons echappé du millieu des Grecz, et par les scadrons Romains penetré jusques au seing de la tant desirée France. Là donq', Françoys, marchez couraigeusement vers cete superbe cité Romaine: et des serves depouilles d'elle (comme vous avez fait plus d'une fois) ornez voz temples et autelz. Ne craignez plus ces oyes cryardes, ce fier Manlie, et ce traitre Camile, qui soubz umbre de bonne foy vous surprenne tous nudz contans la rançon du Capitole. Donnez en cete Grece menteresse, et y semez encor' un coup la fameuse nation des Gallogrecz. Pillez moy sans conscience les sacrez thesors de ce temple Delphique, ainsi que vous avez fait autrefoys: et ne craignez plus ce muet Apollon, ses faulx oracles, ny ses fleches rebouchées. Vous souvienne de votre ancienne Marseille, secondes Athenes, et de votre Hercule Gallique, tirant les peuples apres luy par leurs oreilles avecques une chesne attachée à sa langue.

Fin de la *Deffense et Illustration de la Langue Françoyse.*

To the Ambitious and Greedy Enemy of Good Letters

Sonnet

Serf of favor, slave of greed, you never had power over yourself. I choose to provide myself with such a master that my free mind may nourish itself at will.

Weather, fortune, and human laws have in their hands your miserable wealth. Here the greedy judge has no dominion, nor do the three sisters, nor does the envy of Time.

Then consider which is most to be desired: ease or vexation, the sure or the unstable. As for honor, I hope to be immortal,

For an unblemished name never gives way to death. Your tarnished one promises you nothing of the sort. Thus will you both share the same tomb.

The Muse grants heaven

---

the three sisters: the Fates

The Muse grants heaven: du Bellay's often repeated motto, taken from Horace, *Odes* 4.8.29

A l'ambicieux et avare Ennemy des bonnes Lettres

Sonnet

Serf de faveur, esclave d'avarice,
Tu n'heus jamais sur toymesmes pouvoir,
Et je me veux d'un tel maitre pourvoir,
Que l'esprit libre en plaisir se nourisse.

L'air, la fortune, et l'humaine police
Ont en leurs mains ton malheureux avoir.
Le juge avare icy n'a rien à voir,
Ny les troys Seurs, ny du Tens la malice.

Regarde donc qui est plus souhaitable,
L'ayse ou l'ennuy, le certain ou l'instable,
Quand à l'honneur, j'espere estre immortel:

Car un cler nom soubz mort jamais ne tumbe.
Le tien obscur ne te promet rien tel.
Ainsi, tous deux serez soubz mesme tumbe.

Caelo Musa beat

To the Reader

Friend Reader, you will perhaps find it odd that I have so briefly treated a topic as fertile and copious as the enrichment of our French poetry, which is surely capable of greater adornment than many think. Yet you must realize that the arts and learned disciplines have not achieved their perfection all at once and from a single hand. Rather, through the course of many years, with each contributing some portion of his effort, they have attained the summit of their excellence. Receive then this little work as a sketch and outline of a great and laborious edifice that I may perhaps undertake to complete as my leisure and my knowledge increase and if I know that the French nation is favorably disposed toward this my goodwill, a will (I say) that in the greatest undertakings has always deserved some praise.

As for the spelling, I have more closely followed the common and ancient usage than reason, for this new (but, in my judgment, legitimate) way of writing has been so badly received in many places that its novelty could have made the work, hardly commendable in itself, disagreeable—indeed, contemptible—to readers. As for the faults that may be found in the printing, such as letters transposed, omitted, or superfluous, the first edition will excuse them and the understanding of the learned reader, who will not pause over such petty things.

Farewell, Friend Reader.

---

this new . . . way of writing: the spelling reform promoted by Louis Meigret

Au Lecteur

Amy Lecteur, tu trouverras etrange (peut estre) de ce que j'ay si brevement traité un si fertil et copieux argument, comme est l'illustration de nostre poësie Françoyse, capable certes de plus grand ornement que beaucoup n'estiment. Toutesfois tu doibz penser que les arz et sciences n'ont receu leur perfection tout à un coup et d'une mesme main: aincoys par succession de longues années, chacun y conferant quelque portion de son industrie, sont parvenues au point de leur excellence. Recoy donques ce petit ouvraige, comme un desseing et protraict de quelque grand et laborieux edifice, que j'entreprendray (possible) de conduyre, croissant mon loysir et mon sçavoir: et si je congnoy' que la nation Françoyse ait agreable ce mien bon vouloir, vouloir (dy-je) qui aux plus grandes choses a tousjours merité quelque louange.

Quant à l'orthographe, j'ay plus suyvy le commun et antiq' usaige que la raison: d'autant que cete nouvelle (mais legitime, à mon jugement) façon d'écrire est si mal receue en beaucoup de lieux, que la nouveauté d'icelle eust peu rendre l'œuvre non gueres de soy recommendable, mal plaisant, voyre contemptible aux lecteurs. Quand aux fautes qui se pouroint trouver en l'impression, comme de lettres transposées, omises ou superflues, la premiere edition les excusera, et la discretion du lecteur sçavant, qui ne s'arrestera à si petites choses.

A Dieu, Amy Lecteur.

Bibliography

Because of du Bellay's position as one of the central figures of early modern French literature, his works have been issued in numerous editions over the centuries and have been the subject of hundreds of critical studies. This bibliography does not pretend to give a full account of that huge and ever growing body of material. Instead, it includes a selection of both scholarly and more popular editions and critical works with an emphasis on studies written in English and those that focus on the *Regrets*, the *Antiquities of Rome*, and the *Defense and Enrichment of the French Language*. The original editions on which all modern editions, including the present text, are based—the 1549 l'Angelier edition of the *Defense* and the 1558 Morel editions of the *Regrets* and the *Antiquities of Rome*—can be seen online at Gallica, a service of the French Bibliothèque Nationale (http://gallica.bnf.fr).

Editions

Aris, Daniel, and Françoise Joukovsky, eds. *Œuvres poétiques.* 2 vols. Paris: Classiques Garnier, 1993. Frequently cited edition of du Bellay's French poems, with good introduction, notes, bibliography, and glossary.

Chamard, Henri, ed. *La Deffence et Illustration de la Langue Françoyse.* Paris: Société des Textes Français Modernes, 1997. Originally published in 1904 and then extensively augmented in 1948, this richly annotated edition, which has been reissued with an introduction by Jean Vignes and an updated bibliography, remains in many ways the most useful edition of the *Defense.*

———. *OEuvres poétiques.* 6 vols. Paris: Société des Textes Français Modernes, 1908-1931. Now superseded by various more recent editions, this was long the standard edition of du Bellay's French poetry and is still frequently consulted. Demerson's edition of the Latin poems was published in 1984-1985 as volumes 7 and 8 of this edition.

Demerson, Geneviève, ed. *OEuvres latines.* 2 vols. Paris: Société des Textes Français Modernes, 1984-1985. This edition of du Bellay's Latin poems with French translations was published as volumes 7 and 8 of Chamard's *OEuvres poétiques.* Volume 7 contains the *Poemata,* the collection of Latin poetry du Bellay wrote and published in tandem with the other work he produced during his four years in Rome. Volume 8 contains du Bellay's other Latin poems.

Joliffe, J., and M. A. Screech, eds. *Les Regrets et autres oeuvres poëtiques suivis des Antiquitez de Rome.* 1966; 3rd edition, Geneva: Droz, 1979. A carefully annotated edition of the *Regrets* and the *Antiquities of Rome* with an important introduction by Screech.

Millet, Olivier, ed. *OEuvres complètes.* Paris: Honoré Champion, 2003- . This projected multivolume, chronological edition of du Bellay's complete works, has begun with a first volume devoted almost entirely to the *Defense* and a second volume containing the poems du Bellay published in the year following the *Defense.* Volume 1, which was prepared by Francis Goyet and Olivier Millet, includes a 279-page commentary on the *Defense* by Goyet that gives painstaking attention to three primary "matrix-texts": Étienne Dolet's 1540 treatise on translation, Cicero's *Orator,* and Sperone Speroni's 1542 *Dialogo delle lingue.*

Monferran, Jean-Charles, ed. *La Deffence, et Illustration de la Langue Françoyse.* Geneva: Droz, 2001. A richly annotated edition of the *Defense* with a substantial introduction, a good bibliography, and a valuable dossier that includes du Bellay's primary source, Sperone Speroni's *Dialogo delle lingue,* in both the Italian original and a sixteenth-century French translation along with texts from the contemporary debate that raged over the *Defense.*

Sacy, S. de, ed. *Les Regrets précédé de Les Antiquités de Rome et suivi de La Défense et Illustration de la Langue Française.* Paris: Gallimard, 1967. A frequently reprinted edition of the *Regrets,* the *Antiquities of Rome,* and the *Defense* in modern French spelling with an introduction by Jacques Borel.

English Translations

Shapiro, Norman R. *Lyrics of the French Renaissance.* New Haven, Conn.: Yale University Press, 2002. Selected poems of Marot, du Bellay, and Ronsard in translations that imitate the formal features of the French originals and aim at something of a sixteenth-century English diction. Includes, along with other poems by du Bellay, six sonnets from the *Antiquities of Rome* and sixteen from the *Regrets.*

Sisson, C. H. *The Regrets.* Manchester: Carcanet Press, 1984. A very free, unrhymed verse translation of the first 130 sonnets of the *Regrets* with the French text on facing pages.

Slavitt, David R. *The Regrets.* Evanston, Ill.: Northwestern University Press, 2004. Like Sisson's, this is a lively and very free verse translation—though in rhymed rather than unrhymed verse—of the first 130 sonnets of the *Regrets* with facing French.

Smudlers, Elizabeth. *The Defence and Glorification of the French Language.* M.A. thesis, University of Pretoria, 1935. This unpublished thesis presents a fairly literal translation of the *Defense.*

Spenser, Edmund. *Antiquitez de Rome.* Edited by Malcolm C. Smith. Binghamton, N.Y.: Medieval and Renaissance Texts and Studies, 1994. Spenser first translated eleven of the sonnets from du Bellay's *Songe* (*Dream*) for Jan van der Noot's *Theatre for Worldlings* (1569). He then revised these translations and added versions of the remaining four *Dream* sonnets as *The Visions of Bellay* and translated du Bellay's *Antiquities* as the *Ruines of Rome,* both of which were published in his *Complaints* (1591). These translations can be found in any complete edition of Spenser's poetry. The edition mentioned here reprints them all with du Bellay's originals, van der Noot's woodcuts, and notes by Malcolm Smith.

Turquet, Gladys M. *The Defence and Illustration of the French Language.* London: Dent, 1939. A very literal, though not always dependable, translation of the *Defense* that does its best to imitate sixteenth-century English.

Books on du Bellay and His Literary Milieu

Argod-Dutard, Françoise. *L'Écriture de Joachim du Bellay.* Geneva: Droz, 2002. A heavily quantitative linguistic study of the *Regrets* in comparison with the style, including the orthography, of du Bellay's surviving letters.

Bellenger, Yvonne. *Du Bellay: Ses "Regrets" qu'il fit dans Rome . . . .* Paris: A.-G. Nizet, 1975. An excellent introduction to the *Regrets* with a dossier that includes parallel poems by Olivier de Magny and Jacques Grévin and letters by du Bellay himself.

Bizer, Marc. *Les Lettres romaines de Du Bellay.* Montreal: Les Presses de l'Université de Montréal, 2001. Reads the *Regrets* as an epistolary work, giving useful attention to each of du Bellay's principal correspondents.

Castor, Grahame. *Pléiade Poetics: A Study of Sixteenth-Century Thought and Terminology.* Cambridge: Cambridge University Press, 1964. A careful study of such key terms as *inspiration, imitation, invention, imagination, nature,* and *art* in the work of du Bellay and his contemporaries.

Cave, Terence. *The Cornucopian Text: Problems of Writing in the French Renaissance.* Oxford: Clarendon Press, 1979. This seminal examination of sixteenth-century French theories of writing includes a valuable discussion of du Bellay's idea of *illustration*—that is, enrichment and glorification—through imitation.

Chamard, Henri. *Histoire de la Pléiade.* 4 vols. 1939. Reprint, Paris: Didier, 1961. A massive account of the work of du Bellay and the other members of the Pléiade: Pierre de Ronsard, Jean-Antoine de Baïf, Étienne Jodelle, Jacques Peletier, Pontus de Tyard, and Rémi Belleau.

———. *Joachim du Bellay, 1522-1560.* 1900. Reprint, Geneva: Slatkine, 1969. Now more than a century old, this biographical and critical survey had an important role in inaugurating modern du Bellay studies. Much of the book reappears unchanged in the du Bellay chapters of Chamard's *Histoire de la Pléiade.*

Coleman, Dorothy Gabe. *The Chaste Muse: A Study of Joachim Du Bellay's Poetry.* Leiden: E. J. Brill, 1980. A sensitive reading of du Bellay's poetry in the light of Renaissance literary expectations.

Demerson, Geneviève. *Joachim Du Bellay et la belle romaine.* Orléans: Paradigme, 1996. This collection of Demerson's essays on du Bellay's Latin poetry includes valuable discussions of his divided linguistic loyalties, of his work as a translator of himself, and of his debt to various Roman poets.

Dickinson, G. *Du Bellay in Rome.* Leiden: E. J. Brill, 1960. This detailed account of mid- sixteenth-century Rome provides a very helpful accompaniment to the local and topical dimensions of the *Regrets.*

Ferguson, Margaret W. *Trials of Desire: Renaissance Defenses of Poetry.* New Haven, Conn.: Yale University Press, 1983. A valuable comparative study of du Bellay's *Defense* alongside Philip Sidney's *Defence of Poesie* and the *Apologia* Torquato Tasso wrote in defense of his *Gerusalemme liberata.*

Gadoffre, Gilbert. *Du Bellay et le sacré.* Paris: Gallimard, 1978. This reading of du Bellay pays special attention to the Gallican position of his Roman sonnets and provides a revealing "decoding" of the *Dream,* suggesting that du Bellay's elusive apocalyptic work is as much concerned with modern papal Rome as with ancient imperial Rome.

Goyet, Francis, ed. *Traités de poétique et de rhétorique de la Renaissance.* Paris: Librarie Générale Française, 1990. This useful supplement to du Bellay's *Defense* reprints treatises by Sébillet, Aneau, Peletier, Antoine Fouquelin, and Ronsard with an introduction by the editor.

Gray, Floyd. *La Poétique de Du Bellay.* Paris: Nizet, 1978. Examines the predominance of stylistic concerns in du Bellay's sonnet sequences. Includes a lengthy discussion of the *sermo pedestris,* the middle style, of the *Regrets.*

Greene, Thomas M. *The Light in Troy: Imitation and Discovery in Renaissance Poetry.* New Haven, Conn.: Yale University Press, 1982. This important comparative study of the theory and practice of poetic imitation from Petrarch to Ben Jonson includes a much-cited chapter on du Bellay's *Antiquities* as an attempted "disinterment of Rome."

Griffin, Robert. *Coronation of the Poet: Joachim Du Bellay's Debt to the Trivium.* Berkeley: University of California Press, 1969. A study of du Bellay's work in the light of the sixteenth-century teaching of grammar, logic, and especially rhetoric. Includes chapters on the *Antiquities* and the *Regrets.*

Hall, Kathleen M., and Margaret B. Wells. *Du Bellay: Poems.* London: Grant and Cutler, 1985. A brief introduction to du Bellay's principal collections of French verse, including the *Regrets* and the *Antiquities,* and to the criticism on those collections.

Hampton, Timothy. *Literature and the Nation in the Sixteenth Century: Inventing Renaissance France.* Ithaca, N.Y.: Cornell University Press, 2001. This study of literary nationhood in sixteenth-century France includes an important chapter on du Bellay and "the lyric invention of national character."

Hartley, David. *Patriotism in the Work of Joachim du Bellay: A Study of the Relationship Between the Poet and France.* Lewiston, N.Y.: Edwin Mellen Press, 1993. A study of the literary sources for du Bellay's patriotism and its expression in his works. Suggests that "patriotism is not incidental to Du Bellay's poetry, but arguably its most important theme."

Katz, Richard A. *The Ordered Text: The Sonnet Sequences of Du Bellay.* New York: Peter Lang, 1985. Argues for the thematic and structural unity of each of du Bellay's three sonnet sequences, *Olive, The Regrets,* and *The Antiquities of Rome.*

Keating, L. Clark. *Joachim du Bellay.* New York: Twayne, 1971. A belletristic account of du Bellay's life and works.

Kennedy, William J. *The Site of Petrachism: Early Modern National Sentiment in Italy, France, and England.* Baltimore: Johns Hopkins University Press, 2003. A comparative study of Petrarchan poetry as a site for national self-expression. The four chapters on France all center on du Bellay and claim a stronger adherence on du Bellay's part to the practice of such French predecessors as Clément Marot, Antoine Héroët, Mellin de Saint-Gelais, and Maurice Scève than du Bellay admitted or than most scholars would recognize.

MacPhail, Eric. *The Voyage to Rome in French Renaissance Literature.* Saratoga, Calif.: Anma Libri, 1990. A richly informed study of the literal and figurative meanings of the voyage to Rome in sixteenth-century French literature. Includes an excellent chapter on du Bellay.

McGowan, Margaret M. *The Vision of Rome in Late Renaissance France.* New Haven, Conn.: Yale University Press, 2000. This handsome and lavishly illustrated book reads du Bellay's Roman poems in relation to other sixteenth-century French responses to Rome.

Meerhoff, Kees. *Rhétorique et poétique au XVIe siècle en France: Du Bellay, Ramus et les autres.* Leiden: E. J. Brill, 1986. This study of the early modern intersection of rhetorical theory and poetics in France devotes eight chapters to du Bellay's *Defense,* its sources, and reactions to it.

Prescott, Anne Lake. *French Poets and the English Renaissance: Studies in Fame and Transformation.* New Haven, Conn.: Yale University Press, 1978. An important study of the English response to five sixteenth-century French poets: Marot, du Bellay, Ronsard, Philippe Desportes, and Guillaume du Bartas.

Rieu, Josiane. *L'Esthétique de Du Bellay.* [Paris]: SEDES, 1995. An attempt to define the "system of representation" underlying du Bellay's work. Argues for a religiously motivated "Gallican" style.

Rigolot, François. *Poésie et Renaissance.* Paris: Éditions du Seuil, 2002. A lively, engaging, and extraordinarily well informed introduction to French poetry from 1490 to 1610 by one of the leading scholars in the field. Du Bellay figures prominently in several chapters.

Roudaut, François. *Joachim du Bellay:* Les Regrets. Paris: Presses Universitaires de France, 1995. A comprehensive introduction to the *Regrets* that pays particular attention to its literary self-reflexivity.

Sabatier, Robert. *La Poésie du seizième siècle.* Paris: Albin Michel, 1975. The sixteenth-century volume of Sabatier's popular multivolume history of French poetry. Discusses du Bellay in the company of Ronsard and other poets associated with the Pléiade.

Saulnier, V.-L. *Du Bellay.* 1957; 4th edition, Paris: Hatier, 1968. A biographically oriented introduction to du Bellay and his poetry intended to update and supplant Chamard's *Joachim du Bellay.*

Skenazi, Cynthia. *Le Poète architecte en France: Constructions d'un imaginaire monarchique.* Paris: Honoré Champion, 2003. This study of architecture, poetry, and politics in early modern France includes an insightful discussion of du Bellay's *Regrets* and *Antiquities.*

Tucker, George Hugo. *Homo Viator: Itineraries of Exile, Displacement and Writing in Renaissance Europe.* Geneva: Droz, 2003. Includes a chapter on du Bellay's Roman "exile."

———. *The Poet's Odyssey: Joachim du Bellay and the* Antiquitez de Rome. Oxford: Clarendon Press, 1990. A study of the *Antiquities* (including the *Dream*) in relation to du Bellay's poetic career and to classical, medieval, and Renaissance writings on Rome. Pays special attention to the layout of the 1558 edition.

———. *Les Regrets et autres oeuvres poëtiques de Joachim du Bellay.* Paris: Gallimard, 2000. An introduction to the *Regrets* that attends particularly to the arrangement of the 1558 edition. Includes a dossier of contemporary documents and other materials.

Villey, Pierre. *Les Sources italiennes de la* Deffence et illustration de la langue françoise *de Joachim du Bellay.* Paris: H. Champion, 1908. The book that revealed du Bellay's extensive borrowings in the *Defense* from Sperone Speroni's 1542 *Dialogo delle lingue.*

Collections of Essays

Bellenger, Yvonne, ed. *Du Bellay et ses sonnets romains: Études sur les* Regrets *et les* Antiquitez de Rome. Paris: Honoré Champion, 1994. Eleven essays on the *Regrets* and the *Antiquities* with an introduction and bibliography by the editor.

Cesbron, Georges, ed. *Du Bellay: Actes du Colloque International d'Angiers du 26 au 29 Mai 1989.* 2 vols. Angers: Presses de l'Université d'Angers, 1990. This collection contains fifty-one essays by some of the of the best-known specialists in du Bellay and French Renaissance literary studies.

Dauphiné, James, and Paul Mironneau, eds. *Du Bellay: Actes des secondes journées du Centre Jacques de Laprade tenues au Musée national du château de Pau les 2 et 3 décembre 1994.* Les Cahiers du Centre Jacques de Laprade 2 (1994). Collection of eleven essays on the *Antiquities* and the *Regrets.*

Joachim du Bellay. Special issue of *L'Esprit créateur* 19.3 (Fall 1979). Four of the six

essays in this special edition concern the *Defense*, the *Regrets*, and/or the *Antiquities.*

Rieu, Josiane, ed. *Du Bellay: Antiquité et nouveaux mondes dans les recueils romains. Actes du Colloque de Nice (17-18 février 1995).* Nice: Publications de la Faculté des lettres, arts, et sciences humaines de Nice, 1995. Ten essays on the poems, including the *Regrets*, the *Antiquities*, and the Latin elegies, that du Bellay wrote during his stay in Rome.

Articles

Ahmed, Ehsan. "Du Bellay, Sébillet, and the Problematic Identity of the French Humanist." *Neophilologus* 75 (1991): 185-193.

Barkan, Leonard. "Ruins and Visions: Spenser, Pictures, Rome." In *Edmund Spenser: Essays on Culture and Allegory.* Edited by Jennifer Klein Morrison and Matthew Greenfield. Aldershot: Ashgate, 2000. Pp. 9-36.

Bizer, Marc. "'Qui a pais n'a que faire de patrie': Joachim Du Bellay's Resistance to a French Identity." *Romanic Review* 91 (2000): 375-395.

Brown, Richard Danson. "Forming the 'First Garland of Free Poesie': Spenser's Dialogue with Du Bellay in *Ruines of Rome.*" *Translation & Literature* 7 (1998): 3-22.

Carron, Jean-Claude. "Imitation and Intertextuality in the Renaissance." *New Literary History* 19 (1988): 565-579.

Coldiron, A. E. B. "How Spenser Excavates Du Bellay's *Antiquitez*: Or, The Role of the Poet, Lyric Historiography, and the English Sonnet." *Journal of English and Germanic Philology* 101 (2002): 41-67.

Collins, Karen. "*Les Antiquitez de Rome*: Du Bellay Crosses the Rubicon." In *Rome in the Renaissance: The City and the Myth.* Edited by P. A. Ramsey. Binghamton: Medieval and Renaissance Texts and Studies, 1982. Pp. 293-300.

Cooper, Richard. "Poetry in Ruins: The Literary Context of Du Bellay's Cycles in Rome." *Renaissance Studies* 3 (1989): 156-166.

Defaux, Gérard. "'Moy ton Poete, ayant premier osé. . .': Du Bellay, Ronsard et l'Envie." In *Cité des Hommes, Cité de Dieu.* Edited by Alain Meyer. Geneva: Droz, 2003. Pp. 197-205.

Demerson, Guy. "Le *Songe* de J. Du Bellay et le sens des recueils romains." In *Le Songe à la Renaissance.* Edited by F. Charpentier. Saint-Étienne: Presses de l'Université de Saint- Étienne, 1987. Pp. 169-178.

Ferguson, Margaret. "'The Afflatus of Ruin': Meditations on Rome by Du Bellay, Spenser, and Stevens." In *Roman Images: Selected Papers from the English Institute.* Edited by Annabel Patterson. Baltimore: Johns Hopkins University Press, 1984. Pp. 23-52.

———. "Joachim du Bellay." In *The Spenser Encyclopedia.* Edited by A. C. Hamilton. Toronto: University of Toronto Press, 1990. Pp. 83-85.

———. "An Offensive Defense for a New Intellectual Elite." In *A New History of French Literature.* Edited by Denis Hollier. Cambridge, Mass.: Harvard University Press, 1989. Pp. 194-198.

Greene, Thomas M. "Regrets Only: Three Poetic Paradigms in Du Bellay." *Romantic Review* 84 (1993): 1-18.

Hartley, David. "Religion and the State: Joachim du Bellay's Views on the Duties of the Most Christian King and His Subjects." In *The Sixteenth-Century French Religious Book.* Edited by Philip Conner, Paul Nelles, and Andrew Pettegree. Aldershot: Ashgate, 2001. Pp. 127-37.

Helgerson, Richard. "Remembering, Forgetting, and the Founding of a National

Literature: The Example of Joachim du Bellay." *REAL: Yearbook of Research in English and American Literature* 21 (2005): 19-30.

Legrand, Marie-Dominique. "Exile et poésie: Les *Tristes* et les *Pontiques* d'Ovide, les *Souspirs* d'O. de Magny, les *Regrets* de J. Du Bellay." *Littératures* 17 (1987): 33-47.

———. "Le Modèle épistolaire dans *Les Regrets* de Joachim du Bellay." *Nouvelle revue du seizième siècle* 13 (1995): 199-213.

Lloyd-Jones, Kenneth. "Du Bellay's Journey from *Roma Vetus* to *La Rome Neufve*." In *Rome in the Renaissance: The City and the Myth*. Edited by P. A. Ramsey. Binghamton: Medieval and Renaissance Texts and Studies, 1982. Pp. 301-319.

———. "L'Originalité de la vision romaine chez Du Bellay." *Réforme, Humanisime, Renaissance* 12 (1980): 13-21.

Lupton, Julia Reinhard. "Undressing Alcina: The *Orlando furioso* in Du Bellay's *Les Regrets*." *French Forum* 14 (1989): 291-301.

MacPhail, Eric. "Nationalism and Italianism in the Work of Du Bellay." *Yearbook of Comparative and General Literature* 39 (1993): 47-53.

———. "The Roman Tomb or the Image of the Tomb in Du Bellay's *Antiquitez*." *Bibliothèque d'Humanisme et Renaissance* 48 (1986): 359-372.

Martin, P. M. "Les Rome de Joachim du Bellay, à travers les *Antiquitez de Rome* et les *Regrets*." *Études Classiques* 51 (1983): 133-150.

Melara, Miriella. "Du Bellay and the Inscription of Exile." *Renaissance and Reformation/ Renaissance et Réforme* 27 (1992): 5-19.

Melehy, Hassan. "Du Bellay and the Space of Early Modern Culture." *Neophilologus* 84 (2000): 501-515.

———. "Du Bellay's Time in Rome: The *Antiquitez*." *French Forum* 26 (2001): 1-22.

———. "Joachim Du Bellay's Dream Language: The *Songe* as Allegory of Poetic Signification." *Renaissance and Reformation/Renaissance et Réforme* 24 (2000): 3-21.

Monferran, Jean-Charles, and Olivia Rosenthal. "À quoi sert de nommer? Politique du nom dans *Les Regrets* de Du Bellay." *Nouvelle revue du seizième siècle* 15 (1997): 301-323.

Navarrete, Ignacio. "Strategies of Appropriation in Speroni and Du Bellay." *Comparative Literature* 41 (1989): 141-154.

Norton, Glyn P. "Du Bellay and the Emblematics of Regret." In *Writing the Renaissance: Essays on Sixteenth-Century French Literature in Honor of Floyd Gray*. Edited by Raymond C. La Charité. Lexington, Ky.: French Forum, 1992. Pp. 131-148.

Paré, François. "Du Bellay et l'institution littéraire au XVIe siècle." *Studi Francesi* 105 (1991): 469-473.

Pigman, G. W., III. "Du Bellay's Ambivalence toward Rome in the *Antiquitez*." In *Rome in the Renaissance: The City and the Myth*. Edited by P. A. Ramsey. Binghamton: Medieval and Renaissance Texts and Studies, 1982. Pp. 321-332.

Poliner, Sharlene May. "Du Bellay's *Songe*: Strategies of Deceit, Poetics of Vision." *Bibliothèque d'Humanisme et Renaissance* 43 (1981): 509-525.

Prescott, Anne Lake. "Du Bellay in Renaissance England: Recent Work on Translation and Response." *Oeuvres & Critiques* 20 (1995): 121-128.

———. "Spenser (Re)Reading Du Bellay: Chronology and Literary Response." In *Spenser's Life and the Subject of Biography*. Edited by Judith H. Anderson, Donald Cheney, and David A. Richardson. Amherst: University of Massachusetts Press, 1996. Pp. 131-145.

Rebhorn, Wayne A. "Du Bellay's Imperial Mistress: *Les Antiquitez de Rome* as Petrarchist Sonnet Sequence." *Renaissance Quarterly* 33 (1980): 609-622.

Regosin, Richard L. "Language and Nation in Sixteenth-Century France: The *Arts poétiques*." In *Beginnings in French Literature*. Edited by Freeman G. Henry. New York: Rodopi, 2002. Pp. 29-40.

Rigolot, François. "Du Bellay et la poésie du refus." *Bibliothèque d'Humanisme et Renaissance* 36 (1974): 489-502.

Russell, Daniel. "Du Bellay's Emblematic Vision of Rome." *Yale French Studies* 47 (1972): 98-109.

Wells, Margaret W. "What Did Du Bellay Understand by *Translation*?" *Forum for Modern Language Studies* 16 (1980): 175-185.

Index of Names

This index includes the historical and mythological persons and the places mentioned in du Bellay's texts, in the notes to those texts, and in the introduction. Names from sonnets and/or the notes attached to them are identified by the sonnet number and the page number in parentheses. For the longer poems, the dedication of *The Regrets* to d'Avanson (d'A) and the three Latin elegies, I also include the line number from the original. To identify the poem collections, I use the following abbreviations: *R* = *Regrets*, *A* = *Antiquities of Rome*, *S* = *Songe ou Vision* (*Dream or Vision*), and *E* = *Elegies*, where *E* 2 is "Romae descriptio" (Description of Rome), *E* 6 is "Ad P. Ronsardum" (To P. de Ronsard), and *E* 7 is "Patriae desiderium" (Longing for His Fatherland). Names from the *Defense and Enrichment of the French Language* and the notes attached to it are indicated by *D* and are identified by book and chapter numbers followed by the page number in parentheses. References to the introduction are indicated by I and are identified by page number without parentheses. These references to the introduction do not include modern critics and editors, who are listed with their works in the bibliography. For historical persons especially, the first entry in each of du Bellay's works will normally supply the fullest identification. Because of their ubiquity, there are no entries for "Rome," "France," "Italy" (or "Ausonia"), "Muse," or "Muses." The entry for "Du Bellay, Joachim" refers only to passages where the poet specifically names himself and to Jean Dorat's commendatory poem about him. For *The Regrets*, sonnet numbers are italicized when the subject of the index heading is the addressee of the poem.

Index of First Lines

Poems are identified both by their number in the collection in which they occur (*R* = *Regrets*, *A* = *Antiquitez*, *S* = *Songe*) and by page number in this edition.

www.ingramcontent.com/pod-product-compliance
Lightning Source LLC
Chambersburg PA
CBHW030828310726
48980CB00006B/679/J

* 9 7 8 0 8 1 2 2 3 9 4 1 6 *